ECONOMICS *as* **RELIGION**

Robert H. Nelson

ECONOMICS *as* RELIGION

from Samuelson to Chicago and Beyond

foreword by Max Stackhouse

THE PENNSYLVANIA STATE UNIVERSITY PRESS
University Park, Pennsylvania

LIBRARY OF CONGRESS CATALOGING-IN-PUBLICATION DATA

Nelson, Robert H. (Robert Henry), 1944–
    Economics as religion : from Samuelson to Chicago and beyond / Robert H. Nelson.
        p.   cm.
    Includes bibliographical references and index.
    ISBN 0-271-02095-4 (alk. pbk.)
        1. Economics—Philosophy.   2. Economics—Moral and ethical aspects.
    3. Religion—Economic aspects.   I. Title.
    HB72.N45 2001
    330.1—dc21

                                                                00-052444

It is the policy of The Pennsylvania State University Press to use acid-free paper for the first
printing of all clothbound books. Publications on uncoated stock satisfy the minimum
requirements of American National Standard for Information Sciences—Permanence of
Paper for Printed Library Materials, ANSI Z39.48–1992.

IN MEMORY OF PAUL HEYNE (1931–2000),

Whose Life Exemplified the Search for Truth

CONTENTS

FOREWORD

Max L. Stackhouse
Princeton Theological Seminary

When Robert H. Nelson wrote *Reaching for Heaven on Earth: The Theological Meaning of Economics* nearly a decade ago, he helped initiate a fresh self-consciousness among social scientists about the deeper value constellations that stand behind much of what they do. That volume sparked discussion not only among economists and among theologians but sometimes between them—a discussion that has had sporadic episodes since.

That study was indicative of a modest reversal of the tendency of those economists who wanted their work to be seen as purely value-free. Some had come to use the term "theology" to skewer speculative and value-laden theories for which there was no evidence. But his insightful historical analysis showed that many of the classic founders of the field of economics not only were guided by theological assumptions but also viewed the field in messianic terms. That is, they presumed that the primary reason for human pain, suffering, and death (what theologians identify as a consequence of sin in a fallen world) is that we are in a state of scarcity. Moreover, we can only be delivered from this perilous existence by the overcoming of material deprivation—a prospect that can only come from rightly formulated, rightly believed, and rightly lived principles and policies. Economics can deliver us, bring about a redeemed state of affairs on earth, and lead us to abundant living—the materially incarnate form of salvation.

His argument was not that all economists act like those priests who would read the signs of the times (looking for auspicious moments to invest in new adventures) and the entrails of animals (tracing the effects of consumption) in order to advise rulers and wealthy patrons, although many seem willing, even eager, to do just that. Nor was his argument quite the sort of thing that Marx argued in *On the Jewish Question,* or that Weber argued in *The Protestant Ethic and the Spirit of Capitalism,* and today is under discussion in still a third form in regard to "Confucian values" and the East Asian industrial successes and financial crises, namely, that certain kinds of religious orientations have profound, if unintended, material effects, although none of these are entirely ruled out.

Rather, his argument was that the major theories of economics as they developed in the intellectual history of the West can best be understood in terms of one or another of the great contrasting traditions of theology—especially Roman Catholic and Protestant, each with its philosophical antecedents and dispositional corollaries. In distinctive ways, each deals with the most profound issues of existence. One view involves a developmental, rational optimism about human abilities—morally, spiritually, and socially—to improve the common condition, and offers an institutionalized set of mediating procedures to make that possible. We find this view not only in Aristotle and Aquinas and much of Anglicanism, but in more secular forms in Claude Saint-Simon and John Maynard Keynes.

The second tradition is more pessimistic and radical, sometimes even apocalyptic, for it presumes that a dramatic intervention must occur within persons or in the society as a whole and bring about an alleviation of pervasive evil. Otherwise, very little can be changed; improvements are modest and marginal, and real life often involves only a choice for the lesser of evils. One can find philosophical parallels in Plato, in Augustine, and in such Reformers as Luther, Calvin, and the Puritans. This stream splits in the modern age, Nelson argued, into several branches, and it can go toward Marxism, toward the Social Darwinists, or toward modern theories of economic alienation.

Nelson, then a research economist for the Department of the Interior, traced these themes from the earlier directly religious theories of economic life through the development of the field in the early days of this century, and shows how motifs from these theories have appeared in our time, especially in popular advocacy movements that influence public policy in the name of liberation, ecological, communitarian, or libertarian sectarian doctrines. It may be, of course, that as the discipline of economics—and popular responses to economic complexity—developed, they discovered what theologians had previously found out—that there are only a few basic alternative approaches to the ultimate questions, that the approach chosen has great consequences for every effort to seek a remedy to what ails humanity, and that every basic theory when it is adopted on faith among the people takes on unforeseen forms with unforeseen consequences.

It is equally if not more likely, however, that the profound religious traditions that shaped Western culture framed, inevitably, the intellectual contours of economics more than most leaders in the discipline have admitted, and that they operate still as the deep background beliefs of those who have largely forgotten whence they came. After all, scholarship in other fields has found out that "modernization" did not bring about the secularization of life, as expected, but a host of new developments that go under the name of "globalization" wherein we now face a nearly universal resurgence of religion.[1] Moreover, scholars in many fields may remain personally, even adamantly secular, in their methods and arguments, but are not only discovering that they must study religious matters when they seek to understand cultures other than those of the West but are forced by deeper historical studies to recognize anew the rootage of their presumed "secular outlooks" in religious and theological developments.[2] Nelson has, in fact, himself explored a number of such themes in a series of articles over the last several years—articles that can now be seen as the preliminary probings that have led to this fresh work.

In this new study of *Economics as Religion,* Nelson, himself an accomplished economist within the profession and now Professor in the School of Public Affairs at the University of Maryland, extends his research by examining the basic presuppositions among the most influential contemporary economists. Taking up the story as the redemptive schemes of Marx and Keynes fade, he discerns, quite accurately, I think, the faith presuppositions that are behind the work of Paul Samuelson and other Harvard and MIT economists who represent the "Cambridge School," on the one hand, and Milton Friedman, Gary Becker, and other leading figures of the "Chicago School," including the younger thinkers who are poised to shape the immediate future. If the previous study demonstrated by more classic historiographic methods that theology influenced the deep history of the discipline, this study shows by an acute analysis of contemporary writings that unacknowledged religious assumptions pervade the commitments of currently distinguished and influential figures.

This study is not postmodern in its methods, but it is postfoundational in its results. That is, it shows that the foundations of the discipline are not self-evident, entirely based on fixed rational or empirical foundations, or proven

1. See Peter Berger, Tu Wei Ming, and Abdullhi An-Na'im et al., *The Desecularization of the World: Resurgent Religion and World Politics* (Grand Rapids: Eerdmans, 1999).

2. See, for examples, on law, Harold Berman, *Law and Revolution: The Formation of the Western Legal Tradition* (Cambridge: Harvard University Press, 1983); on science and education, Toby Huff, *The Rise of Early Modern Science* (New York: Cambridge University Press, 1993); on technology, David F. Noble, *The Religion of Technology: The Divinity of Man and the Spirit of Invention* (New York: Knopf, 1998); on political science, Oliver O'Donovan, *The Desire of Nations* (New York: Cambridge University Press, 1996), and Ralph Hancock, *Calvin and the Foundations of Modern Politics* (Ithaca: Cornell University Press, 1989); and, on comparative social development, Lawrence E. Harrison and S. P. Huntington, eds., *Culture Matters: How Values Shape Human Progress* (New York: Basic Books, 2000); David Landes, *The Wealth and Poverty of Nations: Why Some Are So Rich and Some So Poor* (New York: Norton, 1998), and Francis Fukuyama, *Trust: The Social Virtues and the Creation of Prosperity* (New York: Free Press, 1995).

by analysis or theorem. In fact, many are rooted in unexamined presuppositions that are more like faith commitments than in "pure" scientific hypotheses, and that they are often obscure to and obscured by the advocates of the field itself. As such, they can be, and in a certain sense must be, treated in terms that echo classic theological themes and categories. They are, in short, morally and spiritually laden—a fact that does not necessarily make them less truthful or less accurate, unless their own bases are denied.

This is not done, as I read it, to discredit any thinker or the field as a whole. The values that are exposed, as held by the economists under examination, are sometimes better than the arguments for them made by their proponents—precisely because they are more deeply rooted in time-tested and critically examined presuppositions than their current advocates acknowledge or perhaps even know. There are, however, disadvantages to the lack of awareness of and attentiveness to them. If and when they become distorted, there is very little philosophical, historical, or theological self-awareness in place to correct them. For instance, an enormous amount of economic theory ends up being focused on nationalistic policies, a tendency that makes certain culturally particular patterns of economic life appear to be more universal natural laws than they actually are, and that simultaneously blinds us to certain global and/or local patterns of belief and morality that have economic consequences. It also means both at home and abroad that relationships between facts and values, between descriptive and normative modes of discourse, or between analyses of marginal gains and the social, moral, and spiritual effects of policies based on calculations of these gains are not examined by those who advance them.

This new volume extends Nelson's previous work in subject matter, method, and pertinence to current issues. The distinctive contribution is that it takes up a neglected question—one largely ignored both by many economists and by practitioners of the sister social sciences, and often only ideologically treated by social critics of our current economic and social system (including no small number of religious leaders). That question is: What are the values that are built into the dominant, contemporary economic theories that specialists generate, managers and policymakers use, popular movements turn into slogans, and ethicists try to investigate and philosophers and theologians seek to understand and subject to normative criticism? These theories cannot be summarized or dismissed by saying that they are "a function of late-capitalism" that is "only interested in profits" and dedicated to "materialism" and "the commodification of the world."

To be sure, it is difficult to exhume the values that are built into these theories when the theories are designed to be as "value-neutral" as possible.

But, as this volume shows, the authors and key interpreters of these theories, those who have defined this or that aspect of the discipline, sometimes have treated the value questions more overtly than their science says they should. More often they reveal, quite unconsciously, even contrary to their intentions, more about the clusters of values that are operating in the back of their minds as they argue for or refine a theory than they intend, even as the foregrounds of their minds focus on what seems to be purely evidential or logical or analytical arguments. By drawing the connections between the overt statements and the half-concealed commitments, Nelson draws our attention to the fundamental presuppositions behind these value clusters and shows why it is proper to identify them as religiously held doctrines.

It has, as everyone who has been paying attention knows, become fashionable to see every theory as a social construct, as a weapon of the winners in life to justify their own dominance and to keep the losers in a situation of subordination or marginalization. Much postmodern literature is eager to deconstruct the work of theorists in every field and to show the latent colonial or imperial (or racist, sexist, classist, or gender) interests behind purportedly "objective" theory. Professor Nelson is not among these debunkers of modern academia who know only how to argue from a "hermeneutics of suspicion" and see every claim as another power play. He does, however, want economists, plus ethically alert citizens and socially active believers in religious traditions, to recognize that very profound assumptions about the ultimate issues of life are inevitably built into the apparently arid economic theories that shape how we live. He does not want us all to come to this recognition because that would discredit the scientific character of the field, but because it could improve it. He wants economists (and those of us who are not professional economists but who fuss a good deal with economic matters from the perspectives of other disciplines) to come clean about the fact that Economics, no less than other social and historical sciences, however much they use what appear to be morally and spiritually sanitized formulas and complex econometric models, bear within them values in a subtle mix with facts, moral presumptions in a complex blend with argument, matters of faith interwoven with matters of analysis. In fact, ethical, religious, and specifically theological assumptions are not foreign to economic life or economic thought, but pervade them.

In sum, this volume, more than any other published study I have seen, allows us to see in the writings of the major economists of contemporary life which clusters of value assumptions are in play—in them and often in us. That recognition could allow the critical examination of the values that are present from a more discerning point of view and allow the discipline to take its honored place at the crossroads of the sciences and the humanities. Indeed, it could also then articulate, and critically refine, the ethical and theological presumptions hiding in it more clearly and more honestly than it presently allows. Even if the reader is inclined to argue with this or that point as the argument unfolds, it is a striking contribution to our understanding of motifs driving both our intellectual orientations and much of the common life.

PREFACE

Economists think of themselves as scientists, but as I will be arguing in this book, they are more like theologians. The closest predecessors for the current members of the economics profession are not scientists such as Albert Einstein or Isaac Newton; rather, we economists are more truly the heirs of Thomas Aquinas and Martin Luther. Economists think that their role in society is to provide technical knowledge to operate the economic system. The members of the economics profession do make important contributions in this regard. The inflation, unemployment, and other data collected by economists, for example, are critical to monitoring the current state of the economy. However, another basic role of economists is to serve as the priesthood of a modern secular religion of economic progress that serves many of the same functions in contemporary society as earlier Christian and other religions did in their time.* Economic efficiency has been the greatest source of social legitimacy in the United States for the past century, and economists have been the priesthood defending this core social value of our era.

The view of economics as the basis for a religion has been a long time coming for me. I am by training an economist. While I was pursuing my doctorate at Princeton University in the late 1960s, not one of my professors described economics in religious terms. I am in my own beliefs a typical modern representative of the secular world; my own social community has been found largely outside traditional church circles. How, then, have I come to believe that the most important social role of economists is best understood as religious in character?

The story begins with my taking a job in 1975 in the Office of Policy

---

* It should be recalled that theologians in earlier eras not only explored the greater mysteries of God but also issued pronouncements on many questions of daily life, including economic ones. In Judaism, for example, dietary laws controlled the very practical matter of what people could eat. Theological pronouncements on "just price" doctrine could determine the acceptable forms of market transactions. Usury rules of the church commonly prohibited the explicit charging of interest on loans. The various schools of modern economics, addressing both transcendent and mundane questions, can be traced back to previous leading schools of belief within Judaism and Christianity. For a further discussion of these themes, see Robert H. Nelson, *Reaching for Heaven on Earth: The Theological Meaning of Economics* (Lanham, Md.: Rowman and Littlefield, 1991).

Analysis in the Office of the Secretary of the U.S. Department of the Interior. I soon discovered that the details of formal economic calculations had little to do with most policy decisions reached in the department.★ If economists had any influence—which they sometimes did, if rarely decisive—it was seldom as literal "problem solvers." Rather, the greatest influence of economists came through their defense of a set of values. Much of my own and other efforts of Interior economists were really to persuade others in the department to act in accordance with the economic value system, as compared with other competing priorities and sets of values also represented within the ranks of the department.[1]

Before coming to the government, I had expected that economic reasoning would often be in conflict with powerful interest-group pressures. It did turn out that an important role of the economist in government was to speak for a wider national interest against the many parochial influences at work throughout government. This role did not depend as much on any unique access to economic insights as on the differing "professional" motivations of economists as compared with the more "opportunistic" motivations of many other participants in government decision making. At this point the role of the economist in government was already assuming an ethical dimension. Little in my professional training had addressed the ethics of the economist as a member of a profession. Although there clearly was a powerful professional ethic of this kind, it was largely implicit and instilled more by the example of fellow economic (and other) professionals than by any explicit instruction.

I was more surprised, however, to discover that the Interior Department was often a battleground for a modern form of religious disputation. Economists and environmentalists in particular were often pitted against one another in these disagreements that now frequently looked to me like old clashes among Christian sects. Yet I might have been less surprised if I had stopped to consider that the Interior Department is responsible for management decisions concerning many of the most important shrines of the American nation, including the Lincoln Memorial, the Grand Canyon, the Gettysburg battlefield, and Yosemite Valley. For many visitors, wilderness areas on public lands are places of religious inspiration, in essence secular

---

★ I remained at the Interior Department until 1993, when I left to join the faculty of the School of Public Affairs at the University of Maryland. My experiences in the Interior Department eventually led to a number of books and articles on the character of the policy-making process—including the role of economists—at the federal level. See Robert H. Nelson, *The Making of Federal Coal Policy* (Durham: Duke University Press, 1983); "The Economics Profession and the Making of Public Policy," *Journal of Economic Literature* 25 (March 1987); and *Public Lands and Private Rights: The Failure of Scientific Management* (Lanham, Md.: Rowman and Littlefield, 1995).

cathedrals of the modern age. Public land agencies are today being asked to resolve theological questions such as whether the use of permanent rock anchors by mountain climbers is "consistent with" (would not desecrate) their wilderness character.[2]

The Endangered Species Act, administered by the Fish and Wildlife Service of the Interior Department, has been publicly defended by a secretary of the interior, Bruce Babbitt, as a secular version of God's command to Noah in the Bible to preserve two of every species.[3] The requirement of the act that the preservation of a species must trump every other social or economic consideration—even with the recognition that this requirement is impossible to realize in practice—is the expression of a religious ideal.[4]

With a growing conviction that the policy clashes within the Interior Department are often religious in character (although this fact is often obscured by a large overlay of secular rhetoric), I gradually came to the conclusion that a full understanding of the basis for Interior policies must mean entering into the realm of theology in all its modern diversity. Theology can be defined as the systematic study of religious thinking and practice, which I now proposed to apply to the religious forces at work as I was seeing them in the management of the lands and natural resources of the United States. At this point I was also led to recall that the true relationship between humans and nature (understood broadly) has long been a central question of religion, dating in Judaism and Christianity to the consequences of the Fall in the Garden of Eden.[5]

To be sure, I was, as most economists would be, initially reluctant to inquire in a formal way into such matters. As an economics graduate student, I had been taught that value preferences are given, and that the professional study of economics begins from there. As an economist, I thus had no particular formal training in issues of value formation and debate, to say nothing of religion and theology. Eventually, however, I decided to take the plunge. One important question was the following: what specifically were the underlying values of professional economics and what was the justification for favoring these economic values—as I clearly often did in my own policy recommendations—over others? It was also important to ask what elements of economics caused others to regard it as an alien value system and what values—also grounded in a religion of one kind or another, as it seemed to me—they proposed instead.

Thus, rejecting the counsels of my professional elders to maintain a clear separation of the domains of economics and value formation, by the mid-1980s I had begun the study of what I now would describe as the theological foundations of modern economics. I was entering into a field that might be called "economic theology." *

In recent years there has been a rapidly growing scholarly interest in the social functions of religion. A number of economists, as I will describe in later sections of this book, have begun to explore the practical roles that religion can serve in an economic system. If people behave in a more honest and trustworthy fashion, and otherwise behave more ethically, it can greatly reduce the "transaction costs" to an economy. Hence, as is an increasingly common observation, religion can be practically useful—it can be "efficient"—in even a narrowly economic sense.[6]

However, economists have had almost nothing to say about how religion comes to be believed in the first place. In the end, religion is about making claims to truth—as economists see their own economic research in this light. Religion is about changing people to make them better understand the truth as it is seen by the initiated and thereby also changing their behavior—as in Christian efforts to persuade sinners to see their fallen ways and to give up their sinful behavior (and economists' efforts to teach people to be more "rational"). If economists typically assume a preexisting preference structure, much of religion is about changing the preference structure. Religion often teaches us to want different things or to be happier with what we have.

In all these respects it is difficult to fit discussion of religion into the standard framework of economic thought.[7] An economist might ask the question, How much is a belief in a heaven in the hereafter worth in dollar terms? or, What is the economic value to an individual of believing in God? These are simply absurd questions from the perspective of the religious true believer.[8]

Ultimately, the discussion of religion is not about the efficiency-enhancing character of religion for overall economic performance, or the higher level of utility that religious belief may offer a person. Serious theology will address such things as the correct initial framework of thought—for

---

* Economic theology, as I am using the term here, should be distinguished from the economic study of religion. Although economists are now showing a new interest in religion, they typically put religion within the economic framework of thought. The church is one more institution whose behavior is driven by economic incentives. And the existence of a religion can shape preferences and otherwise affect individual behavior in ways that promote or inhibit economic efficiency. See, for example, Kelly Olds, "Privatizing the Church: Disestablishment in Connecticut and Massachusetts," *Journal of Political Economy* 102, no. 2 (1994); and Douglas W. Allen, "Order in the Church: A Property Rights Approach," *Journal of Economic Behavior and Organization* 27 (June 1995). For surveys of the growing literature on the economics of religion, see Laurence R. Iannaccone and Brooks B. Hull, "The Economics of Religion: A Survey of Recent Work," *Bulletin of the Association of Christian Economists* (Fall 1991); and Laurence R. Iannaccone, "Introduction to the Economics of Religion," *Journal of Economic Literature* 36 (September 1998).

the practice of eco-nomics (which also must begin from somewhere) or otherwise. It will address matters such as how an initial framework of thought can ever be developed, when this development seems to presuppose the very thing—a framework of thought—that is supposed to be the outcome.★ Where might it be necessary for some elements of "faith" to come in, as economists may themselves also have to take some articles of economic belief on faith? It will ask how rational the world is, and to what extent human beings are capable of discovering this rationality through their own efforts, which may or may not lead them to act in a genuinely rational fashion in their actual behavior. Such subjects have been a central concern historically not only of economic writers but also of many leading theologians of centuries past.

Like others before them, current economists have a framework of thought and a set of presuppositions that define their basic outlook on the world. Most of them, for example, are among the true believers in the potential for a rational world. Many economists believe in economic progress in a religious way, as something that is significantly improving the basic

---

★ One of the few economists who has addressed such subjects is Amartya Sen, the winner of the 1998 Nobel Prize in economics. It partly reflects the greater uncertainty with respect to a proper frame of economic reference when considering the development of a nation such as his native India, where the processes of economic development often involve obvious conflicts with traditional values. Addressing issues of what might be called "economic theology," Sen (with Martha Nussbaum) thus writes that

> [it is important to recognize] that values cannot be treated, as they often are in the literature on "economic development," as purely instrument objects in promoting development. Indeed, the very idea of "development"—whether seen from within a culture or in the stylized impersonal context of development economies—is inevitably based on a particular class of values, in terms of which progress is judged and development is measured.
>
> There are two distinct issues involved in recognizing the importance of the "value-relativity" of the concept of development. The first is the elementary but far-reaching fact that without some idea of ends that are themselves external to the development process and in terms of which the process may be assessed, we cannot begin to say what changes are to count as "development." In judging development in the context of a culture the values that are supported and are sustainable in that culture provide an essential point of reference.
>
> The second issue concerns the possible undermining of traditional values that may result from the process of change. . . . This "undermining" may take two rather different forms, which have to be distinguished. It could be that the *objects of valuation* that a particular traditional value system treasures—such as a particular lifestyle—may become more difficult to obtain and sustain as a result of material change. The other way that the values may be "undermined" is a weakening of the hold of those *values themselves* on the subjects.

See Martha C. Nussbaum and Amartya Sen, "Internal Criticism and Indian Rationalist Traditions," in Michael Krausz, ed., *Relativism, Interpretation, and Confrontation* (Notre Dame: University of Notre Dame Press, 1989), 299–300.

human condition for the better. Yet, on the whole, they are remarkably un-reflective on such foundational matters.[9] One of my aims in this book is to offer some preliminary explorations in these theological domains, as labeled here economic theology.

There is some but not much literature to draw on from professional econ-omists in these regards.[10] To the extent that helpful writings are available, they can be found in the theological literature as well.[11] In the 1980s, delving for the first time into formal theology, I discovered a new respect for theo-logical thinking.* Economists tend to think of theologians as naive in their lack of economic knowledge, but in fact most economists are themselves also naive about the character and grounds for their most basic presuppositions. They are embedded in an economic culture where such questions are rarely raised and the economic way of thinking is simply taken for granted as the correct way of thinking—the best means of access to genuine knowledge about the world. If religion is the correct means of access to truth, as it should properly be understood (and Christianity has always understood it—recall the biblical message that "the truth shall make us free"), most economists take their economic religion on faith.†

The first systematic product of my explorations in these domains was my 1991 book *Reaching for Heaven on Earth: The Theological Meaning of Econom-ics.*[12] Somewhat to my relief, given the large leap in thinking it represented for me, it was on the whole well received among a number of economists (and a few theologians)—although, to be sure, there were many points of criticism and some harsh overall reactions. The economics profession, I ar-gued for the first time in that book, is the priesthood of a powerful secular religion—or more accurately a set of secular religions, as they have been de-veloped in the theories of leading schools of economics of the modern age.[13] Beneath the surface of their formal economic theorizing, economists are en-gaged in an act of delivering religious messages. Correctly understood, these messages are seen to be promises of the true path to a salvation in this world—to a new heaven on earth. Because this path follows along a route of economic progress, and because economists are the ones—or so it is believed by many people—with the technical understanding to show the way, it falls

---

* The greatest influence on the development of my new understanding of formal theology was Paul Tillich's *A History of Christian Thought: From Its Judaic and Hellenistic Origins to Existentialism* (New York: Simon and Schuster, 1967). This is not only a good introduction to the history of Christian the-ology but also a marvelous example of the sophistication of theological reasoning at its highest.

† Ellen Charry, a professor of systematic theology at Southern Methodist University writes of the development of Christian theology; "Traditionally, the overriding concern has been for the criterion of truth understood as coherence and intelligibility on the grounds of intellectual honesty." See Ellen T. Charry, "Academic Theology in Pastoral Perspective," *Theology Today* 50 (April 1993): 102.

to the members of the economics profession (assisted by other social scientists) to assume the traditional role of the priesthood.

I also explored in my 1991 book how the differences among the secular religions of various economic schools mirror the history of Judeo-Christian religion. Some schools of economics have a more "Roman" character, as I labeled one main tradition much discussed in the literature of Western theology, and others a more "Protestant" character, as I labeled a second main tradition.[14] American economics follows more closely in the Roman tradition, associated with ideas of natural law as revealed through exercise of faculties of human reason, given a leading theological exposition by Thomas Aquinas and others in the Roman Catholic Church.* Overall, Judeo-Christian influences have had an extraordinary staying power in the Western world at the level of fundamental assumptions concerning the motives for human behavior and the meaning of history. Judeo-Christian beliefs—if often in modern secular disguises—continue today to exert a much greater influence on their thinking than most current economists and other social scientists have seemed prepared to understand.[15]†

Since 1990, I have also applied the same lens of theological analysis to the modern environmental movement, reaching similar conclusions. Contem-

---

* The greatest figures in the "Roman" tradition of seeing a rational world that is guided by natural law follow from Aristotle to Aquinas to Adam Smith to the positive economics of the twentieth century. The greatest figures in an opposing "Protestant" tradition—seeing a sinful and alienated world at present where the powers of human reasoning have been fatally weakened by the general corruption of human nature—follow from Plato to Augustine to Martin Luther to Karl Marx (along with Herbert Spencer and other social Darwinists). A main purpose of my *Reaching for Heaven on Earth* was to trace the evolution of thinking about economic aspects of life through the theologies (traditional and secular) of leading figures in each tradition. As some of my critics found fault, few great thinkers fit perfectly in either tradition (and I do not disagree), but I do contend that in the cases above (and many others) their thought contains a predominant emphasis derived from one or another of these traditions.

† Although he fails to give full due to the many benefits of a market system, Harvard theologian Harvey Cox is correct in seeing close parallels between contemporary economic ideas and the historical tenets of Judeo-Christian religion:

> The lexicon of *The Wall Street Journal* and the business sections of *Time* and *Newsweek* . . . bear a striking resemblance to Genesis, the Epistle to the Romans, and Saint Augustine's City of God. Behind descriptions of market reforms, monetary policy, and the convolutions of the Dow, I gradually made out the pieces of a grand narrative about the inner meaning of human history, why things had gone wrong, and how to put them right. Theologians call these myths of origin, legends of the fall, and doctines of sin and redemption. But here they were again, and in only thin disguise.

See Harvey Cox, "The Market as God: Living with the New Dispensation," *Atlantic Monthly,* March 1999, 18.

porary environmentalism offers a story line beneath which lies yet another secular theology, also a message that follows closely in the Judeo-Christian tradition.[16] The distinguished environmental lawyer and scholar Joseph Sax has written that he and many of his fellow American environmentalists are "secular prophets, preaching a message of secular salvation."[17] Indeed, the conflicts between economic and environmental values that dominated many of the policy outcomes during my years at the Interior Department are best understood as new variations on earlier religious disagreements among followers in branches of Jewish and Christian religion.[18]

Although few economists have given much attention to the issues explored in this book, other social scientists have shown a greater intellectual curiosity. There is in fact a growing recognition at the beginning of the twenty-first century that secular religions—usually grounded in scientific claims—are actual categories of religion, often now competing directly with more traditional faiths for followers and for influence on society.[19] As a writer in *Science* magazine acknowledged not long ago, we live "in a world in which science has replaced religion as the most powerful of orthodoxies."[20] Sociologist Robert Bellah finds that "we can say that in contemporary society social science has usurped the traditional position of theology. It is now social science that tells us what kind of creatures we are and what we are about on this planet. It is social science that provides us images of personal behavior and legitimations of the structures that govern us. It is to social science that the task is entrusted, so far as it is entrusted at all, of, in whatever the contemporary terms for it would be, 'justifying the ways of God to man.' "[21]

While most members of the economics profession have paid little attention to such matters, there are a few, perhaps most prominently D. McCloskey, who have argued that the values communicated by economic writings are often more important than the research results themselves. As McCloskey has said, economics promises objective science but actually delivers a hidden metaphysics.[22] Behind their formal theorizing, economists are engaged in telling stories that have powerful symbolic messages that often have a philosophical (and theological) content.[23]

McCloskey does not emphasize, as I will in this book, that these stories contain a predominantly religious content.* However, McCloskey's choice

---

* There is, to be sure, a considerable literature by economists outside the professional mainstream that finds in economics many of the behavioral characteristics of a religion. Among the many examples that could be cited, one writer explained that the "hard core of economic principles is a little like the Ten Commandments"; that these principles tend to be treated "as axioms or almost as self-evident truths;" and that in a number of respects "economics . . . is closer to religion than to science." See Craufurd D. Goodwin, "Doing Good and Spreading the Gospel (Economic)," in David Colander and A. W. Coats, eds., *The Spread of Economic Ideas* (New York: Cambridge University Press, 1989), 172.

of adjectives and metaphors to characterize the actions and thinking of economists often suggests a religious inspiration. At one point McCloskey observes that economics offers a new kind of "modernist faith." If taking a secular form, it has its own "Ten Commandments and Golden Rule," its "nuns, bishops, and cathedrals," its "trinity of fact, definition, and holy value." What was once a young and vigorous "crusading faith" has now "hardened into ceremony."[24] Like the priesthoods of old, the economics profession has often become defensive, sometimes as concerned with preserving its prerogatives as with the saving of the world.

Although many economists are skeptical, outside observers of the research and public policy activities of economists often come to much the same viewpoint. Philosopher Mark Sagoff has commented that the policy interactions of economists and environmentalists involve a new form of "wars of religion" between "two faith communities—one believing in the equilibria of ecosystems, the other in the equilibria of markets." At issue in these controversies are mat-ters such as whether "preference satisfaction" is the "true and only" path to "Heaven" on earth.[25]

Other philosophers such as Richard Rorty now tell us that the very idea of a scientific base of objective truth that is "value-neutral" has always been a chimera.[26] Even the physical sciences rest in the first instance on a foundation of original conceptions that cannot be derived by rational methods alone or demonstrated to be objectively true in an ultimate sense.[27] By comparison, the claims of social scientists to value neutrality are much more fragile.[28] The Freudian "science" of psychoanalysis is widely seen today as closer to a form of religion than to a genuine science.★

We live in an age of philosophical and value pluralism that shows deep skepticism toward the claims of any group to possess unique truths. Indeed, this skepticism is found in the attitudes of the up-and-coming generation of economists. A survey in the mid-1980s found that 83 percent of Harvard graduate students in economics and 75 percent of MIT students no longer believed in the old distinctions between positive and normative economics, leading the surveyors to conclude that "the scientific status of economics is clearly in doubt among students."[29] Yet if economics is not a form of science, few economists have undertaken to ask in a systematic way just what it is.

Leading theologians have also addressed the breakdown of the old dis-

---

★ Richard Webster notes "the numerous similarities between Luther's view of the human condition and that found in psychoanalysis." Much as is argued in this book with respect to some of the main elements of modern economic thought, Webster suggests that twentieth-century psychoanalysis has contained "a subtle reconstruction in a challenging and modern form of some of the most ancient religious doctrines." See Richard Webster, *Why Freud Was Wrong: Sin, Science, and Psychoanalysis* (New York: Basic Books, 1995), 5.

tinctions between religion and the social and physical sciences. Reinhold Niebuhr, a figure better remembered today by the general public than is his colleague Paul Tillich, once said of Tillich that he was "by general consent the most creative philosopher of religion of our generation," a man known to his fellow theologians for "the breadth and depth of his erudition and the wisdom of his judgments."[30] Tillich emphasized that the idea of a "Personal God" is essential to Christianity. Yet, contrary to the language of much popular religion, this concept of the divine does not mean literally "a being," analogous to human beings, who demonstrates his existence and powers by supernatural miracles in the world.[31] This kind of humanized concept would threaten to put God in the same category as the comic-strip character Superman of our day, who also uses supernatural powers to help people in need.* Rather, for Tillich God was the underlying ordering principle giving meaning to and establishing the direction of events in the universe: God was "ultimate reality, being itself, ground of being, power of being."[32] In the Judeo-Christian tradition God works his ways in the world through the events of history. Indeed, it is only due to the presence of God that human beings and history have any real meaning. The message of the Bible is at heart the message of a historical prophesy for humankind, or set of prophesies. Marxist, progressive, social Darwinist, and other secular religions have typically offered their own interpretations of the events and meaning of history—in essence, therefore, their own competing religious understandings. Tillich thus said at one point that he rated Karl Marx as "the most successful of all theologians since the [Protestant] Reformation"—an assessment difficult to dispute in terms of the influence of Marx on the world (if not the logical quality of his thought).[33]

A recent legal commentary on Supreme Court church-and-state jurisprudence finds that the court—in part borrowing explicitly from Tillich—has defined religion as "an individual's 'ultimate concern,' to which all other concerns, including self-interest, are subordinate." In seeking to define "religious" actions immune from "state" interference, the court has accepted a wide range of "belief systems" as valid religions even when they "avoided any reference to supernatural entities or forces."[34] Many American religious leaders now find that the boundaries between traditional religious beliefs and secular ideas are much fuzzier than previously thought.† The

---

* Tillich's perspective in this regard reflects a long-standing view in Judeo-Christian theology. For example, David Novak writes: "For Maimonides, . . . bad monotheistic theology . . . takes the anthromorphic language of Scripture literally. Good theology takes scriptural language that attributes physical properties to God to be largely figurative. It is a concession to human imagination." See David Novak, "The Mind of Maimonides," *First Things,* February 1999, 30.

† Many believers in secular faiths also accept the characterization of their belief system as a "religion." In his *Religions of America,* editor Leo Rosten included secular humanism in his list. In explain-

1990 edition of the *Dictionary of Christianity in America* states: "Since the 1970s there has been much discussion as to whether secular humanism is a religion and should be regarded legally as such. This question hinges on one's definition of religion. If belief in a god is necessary to define a religion, secular humanism does not qualify. If on the other hand, religion (or a god) is defined as one's ultimate value, then secular humanism is a religion." [35]

This book, then, offers a theological exegesis of the contents of modern economic thought, regarding the economic way of thinking as not only a source of technical understanding of economic events, but also for many economists and noneconomists alike a source of ultimate understanding of the world. It is a new kind of theological study of the most powerful set of religious beliefs, as I have come to conclude, of the modern era. The intended audience includes other economists, but they should recognize that my method of analysis is as much in the mode of history and of theology as of formal economic theorizing. In this book I have gone beyond my training as an economic professional to try to develop a wider view of the human condition. The book should also be of interest to theologians, especially those studying the interactions of theology and economic affairs.

Beyond the economists and theologians, I believe that readers in other disciplines could profit from paying attention to the issues to be explored in the pages to follow. Indeed, these issues are potentially of concern to any person with an inquiring mind who is seeking to understand the condition of the American economy and culture today.

ACKNOWLEDGMENTS

This book has benefited from the comments and encouragement of a number of people at various stages. Timur Kuran deserves special thanks for his comments and criticisms on several drafts, and especially for encouraging me to extend the scope of the book from an initial focus on Samuelson to cover

---

ing its defining beliefs, a representative of the New York Society for Ethical Culture, Edward L. Ericson, declared that "a humanist, who may also be a secularist, believes that man must look to human experience for moral and spiritual guidance, without believing that there is a supernatural God or divine power to support him. Many humanists, however, define humanism as a religious movement in its own right—a religion without revelation or God." Ericson noted that "humanists find their immortality in the human community," and believe so strongly in such convictions that they may "go to their death before they betray the values they prize most highly"—certainly meeting the criteria for a religion as an "ultimate value" or "ultimate reality." Indeed, as Ericson reports, "under federal and state legal practice, leaders and counselors in Ethical Culture and humanist groups are legally qualified to function as ministers of religion." See Leo Rosten, ed., *Religions of America: Ferment and Faith in an Age of Crisis* (New York: Simon and Schuster, 1975), 257, 259, 258.

as well the Chicago school and the new institutional economics. Anthony Waterman provided a detailed and very helpful critique of the Samuelson discussions at an early stage as well as other useful suggestions. Paul Heyne, Robert Lerman, Mark Sagoff, Steinar Ström, and Sandy Thatcher read one or another draft in its entirety and made many valuable comments. Others whom I wish to thank for their helpful comments are Peter Boettke, Peter Brown, Herman Daly, Kenneth Elzinga, Bert Foer, and Deirdre McCloskey.

INTRODUCTION: THE MARKET PARADOX

The maintenance of a market economy involves a basic paradox. For centuries writers such as Adam Smith have argued that the workings of the market should be based on the individual pursuit of self-interest. Yet, if the pursuit of self-interest goes too far in society, the very existence of the market may itself be endangered. If "opportunistic" behavior encompasses too many forms of social action, as seen in recent years in Russia, a market economy may function very poorly.* There is a wide range of behavior—including dishonest and "corrupt" transactions within the

---

* The difficulties of the Russian economy in the 1990s in fact served to highlight for many observers the importance of a normative foundation that is often simply taken for granted in successful market economies. A few leading economists have been more aware of this necessary element in market workings. A commentary on the work of Friedrich Hayek—ranking him among the most influential economists of the twentieth century—noted:

> Capitalism had proved remarkably effective at raising living standards, Hayek argued, but its success wasn't automatic; it depended on the existence of a generally accepted set of social norms (among them the sanctity of private property), a system of laws reflecting these norms, and a government that enforced the laws fairly, rather than discriminating arbitrarily among individuals. If any of these things were absent, economic development would be stymied. The pertinence of Hayek's analysis has been amply demonstrated since the collapse of communism. Many Western economists, including most of those who acted as advisors to the post-Communist governments, believed that the collectivist economies could be transformed merely by freeing prices and privatizing state-owned firms. In Hungary, Poland, and Czechoslovakia—where capitalism predated Communism, the rule of law was firmly established, and governments tended to respect private contracts—the optimists were pretty much proved right. In the former Soviet Union—where capitalism had never taken deep root, legal contracts were an alien tradition, and official corruption was rampant—the optimists got it horribly wrong.

See John Cassidy, "The Price Prophet," *New Yorker,* February 7, 2000, 50. See also "Russian Organized Crime: Crime Without Punishment," *Economist,* August 28, 1999, 17–19; and R. Jeffrey Smith, "Croats Find Treasury Plundered: State Says Former Regime Stole or Misused Billions" *Washington Post,* June 13, 2000, A1.

institutional framework of the market, "rent seeking" in government policy and administration, and actions that destroy trust in the legal system—that have the potential for undermining the efficient workings of markets.

Although few economists have so argued, it may be that finding a satisfactory resolution of the conflicting roles of self-interest in society—those areas where it can be encouraged and other areas where it must be actively discouraged—is more important to economic outcomes than the technical knowledge provided by economists. The formal idea of "social capital" traces back at least to James Coleman, who wrote in 1987 that "social norms constitute social capital."[1] In the 1990s there has been a growing literature in economics as well that emphasizes the importance of social capital in determining economic outcomes.[2] Some leading social scientists now assert that the social form of capital may be equally or more important to economic performance as compared with physical and human forms of capital.[3] A number of recent commentators have stated that a culture of "trust" is an essential element in maintaining a successful market (or other) economic system.[4] One of the most respected economists of the past fifty years (and winner in 1972 of the Nobel Prize in economics), Kenneth Arrow, recently declared that economists in the future will routinely have to incorporate new forms of analysis of "social variables"—objects of analysis on which the traditional individualistic assumptions of ordinary economic thinking may shed little light.[5]

However it might be achieved, a suitable value-foundation for the market should approve the pursuit of self-interest when it is expressed "legitimately"—for example, in the normal pursuit of business profits in the marketplace. However, there should also be a strong social sanction against various forms of opportunistic activity that represent "illegitimate" expressions of self-interest—for example, bribing government officials to deny operating licenses to potential business competitors.* Society as a whole

---

* Terms such as "corruption" suggest immoral and illegal actions, and such actions are in fact seen as such from the modern economic perspective. It is important to keep in mind, however, that what is "corrupt" in a modern economic system may be socially acceptable and ethically legitimate in many premodern societies. The development of a modern economy thus requires not only tighter enforcement of laws against corruption but also a cultural shift, part of the process by which the very character of a corrupt practice is redefined as such. This is yet another example of how an understanding of economic development sees it as requiring a social transformation that is inextricably interwoven with many cultural factors. Michael Novak has explained:

> Multinational corporations encounter many moral dilemmas in doing business overseas. In most traditional societies, bookkeeping is not public, nor bound solely by law. Custom and tradition have a familiar base. Ruling families consider it a right, perhaps a duty, to take a percentage of all commercial transactions, much as the governments of developed states levy taxes. In developed societies, such extra-legal but traditional pay-offs are considered bribes, and are both

benefits from a well-functioning market, but many individuals could in fact themselves gain significantly from corrupt and other self-interested actions. Such a tension between individual and common interests is found in many collective action problems. Often the solution is to establish a powerful social sanction against individually motivated actions that harm the wider group.[6] The novel element here is that the requisite normative foundation for the market requires a dual attitude with respect to self-interest—strong cultural inhibitions against the expression of self-interest (of opportunistic motives) in many areas of society, but at the same time strong encouragement for another powerful form of "opportunism," the individual pursuit of profit within the specific confines of the market.

A similar tension in the workings of political systems has been attracting growing attention among political scientists—the conflict between "liberal" attitudes granting a greater legitimacy for the individual pursuit of self-interest and the requirement for a certain degree of civic "virtue" in order to sustain the democratic institutions of a free society. As one political philosopher writes:

> In spite of the considerable evidence for the proposition that the liberal-republican polity requires no more than the proper configuration of rational self-interest, this orthodoxy has in recent years come under attack from scholars who argue that liberal theory, institutions, and society embody—and depend upon—liberal virtue.
>
> The thesis that liberalism [in the old sense of a free market and an individualist and democratic politics] rests in some measure on virtue is not the palpable absurdity that the liberal polity requires an impeccably virtuous citizenry, a "nation of angels." Nor is it incompatible with the mechanical-institutional interpretation of liberalism, for clearly the artful arrangement of "auxiliary precautions" can go some distance toward compensating for the "defect of better motives." Nor, finally, does this thesis maintain that the liberal polity should be understood as a tutelary community dedicated to the inculcation of individual virtue or excellence. The claim is more modest: that the operation of liberal institutions is affected in important ways by the character of citizens (and leaders) and that at some point the attenuation of individual virtue will create pathologies with which liberal

---

illegal and immoral. In traditional societies, neither custom nor tradition so regard such activities.

See Michael Novak, "God and Man in the Corporation," *Policy Review* (Summer 1980): 19.

political contrivances, however technically perfect their design, simply cannot cope. To an extent difficult to measure but impossible to ignore, the viability of liberal society depends on its ability to engender a virtuous citizenry.[7]

In Africa today, one finds many people who pursue their own happiness and self-interest with gusto. Yet the history of Africa offers little sense of a boundary between "legitimate" self-interest in the market and "illegitimate" self-interest in other key aspects of social interaction. There exist powerful forces for collective action in African society, but the boundaries of community seldom extend much beyond the clan and the tribe, an arena much smaller than that required for the realization of the full benefits of competitive markets. Corruption is in fact rampant in most African countries; governments commonly intervene politically to undermine market workings; the rule of law in many places hardly exists.* In this political and economic environment, the workings of markets offer many fewer economic benefits than elsewhere in the world. As the *1998/99 World Development Report* of the World Bank put it, "Developing countries have fewer institutions . . . and the institutions they do have are weaker than the counterpart institutions in industrial countries. These institutional deficiencies mean that markets often wither rather than thrive" in Africa and elsewhere.[8]

Economists once believed that a shortage of financial capital was at the heart of the problem of economic underdevelopment. Over the past forty or so years since most African nations achieved independence, however, the developed nations of the world have poured many billions in public and private capital into many of these nations, with little impact on economic growth (in a number of countries gross national product [GNP] per capita has actually declined since the 1960s).† Zambia, for example, for years has been one of the largest recipients of foreign aid in Africa. As the World Bank reported, if all the money directed to Zambia had simply earned a normal rate of busi-

---

* As I make this observation, I am spending six months in Harare, Zimbabwe. It seems that the local newspapers reveal almost every day a new story of corruption. One recent report relates how "investigations into the troubled national oil procurement company, National Oil Company of Zimbabwe . . . have been completed . . . with massive corruption again being unearthed." The investigation by the National Economic Conduct Inspectorate revealed that "the oil procurement company was in shambles," characterized by "rampant maladministration, looting, lack of control and cheating by top managers as they enriched themselves through dubious deals with some international oil agencies." See Sandra Nyaira, "Probe Reveals More Graft at Noczin," *Daily News* (Harare), September 6, 1999, 1.

† As described in a 1998 report of The World Bank, it was the set of past "beliefs about development strategy [that] structured organizations, instruments and implementation of [foreign] aid. But

ness return, the GNP of Zambia would have risen from around six hundred dollars per capita at independence in 1964 to more than twenty thousand dollars per capita today. In actual fact, the GNP per capita of Zambia was less in the 1990s than it was in 1964.[9]

If not wasted altogether, a large part of the foreign assistance directed to Africa has gone into the pockets of a ruling class, part of what a leading analyst of African economic development describes as the typical "predatory state" that exists throughout much of the continent.[10] The opportunistic habits of this ruling class—which often genuinely advances its own self-interest as a consequence—undermine the effective workings not only of governments but of markets as well. The lack of an adequate value-foundation also comes down in the end to matters of dollars and cents. Mancur Olson concluded that "the sums lost because the poor countries obtain only a fraction of—and because even the richest countries do not reach—their economic potentials are measured in the trillions of dollars." Much of this was attributable to a prevalence of opportunistic behavior, encouraged by an absence of suitable normative traditions in the presence of faulty institutional design:

> Though the low-income countries obtain most of the gains from self-enforcing trades, they do not realize many of the largest gains from specialization and trade. They do not have the institutions that enforce contracts impartially, and so they lose most of the gains from those transactions (like those in the capital market) that require impartial third-party enforcement. They do not have institutions that make property rights secure over the long run, so they lose most of the gains

---

these beliefs have undergone enormous, and accelerating change" in light the dismal development record of many countries in Africa and elsewhere. As the World Bank was forced to conclude:

> Sadly, experience has long since undermined the rosy optimism of aid-financed, government-led, accumulationist strategies for development. . . . The past 20 years have seen the death of centrally planned economies, stagnation in the leading import-substitution models of the 1970s (Mexico and Brazil), and broad economic failure (if not absolute disintegration) of post-independence Africa.
>
> Developing countries with sound policies and high-quality public institutions have grown much faster than those without. . . . Put simply, failures in policymaking, institution building, and the provision of public services have been more severe constraints on development than capital markets.

See the World Bank, *Assessing Aid: What Works, What Doesn't, and Why* (New York: Oxford University Press, 1998), 9–11.

from capital-intensive production. Production and trade in these societies is further handicapped by misguided economic policies and by private and public predation. The intricate social cooperation that emerges when there is a sophisticated array of markets requires far better institutions and economic policies than most countries have.[11]

If cultural and institutional causes undermine the economies of many poor countries, it is a corollary that rich countries must have more of the requisite foundation of values and institutions in place. Yet economists have devoted little effort over the past fifty years to the study of such influences on the economy. They have focused instead on fiscal and monetary policy, taxes, regulation, anti-trust, installation of infrastructure, and other instruments in the hands of governments. It is only recently that "culture" has begun to enter into the mainstream of economic analysis. The impetus has come mainly from the field of development studies. Economists have been forced there to take up cultural subjects simply in order to have any prospect of explaining the poor economic performance of so many countries around the world.[12] However, when it comes to the other side of the coin—the cultural roots that have made for prosperity in the United States and other highly developed nations—the literature is sparse indeed. A whole area of significant influences on the efficiency and other aspects of national economic performance has been largely ignored in mainstream economic analysis.

Culturally, as noted above, a key requirement for a market system will be a set of values in society that offer vigorous encouragement to self-interest in the market and yet maintain powerful normative inhibitions on the expression of self-interest in many other less socially acceptable areas. This all creates a paradox. How will it be possible to maintain a value system in society containing such seemingly conflicting attitudes with respect to the legitimate expression of self-interest? A free market might be described as in some ways the institutionalization and legitimation of "bribery" on a grand scale, but the social approval for acts of bribery nevertheless must not extend to every area of society.

One way of resolving this market paradox could be a religion with the following special tenets of belief. Whatever the theological grounds might be, one tenet of the religion should dictate strong approval of ordinary efforts to maximize business profits in the market. However, another tenet should impose a strong religious disapproval of the many other kinds of self-interested actions that might tend to undermine the workings of markets and to have other undesirable social consequences. When self-interest is confined to constructive market channels, the market is in fact an immensely useful instrument for organizing the production of goods and services. In its essence, the market is a system of exchange that greatly facilitates trading among any group larger than a few people. As an alternative to a political or other type of barter regime, the enormous advantages of an economic system based on the use of money and prices for the processes of exchange requires little further explanation in this day and age.

Yet, if self-interest is to reign, why should it not reign everywhere? The answer can not be found in any formal models of current economics. Even outside of economics, while there is a rapidly growing literature emphasizing that economic growth requires an adequate foundation of "social capital," this literature says little about the means of creating and sustaining such a foundation.* How does a social climate of "trust" come into existence? How is a cultural environment of honesty in economic transactions established and maintained? Admittedly, a good individual reputation for honesty and fair dealing is important in any business or political system where social interactions occur repeatedly, but a "reputation" need be upheld only so long as it serves self-interest. A good reputation can be faked in the short run and then violated whenever convenient. Good reputation is not the same as a culture in which trust is ingrained as a generalized social expectation and reality.[13]

Describing such a culture is difficult in the ordinary language of the social sciences. It may help to turn to the artistic imagination. It is said that the eighteenth century was the century of France; the nineteenth, of England; and the twentieth, of America. Commenting in 1872 on the real sources of England's advance in the nineteenth century, George Eliot winds up the novel *Middlemarch* with the following words: "The growing good of the world is partly dependent on unhistoric acts; and that things are not so ill with you and me as they might have been, is half owing to the number who lived faithfully a hidden life."[14] Good acts that are "hidden" do little to advance reputation as might then contribute to individual private gain. Eliot

---

* The necessity of a culture that sustains economic growth also does not mean that there is only one such culture. Historian David S. Landes, in his recent *The Wealth and Poverty of Nations: Why Some Are So Rich and Some So Poor* (New York: Norton, 1998), asserts that "if we learn anything from the history of economic development, it is that culture makes all the difference." In a review of this book, Columbia University economist Jagdish Bhagwati finds that Landes puts too much emphasis on the specific role of "underlying values as defined by the Judeo-Christian, and especially the Protestant, universe." Bhagwati concludes that "the precise role of culture in economic behavior remains elusive. The encouraging truth appears to be that growth-inducing institutions . . . are resilient and compatible with a range of cultures." See Jagdish Bhagwati, "The Explanation," *New Republic*, May 25, 1998, 32, 34, 36.

Yet, in support of Landes, one might note that the Judeo-Christian value system spread around the world in the twentieth century in predominantly secular forms. One would be hard pressed to find any nation that has been economically successful without having adopted a large dose of "modern" values, but these are values that originated in large part in European civilization, where they were shaped in significant degree by Judeo-Christian religion (which now exerts its most powerful influences in such secularized forms).

was reminding us that a successful society may require many people who do "the right thing" for no other reason than that.

No less an authority than James Q. Wilson has written that human nature involves both a "self-interested" side and an "altruistic" side. Contrary to the almost exclusive emphasis on the former in economic analysis, Wilson concludes after a lifetime of close observation of political and economic affairs that "on balance, I think the other-regarding features of human nature outweigh the self-regarding ones." There exists in most human beings a tendency "to sociability and hence to morality, although it is only a disposition and not a rule." Much of life cannot be explained in ordinary economic terms. For example, "why do women have children? There is no economic gain to them and much pain in the process." It is not only family life but the economic life of whole societies that may depend on these social elements that lie outside traditional economic forms of explanation.[15]

Economists have particular difficulties with such an area of inquiry because almost inevitably it brings up the subject of religion, and the real basis for religious belief. The practical consequences of religion can be integrated easily enough into economic analysis—treating religious values as a key influence in shaping a given individual structure of "preferences." But the sources of religious belief represent a much less familiar and much less comfortable ground for economic analysis. Yet the successful workings of an economic system may depend heavily on the specific character of religious beliefs that serve to provide a normative foundation for the market. Achieving a more efficient economy may depend on having a more "efficient" religion.

A surprising possibility is thus raised: it might not be economists but theologians who are the most important members of society in determining economic performance. The nations that grow most rapidly may be the nations with the "better" religions, the religions that are able to establish a set of cultural norms that create a higher level of social capital for their economies—religions that, among other things, resolve the market paradox in a satisfactory way.[16] However, a still more radical possibility exists. It may that economists themselves been acting in the requisite religious capacity. Startling as the thought must be to most current economists, it may be that their most important social role has been as preachers of a religion with the special character that it acts to uphold the normative foundation required for a rapidly growing modern economy.

Indeed, in this book I will make precisely this argument. Economists played their most important role in American society in the twentieth century as theologians and preachers of a religion. Religion has long provided evidence that it is capable of inspiring a powerful dedication to work for the common good, ranging from the acts of Christian martyrs who sacrificed their lives to less extreme forms of sacrifice of individual interest. But the defense of a market economy cannot rest on any ordinary religion. It requires a religion with the particular characteristic that it advances the pursuit of self-interest in appropriate domains but tightly restrains it in others.

As is argued in this book, the mainstream "economic religion" in the United States today (it has not always been true, as, for example, in the progressive orthodoxies early in the twentieth century) offers such a market sustaining set of norms. Leading economists teach the acceptability of self-interest in the market but the "sins" of similarly opportunistic behavior in "politics." Within the marketplace, economists warn of the dangers of a tolerance for "corruption" in economic interactions. Economists are strong advocates of a rule of law that rigorously defends property rights and promotes adherence to contracts, again dependent on a cultural environment of long-term honesty and trust. All these things are reinforced by a religious/moral system that encourages self-sacrificing actions for the greater good of "the market system."

The manner in which economists have accomplished the necessary delicate balancing act between self-interest and commitment to a greater public good will be analyzed in full detail in subsequent chapters. However, the essence of the argument can be previewed here. In economic religion, the existence of a market economic system itself serves a religious purpose. Hence, while perhaps objectionable in other contexts, the full expression of self-interest within the setting of the market is therefore blessed by a religious cause. The religious purpose of the market is to ensure maximal efficiency in the use of the material resources of society, and thus rapid movement of American society along a route of economic progress in this world.

Economic progress is so important because progress is seen as the path to the attainment of a new heaven on earth, to a secular salvation. If the love of money is, as many have believed, the root of all evil, the end of scarcity and the arrival of an era of full material abundance can mean the end of evil in the world. The Fall in the Garden of Eden will finally be reversed, now in our own age by the application of economic knowledge to sustain rapid economic progress. Because the market in this gospel has such an exalted function in society, it is the duty of every follower in the faith to defend the market system, forgoing the opportunistic pursuit of a large number of potentially advantageous but "unethical" actions, actions that might in fact serve the self-interest of the individual, although undermining the efficiency of the market.

There could be other religious paths to the same outcome. God (or his representatives in the church on earth) might decree that the pursuit of self-interest within the marketplace is within the divine plan, but other forms of self-interest outside the market—actions that would tend to subvert its workings—would violate God's commands.[17] In the modern era, however, as older religions have had less influence in the conduct of the affairs of society, such a traditional religious blessing for the market system would have been less persuasive to a secular society. It has instead fallen to a new priesthood in the economics profession to provide a normative foundation for the market, now necessarily taking a secular religious form.

In contrast to the tenets of this modern economic religion, those of many religions throughout history have condemned the pursuit of self-interest in almost every domain of society, including the market.* Marxism and socialism had such worldwide appeal partly because they had so many predecessors in history (and contrary to their claims, many of the real effects and much of the appeal of Marxism and socialism were conservative, acting to perpetuate premodern forms of existence—communism in the former Soviet Union thus tending to continue many of the old arrangements of Russian czarism in the face of looming market and democratic forces in the early twentieth century). It takes a special religion with special theological characteristics to resolve the market paradox. However much at odds with their own self-image, economists in the United States (and perhaps other European and non-Western countries, but that is a subject that will have to be studied more closely at another time and place) have played their most important role in society in establishing the necessary cultural foundation—the

---

* And many Americans today as well still feel a deep ambivalence about the potential impact of market motives and incentives on other aspects of their lives. A three-year research project "Religion and Economic Values," at Princeton University surveyed more than two thousand people. Robert Wuthnow reported the results:

> In the survey, 89 percent agreed that "our society is much too materialistic." 74 percent said that materialism is a serious social problem; and 71 percent said society would be better off if less emphasis were placed on money. Many of the people we talked to described the corrosive effect of materialism on their families.
>
> Most of us are quite sincere when we express concern about our society's pervasive materialism. We sense that our wants are spiraling out of control. We know there is more to life than having nice things. For many of us, a religious factor may also prompt our misgivings. We are dimly aware of biblical teachings contrasting the worship of God and mammon. When journalists write of greed, we remember that religious authors have had something to say on the topic as well. Secular as our culture is, 71 percent agree that "being greedy is a sin against God."
>
> Thinking that materialism is a serious problem, however, seems to have little connection with how we actually live our lives. Money and material possessions are, in fact, among the things we cherish most deeply. . . . 84 percent admitted "I wish I had more money than I do."

See Robert Wuthnow, "Pious Materialism: How Americans View Faith and Money," *The Christian Century*, March 3, 1993, 238–39.

social capital—in support of the competitive market as an institution for broad social benefit.★

BEING A PROFESSIONAL

The dichotomous treatment of self-interest as found in economic morality—blessing it in some realms of society, condemning it in others—is illustrated by the ethics of economic professionalism. Although most professional economists actively encourage the assertion of self-interest in the market, in their own role in society as economic professionals the expression of self-interest in many forms is disapproved. The economist can of course work for money. However, the economist as professional (admittedly an ideal sometimes more professed than upheld) is ethically bound in his or her professional capacity to reject offers of money to bias or distort economic advice in favor of one or another party—even if there is no chance of this being discovered, and it would in fact genuinely serve the self-interest of the economist. The morality of professionalism is not that of the marketplace but of the priesthoods of old whose members have always been able to accept money for their services but only in limited and appropriate circumstances.

Like some priests of the past, some economists today are motivated in practice by the opportunity for private gain—for cushy university appointments, lucrative consulting contracts, or other personal benefits. Yet many economists have been sacrificing and continue to sacrifice monetary gain in the pursuit of religious truth, in this case the truths of economic efficiency and the path of material progress in society. Even in a market economic system grounded in the pursuit of individual self-interest, it is necessary to have such a priestly class, religiously dedicated to protecting the market system

---

★ A fascinating example of a priesthood that failed to resolve the ethical tensions with respect to the market and instead acted powerfully to inhibit economic growth is found in China. In the 1400s China was not only the most economically developed society in the world but also a maritime power, exploring as far as the eastern coast of Africa with large and technically sophisticated sailing vessels, led by Admiral Zheng He. These efforts, however, ran afoul of the Confucian scholars who had great influence in the court of the Chinese Emperor. Eventually, they succeeding in halting the voyages of exploration, imposed a ban on construction of new ships, and even destroyed the maritime records. These actions were partly a reflection of the tenets of Confucian religion: "The dominant social ethos in ancient China was Confucianism and in India it was caste, with the result that the elites in both nations looked down their noses at business. Ancient China cared about many things—prestige, honor, culture, arts, education, ancestors, religion, filial piety—but making money came far down the list. Confucius had specifically declared that it was wrong for a man to make a distant voyage while his parents were alive, and he had condemned profit as the concern of 'a little man.' " See Nicholas D. Kristof, "1492: The Prequel," *New York Times Magazine,* June 6, 1999, 85.

against political rent seeking and various other potentially destructive forms of individual opportunism.

However, as I will also explore in this book, today there is a crisis of social legitimacy facing the members of the economics profession, and economic religion more broadly.[18] Enormous material advance has in fact been achieved by nations in the developed world in the modern era, accelerating in the twentieth century.[19] It is more and more being recognized, however, that the main corpus of economic theory does a poor job of explaining all this economic growth and development.[20] As will be examined in later chapters of this book, the members of the economics profession have themselves been declaring with increasing frequency that their own past "scientific" efforts to understand the mechanisms of economic growth and development have fallen well short of expectations.★

Yet the more important crisis now facing economics reflects deeper concerns. There is a wide loss of faith today in the redeeming benefits of economic progress itself. At the beginning of the twentieth century, there was a sure conviction throughout the Western world that the solution to the material problems of the human condition must also mean the solution to crime, drug addiction, suicide, hatred, and war and indeed a general spiritual transformation in the human condition for the better. If the market (or any other economic system) could guarantee continuing rapid economic growth, it would be the route to salvation in this world.

People had behaved so badly throughout previous history, it was thought in those more optimistic days, because they had been driven to it by material deprivation. In a world always before characterized by severe material shortages for most people, it had seemingly been necessary to cheat and steal simply in order to survive at all. Wars between nations were mostly the product of competition for land and resources. All this would be changed, however, when modern economic growth and development had provided a full abundance of every good and service for all.

★ Economists, for example, were once confident that they could scientifically model an economy and predict with reasonable accuracy its future course. Illustrative of a broader loss of confidence in society in the technical capabilities of economists, repeated failures of prediction have now yielded a public attitude of deep skepticism toward such efforts by economists. Economics writer Steven Pearlstein recently commented on the follies of the "hapless forecasters" among the members of the economics profession. See Steven Pearlstein, "An Economy That Just Keeps On Growing," *Washington Post,* May 2, 1998, A1. Advising on the usefulness of economics to investors in the stock market, the former head of the Fidelity Magellan Fund, Peter Lynch, declared that "if you spend over 14 minutes a year on economics, you've wasted 12 minutes." Quoted in William Power, "Heard on the Street," *Wall Street Journal,* December 3, 1992, C1.

Yet, as matters turned out, the terrible wars, genocides, and other events in the history of the twentieth century belied this faith.[21] A nation such as Germany could be a scientific leader of the world, have a modern economy with a much higher standard of living in comparison with most previous conditions of human existence, and yet be taken over—let us not mince words— by pure evil. All this was virtually incomprehensible in the rational terms of the modern religions of economic progress. Looking back at these awful events, even if the claims of economists to show the true scientific (rational) route to economic advance are still accepted, society is less inclined to recognize the religious authority of the economic priesthood.*Apparently, the search for a new heaven on earth will have to be abandoned, or an alternative route of secular salvation outside material realms alone will have to be discovered.

Then, the very practical functions served by economists—priestly functions in defense of the common good that may be little related to the formal contents of high-level economic theory—may thereby also be jeopardized. This is a significant problem not only for the members of the economics profession but for society as a whole. Society will always require the services of some kind of priestly class, economic or otherwise, in order to assist in fending off the widespread rent seeking and other multiple forms of opportunism that always threaten the bonds of social cohesion. If economists (aided by other social scientists) no longer have the requisite social authority to perform this role, to whom will it fall?

As these observations suggest, I believe that the American economics pro-

---

* From the vantage point of the end of the twentieth century, historian Gertrude Himmelfarb summarized the new thinking about progress.

> Science and technology, like progress itself, can be morally equivocal. It was not a millenium ago but in this very century that we experienced one of the most monstrous events in human history, the Holocaust, and discovered, not for the first time, that both science and technology can be put to the most heinous uses. We have also been obliged to reconsider the Enlightenment, which bequeathed to us many splendid achievements but also some dangerous illusions.
>
> In our post-Enlightenment world, we have had to relearn what ancient philosophy and religion had taught us and what recent history has brought home to us: that material progress can have an inverse relationship to moral progress, that the most benign social policies can have unintended and unfortunate effects, that national passions can be exacerbated in an ostensibly global world and religious passions in a supposedly secular one, and that our most cherished principles (liberty, equality, fraternity, even peace) can be perverted and degraded—that, in short, progress in all its spheres, not only in science and technology, is unpredictable and undependable.

See Gertrude Himmelfarb, "Two Cheers (or Maybe Just One) for Progress," *Wall Street Journal,* May 5, 1999, A22.

fession is on the verge of fundamental change. The profession emerged at the end of the nineteenth century as part of an earlier wave of basic change in American society, led by economic, political science, and other theorists of the American Progressive movement. The economics profession was part of a general effort to develop the institutional apparatus of professional expertise, then considered an essential element in achieving the scientific management of society, a critical step on the route to heaven on earth. In the university world, for example, as the teaching of technical skills in many fields took the place of the old mission of Protestant education; the knowledge provided by the modern university would now lay the basis for a new salvation in this world. One religious role for the university had in effect succeeded another. Superceding the institutional Christian churches of old, as George Marsden comments, Progressivism now made "the nation its church"—and Washington, D.C., would become in effect a new Vatican (and like the Vatican, Washington would be a unique governing jurisdiction separate in its sovereignty from the rest of the nation).[22] Indeed, the efforts of Progressive Era social scientists paved the way for the full development of the American welfare and regulatory state of the twentieth century, headquartered in Washington.[23]

However, as the twentieth century ended, the old progressive ideas had about played themselves out. There is a search now in many quarters for new models of governance, including a working out of new roles in the governing process for professional groups such as economists.[24] As I will argue in the present volume, economists may themselves have to rethink at a fundamental level what it means to be a member of a profession such as economics. Economists may have to learn to think of themselves more like members of the priesthoods of old—the defenders of a core social ethic grounded in a religious truth—than as research scientists.

An important concern of this book thus is the very social meaning of "being a member of the economics profession." There have been a number of historical studies (mostly by noneconomists) of the development of the idea of professionalism in the Progressive Era and its later evolution.[25] However, typical of a lack of introspection with respect to their own role in society, economists themselves have been rather unreflective about the social meaning and consequences of their professional identities.[26] If asked what it means to be an economic professional, many current economists would probably be somewhat surprised or puzzled by the question. They might simply assert that to be a professional economist means to pursue scientific truth with respect to the operation of the economy and to apply this truth to improve economic performance and public policy more generally.

However, this answer would be a strained one for most economists. It would assert a collective purpose and social idealism in the role of the econ-omist as professional at odds with the "methodological individualism" and "rational actor" forms of analysis characteristic of economic thinking in al-most all other domains. A more consistent answer for an economist would be that the role of the economic professional means using the social prestige of professionalism to get a good job with reasonable pay, interesting work, and a comfortable surrounding environment—asserting the special status of a professional as a good way to maximize the individual well-being (the "utility") of an economist.

As in other collective action situations, it is very unlikely that the efforts of any one economist will make any difference to the future overall perform-ance of an economic system as large as that of the United States. So substan-tial shirking on economic work effort (especially after receiving tenure) would also be a logical response for an economic professional acting accord-ing to the standard behavioral assumptions of economic models. Why should any economist work day and night to discover economic truth? Why should an economist try to "do his or her small part in society" in the larger strug-gle to adopt sound economic policies that promote growth and develop-ment around the world? Just as the act of voting by an individual in an election will virtually never influence the election outcome, the actions of any individual economist will be virtually meaningless in terms of any broader economic outcomes in society.

Yet, if not all economists, there have been many past and present econo-mists who are in fact strongly motivated to do good in the world (if perhaps often falling well short in practice). How can economists justify telling others to actively pursue their self-interest as the best way to serve society, when many of them behave otherwise? The answer, it would seem, will have to be found in some form of "noneconomic" explanation (or one that is "eco-nomic" but in a much broader sense than is traditionally offered). Many econ-omists—as well as many millions of ordinary citizens of nations in the developed world—have in fact been true believers in an economic religion of progress that promised finally to reverse the consequences of the Fall in the Garden of Eden. This religion had the additional practical consequence that it resolved the market paradox and in this way promoted markets even while sustaining the normative foundations of modern economic professionalism.

CAMBRIDGE VERSUS CHICAGO

In pursuing in further detail the questions raised thus far, I will develop my analysis by examining the theories and writings of a number of modern

American economists from the perspective of "economic theology." I concentrate on the history of the American economics profession in the twentieth century and mainly the years since World War II.* For the first two or three decades after this war, American economics was dominated by ideas originating in Cambridge, Massachusetts. Paul Samuelson was a professor in the economics department at the Massachusetts Institute of Technology (MIT) and the leading economist at Cambridge. His *Foundations of Economic Analysis* and other writings led a methodological revolution in American economics in the years after World War II, the main reason that in 1970 Samuelson was the first American and third winner overall of the Nobel Prize in economics (the prize was not given in economics until 1969, when Ragnar Frisch of Norway and Jan Tinbergen of Holland became the first recipients). In the years following Samuelson's arrival, MIT would become the most prestigious economics department in the United States. If MIT had been founded as a school of engineering, it was perhaps fitting that the MIT economics department would now become the leading American advocate for a new scientific form of social engineering of the American economy on a grand scale.

Yet, among Samuelson's writings, it was not the *Foundations* that had the greatest influence on American society at large. The closest thing to a bible of economics during the several decades after World War II was Samuelson's introductory textbook *Economics.* Hence, as an especially illuminating means of exploring the implicit religious messages contained in the writings of post–World War II economics, Parts I and II below focus on the religious elements of *Economics.*

First introduced to the market more than fifty years ago, *Economics* is now in its sixteenth edition (with a co-author, William Nordhaus, in the more recent editions), has sold more than 3.5 million copies, and has been translated into at least forty-six languages.[27] *Economics* created the model emulated in almost every introductory economics textbook for the following fifty years.[28] Although it has not led the market since the 1960s, *Economics* was until then the leading textbook in annual sales.[29] *Economics* both promoted and reflected a value system of rationally directed progress that was dominant in American society from the end of World War II into the 1960s, and is still very influential today. If economists have in the end been priests of a secular religion, the "theology" of economics was particularly well expressed in *Economics.* How-

---

* In my previous book on economic theology, *Reaching for Heaven on Earth: The Theological Meaning of Economics,* I explored the interaction of ideas about economics and theology as far back as the ancient Greeks. In contrast to the current volume, much of that book covers the history of economic thought prior to the twentieth century.

ever, consistent with the stated goal that economics should be "value neutral," the powerful value elements were for the most part overtly suppressed and instead would now show up in an underlying and implicit fashion.

Yet, as will be demonstrated in Part II of this book, many of the key conclusions of *Economics* do not follow logically, if implicit theological assumptions are not made to sustain the argument. It is as though a mathematician had provided the proof of a theorem but had left out one-quarter of the steps necessary to the end result—and in *Economics* the missing steps were typically the ones that belied the value-neutral claims of the book. If we penetrate below the surface in this way, *Economics* is revealed to be a religious work grounded in articles of progressive faith, as well as a conventional analysis of economic forces at work.

Since *Economics* has had sixteen editions, it is a bit misleading to speak of it as one book. For the purposes of the analysis of this book, I will focus on the first edition.[30] It was the publication of this edition in 1948, and its almost immediate success, that set the stage for not only Samuelson's subsequent efforts but also those of other introductory textbook writers in economics. While Samuelson later made extensive revisions to some sections, and has added new topics as the areas of greatest current policy interest have shifted, the core ideas and values have remained fairly consistent through successive editions of *Economics.*★ Indeed, Samuelson stated in 1992 that "I do not perceive that my value-judgment ideology has changed systematically since the age of 25."[31]

From the 1960s onward, social values in American life would change rapidly. The value system of *Economics* no longer fit the prevailing American ethos as well as it had in the first two decades of its existence. At the same time a new school of economics based at the University of Chicago took center stage in American intellectual life. It was not a coincidence, as I will argue below, that Chicago replaced Cambridge as the focal point for American economics.

★ There may also be an advantage to using the first edition, since Samuelson may have been somewhat more revealing there of his own foundational values. It was written at a moment of great postwar optimism about the capacity of experts to manage society through the use of professional knowledge such as provided in *Economics.* Over time, while these values still remained at the core of the book, there have been greater doubts. Samuelson has always been one to pay attention to changing trends, and it has become perhaps more difficult to disentangle his core philosophy from other materials.

Yet Samuelson commented in October 1997 that on his rereading the original 1948 edition, it had "been a pleasant surprise to discover how much of the original verve and relevance is still there." He noted that other introductory-textbook authors had followed in the path of ideas that "had first entered the public domain in the present commemorative volume." Samuelson now regards his textbook as a grand "cathedral" he built for the economics profession—a kind of personal monument for which a religious metaphor is appropriate. See Samuelson's new foreword to the commemorative reprint of the first 1948 edition of *Economics* (New York: McGraw Hill, 1998).

Chicago exhibited a hostility to many of the projects of the American progressive tradition just as progressive ideas and institutions were losing favor in American society. If MIT had been the center in the United States for the evolving self-concept of economics as a "science," the founder of the Chicago school, Frank Knight, rejected both the goal itself and the practical feasibility of the scientific management of society. It was perhaps symbolic of the differences in viewpoint that some of the leading economists at Chicago wrote in old-fashioned prose comprehensible to the ordinary person.

In this book I also explore the fundamental values expressed—the underlying "theology"—in the economic thinking at Chicago. With origins going back to the 1930s, and as might be expected for a school that is nearing seventy years old, there is greater diversity of thought among the various practitioners of Chicago economics than in the writings of a single economist such as Samuelson. Chicago economics falls in the tradition of the "protesters" against the mainstream orthodoxies of the times—one might thus see the Chicago school as a modern, secular continuation in the tradition of Protestant Reformers such as Martin Luther and John Calvin. Indeed, the connections to Protestant theology found at Chicago go beyond this sociological observation. The welfare and regulatory state of the twentieth century has in many respects served as the modern equivalent of a church. If progressive religion has served as the gospel of this national church of America, the Chicago school of economics has protested that American Progressivism preaches a false religion, and that the church itself has been corrupted to serve special interests and other private purposes. Washington, D.C., is the new Rome where the original American virtues have been lost.

In condemning both the sustaining faith and the institutional forms of the modern welfare and regulatory state, Chicago has also promoted a new libertarian trend within economics. It is a libertarianism that has closely mirrored a broader spread of individualistic values in American society since the 1960s, going well beyond economic affairs. This new individualism is manifested in no-fault divorce, abortion "choice," student "liberation" from traditional college supervision, increased sexual freedom, and the relaxation of many other social constraints on individual behavior. Chicago economics did not create these trends but—much as Samuelson blessed progressive values—the Chicago school has put its priestly imprimatur on a newly libertarian set of values in American life.*

---

* A recent analysis of basic trends in American politics since the 1960s finds that there has been a fundamental shift in power to "citizens groups" associated with the civil rights, environmental, feminist, antiabortion, and other causes. The members of such groups "place aesthetics, morality, rights and

As the twenty-first century begins, it seems increasingly clear that a new religion, belief system, guiding paradigm—whatever one chooses to call it—will be required to replace the past role of the progressive gospel of the twentieth century in shaping and legitimizing the governing institutions of American society. One might even go so far as to say that in some fundamental sense the idea of elevating science to the status of a religion—the "modern project" of the past three hundred years in the Western world—increasingly seems to be failing.[32] Despite long-standing wide hopes, it has proved difficult to transfer the extraordinary powers of science in explaining matters of physical nature to a corresponding set of explanatory and predictive powers in human society. Whatever its astonishing successes in creating a power to control physical nature for human purposes, the scientific method has been much less successful in corresponding social efforts. Science seemingly cannot provide the complete explanation for all questions important to human beings. And as more and more people also now seem to be saying, this is perhaps fortunately so.

THE PLAN OF THE BOOK

This book is organized as follows. In Part I, I examine the values of the American Progressive movement at the end of the nineteenth and the early part of the twentieth century. Progressives saw in economic progress the route to a new heaven on earth, a future of full material abundance where past evils of human behavior resulting from the fierce competition for economic resources would finally be abolished. Part II shows how Samuelson in *Economics* adapted this American secular religion—a progressive "gospel of efficiency," as the historian Samuel Hays once called it—to the new intellectual climate of the United States in the years after World War II.[33]

Economists at the University of Chicago played a central role in showing

---

other nonmaterial political objectives above the pursuit of economic gain or enhanced physical security." As their political influence has grown, the U.S. Congress has become "less concerned about the needs of business and more concerned about how to protect the earth and preserve our souls." This is a reflection of the fact that these predominantly "liberal citizen groups . . . don't share the view that the solution to most of our problems is more prosperity." In understanding the decline in political power of the AFL-CIO, and the rise of the Sierra Club, "America's embrace of postmaterial values lies at the foundation of the changes observed." If Chicago economics captured the declining faith in traditional progressive themes more accurately than other parts of economics, it also reflected more closely a libertarian trend in American social values associated with some of these same "postmaterial values." See Jeffrey M. Berry, *The New Liberalism: The Rising Power of Citizen Groups* (Washington, D.C.: The Brookings Institution, 1999), 36, 37, 86, 119.

the fundamental deficiencies of *Economics* and other writings by progressive economists grounded in similar foundational values and assumptions. Part III of the book follows the development of the Chicago school of economics, including the value systems—implicit theologies, as this book finds them—of some of its leading members. It shows how prominent figures in the Chicago school have played a central part in the development and legitimization of a new individualistic and libertarian ethic in American life since the 1960s.

In that same period the neoclassical framework of economic analysis—the core ideas as developed for popular consumption in Samuelson's *Economics*—has been undermined by the theoretical framework of a "new institutional economics."[34] A new institutional school today has become an important part of American economic thought, finding many proponents among the faculty members at the most prestigious of American economics departments.[35] As will be examined in Part IV, the new institutional economics, including a new appreciation of the economic significance of religious beliefs, may also point the way to the future of economics in the twenty-first century. For readers outside the economics profession, Part IV can also serve as a brief overview of a basic redirection toward institutional concerns that has taken place within American economics during the past thirty years.

Finally, in Part V I further develop the view that, although economists have served an important function in generating a working knowledge of the behavior of the U.S. and global economic systems, a still more important role has been in providing a defense for certain values in American society. The members of the economics profession have helped to provide a value foundation of civic-mindedness grounded in a religious belief in the redeeming benefits of economic progress. For much of the twentieth century this value-foundation had the particularly important property that it approved the expression of self-interest in the market even while successfully denying legitimacy to many other forms of harmful "opportunism" in other areas of society. Rather than being value-neutral technicians, members of economic schools since Adam Smith have been the most influential priests of the modern age. It has been their special religious task to find a satisfactory moral resolution to "the market paradox."

In the Conclusion I speculate briefly on how the self-image and the practices of American economics may be transformed in the twenty-first century, as the long-term trends explored in this book take greater hold in society.

part **ONE**

THE LAWS OF ECONOMICS AS THE NEW WORD OF GOD

In the early decades of the twentieth century, a minority of economists such as Thorstein Veblen and Wesley Clair Mitchell, associated with the institutionalist school of American economics and the Progressive movement, advocated the "scientific management" of society through the instrument of government. Much of the economics profession, however, continued to believe in the merits of markets with a minimum of government intervention. By the 1940s, even the minority of institutional economists was rapidly disappearing from the American scene.

The role of Paul Samuelson's *Economics* in the history of American economic thought was to revive the progressive message. In doing so, Samuelson could draw on a new design for the scientific management of society as developed in the 1930s by John Maynard Keynes in England. Samuelson abandoned the common progressive faith that government should replace the market in many areas of society and directly administer economic actions. The U.S. Forest Service, for example, was created in 1905 as a superior administrative instrument for obtaining maximum long-run productivity from the forests of the nation. Instead, in Samuelson's newer version of progressivism (a "neoprogressivism," one might call it) the market would remain the basic instrument of production. Although the functions of government would be less encompassing, many important tasks would remain, including the government management of the market to maintain full employment and for other social purposes—a task now believed to be feasible with the advances in scientific economic understanding achieved by Keynes and other modern economists.

Samuelson also sought to rework progressive ideas into a more rigorous and mathematic form, in this manner aiming to give them a new prestige and authority. In the wake of the New Deal transformation in the role of the federal government in American life, the growing acceptance of Keynesian remedies, and the great expansion of government as a whole during and after World War II—even while maintaining the core of a market system—American society was newly receptive to the new progressive message as developed in *Economics*. It offered not only a prescription for the federal government's active management of the economy but also provided a strong message of inspiration for the traditional value system of American progressivism—a conviction that economic progress is achieving a basic transformation of the world for the better, that the new scientific understanding of society will guide the way to a triumph of material progress that will mean a secular salvation here on earth.

In Part I, I briefly examine the origins in the late nineteenth and early twentieth century of a progressive value system that would inspire *Economics*. The belief that modern science and industrial advance were solving the basic problems of the human condition was widespread at that time and was held by economists as diverse as Karl Marx, John Maynard Keynes, and many American progressive economists. The ways in which Samuelson's new textbook in 1948 would then spread this secular faith in progress to a new generation of American readers with great persuasiveness will be explored in Part II.

chapter ONE

TENETS OF ECONOMIC FAITH

To the extent that any system of economic ideas offers an alternative vision of the "ultimate values," or "ultimate reality," that actually shapes the workings of history, economics is offering yet another grand prophesy in the biblical tradition. The Jewish and Christian bibles foretell one outcome of history. If economics foresees another, it is in effect offering a competing religious vision. The prophesies of economics would then be a substitute for the traditional messages of the Bible. Perhaps the biblical God has reconsidered. Perhaps, instead of Jesus, he has now chosen economists to be a new bearer of his message, replacing the word of the Old and New Testaments that has now become outdated for the modern age—as Islam advertised the Koran as a later and more accurate statement of God's real plans for the world. Perhaps God has decided that the underlying ordering forces of the world, the ultimate reality that will shape the future outcome of history, will truly be economic.

To be sure, for many thinkers, such a message of economic prophesy has not depended on the necessary existence of any god in the hereafter. In this case their belief system results not in a Judeo-Christian heresy, but in an entirely new and secular religion—although one that draws many of its themes from the biblical tradition, now typically reworking them in a less direct and mostly implicit fashion.[1]

THE MARXIST EXAMPLE

No economic thinker, for example, was more outwardly antagonistic to religion than Karl Marx.[2] Religion was for him the "opiate" of the masses. Yet, in retrospect, no social scientist better illustrates the power of underlying religious influences than Marx.★ Beneath his confused economic analysis and grand pronouncements on the economic laws of history lies a simple biblical eschatology. Humankind has fallen into evil ways, corrupted by the workings of the forces of the class struggle. The resulting "alienation" for Marx has virtually the same meaning for the human situation as "original sin" in the biblical message. Human beings are today still living in a state of darkness, depravity, and corruption.

The prospect of escape from this terrible condition, however, is close at hand. God (now replaced in Marx by the economic laws of history) has promised to deliver the world from sin (alienation). There will be a fierce struggle and a great cataclysm (a final war in history between the capitalist and the working classes), followed by the arrival of the kingdom of God on earth (the triumph of the proletariat and the arrival of pure communism). In Christian theology the twin coercive instruments of government and property are both products of the fallen condition of mankind in this world since the Garden of Eden, and in heaven neither will exist. In Marxist theology as well, the end of the class struggle, the end of alienation (sin), will bring about the abolition of government and property alike. Secular religion, as this example shows, can follow remarkably closely in the path of Judeo-Christian religion.

Marx thus is best understood not fundamentally as an economist at all, but as another Jewish messiah—like Jesus—with another message of salvation for the world. If the message of Jesus had conquered the Mediterranean and European world, the Marxist gospel in the twentieth century would spread over Russia, China, and many other nations—to billions of people throughout the globe. As Paul Tillich said in his history of Christian religion, and however distorted the Marxist gospel, Marx was one of the most influential "theologians" who ever lived.[3] To be sure, as D. McCloskey has said is true for of the value systems embodied in the work of many current economists as well, this value system of Marx with its roots in Judeo-Christian eschatology is never made explicit; instead, the religion is left buried under a large body of ostensibly "scientific" arguments.[4]

Thus, the libertarian and Austrian economist Murray Rothbard considered Marxism to be an "atheized variant of a venerable Christian heresy"

★ *The Encyclopedia of the World's Religions* includes a chapter on Marxism, declaring that it meets all the essential requirements of a religion. See R. C. Zaehner, "Dialectical Materialism," in R. C. Zaehner, ed., *Encyclopedia of the World's Religions* (New York: Barnes and Noble Books, 1997).

that offered a "messianic goal" to be realized by the "apocalyptic creation" of a new world order. Joachim of Fiore and other Christian visionaries had preached messages of a communist "final state of mankind as one of perfect harmony and equality," inspiring among others the later Anabaptist revolutionaries of the Protestant Reformation. The greatest new element introduced by Marx and his followers in the modern age was that these ancient themes now assumed a "secular context."[5] Aside from this, Rothbard saw Marxism as the application of an ancient formula:

> [For Marx] history is the history of suffering, of class struggle, of the exploitation of man by man. In the same way as the return of the Messiah, in Christian theology, would put an end to history and establish a new Heaven and new Earth, so the establishment of communism would put an end to human history. And just as for . . . Christians, man, led by God's prophets and saints, would establish a Kingdom of God on Earth, . . . so for Marx and other schools of communists, mankind, led by a vanguard of secular saints, would establish a secularized kingdom of heaven on earth.[6]

The success of Marxism in Russia, according to one leading interpreter, was attributable to its ability to draw on a long-standing "'religious conception of the czar's authority' and a deep belief that land belonged to God." The powerful religious faith of the Russian people was capable of "switching over and directing itself to purposes which are not merely religious, for example, to social objects," part of a process in which Russians "could very readily pass from one integrated faith to another" as found in the Marxist gospel. Indeed, as perceived by many Russians, "the world mission of the [Communist Party] Third International echoed Orthodox Christian messianism, which saw Moscow as the Third Rome." Under Stalin, the members of the communist party functioned "less as members of a political party than as clergy under an infallible pope."[7]

Marxist economics clearly met Tillich's requirement that a genuine religion must offer a vision of "ultimate reality." For Marx everything that happened in the history of the world was controlled by economic laws. Altogether blind to the obvious religious character of his own economic system, Marx said that every form of religious belief is merely a product of a particular economic stage of the class struggle. Echoing this tenet of Marxist faith, for example, in the bible of Chinese communism, the "red book," Mao Tse-Tung would say that "in the general development of history the material determines the mental and social being determines social consciousness."[8]

Religion for Marxism thus can have no objective content; it merely provides a convenient rationalization for the relations of economic power of the moment. If capitalists are the dominant economic class today, then the current religion of society will be determined by the objective needs of capitalism at this particular time. If capitalists actually believe in the truth of their religion, this grand self-delusion merely shows the warped and distorted quality of human thought in the current state of deep human alienation (a secular restatement of the sinfulness of fallen men and women).

Marx regards everything else in society in the same perspective. Political organizations, social theories, the legal system, the role of universities, all the institutional features of society are designed to serve the existing relationships of economic power, as manifested in and determined by the current stage of the class struggle. As a new "ultimate reality," the laws of economics have literally taken the very place of the laws of God in ordering the world. The economic god of Marx is, moreover, a harsh god in the biblical tradition; he has condemned the present world to constant fighting and destruction and most human beings to lives of deception and depravity.

To be sure, Marx may have offered an exaggerated version, but he was hardly alone in thinking in this religious way. Just as the biblical message was recorded by Matthew, Mark, Luke, and John in different versions, the god who works through economic history has also had multiple interpreters. Jean-Jacques Rousseau, according to one authority, believed that "it was property alone which induced crime and wars," corrupting the original happy state of nature by conflicts over material possessions.[9] Also in the eighteenth century, David Hume had said: "Let us suppose that nature has bestowed on the human race such profuse *abundance* of all *external* conveniences, that . . . every individual finds himself fully provided with whatever his most voracious appetite can want, or luxurious imagination wish or desire." If this state of affairs should ever be reached, Hume suggested, "it seems evident that, in such a happy state, every other social virtue would flourish, and receive tenfold increase." Property and the divisions in society it fosters would cease to have relevance in a world of perfect abundance; issues of social justice would no longer be a concern, because there would be little or no crime or conflict. It would be a world of "unlimited abundance" where "justice, in that case, being totally useless, would be an idle ceremonial."[10]

By the late nineteenth century and well into the twentieth, social scientists of all kinds and stripes were occupying themselves in showing how economic forces in the long run determine almost everything important that happens in history. A few have been grand synthesizers on the order of Marx, such as Herbert Spencer with his message of social Darwinism. Many others have focused on the illustration of one or another specific case of the controlling power of economic forces in history. In American history, for example, Charles Beard claimed to show that the American Constitution was not really the outcome of a battle of ideas about freedom but was the result of a clash of economic interests in the late eighteenth century.[11] Others would argue that the Civil War was not about the morality of slavery or about preserving one union grounded in a common American civil religion but was actually the product of a conflict between powerful economic interests of the North and the South.

Thorstein Veblen would contend that the entire economic system and the relationships of property ownership in this system were being driven by the exigencies of technological change in the newly industrializing United States, that the economic realities of modern industrial society entirely "shapes their habits of thought" for those directly involved in its workings.[12] John Kenneth Galbraith would echo Veblen's vision when he claimed in the 1960s that the technological imperatives of modern government and industry had displaced the formal owners of capital and empowered a new "technostructure" of scientific and administrative experts to run the affairs of the nation.[13]

Outside the United States, the French Revolution was recast by leading intellectuals as an economic power struggle, the means by which the rising middle class finally displaced the old feudal order. Max Weber, while he found many of the economic details of Marxism inaccurate, nevertheless often looked at noneconomic aspects of society in terms of the workings of economic forces. The important thing about Calvinism for Weber was not the objective reality of its truth claims about the human condition. Rather, the more significant element was that Calvinism provided a powerful economic motive for and rationalized the existence of a new economic class—the emerging new commercial and other business groups in Europe, the very groups among whom Calvinism had first found favor.[14] Much in the manner of Marx, Weber was seeming to agree that the form and character of religion was shaped by necessities to be found in the underlying workings of economic forces.*

A COMING AGE OF ABUNDANCE

The Marxist assumption that the working of the laws of economics will yield a new species of human being, the "new man" of the communist utopia, has often been derided as an example of the folly of Marx's overall scheme. However, the hope for a new human condition as a result of eco-

---

* More recent reviewers, it should be noted, have found many aspects of Weber's argument to be deficient. See Kurt Samuelsson, *Religion and Economic Action: The Protestant Ethic, the Rise of Capitalism, and the Abuses of Scholarship* (Toronto: University of Toronto Press, 1993).

nomic progress is not unique to Marxism; indeed, the same kind of thinking was manifested in western European socialism, American Progressivism, and other leading economic belief systems of the twentieth century. As Kate Soper has commented, the great attraction of socialism derives from the "satisfaction it permits to the ethical demand for justice and equity in the distribution of goods, as [much as] it has to do with the material gratification afforded by those goods." [15]

In the economic gospels, the existence of evil behavior in the world has reflected the severity of the competition for physical survival of the past. Human beings have often lied and cheated, murdered, and stolen, were filled with hatreds and prejudices, because they were driven to this condition by the material pressures of their existence.* If the choice was to live or die in the struggle for control over resources, few people were likely to choose to sacrifice themselves in order to save others. Thus, the state of material deprivation is the original sin of economic theology.† Then, if this diagnosis is correct, the cure for evil in the world follows directly enough. If sin results from destructive forces brought into existence by material scarcity, a world without scarcity, a world of complete material abundance, will be a world without sin. [16]

The contemporary philosopher Will Kymlicka thus comments that in Marxism "it is material abundance which allows communist society to over-

---

* Although there are many fewer people today who believe that economic influences are so important, such views that conflicts are stirred by material deprivation are still widely expressed. Among many examples that could be cited, one 1995 report in *Washington Post* finds that "South Korean President Kim Young Sam and other officials have warned that hunger and economic desperation could tempt North Korea's leaders to consider a military strike against South Korea." See Kevin Sullivan, "Food Shortages Fuel Alarm over N. Korea," *Washington Post,* December 23, 1995, A11.

† Another way of putting this is to say that it is material deprivation that gives rise to the "craving for belongings" and that evil behavior arises because human beings have been "thoroughly warped" by this intense desire for possessions. The secularization of the idea of original sin in this manner became a principal theme of Rousseau and other French intellectuals in the eighteenth century. One of them, writing anonymously, declares: "The only vice which I know in the universe is *avarice;* all the others, whatever name one gives them, are merely forms, degrees of it: it is the Proteus, the Mercury, the base, the vehicle of all the other vices. Analyze vanity, conceit, pride, ambition, deceitfulness, hypocrisy, villainy; break down the majority of our sophisticated virtues themselves, all dissolve in this subtle and pernicious element, *the desire to possess."* See Richard Pipes, *Property and Freedom* (New York: Vintage Books, 1999), 41.

Then, if evil in the world could be traced to material causes, it followed logically enough that the remaking of the material world by human effort had the potential to abolish evil. Humankind could refashion social and economic circumstances to perfect the condition of the world—to achieve a new heaven on earth. Inspired by their hopes for such a secular salvation, the first to make the effort were the French during the French Revolution. It was a new species of religious revolution where God was now dropped from the essential vocabulary. Many others would come later in the modern age, following one or another economic theory of the elimination of scarcity and thus the elimination of the very grounds for the existence of material cravings and for evil behavior on earth.

come the need for justice." It is not because "individuals cease to have conflicting goals in life, or when a 'more developed form of altruism' arises." Rather, evil currently exists in the world because the economic relations of production create a material circumstance in which "the social creations of an individual take on an alien independence, 'enslaving him instead of being controlled by him.' These include the imperatives of capitalist competition, role requirements of the division of labor, rigours of the labour market, and what Marx calls the 'fetishism' of money, capital and commodities." Thus, "material scarcity" is the "crucial circumstance," but it also creates the possibility that the present state of alienation "can be eliminated." The perfection of the world for Marx "is impossible without abundance" but following the triumph of the proletariat "is guaranteed by abundance."[17] As Marx himself stated:

> In a higher phase of communist society, after the enslaving subordination of the individual to the division of labor . . . has vanished; after labour has become not only a means to life but life's prime want; after the productive forces have also increased with the all-round development of the individual, and all the springs of co-operative wealth flow more abundantly—only then can the narrow horizon of bourgeois right be crossed in its entirety and society inscribe on its banners: From each according to his ability, to each according to his needs![18]

Engels had written as early as 1847 that "private property can be abolished only when the economy is capable of producing the volume of goods needed to satisfy everyone's requirements. . . . The new rate of industrial growth will produce enough goods to satisfy all the demands of society. . . . Society will achieve an output sufficient for the needs of all members."[19] Marxism thus has an ambivalence that some might find surprising with respect to the existence of the capitalist economic system based on competition in the marketplace. Although the workings of this system may degrade the laboring classes today, without the marvelous advances in economic productivity due to the profit incentive and other elements of the market system, the future salvation of the world would not be possible. Capitalism is thus a necessary economic stage on the road to heaven on earth. If the date of its arrival could not be precisely fixed, Marx would "hail each important new invention as *the* magical 'material productive force' that would inevitably bring about the socialist revolution."[20] The scientific development of electricity with its amazing and transformative economic capabilities, Marx was sure, had significantly advanced the timetable for the arrival of his new heaven on earth.

THE KEYNESIAN GOD

It would be hard to imagine a temperament more the opposite of Marx's than that of John Maynard Keynes. If Marx was prophetic and bombastic, Keynes had the manner of the worldly wise. If Marx was a social misfit and bohemian, the urbane Keynes designed economic blueprints for the British Treasury, and yet at the next moment might be consorting with the artistic elite of Bloomsbury.[21] Keynes also differed sharply from Marx in his prescription for solving unemployment and other economic problems. Yet in terms of ulti-mate values, Keynesianism was only a modest variation on Marx—on the re-cent revelation of God's actual plan for the world, that the Christian Bible is apparently mistaken, that God actually works in history through economic forces and is planning a glorious ending to the world based on the workings of rapidly advancing material productivity.

In his 1930 essay "Economic Possibilities for our Grandchildren," Keynes agreed with Marx (and Jesus) that capitalism—necessarily grounded in the desire for money and the competitive workings of self-interest in the mar-ket—is a "disgusting" system, characterized by motives unworthy of human beings. Christianity, and later Marxism, were right to believe that "avarice is a vice, that the exaction of usury is a misdemeanor, and the love of money is detestable." Keynes also agreed that it was the force of economic pressures— the result of material scarcity in the world and the resulting fierce struggle for mere physical survival—that had separated human beings from their inner better selves. Marx was right to say that the economic workings of capitalism (and feudalism and other economic systems before that) had alienated human beings from their true natures (as the Fall in the Garden had previ-ously been thought to be the true cause of this separation). As Keynes him-self put it, the economic individual had been required to suppress a natural instinct to "pluck the hour and the day virtuously and well," to be able to take spontaneous and "direct enjoyment in things," as was possible for the "lilies of the field who toil not, neither do they spin."[22]

The modern god of Keynes who spoke to humankind through the work-ings of economic forces in history had the same basic plan for a secular salva-tion as had the god of Marx. Both relied on the marvelous productive powers of capitalism to bring on a final stage of history.* It will be an era of

---

* While economists have often been blind to the underlying values in their economic messages, Christians theologians—lamenting the substitution of secular beliefs for traditional Christian teach-ings—have often been more perceptive in seeing the core religious quality of these beliefs. Thus, Richard Niebuhr in the 1930s came to think that "the Social Gospel, with its focus on human striving, was in-sufficiently centered on God." The Christian churches of America were located in a "culture caught up

abundance, ending the corrosive and corrupting influence of economic scarcity, thus bringing on a time of great human virtue, equality, and contentment. Keynes, like Marx, sees a new man and woman being born: "All kinds of social customs and economic practices, affecting the distribution of wealth and of economic rewards and penalties, which we now maintain at all costs, however distasteful and unjust they may be in themselves, because they are tremendously useful in promoting the accumulation of capital, we shall then be free, at last, to discard." It will all come about, Keynes writes, as a result of "the greatest change that has ever occurred in the material environment of life for human beings in the aggregate." After this happens, we will finally be "able to rid ourselves of many of the pseudo-moral principles which have hag-ridden us" for centuries.[23]

Keynes's timetable was hardly less optimistic than that of Marx. Like the early followers of Jesus in biblical times, Keynes thought that the arrival of the kingdom of heaven on earth was near at hand, to occur in perhaps one hundred years or so. The continued rapid advance of economic progress in the world would soon "lead us out of the tunnel of economic necessity into daylight."[24]

In terms of the path to heaven on earth, there was one key difference between Keynes and Marx. Marx was what in Christianity is called a "premillennial" prophet; Keynes was instead a "postmillennial."[25] The premillennials, like Marx, see humankind as mired today in such fundamental depravity that the only hope—which God (or the economic forces of history) fortunately has predestined—is an apocalyptic transformation of the human condition. This transformation will often be prefigured by catastrophes of the worst kind. For postmillennials, in contrast, the millennium has already begun; human progress toward heaven on earth is already taking place at this very moment; humankind has an important continuing role to play within the divine plan for bringing about the salvation of the world.

As Keynes said, being careful to distinguishing himself from Marx in this regard, the coming era of economic abundance would not be experienced initially "as a catastrophe." Instead, like a good Christian postmillennial, Keynes writes that "I look forward, therefore, in the days not so very remote" to great changes in the human condition for the better. "But, of course, it will all happen gradually. . . . Indeed, it has already begun."[26]

---

in idolatrous faiths which take partial human communities, activities and desires as cherished objects. Nationalism focuses on one's country, capitalism on economic production and racism on a particular group. The church has been infiltrated by these social faiths" but must now seek a future "emancipation from cultural bondage" with its pervasive "idols" such as "economic production." See Douglas F. Ottati, "God and Ourselves: The Witness of H. Richard Niebuhr," *Christian Century,* April 2, 1997, 346.

Keynes included his essay "Economic Possibilities for Our Grandchildren" as the closing chapter in *Essays in Persuasion*. This was not the only time that Keynes chose to wrap up on important book in this manner—to indicate that the details of his prior economic theorizing were designed in the end to serve a grand moral purpose. In the concluding chapter of *The General Theory*, Keynes repeats similar themes, if in a somewhat more subdued and cautious language, also reflecting the different conventions of the academic audience to which this work was directed. Moreover, by the mid-1930s Hitler was already becoming a threat to the world, and Keynes's assessment of the human condition was shifting accordingly.

Thus, Keynes writes at the end of *The General Theory* that there are "dangerous human proclivities" at work in a sinful world that pose the prospect of "cruelty, the reckless pursuit of personal power and authority, and other forms of self-aggrandizement." Capitalism could serve an important short-run function because "it is better that a man should tyrannise over his bank balance than his fellow citizens." Moreover, there were "valuable human activities" that depended on the "motive of money-making and the environment of private wealth-ownership for their full fruition." [27]

Yet, in the longer run, if society would heed the prescriptions of *The General Theory*, the resulting steady economic growth would mean—much as Marx had prophesied—"the euthanasia of the cumulative oppressive power of the capitalist class to exploit the scarcity value of capital." The current capitalist system was merely a "transitional phase" after which the world would experience a "sea-change." [28] If Keynes did not give many details concerning the consequences of this change in *The General Theory*, one can assume that he meant something of the kind that he had already described in *Essays in Persuasion*.

Keynes of course did not advertise *The General Theory* as a work of theology. Instead, as the title reflected, he seemed to suggest that readers should see his efforts more as following in the footsteps of Albert Einstein. Einstein had discovered a general theory of time and space; Keynes had now discovered a general theory of economic interactions. Einstein's theory of relativity had shown that dynamic factors could fundamentally alter the conclusions of Newtonian physics; Keynesian economics would now show that dynamic factors could yield new and unexpected laws fundamentally altering the behavior of a market economy. Thus, like Marx, Keynes presented himself in the role of a true scientist of society—an essential element in the enormous influence both would have on the history of the twentieth century.

D. McCloskey may be right, however. Despite the scientific aspirations of *The General Theory* (which have not held up well over time), the more important content may have been an implicit theological message. Contrary to

Marx, Keynes was saying, the salvation of the world would take time, it would require patience. Both agreed that capitalism was a debased form of existence, yet Marx no less than Keynes now thought that capitalism at present was indispensable to the economic growth that would end economic scarcity and bring on a new stage of abundance in history. However, as Keynes now thought, attempts to accelerate the schedule for the end of capitalism, acted out under the duress of the economic conditions of the depression years, would be disastrous in the long run. The millennium had already begun; the human condition was steadily improving already. With patience and trust in the economic forces in history, the underlying moral theology of *The General Theory* was that the capitalist stage of economic history would soon enough be ended (in one hundred years or so), and no great economic cataclysm or other great disaster would be necessary to fulfill the looming material and spiritual perfection of the world.* No dictatorship of the proletariat was necessary or desirable; it was necessary only to use the instrument of existing democratic government to make further incremental adjustments in the workings of the current market system.

This secular Keynesian theology would become "the new gospel" for the economics profession in the years following World War II.[29] As Milton Friedman has commented, it was "tremendously effective" in the United States in influencing the direction of public policy. Friedman recalled how a whole generation of "economists, myself included, have sought to discover

---

* As a postmillennial, Keynes was following closely in the tradition of John Stuart Mill, more so than of the premillennial, apocalyptic Marx. Mill in his *Principles of Political Economy* offered a view of the future strikingly similar to that later developed by Keynes in "Economic Possibilities for our Grandchildren." Agreeing with Keynes, Mill describes the current stage of industrial development, characterized by the "trampling, crushing, elbowing, and treading on each other's heels" of the competitive process, as impossible to consider "anything but the disagreeable symptoms of one of the phases of industrial progress." Mill also agrees with Keynes (and Marx) that capitalism may be a "necessary stage"; it would be important for some time to come that "the energies of mankind should be kept in employment by the struggle for riches," especially because in the present material circumstances of mankind the alternative might be (as Keynes would also warn) "the struggle of war."

But capitalism should be regarded, Mill says, as a "very early stage of human improvement" that will eventually be superceded by a much better "ultimate type." In the current stage it is necessary to exalt degraded values such as the "increase of production and accumulation." However, in the longer run such economic motives will be of "little importance." The current environment, with its prevailing motive "to grow as rich as possible," will be replaced by a world in which "no one desires to be richer." This "steady state," as Mill's characterizes it, "would be, on the whole, a very considerable improvement on our present condition."

It would be, as Marx and Keynes also emphasized, the transforming power of material progress that would lead to this new world in which "a much larger body of persons than at present, [would be] not only exempt from the coarser toils, but with sufficient leisure, both physical and mental, to cultivate freely the graces of life." Progress would no longer be conceived in economic terms, but in the steady state, as Mill believes, "there would be as much scope as ever for all kinds of . . . moral and social progress; as much room for improving the Art of Living, and much more likelihood of its being im-

how to manipulate the levers of power effectively, and to persuade—or educate—government officials regarded as seeking to serve the public interest." [30] The most important form of manipulation would be that of the "market mechanism." Keynes sought especially to ward off the ideas of Marxists, doctrinaire socialists, and other potentially harmful influences on public opinion, the kinds of people whom Keynes himself characterized as most likely in practice actually "to serve not God but the devil." [31]

If false religions were at work in the land, Keynes found it necessary to fight fire with fire. As Joseph Schumpeter would relate, Keynes's own efforts inspired a band of followers who exhibited a new religious fervor:

> A Keynesian school formed itself, not a school in that loose sense in which some historians of economics speak of a French, German, Italian school, but a genuine one which is a sociological entity, namely, a group that professes allegiance to One Master and One Doctrine, and has its inner circle, its propagandists, its watchwords, its esoteric and its popular doctrine. Nor is this all. Beyond the pale of orthodox Keynesianism there is a broad fringe of sympathizers and beyond this again are the many who have absorbed, in one form or another, readily or grudgingly, some of the spirit or some individual items of Keynesian analysis. There are but two analogous cases in the whole history of economics—the Physiocrats and the Marxists. [32]

Samuelson's *Economics* would be the means by which the Keynesian gospel was communicated to millions of American college students in the postwar years. Samuelson was an unabashed admirer not only of the Keynesian economic theories but also of Keynes himself, whom he declared to be a true "many-sided genius" of our time who was eminent not only in economics but also in "the field of mathematics and philosophy." [33] Samuelson's mission in *Economics* was to communicate persuasively not only the technical details but also the moral philosophy—the implicit secular religion—of Keynesianism. Samuelson's great accomplishment was to devise a way of accomplishing this task ideally suited to his specific time and place in American history.

---

proved, when minds ceased to be engrossed by the art of getting on" economically. If any further economic growth did occur, it would not be used to increase levels of consumption that would already be ample to meet any real needs but with "abridging labour" and thus opening the way for greater leisure and personal development.

In short, Mill is yet another of the leading economists of the past two hundred years who sees material progress not as the end in itself but as the short-run means of reaching for a long-run future heaven on earth. See John Stuart Mill, "The Stationary State," chap. 6 in bk. 4 of *Principles of Political Economy* (1871; reprint, Fairfield, N.J.: Augustus M. Kelley, 1987), 746–51.

chapter **TWO**

A SECULAR GREAT AWAKENING

Keynes was the most important, but there were many other important social thinkers in the first half of the twentieth century who preached a similar message of secular salvation through the efficiency of modern industrial society. The American proponent of scientific management in business Frederick Taylor believed that the application of his ideas would so increase the productivity of American companies that it would bring on a "complete mental revolution," as well as a revolution in physical production processes. An efficiency revolution in American business would "eventually end . . . material scarcity," a result that Taylor believed would also abolish "the age-old antagonism between workers and bosses."[1] Taylor thus foresaw the same basic future as did Marx and Keynes: scientific knowledge bringing on an end to scarcity and the arrival of a new era of abundance, thereby ending the alienating and debilitating struggles among contending economic interests in society.

Taylorism was merely one instance of a much broader rage for efficiency that swept over American society in the Progressive Era, typically dated by historians as running from 1890 to 1920. A leading Progressive, Gifford Pinchot, one of the closest advisors to President Theodore Roosevelt, who founded the Forest Service in 1905 and was later governor of Pennsylvania, declared that his lifetime mission was "to help in bringing the Kingdom of God on earth."[2] A later chief of the Forest Service would comment that the agency was "born in controversy and baptized with the holy water of reform."[3]

Historians have labeled the progressive message the "gospel of efficiency."[4] One said that the Progressive movement was characterized by "an efficiency craze" that amounted to "a secular Great Awakening."[5] Another historian spoke of "the efficiency movement" that was offered "as a panacea for the ills of mankind" and exhibited "a moral fervor that had all the earmarks of a religious revival."[6] Dwight Waldo would observe that in the Progressive Era in the United States "efficiency" assumed a "position of dominance" relative to all other values; events came to be "degraded or exalted" according to their perceived impact on the efficiency of American society.[7]

Efficiency did not assume this great importance simply because Americans were suddenly consumed by a fierce new desire for greater material possessions. The United States, as it has been said, is "a nation with the soul of a church."[8] Great religious movements—at first taking traditionally Judeo-Christian forms, as in earlier religious awakenings, and more recently taking secular forms—sweep periodically over the politics and intellectual life of the United States. The progressive gospel of efficiency was one such religious revival. Environmentalism, it might be noted, is such a secular religion today, often in opposition to the earlier progressive faith in science and material progress.[9]

Each such religious wave in American life has its own plan for saving the world. It began with the Puritans building a "City on the Hill" in the Massachusetts wilderness, which would serve as a beacon for all humankind.*

---

* In his farewell address in January 1989, Ronald Reagan again invoked this Puritan image in reflecting on his guiding conviction throughout his career that Americans are a chosen people with a fundamental religious mission to lead the world:

> The past few days when I've been at the window upstairs, I've thought a bit of the shining "city upon a hill." The phrase comes from John Winthrop, who wrote it to describe the America he imagined.
>
> I've spoken of the shining city all my political life. . . . In my mind it was a tall proud city built on rocks stronger than the oceans, wind swept, God blessed, and teeming with people of all kinds living in harmony and peace—a city with free ports that hummed with commerce and creativity, and if there had to be city walls, the walls had doors, and the doors were open to anyone with the will and the heart to get here.
>
> And how stands the city on this winter night? . . . After 200 years, two centuries, she still stands strong and true on the granite ridge, and her flow has held steady no matter what storm.
>
> And she's still a beacon, still a magnet for all who must have freedom, for all the Pilgrims from all the lost places who are hurtling through the darkness, toward home.

See "Text of President's Farewell Address to the American People," *New York Times,* January 12, 1989, B8.

It would be difficult to overestimate the importance to American politics and society of this long-standing vision of America as an instrument of God's purpose. Reagan was such a political success in part because he had a rare ability to articulate these core values of the American electorate.

Later, the American Revolution would offer a model of liberty, equality and democracy for all the people of the world to follow. In the Progressive Era, the redemptive hopes of Americans turned to building a perfectly efficient economic system, an outcome that would bring moral and spiritual perfection to the United States—and again eventually the rest of the world as well.

THE GOSPEL OF EFFICIENCY

Looking back to the mid-nineteenth century, the Progressives had already witnessed an astonishing growth of productivity of the American economic system, built in part on a wave of marvelous scientific inventions. Indeed, such economic events, escalating from mid-century onward, seemed to raise the real and astonishing prospect that for the first time in human history the material deprivations of the past might actually be eliminated. The Progressives were in fact accurate in their view that a brand-new era in human history was looming. In the United States today, at the beginning of the twenty-first century, in terms of health care, food, transportation, communications, and a number of other important matters, a middle-class person enjoys a standard of living above that of kings and queens of a mere three hundred years ago.

This transformation of the material circumstances of humankind (or at least in the economically most developed nations of the world) was confidently expected by the Progressives to transform everything else as well—including matters of morality and spiritual well-being. It would lead, they believed, to the arrival of a new heavenly paradise on earth. More generally, as Charles Hopkins has said, the social gospelers of the Progressive Era sought the "social salvation" of humankind, which would mean "the coming to earth of the kingdom of heaven."[10]

Traditional Jewish and Christian religions found it difficult to compete with this prospect. Their traditional assurances of a future arrival of a messiah bringing heaven on earth—or of individuals reaching a heaven in the here-after—were based on biblical statements of the word of God of uncertain reliability, now almost two thousand years old, and with the exact future timing of events also uncertain. The progressive gospel of efficiency in the United States became one of the triumphant denominations in a worldwide "religion of progress" that shaped the dominant secular religions of much of the twentieth century. In country after country, traditional Christian and Jewish faiths were marginalized over the course of the century; in western Europe they virtually disappeared in some countries as significant influences on public affairs. If the wars of religion four hundred years earlier had been fought among Catholics and diverse Protestant denominations within Christianity, the great wars of religion of the twentieth century were now fought among socialist, Marxist, fascist, American progressive, capitalist, and other branches of an overarching religion of progress.

If salvation was now to be a matter of ending material scarcity, leading humankind into a new era of economic abundance, it followed logically that the new chief priesthood should consist of economists. The members of the economics profession would, to be sure, need the help of many other disciplines that would provide expert knowledge in particular fields. In the late nineteenth century new American universities such as Cornell, Johns Hopkins, and the University of Chicago were created to supply the professional experts with the requisite technical skills. Old universities such as Harvard and Yale, which had formerly educated the ministry for Protestant America, were retooled to perform a new kind of religious mission.[11] They largely abandoned their old Christian subject matter and were reorganized into disciplinary specializations to educate the corps of professional experts to lead the way to the secular salvation of American society.

One of the new proselytizers was George Gates, in the 1890s the president of Grinnell College in Iowa, yet another of the new institutions of higher education created to serve the progressive cause. Gates considered the mission of the college to be to "teach the actual applicability of the principles of Jesus Christ to every department of human life."[12] He summarized his overall purpose as follows: "The Kingdom of heaven and the Kingdom of God does not refer to a life beyond the grave; the Kingdom of God does not mean the Church or any other institution; such an identification of the Kingdom with the Church either concrete or invisible being 'one of the most dangerous of heresies'; the Kingdom of God [means] a society upon this earth in which all human affairs exhibit the nature and spirit of God."[13]

The modern university must assume such a critical role in realizing this vision, Progressives believed, because it must be the leading generator and repository of scientific knowledge of both physical nature and human society. As Eliza Lee has commented in reviewing the history of public administration in the United States, Progressivism offered a "vision of scientific management as morally uplifting" that went "far beyond the idea of making public administration more businesslike." Leading political scientists of the time such as Francis Lieber, John Burgess, Woodrow Wilson, Frank Goodnow, and W. W. Willoughby saw their mission as "to reform the liberal state through science." In their thinking, "science was regarded as the method of understanding and controlling changes. Extravagant faith was invested in science and technology as the engine of progress." The overall guidance for this process would come from the institutions of government, which must be radically recast to meet the requirements of the new era. Progressive political theorists thus provided "the ideological and institutional apparatus for the rise of the administrative state" over the course of the twentieth century.[14]

Professional economics and other social sciences had a central role to play in all this. As Lee writes, Progressives assumed that there existed a one true "natural science of society" whose knowledge would provide the technical basis for governing. Hence, social science researchers must work "to discover the immutable laws of society." In this way, it would be possible for "the truth and objectivity of science" to substitute for the interest-group favoritism, for "the unenlightened majority" of past American politics, thus providing a much firmer "basis of [American] democracy." This would stimulate a new "sense of political community" in the United States, based on "the adoption of science as the common language of discourse, bringing about an end to irrationality, rivalry of power, and authoritarianism." It reflected a view that the tasks of government administration are mainly "objective, universal, natural, altogether devoid of historical and cultural contexts, and dictated only by scientific laws." The "social significance of science" was that it would now provide "the legitimate basis of public authority" for American government.[15]

As part of this grand project, Progressives sought to curtail the old political role of the special interests, thereby putting government decision making on an objective scientific basis in the service of the overall public interest. Progressive political reforms such as the direct election of senators, the development of the primary for selecting candidates for office in elections, the adoption of universal suffrage, and still others were designed to curb the old patterns of narrow exercise of private power. Instead, the new progressive vision of "scientific politics took technical rationality as the criteria of political action and sought to technically control and engineer social and political processes, with scientists, experts, and professionals as legitimate bearers of such knowledge." It resulted in a "centralization of power in the hands of political and administrative elites [that] was justified as the science of democracy," the means by which government would transcend private concerns and act for the benefit of all the people. Technical rationality included as a central preoccupation "the demands for efficiency" in government and society as a whole.[16] All this produced among the progressive faithful a typical conviction that a secular "salvation would come from 'science,' 'primary sources,' 'relevance,' 'democracy,' and 'progress.'"[17]

Progressivism strongly encouraged the turn of the civic allegiance of Americans from the local community to the nation as a whole. If good government required the application of the best scientific knowledge, scientific institutions at the national level could be expected to achieve the highest quality of science, produced by the most gifted scientists gathered from throughout the country and the world. The national government could plan and coordinate economic and administrative tasks on the broadest possible scale, encompassing the entire nation. Professional associations could be organized at the national level to communicate expert knowledge and skills to every section of the United States. Hence, as William Schambra observes, Progressives sought "to create a national community through bureaucratization, rationalization, centralization, and the centripetal moral impulse of the national idea [that] bespoke an active hostility to civil society's intermediate institutions." Indeed, "every great liberal president of the twentieth century following Wilson made the cultivation of the national community the central goal of his administration, expanding the power and reach of the national government, and calling upon Americans to put aside self-interest and local allegiances on behalf of the national idea." [18]

In the progressive value system, there were "serious doubts about [traditional] religion, traditional morality, and the local civic manifestations," because they posed an obstacle to the "new reliance on rational, scientific principles and institutions to create a national community." [19] Instead, as Schambra comments, Progressives turned to new secular faiths in place of an outmoded Christianity:

> Many of the Progressives understood the new social sciences and their seeming capacity to reorder society into a coherent and orderly whole to be a secular evolution from or substitute for religion, a realization of the Kingdom on Earth—to recall [Herbert] Croly's formulation, a "religion of human brotherhood." Sociologist Albion Small considered his discipline "a science . . . of God's image," "the holiest sacrament open to men," teaching that "we live, move and have our being as members one of another" (rather than as children of "our heavenly Father," as taught by discredited conventional Christianity). John Bascom argued that "a theology which seeks the regeneration of society in ignorance of social laws is doomed to failure," while a government that grasped such laws was "a surrogate for the churches and voluntary societies." Progressives generally shared Bascom's view that traditional, local civic institutions—as he put it, "rambling, halting voluntaryism"—based on traditional moral principles could only obstruct and delay the creation of a new, sleek, streamlined, rational centralized order. [20]

Traditional Christianity thus was often displaced among the American elite by the new progressive thinking, although the "social gospel" movement within American Protestantism sought a reconciliation by incorporating in its creed significant elements of the progressive faith. Theodore Roosevelt, for example, was the most prominent political spokesperson of his generation for the progressive plan for government. Bernard Ruffin reports that Roosevelt "apparently did not believe in life beyond the grave"; he subscribed to "a totally this-worldly faith."[21] Roosevelt himself declared that "the religious man who is most useful is not he whose sole care is to save his own soul, but a man whose religion bids him strive to advance decency and clean living and to make the world a better place for his fellows to live."[22] People should go to church, Roosevelt believed, because it would promote the moral qualities that would enable the realization of "the just and democratic society."[23]

PROGRESSIVE ECONOMISTS

Since the deepest aspirations of American society now rested on the attainment of technical efficiency, the route by which continuing economic progress could be assured, it was appropriate that the American Economic Association was the first of the new social science professional associations. It was formed in 1885 as an outgrowth of efforts led by Richard Ely.[24] Like a number of others in the early Progressive movement in the late nineteenth century, Ely sought to adapt the religion of progress to the older forms of Protestant Christianity. He and others in the social gospel movement of the time were not yet prepared to abandon the Protestant institutional churches that until recently had guarded the moral foundations of American life. The American Economic Association thus was created in an explicitly Christian context; among its fifty founding members, twenty were current or former practicing Protestant ministers.

Ely was better known to the American public in the 1880s as a social gospeler, not an economist.[25] He criticized religious leaders for their ambitious plans to reconstruct society that were not grounded in any adequate foundation of social knowledge. Church leaders appeared "like blind leaders of the blind; for they manifestly have never received instruction" in economics and other social sciences. The church assumed that its deep moral passion and obvious good intentions would be enough, but Ely sought to convince the Protestant leadership of America otherwise. If they shared with Ely the deep conviction that "Christianity is primarily concerned with this world,

and it is the mission of Christianity to bring to pass here a kingdom of right-
eousness," the application of scientific methods to all the problems of society
would be necessary—from Taylor's studies of individual business production
methods to Ely's and other economists' studies of the workings of economic
forces more broadly.[26]

For Ely, John R. Commons, John Bates Clark, and a number of other
leading early American economists connected with the social gospel movement, the problems of economics thus were, as Ely put it, "religious subjects." The role of economics was to contribute to the requisite base of social
knowledge in order to succeed in "a never-ceasing attack on every wrong
institution, until the earth becomes a new earth, and all its cities, cities of
God."[27] If God in the Bible had sent Jesus to deliver the great news of the
impending arrival of the kingdom of heaven on earth, a new god—or perhaps the same god with a new messenger—was now saying that the true
route to heaven on earth lay along an economic path in history.

However, Ely's attempt to incorporate economics as an element of the
Protestant social gospel movement soon foundered on the pluralism of
American life. Economists who were Catholics and Jews, for example, were
not comfortable with the close connections of their new professional association with an explicit Protestant religious creed. Moreover, the direct Christian connection was unnecessary, more a residue of the past that served to
preserve an institutional role for the Protestant churches, avoiding an outright break. A salvation of society to be achieved in the here and now required the efforts of scientific experts, not Protestant ministers. Hence, by
the early 1890s Ely faced a revolt among many of his fellow economists.
Economics soon moved on to become the secular field of study that it has
been ever since. As Robert Crunden comments, Ely himself also "learned
from his experiences and turned away from popular and openly religious
work toward more acceptable, professional, scientifically neutral studies."
Nevertheless, the original religious convictions did not disappear but "became implicit within professionalism and a vaguer progressivism." Although
the manner of their expression thus might have been altered, "Ely never
abandoned his original attitudes and goals."[28]

Although he was a friend of Ely, Edwin Seligman was an advocate of the
secularization of the activities of the economics profession. Jewish by birth,
Seligman was professor of economics at Columbia University and in 1903
served as president of the American Economic Association. His views, as developed in his treatise *The Economic Interpretation of History,* reflected assumptions widespread among progressive economists and other intellectuals of the
time. Seligman sought to address the question of whether traditional morality and other convictions historically associated with Jewish and Christian

religion had any absolute validity. He stated, "The conception of right or wrong does not attach invariably to any particular action, because the same action may, under different circumstances and as applied to varying social stages [of history], be both right and wrong. Since social conditions make the social actions of the individual right or wrong, the idea of good or evil itself is a social project."[29]

To be sure, such a relativity of moral conceptions does not deny the objective power of the moral thoughts and feelings as they arise in any individual person at any given historical stage. Indeed, ideas of good and evil along with other religious beliefs have clearly played a major role in many historical events. As Seligman commented, "It would . . . be absurd to deny that individual men, like masses of men, are moved by ethical considerations." Yet it must be recognized that "amid the complex social influences that cooperated to produce it, the economic factors have often been of chief significance—that purely ethical or religious idealism has made itself felt only within the limitations of existing economic conditions."[30]

Improving the moral condition of humanity thus becomes a matter of altering the economic circumstances in which the mass of people live. "The demand of the ethical reformer," Seligman declares in a manner similar to that of Marx, will be unavailing "unless the social conditions . . . are ripe for the change." Indeed, the realization of the existing aspirations for "international justice and universal peace" will depend on a continuation of "the economic changes now proceeding apace." Economic progress throughout the world is a prerequisite because "economic equality among individuals creates the democratic virtues; economic equality among nations can alone prepare the way for international peace and justice."[31]

Hence, while Seligman believes that "the [traditional] ethical teacher" has an important role to play, it is a subordinate role in advancing ethical behavior to that of the economist. That is because "the real battle [for ethical reform] will be fought by the main body of social forces, amid which the economic conditions are in last resort so often decisive."[32] Indeed, as Seligman would explain,

> To permit the moral ideals to percolate through continually lower strata of the population, we must have an economic basis to render it possible. With every improvement in the material condition of the great mass of the population there will be an opportunity for the unfolding of a higher moral life; but not until the economic conditions of society become far more ideal will the ethical development of the individual have a free field for limitless progress.

If by materialism we mean a negation of the power of spiritual forces in humanity, the economic interpretation of history is really not materialistic. But if by economic interpretation we mean—what alone we should mean—that the ethical forces themselves are essentially social in their origin and largely conditioned in their actual sphere of operation by the economic relations of society, there is no real antagonism between the economic and the ethical life.[33]

The perfection of human existence, the arrival of the kingdom of heaven on earth thus is attainable only along an economic route. It was not only radical Marxists and socialists who held such convictions; leading American economists of the Progressive Era such as Seligman shared them as well. Much as Keynes would later envision that one hundred years or so in the future—with rapid economic growth continuing until then—it would be possible to eliminate from the world such unsavory motives as self-interest, Seligman had already spoken earlier in the century of a time in the future "when it will be possible to neglect the economic factor." It will be a material steady-state in which economic conditions "may thenceforward be considered as a constant." With material pressures eliminated from human existence, the moral state of human existence will be perfected, leaving "the economic interpretation of history [to] become a matter for archaeologists" alone to study.[34] Economists, as Keynes famously wrote, would then be no more important to society than dentists.

The progressive economist with the widest public following was Thorstein Veblen. Veblen had a doctorate from Yale, taught economics at the University of Chicago from 1892 to 1906, and for several years was managing editor of the *Journal of Political Economy*. A leading American progressive economist, Wesley Clair Mitchell, would declare that "no other such emancipator of the mind from the suble tyranny of circumstance has been known in social science, and no other such enlarger of the realm of inquiry."[35]

Veblen rejected the laissez-faire economics of the nineteenth century as a "spiritual" set of theories that were grounded in traditionally religious notions of the "order of nature, natural rights, and natural law." Economics had historically performed a "ceremonial" function by which "the instructed common sense of the time" was transformed into a religious "canon of truth."[36] Thus, for Adam Smith "the ultimate ground of economic reality is the design of God."[37]

Veblen regarded the free market as an archaic institution for the twentieth century; market institutions based on old-fashioned trial-and-error methods were promoting "an incredibly wasteful organization of equipment and manpower." He prescribed instead "a revolutionary overturn as will close out the Old Order of absentee ownership and capitalized income." Control over the resources of society must shift to those who have the requisite technical knowledge to make the most efficient use of these resources. These are the social and physical scientists who have joined together in professional associations to advance the public use of their knowledge. Thus, as Veblen would write, control over the industrial system should be assumed by "Production Engineers" and "Production Economists." They should be selected according to their ability to promote "productive efficiency, economical use of resources, and an equitable distribution of the consumable output."[38]

As the "keepers of the community's material welfare," they would be motivated not by a "commercial interest" but by a "common purpose."[39] As Veblen would summarize his views,

> The material welfare of the community is unreservedly bound up with the due working of this industrial system, and therefore with its unreserved control by the engineers, who alone are competent to manage it. To do their work as it should be done these men of the industrial general staff must have a free hand, unhampered by commercial considerations and reservations; for the production of the goods and services needed by the community they neither need nor are they in any degree benefited by any supervision or interference from the side of the owners.[40]

Professional groups were thus to be the new priesthood of progressive religion. Veblen simply took it for granted that economists, engineers, and other professionals would be motivated to serve the common good (as now revealed by science), much as priests of old had followed God's commands (as revealed to them through biblical and other sources). The distinguished American historian of the Progressive Era Robert Wiebe has commented that the new expert professionals of the time found that "the shared mysteries of a specialty allowed intimate communion." Much as in older priesthoods, the self-concept of being a professional again offered a sense of "prestige through exclusiveness," a brotherhood of individuals brought together by their common "desire to remake the world," and a "deep satisfaction" that accompanied a "revolution in identity" that followed initiation into a select class of fellow professionals. The rites of professional life were designed to ensure that "the process of becoming an expert, of immersing oneself in the scientific method, eradicated petty passions and narrow ambitions," justifying the great trust that ordinary people would have to put in the holders of such large responsibilities for the future of American society.[41]

Veblen's language was more colorful and his proposals more radical, but his basic outlook was shared by many others in the Progressive Era. Herbert Hoover stated that "one-hundred thousand professional engineers in the United States, men trained in exact thinking and in administrative responsibility, who were drafted into civilian and military service during [World War I], vindicated the scientific attitude in dealing with the problems of social organization."[42] In 1921, the authors of the "Hoover Report" stated that "engineers come in contact with and influence every activity in industry and as a body possess an intimate and peculiar understanding of intricate industrial problems. . . . It is peculiarly the duty of engineers to use their influence individually and collectively to eliminate waste in industry."[43]

FROM PROGRESSIVISM TO PAUL SAMUELSON

As American economics in the early part of the twentieth century cast off its Protestant trappings, professional economists would soon proclaim that they were engaged in a "value-neutral" search for the scientific laws of the economic workings of society. Yet, the putting aside of the outward religious forms was more a matter of show. The underlying reality was that the application of economics continued to have a mission to bring heaven to earth. Although often described in secular terms, the expectations for this future earthly paradise were in essence borrowed from Judeo-Christian origins; there would be no more stealing, fighting, lying, or other violations of the Ten Commandments; there would be an abundance of all the things necessary for the good life; there would be true equality among all human beings; there would be no coercion, as historically had been manifested in the institutions of both government and private property.

Even many nominally atheistic Progressives invested the crusade for heaven on earth with all the old moral passion that Christians had formerly devoted to fulfilling God's plans for the world.[44] Many devoted their lives to this effort; some, like many Marxists around the world, were even willing to die for the cause. Virtually every historian of the Progressive Era has commented in one way or another—applying terms such as "gospel," "crusade," "great awakening"—on the obvious deep religious passion underlying the American Progressive movement. The historian Richard Hofstadter would explain that American "progressivism can be considered . . . as a phase in the history of the Protestant conscience, a latter-day Protestant revival. Liberal politics as well as liberal theology were both inherent in the response of religion to the secularization of society."[45]

Many of the specific reform proposals of American Progressivism—improving the conditions of labor, cleaning up the slums, greater equality for women, curbing the excesses of American business—were borrowed from the earlier reform agenda of the Protestant social gospel movement. Thus, despite the later casting aside of the old religious framework, one historian would write that "the social gospel . . . was, in a sense, the religion of the progressive movement."[46] In analyzing the history of American social science, Arthur Vidich and Stanford Lyman comment that an early leading sociologist (sociology was then part of economics in most universities), William Ogburn, had made a "shift from the old Social Gospel to the new statistical positivism." Even though now "the language of Christian endeavor was expunged from sociology" and economics, this was all deceptive in a sense because the spirit of Christianity "remained part of the [new] science's catechism."[47]

Harvard economist and sociologist Thomas Carver had built his version of this catechism on the familiar assumptions—"that all social conflict is founded upon economic scarcity of one kind or another," and this opened up the possibility of "industrial prosperity, elimination of class conflict, and appropriately graded prosperity for all." As one early social scientist put it in 1886, before secular trends had come to prevail, "The great remedy for social wrongs will be found in the Christian use of money." In the future, however, as Vidich and Lyman explain, there would be a "secular eschatology" in which social scientists "replaced God with science," substituting "perfectability on this planet" for the former promises of a God in heaven above.[48]

In the sixteenth and seventeenth centuries, mathematics had been considered the "divine language" through which God made accessible "the Book of Nature." Galileo had said that without "mathematical language," trying to understand the world would be like "wandering in vain through a dark labyrinth." Vidich and Lyman comment that "prior to the Reformation, mathematics was a priestly function. After the Reformation the ability and responsibility to know God were transferred to the individual." Then, in American Progressivism and most other religions of progress of the twentieth century, "the secular scientist adopts the Catholic priest's role as God's interpreter." Or, as the American social scientist Franklin Giddings believed, the use of new "statistical methods" grounded in mathematics made possible the achievement of knowledge superior in its fundamental "truth value" to "the haphazard observation of the blunderer" of old.[49]

Yet another aspect of the new progressive "civil religion" was the belief that "public morality is guided by the hidden hand of dynamic equilibrium," whose workings "unites the individual, civil society, and the state in pursuit of a common historical purpose."[50] As the social gospel and other Protestant roots of American social science became more remote, the social sciences made ever greater efforts to separate themselves from religion and to ensure the value neutrality of their efforts. Yet it may not be possible, even in concept, to achieve this objective, because any method of social analysis depends on and inevitably also communicates to others some foundational set of values.

By the 1930s, the progressive tradition in the economics profession, which was strongest among the members of the institutionalist school, was waning. Neo-classical economics, still grounded in a faith in the superiority of markets, was dominant in the professional mainstream. Yet the future of economics did not lie in a restatement of the natural-law theories of Adam Smith, the social Darwinism of Herbert Spencer, or other past defenses of laissez-faire orthodoxy. There would instead be a new American economics in the second half of the twentieth century, reconciling the earlier free-market tradition with the core social values of American Progressivism.

The pivotal figures in providing the new synthesis would be Keynes in England and his disciple Paul Samuelson in the United States. From the neo-classical tradition would be taken the idea that private markets serve to allocate resources most efficiently and thus to maximize the production of goods and services for the benefit of society. From Progressivism would be taken the idea that government must nevertheless act affirmatively to curb unemployment and otherwise to plan and manage scientifically the workings of the market. The engineering of social progress is still necessary, but the key experts for the task of eliminating future scarcities of resources—of attaining the state of human perfection that will come from full abundance in the world—will now be the researchers into the operation of markets and other economic subjects. That is to say, the new leading priests of modern society will be the members of the economics profession.

part **TWO**

THEOLOGICAL MESSAGES OF SAMUELSON'S
ECONOMICS

Samuelson's introductory textbook, *Economics,* does not, of course, advertise any religious contents. Like most other professional economists, Samuelson presents his work, as he states in the first edition in 1948, as a "science" in the same category as "physical or biological" sciences (8).★ He has maintained this stance, if perhaps with more qualifications, throughout subsequent editions. Samuelson believes that "there is only one valid reality in a given economic situation" and professional economists are uniquely capable of revealing it. "Ethical questions," however, belong in a separate realm, where subjective factors may dominate. Thus, on matters of ethics, "each citizen must decide for himself, and an expert is entitled to only one vote along with everyone else" (5).

Samuelson, in short, is a firm believer in the "fact-value," "objective-subjective," "science-religion" distinctions that characterize the

★ I have used the first edition of *Economics,* published in 1948, as my benchmark for *Economics.* All page citations to *Economics* given in Part II (as will be shown in parentheses in the main body of the text) are to the 1948 edition, unless specifically noted otherwise.

belief systems that have been variously labeled as "positivism," "modernism," "progressivism," and other such terms.[1] The political theorists of American Progressivism emphasized yet another version of this distinction, an asserted sharp "dichotomy" between what they considered the value domain of democratic "politics" and the scientific domain of government "administration." Society would set its overall goals in the former arena, but the design of the technical means to implement them should occur in the latter. Samuelson thus says at one point that economists have little to say about the ends sought by society but that their proper task is "to throw light on how successfully an economic system realizes any suggested ethical goals" (590).

Today, to be sure, this distinction has been largely abandoned in most fields, as long ago as the 1940s and 1950s in political science. Leading students of government, for example, were already writing then about the impossibility of the progressive plan to separate politics and administration.[2] When Charles Lindblom in 1959 characterized public decision making as the "science of 'muddling through,' " he was describing an "incremental" and "pluralist" governing system in which fact and value were often inextricably interwoven.[3] The values of society typically were recognized only after the fact, the cumulative product of many individual decisions often made for practical reasons. Lindblom's analysis suggested that the actions of economists as advisors to American society would inevitably mix value elements with technical considerations. To the extent Lindblom was correct (and most political scientists agreed), it would act to undermine a key part of the foundational scheme on which Samuelson's *Economics* rested.

Indeed, when *Economics* is put under a close value lens, or studied with the aim of identifying its implicit religious message, its claims to value neutrality appear as mostly the rhetorical flourishes of an era that suffered from many illusions in this regard. There is a powerful value system, a secular religion in essence, lying at the heart of *Economics*. Its progressive message has reached two generations of American undergraduates, preaching the scientific management of American society, now to be supervised at the highest levels by the members of the American economics profession, who will bring about sustained economic growth and development. Moreover, as material scarcity is ended, and as an era of full abundance is achieved, all this will mean the arrival of a brand-new condition for humankind on earth, ethically as well as materially.

Samuelson was thus a follower in the footsteps not only of Keynes but also of Richard Ely, John R. Commons, Thorstein Veblen, and other American progressive economists (as well as many other progressive intellectuals outside the economics profession). His innovation was to devise a new form of the art of economic persuasion. The old progressive message was adapted by Samuelson to a newly scientific appearance, economics as physics.★ *Economics* in fact looked more like a modern physics textbook than a traditional economic text such as Alfred Marshall's older classic, *Principles of Economics.* In the manner of presentation employed in *Economics,* Samuelson sought, and to a considerable extent actually succeeded for a time in appropriating to economics, the prestige that physics held in American society in the wake of the atom bomb, radar, jet airplanes, television, computers, and a host of other extraordinary applications of scientific understanding of physical processes in nature.[4]

Many of the most powerful forms of religion in the past three hundred years have been secular religions that claimed the mantle of science. As modern forms of religion, they are similar to earlier forms in that they have often been capable of inspiring a religious zeal and a willingness to sacrifice in defense of their principles. *Economics* was meant to instil, and to a considerable extent succeeded in instilling, a religious commitment to the market—now depicted as the "market mechanism"—and a commitment to the priestly authority of economists to manage this marvelously productive instrument for the general social benefit. In this way, Samuelson sought to resolve the difficult ethical problem of encouraging self-interested behavior in the marketplace but excluding self-interest from the management of the market and other key governing institutions of society—that is to say, he had devised a new theological solution to the market paradox well suited to his time.

★ Philip Mirowski comments that from the 1930s to the 1980s, "Paul Samuelson was the very model of a neoclassical man in twentieth-century economics: He set the tone for the appropriate demeanor to be displayed before the altar of Science in the twentieth century, innovating an elaborate rapprochement with the developments in twentieth-century physics. . . . It was Samuelson . . . who by both word and deed was responsible for the twentieth-century self-image of the neoclassical economist as scientist." See Philip Mirowski, *More Heat than Light: Economics as Social Physics, Physics as Nature's Economics* (New York: Cambridge University Press, 1989), 378.

chapter THREE

THE MARKET MECHANISM AS
A RELIGIOUS STATEMENT

Until World War I many progressive social scientists, as historian Dorothy Ross writes, "still spoke in the idiom of Christian idealism."[1] However, this old style of Progressivism would gradually lose favor. It was too emotional, too obviously the bearer of a message of religious inspiration, for the newly skeptical temper of the times. The institutionalist school of progressive American economics was dying by the 1940s. In the wake of two world wars, the Holocaust, Siberian prison camps, the rape of Nanking, and other terrible events of the first half of the twentieth century, the language of the older progressives now seemed naively optimistic. In retrospect, a new hardheaded progressivism would be required, making fewer prophetic utterances, expecting less of human behavior, and devoting greater effort to perfecting the detailed scientific knowledge of society.

Samuelson in *Economics* would reflect the new times. He adapted the basic progressive scheme for the scientific management of American society, and the core values of American Progressivism, to the circumstances of the post–World War II setting.* The original progressive aim to give control of industry and other areas of society

---

* Martin Bronfenbrenner describes *Economics* as embodying "the 'new economics' and 'neoclassical synthesis' of 1945–70, compounded of essentially fiscalist Keynesian macroeconomics and essentially Marshallian microeconomics, with an overlay of imperfect competition." See Martin Bronfenbrenner, "On the Superlative in Samuelson," in George R. Feiwel, ed., *Samuelson and Neoclassical Economics* (Boston: Kluwer Nij-hoff, 1982), 346.

to the engineers and other professional experts—virtually to banish self-interested motives from their past central role in society—would have to be put on hold. The new goal would be to accept a pervasive presence of self-interest in the world but to put it to use in the service of higher progressive values. This was a less ambitious but more feasible project.[2]

In terms of the actual practice of scientific management, Samuelson thus substituted the scientific management of the market for the older progressive vision of the management of society through direct control by government. In Europe, a similar rethinking of orthodox socialist principles was taking place. In the second half of the twentieth century, new forms of "market socialism" increasingly displaced the assumption that direct social ownership of the means of production was a necessary central element of a socialist plan for the future.

Yet, despite Samuelson's modifications, *Economics* still expressed the core progressive values. For those willing to make the effort, it is not difficult to discover in Samuelson's new textbook a hope for the secular salvation of the world. Samuelson still believes, like his progressive predecessors, that the material conditions of a person's existence will shape his or her behavior in ethical and other dimensions beyond economics.

At one point in *Economics,* for example, similar to Edwin Seligman, who offered the view that economic conditions underlay ethical beliefs in society, Samuelson declares in 1948 that "if one can know but one fact about a man, knowledge of his income will prove to be most revealing." A person's level of income will provide solid evidence of "his political opinion, his tastes and education, his age, and even his life expectancy." Income shapes not only "materialistic activities" but also "nonmaterialistic activities," matters such as "education, travel, health, recreation, and charity" (61). Other people might have said that a person's religion—whether they have been saved, for example—is more important than their income in understanding their charitable efforts, intellectual proclivities, recreational tastes, and other social behavior. For Samuelson in 1948, however, income is truly the most important thing, for its ethical and other implications even well beyond material possessions.

The editor of a collection of essays on Samuelson's lifetime achievements commented that Samuelson "is well known for his liberal views."[3] Indeed, Samuelson makes no secret of this. In a 1992 essay, "My Life Philosophy," Samuelson states that "my parents were 'liberals' (in the American sense of the word, not in the European 'Manchester School' sense), and I was conditioned in that general *Weltanschauung.* It is an easy faith to adhere to." At the core of Samuelson's liberalism, he says, is "a simple ideology that favors the underdog and (other things equal) abhors inequality." [4] Although Jewish by birth, he has not been known to be an active practitioner of the Jewish religion. His religion has been an economic Progressivism that has sought to use government to promote economic progress with the material benefits extended as far as possible and as equally as possible to all members of American society—and eventually to the salvation of all the world.

From time to time, Samuelson drops his posture of scientific neutrality and adopts an explicitly moralistic tone that more accurately conveys his fundamental values. At one point in *Economics,* for example, he says that the current unequal distribution of income in the United States is "improper" and in fact an outright "evil" (604). Monopolistic practices by which the powerful exploit the weak are another "evil." Indeed, the use of the term *evil* occurs with surprising frequently throughout the pages of *Economics.*

Although Samuelson seeks objectivity in his scientific works, in his later years he has on occasion acknowledged of himself and other social scientists that "our hearts do often contaminate our minds and eyes." Indeed, this may sometimes be a good thing: "In my heart of hearts I nurture the claim that I have good judgment. Be wise, sweet maid, and let them who will be clever. My theories must run the gauntlet of my judgment, an ordeal more fearsome than mere peer review." [5] Samuelson's "judgment" that he applies to shape his economic thinking is that of a battle-hardened American Progressive who adapted the traditional values of the progressive project to a new realism about human behavior, markets, and the workings of economic institutions more generally.

The most powerful value statements in *Economics* are mostly left implicit.★ They are to be found in the way Samuelson chooses to phrase an issue or to develop an argument. To take an example of no great importance, at one point he is illustrating the principle of comparative advantage, describing a brilliant lawyer who also happens to possess great typing skills (540). Samuelson comments that this man should hire a woman to be his secretary, even though he types much faster than she does. Anyone reading this passage understands clearly that the social division of responsibility is that the best lawyers are men,

---

★ Alfred North Whitehead once commented, "Do not direct your attention to those intellectual positions which [controversialists] feel it necessary to defend." The more important elements of a culture are found in "fundamental assumptions which adherents of all the variant systems within the epoch unconsciously presuppose. Such assumptions appear so obvious that people do not know what they are assuming because no other way of putting things has ever occurred to them." Quoted in Alan Jacobs, "A Bible Fit for Children," *First Things,* May 1997, 22. One might say that, in part at least, the purpose of Parts I and II of this book is to uncover the core underlying value assumptions that informed the very framework of thought that Samuelson adopted—but never felt much need to make explicit—in *Economics.*

and their typists are women. The fact that Samuelson in 1948 is merely repeating a conventional understanding of the time does not diminish the fact that he is offering here a cultural judgment in an implicit fashion.

THE MARKET MECHANISM AS METAPHOR

The much more important implicit statements in *Economics* have to do with his economic theology. Samuelson's portrayal of the "market mechanism" serves as the most powerful statement of his core values—his underlying secular religion. Before examining, later in this chapter, this religious content, it will be helpful to recall the image of the market mechanism, as Samuelson introduced it in 1948, and as the concept would be given yet more prominent treatment in later editions and indeed throughout the economics profession.

Samuelson explains the market mechanism as the basic instrument by which American society solves the three problems that every economy must address—"what commodities" will be produced, "how" they will be produced, and "for whom" they will be produced (12–13). Instead of government attempting to solve these problems by direct allocation decisions, as in traditional socialist planning regimes, the market mechanism offers a "system of rationing by prices" (1981 edition, 53).

The market does this, as members of the economics profession have instructed generations of students, with greater efficiency than does any alternative economic system. Indeed, if a socialist government were wise enough, as Samuelson recommends, it would also employ the market mechanism. In that case, the differences between the "mixed-economy" form of government supervision of private business in the United States and a socialist system would in many respects disappear—consisting perhaps most of all of the "much more nearly equal distribution of income" in the socialist system (602).

In any properly functioning economy, capitalist, socialist, or whatever, it is the responsibility of economic technicians using the market mechanism to act to ensure that society reaches its maximal productive potential—a level of output along what Samuelson calls the "production-possibility curve" (17). Then, as a separate matter, society can set the "final distribution of income" equal to the "ideal distribution" of income, according to its own ethical precepts. Society can best accomplish this "by means of a payment of a lump-sum social dividend to people, depending upon 'needs and wants' but never—like a wage—on effort or performance," because that might have distorting effects on productive incentives (601).

In summary, as Samuelson provides an overview of the workings of the market mechanism in *Economics,* the economic task facing any society is most efficiently handled as follows:

> The correct (equilibrium) set of prices of consumption goods and of productive services, the market quantities of outputs and inputs—all these are "unknowns" whose numerical values are determined by a vast set of "simultaneous equations": the condition that all prices be equal to producers' "marginal costs," and to consumers' relative "extra utilities"; that wages equal "marginal revenue productivities"; that profits be at a maximum, etc.
>
> Given such noneconomic facts as (1) production, (2) technology, (3) tastes, and (4) distribution of ownership of property, there are just enough individual and market relations or equations to determine a unique economic solution. Everything depends on everything else, but all together determine each other in just the way that stationary balls in a bowl mutually determine each other's position.
>
> Who solves the complex equations of economic life? Certainly not mathematicians. Certainly not government bureaucrats or congressmen. Every person—whether a businessman, housewife, farmer, or wage earner—is helping to solve them every time he decides to use one kind of labor and not another, or decides to buy butter and not oleomargarine, or decides to plant more or less intensively so much corn and so much wheat, or decides to quit glass blowing for type setting. We don't have to use slide rules, and we don't have to understand the pricing system to contribute to the solution of "general equilibrium." . . .
>
> Prices keep moving as a result of our readjustments of behavior. If outside factors such as inventions, wars, or tastes were to remain constant long enough, then we might finally approach the "general equilibrium set of prices," at which all the forces of supply and demand, value and costs, might just be in balance, without any tendency to further change. Of course, in the real world, outside factors never stand still, so that as fast as equilibrium tends to be attained it is disturbed. Still, there is always a tendency—at least in a "perfect" competitive system—for the equilibrium to reestablish itself, or at least to chase after its true position. (593–94)

This is the heart of the market mechanism, the central economic vision of *Economics.* To be sure, while Samuelson spends two-thirds of the 1948 edition on the various institutions, parameters, and specific workings that surround the market mechanism, he spends the other one-third on the problems of macroeconomic stabilization. The market mechanism by itself is like "a machine without an effective steering wheel or governor," exhibiting wild tendencies to plunge into periods of severe unemployment such as the recent depression of the 1930s. Fortunately, as Keynes has now shown the world, it will be possible to add a "thermostatic control device," allowing society to put the great capacity of the market for efficient production to good use, steering the market mechanism without having to interfere with its basic productive capabilities (412).

Society thus can set its employment and other goals as an independent social-value decision, and then scientifically engineer the economy through manipulation of the market mechanism to the desired end state. As a former MIT graduate student and Samuelson disciple, Lawrence Klein, would put it in 1947, "The Keynesian economic system is essentially a machine which grinds out results according to where the several dials controlling the system are set. The functional relations are the building blocks of the machine, and the dials are the parameters (levels and shapes) of these functions."[6]

For Samuelson, a basic social goal must surely be full employment. Thus, if society will allow its economic technicians free rein to put their scientific knowledge of the market to full use, macroeconomic stability at full employment can be combined with the unmatched productive efficiency of a market system. Then, the full fruits of this marvelous productive efficiency can be distributed among all the members of society—in as perfectly equal a way as is possible, as the readers of *Economics* can have no doubt is Samuelson's strong preference.

By the 1940s, as a result of debates involving Ludwig von Mises, Friedrich Hayek, and Oskar Lange, among others, there was a growing recognition that the old socialist faith in command-and-control central planning had been a utopian conception. The early American Progressivism had also suffered from much the same naive optimism that engineers and other scientific managers would be able to act directly through the instrument of government to implement central plans and programs, all designed "in the public interest." As Keynes had said at the end of *The General Theory,* and Samuelson now repeated in *Economics,* one of the great attractions of the market mechanism was that it proposed to reduce greatly this direct planning and administrative role of government. Instead of government trying to prescribe the fine details of industrial production and administrative actions, it was much better for it simply to manage the market to achieve its broader purposes.

Hence, Samuelson's image of the market mechanism in *Economics* effectively served to convey the message that society could have the benefits of private market efficiency without having to forgo other value goals of society. Society could have its cake and eat it too. Professional economists had (or would soon acquire) the requisite social-engineering skills based on knowledge of the market mechanism to assure this happy outcome.

AN ECONOMIC TAUTOLOGY

The problem is that this image of the market mechanism of *Economics* is more poetry than science. It is best understood as a compelling metaphor for its time designed to attract converts to a new understanding of the progressive gospel of efficiency. None of the claims Samuelson made for the market mechanism rested on any strong scientific foundation, as leading economists over the next fifty years would increasingly conclude. In retrospect, as in Marxism and other systems of economic thought before it, the greatest attraction of *Economics* was its underlying inspirational message.

As is the case in most of the formal economics done in the two or three decades following World War II, the picture of the economy drawn in 1948 in *Economics* is essentially static. That is to say, it is concerned with comparing one possible equilibrium state of the world with another. In a static world, information problems hardly exist, because eventually (and there is an indefinite amount of time available) all the information needed will accrue to anyone who can make use of it. Thus, it is also reasonable to assume the existence of a world of perfect information—another standard assumption of the traditional neoclassical forms of economic analysis—in conducting economic research into the properties of a static world.

However, as economists in recent years have been coming to understand, a static world has little to do with the essence of any real-world economic situation. There is little reason even to ask the question of whether an economic system is capable of being efficient in a perfectly informed and static world. In these circumstances virtually any economic system works perfectly. As Kenneth Arrow has commented, in a world of perfect information where "every agent has a complete model of the economy, the hand running the economy is very visible indeed. . . . Under these conditions, the superiority of the market over centralized planning disappears" altogether.[7]

Politics, for example, can be regarded as a special form of economic system in that it provides an exchange mechanism that can be used for allocating resources in society. As in logrolling and other familiar political phenomena, much of what goes on in politics is the bartering among groups in society of one good or service for another. In a world of perfect information and zero transaction costs, every participant in the political system would know the full economic potential for exchanges available to all (they would know the full production possibility curve, in Samuelson's terminology). Any conceivable shift in resource allocation that is Pareto optimal in an economic sense will also be desirable and achievable in a political system for allocating the resources of society. If this efficient allocation of resources does not occur within the political system, it will be as a result of a failure of politics (stalemates due to failures to resolve disputes of one kind or another), not of economics. If the assumption of zero transaction costs is taken to rule out political failures as well, by definition a political system will attain to a state of economic efficiency in society no less perfect than a market system.★

Hence, the economic problem arises precisely because the world is not static and perfectly informed, and because different economic systems have different learning, transacting, and information-processing capabilities. An unregulated free market is one such learning system; Samuelson's mixed economy is yet another; central socialist planning is still another; and autarchy (however poorly it is likely to fare on economic grounds) is also a theoretical economic possibility, among many others. All economic systems are trial-and-error systems in some fundamental sense. The most desirable system, in economic-efficiency terms, will be the system that moves toward any desired economic state most rapidly and with the least information, negotiation, contracting, enforcement, and other transactional and transitional costs. Or course, the end state itself will be constantly moving (and may not even be definable in any real world situation), a further fundamental complication.

The costs of economic transition will consist in significant part of the er-

---

★ The equality of perfect efficiency of both market and political outcomes in a world of zero transaction costs is not a new insight. At least as long ago as 1962, Buchanan and Tullock in *The Calculus of Consent* noted that "if full side payments are allowed to take place, *any* decision-making rule for collective action will lead to positions that may properly be classified as Pareto-optimal." The assumption of zero transaction costs necessarily implies an absence of restrictions on the making of side payments. Then, the unrestricted and costless "introduction of [such] side payments" results in the "conversion of all collective decisions to . . . *purely redistributive* elements. Unless a public investment project [by the government] is 'worth while' in a market-value sense, side payments ('bribes') will arise to prevent action from being taken, regardless of the [political] rule for choice. . . . With full side payments, the decision-making rules determine the structure of the net income transfers only."

That is to say, in a world of zero transaction costs—incorporating a perfect ability to make all desired side payments (which could just as well be in-kind forms of side payments as well as monetary forms)—any political rule of choice will achieve the same state of perfect Pareto optimality as is achieved in a market system under the conventional assumption of zero transaction costs. In the political system, to be sure, the initial "assets" driving the distribution of income will consist of voting power; in the market system the assets will consist of initial property holdings. But this difference will not affect the fact of achieving perfect Pareto efficiency of final outcomes in both cases. See James M. Buchanan and Gordon Tullock, *The Calculus of Consent: Logical Foundations of Constitutional Democracy* (Ann Arbor: University of Michigan Press, 1962), 189–91.

rors of the particular trial-and-error process associated with a particular economic system. In the U.S. market system, when the Ford Motor Company produced the Edsel, and then saw its rapid demise, it was no doubt able to convert some of the former Edsel production facilities to other car-making purposes, and to benefit in some ways from the previous training of the labor force in Edsel manufacturing. However, a significant part of the Ford investment to gear up for Edsel production was also surely a deadweight economic loss. These not only were losses to Ford but also represented real resource costs to the American economy at the time.

If less visible, there are many thousands of Edsel equivalents throughout the diverse sectors of the U.S. economy every year. Many restaurants, to take a particularly volatile sector, fail in a year or two. These failures are part of a search process by which the economy is always responding to the forces of changing technology, shifting consumer demands, new resource discoveries, and a host of other economic factors. Two main criteria for judging an economic system will be the speed at which it moves along a path toward any desired end state and the error rate with a resulting deadweight economic cost of transition likely to be associated with moving along a trial-and-error process of that kind.

Samuelson in *Economics,* implicitly if not in so many words, asserts the superiority of the market mechanism, as scientifically engineered by economists, in these regards. However, there is no scientific demonstration to be found in *Economics,* partly because the mainstream of the economics profession had devoted little attention to this broader subject in the 1940s and 1950s. It was not until George Stigler's 1961 article "The Economics of Information" that the profession began the process of redirecting its attention to the complex economic details of the processes of information generation and transmission in a dynamic economy.[8] In the previous year Ronald Coase's article "The Problem of Social Cost"—perhaps the one most influential economic article of the past fifty years—also had directed attention to another crucial aspect of a dynamic economic system, the potential for widely varying transaction costs associated with reaching contractual and other agreements among the many economic actors in a world of less than complete information.[9]

Over the past several decades, the upshot of all this has been startling. The past methods of comparing alternative economic systems, such as employed by Samuelson in *Economics,* many economists now concede, are in essence incapable of achieving their objectives as then stated. In discussions of traditional arguments with respect to international trade, for example, Rachel McCulloch now comments that "most theoretical arguments, old and new, overstate the benefits of change by comparing alternative equilibria without considering costs of moving between them." Although few trade economists have ever sought to calculate such costs, any definitive conclusions about the full benefits of free trade require taking account of the potential high costs of "displaced resources that remain idle for an extended period," during the processes of adjustment to shifting trading patterns. Without such calculations, the commonly asserted economic superiority of free trade is nothing less than a large "leap of faith"—a matter perhaps more of "religion" than of "science."[10]

More broadly, by generally ignoring learning processes, information transmission mechanisms, error rates, contracting complexities, transaction costs, and so forth—and indeed, often simply assuming as a starting point of the analysis that a state of perfect information and equilibrium (the two are virtually equivalent) exists throughout the economic system—the economic arguments of the past, including arguments central to the image of the market mechanism of *Economics,* became virtual tautologies. As Eirik Furubotn and Rudolf Richter comment in their comprehensive review of a recent and rapidly growing literature critical of past economic arguments, there has been a growing conviction among economists that "orthodox neoclassical analysis rests on highly specialized assumptions and is incapable, *without some modification,* of dealing effectively with many problems of interest to theorists, empirical researchers, and policy makers."[11] For example, Avinash Dixit comments that "the neoclassical view" conceived of firms as "production functions" but that the introduction of considerations of transaction costs yields a whole new understanding of the business world that is "novel and revolutionary" in its way of thinking.[12]

Joseph Stiglitz—a former MIT student, editor of Samuelson's collected papers, chair of the Council of Economic Advisors in the Clinton administration and then chief economist at the World Bank—commented in 1994 that, seen from the perspective of the new "information paradigm," standard economic modes of theorizing yield a fundamentally "incorrect characterization of the market economies and the central problems of resources allocation. . . . and the market mechanism." As a consequence, "the standard neoclassical model . . . provides little guidance for the choice of economic systems, since once information imperfections (and the fact that markets are incomplete) are brought into the analysis, as surely they must be, there is no presumption that markets are efficient."[13]

In short, if information, transaction costs, and other costs of dynamic adjustment are the core issues for an economic system, any mode of theorizing based on an assumption of perfect information, zero transaction costs, and perfect equilibrium will have very little to contribute to an understanding of fundamental economic understanding. Yet, as George Akerlof has noted, as recently as the mid-1960s "there was almost nothing about information in economics." Worse than that, there existed a virtual "taboo against writing about information" in the profession.[14] As a contemporary economist from the "Austrian" school, Peter Boettke, has recently elaborated on this problem:

> Samuelson's research program [as its results were communicated to a wider public audience from 1948 onward in *Economics* and its many imitators] eliminated the conscious component from the economic choices facing individuals in a world of uncertainty. Choice was reduced to a simple determinate exercise within a given ends–means framework, something an automaton [or central planner] could master. The task of discovering not only appropriate means, but also which ends to pursue, was left out of the equation. Moreover, it was forgotten that market institutions and practices arise in large part precisely *because* of deviations from the perfect-market model. . . . The imperfections of the real world give rise to the essential institutions and practices that make economic life possible. The complexity of both institutions and individuals is impossible to model precisely, so it was pushed aside by simplifying assumptions [throughout the research agenda of the economics profession, as presented for popular consumption by Samuelson].[15]

Boettke thus finds that in retrospect the economic system of Samuelson is yet another "utopian" vision in a similar category to socialist, Marxist, or other economic utopias of the past. It is also utopian in a political sense because politicians in any real-world democratic system are unlikely to grant economic scientists the necessary autonomy to engineer the market mechanism efficiently.[16] It is utopian, as a matter of economics, because in effect it simply assumes from the outset a perfect solution to the very problem that an economic system is supposed to solve. In short, Samuelson's treatment of the market mechanism becomes virtually a tautology in economic thinking—if not an act of religious faith.

A realistic treatment of the fundamental economic problem, the kind missing in *Economics,* would have focused on the information and transaction roles of alternative institutional arrangements within an economy. As the economic historian (and winner in 1993 of the Nobel Prize in economics) Douglass North has observed, "Throughout most history the institutional incentives to invest in productive knowledge have been largely absent." The key to economic growth in the West has been "institutional innovations that have lowered the costs of transacting." Such costs "arise because information is costly and asymetrically held by the parties to exchange." In particular, differences in information among economic parties give rise to "incentives to cheat, free ride and so forth that will contribute to market imperfections." The fundamental problem for any economic system is to devise a suitable set of institutions that provide "adaptive efficiency" in the means of generating and distributing relevant economic information to the parties in need of it.[17] However, Samuelson, like most leading economists of his time, rejected institutional studies in favor of the "high theory" that would—it was then believed—be more truly "scientific."

As will be examined further in Part IV, North argues that the economics profession today must devote a much greater part of its research to the detailed analysis of institutions. Taking up issues that Samuelson altogether failed to address, economists must "explore much more systematically than we have done so far the implications of the costly and imperfect processing of information for the consequent behavior of the actors." The profession must somehow "come to grips with the subjective mental constructs by which individuals process information and arrive at conclusions that shape their choices." This will require a radical redirection of economic methods. As North puts it, the traditional economic "preoccupation with rational choice and efficient market hypotheses has blinded us to the implications of incomplete information and the complexity of environments and subjective perceptions of the external world that individuals hold."[18]

One of the greatest failings of the Samuelson approach was that it offered no satisfactory theoretical explanation for the existence of the modern corporation. It was not until Oliver Williamson's 1975 book, *Markets and Hierarchies,* that one finds the beginnings of serious theoretical study by economists of the organizational structure of modern industry.[19] As Williamson would later explain, "The modern corporation is mainly to be understood as the product of a series of organizational innovations that have had the purpose and effect of economizing on transaction costs."[20]

Compared with an atomistic market, the corporation often provides better solutions to three types of problems: (1) bounded rationality, (2) opportunism, and (3) asset specificity.[21] Bounded rationality means that, contrary to the standard neoclassical assumptions such as Samuelson made, individuals have limited information and limited capacity to process that information. Opportunism means that some people can be expected to lie, cheat, and otherwise to deceive, especially if such behavior will yield greater profits, and economic actors must take steps to protect themselves from such misleading forms of behavior. Asset specificity means that much economic behavior involves long-run commitments to actions of benefit to particular parties, and yet it is difficult in an uncertain world to write contacts covering many future contingencies. The modern corporation, Williamson argues, represents an institutional solution to these problems, a more successful solution than any set of autonomous free market agents would be able to develop.

Samuelson obviously cannot be faulted for not presenting in 1948 a body of work that did not exist until the later editions of *Economics*. Where he can be faulted is in making definitive statements that included strong policy conclusions and recommendations about the workings of markets on the basis of a theoretical apparatus that manifestly failed to explain even some of the most basic aspects of the organization of economic activity in the United States of his time.

Indeed, the theory of the market mechanism of Samuelson's *Economics* is yet another instance of Herbert Simon's complaint that in economics "most of its 'action'—the force of its predictions—derives from the, usually untested, auxiliary assumptions that describe the environment in which decisions are made," yielding an economic methodology that is essentially "tautological and irrefutable."[22] In the case of the market mechanism, the formal arguments of *Economics* in strict scientific terms accomplished little more than demonstrating the obvious—that an economic system already assumed to be perfectly efficient will in fact turn out on closer examination to be perfectly efficient. As Simon suggests, the initial assumptions were more important than the conclusions, and these assumptions reflected and communicated a powerful value position.

Why, then, given all these grave failures of analysis, was *Economics* such a great success? Perhaps the answer is that *Economics* was not ultimately a scientific undertaking at all. Perhaps Samuelson's efforts in *Economics* should be seen in the light of D. McCloskey's critique of the social function of the economics profession. As McCloskey has stated, the "modernist" methods of economics, as practiced by the members of Samuelson's generation, promise scientific "knowledge free from doubt, free from metaphysics, morals and personal conviction. What it is able to deliver renames as scientific methodology the . . . economic scientist's metaphysics, morals and personal convictions."[23] In *Economics* Samuelson may have had a message of secular religion to deliver to his audience, but he (along with a whole generation of other economists as well) may have chosen to preach this new gospel in the more authoritative voice of science—in particular, of physics.[24] Like other preachers, Samuelson knew his audience and spoke in terms that he knew would prove most persuasive.

To be sure, the success of *Economics* was also partly attributable to the abundant practical observations and descriptions of institutional details that the book provided concerning the American economy. *Economics* was crammed with interesting facts and figures of all sorts. Samuelson gave significant attention to matters such as the spending patterns of state and local governments, relative consumption behavior of people with different incomes, the composition of national income, and many other empirical details of the American economy. Ironically, in light of Samuelson's reputation as the greatest economic theorist of his generation, the greatest failings of *Economics* were not in its descriptions of the details of the American economy (where the book in fact is often very useful), but in the broader theoretical framework in which Samuelson embedded such practical information.

SAMUELSON'S UTOPIA

The intellectual history of Western thought since the Enlightenment is characterized by one utopian vision after another, each finding fault with its predecessors, but then holding out the prospect of yet another, truer—more scientific—path to heaven on earth. The American progressive gospel of efficiency stirred a deep religious fervor because the followers in this new creed believed that they had finally found the correct way to earthly perfection. Samuelson, of course, does not explicitly promise such an outcome to history; his utopianism is revealed only in a set of implicit assumptions necessary to make any sense of the logic of his economic arguments.

The growing body of recent criticism of the economic methodology of Samuelson and other economists of his era has only touched the tip of the iceberg. There are even more fundamental scientific problems than those that Stiglitz, Boettke, and others have raised. Almost without thinking about it, virtually all economists automatically distinguish between what might be described as "valid" social costs and "invalid" costs. In making this distinction, economists automatically communicate a powerful set of social values, implicitly endorsing those values.

For example, in considering the economic burdens of transition from one state of economic equilibrium to another, a valid cost of dynamic adjustment for a current economist would include such things as the expense of hiring moving vans for furniture and other household items. The process of economic transition means that some workers have to move their place of residence from one city to another to find a new job. These represent real commitments of social resources. An invalid cost—or at least a cost that economists of Samuelson's time, or of today, almost never incorporate into their economic thinking—would be any "psychic pain" experienced by that same worker in the process of making the same move. The worker might feel deep grief in having to leave a familiar community behind; in having to move away from family and friends; or in having to leave a home where he or she has grown up. Or the worker may simply feel a deep anxiety in facing the uncertain prospects of a brand-new job and other surroundings.★

Economists automatically exclude these and many other types of costs from their analyses. When several smaller farms are consolidated into one larger and more productive farm, thus helping in fact to improve the overall efficiency of U.S. agriculture, economists do not consider the bruised feelings of the smaller farmers themselves, or the possible distress at their plight that might be felt by neighbors when the smaller farmers are forced out of business. Economists do not consider the impact on the existing sense of community for the remaining residents in a rural area when workers or farmers have to leave, because the rural economy will no longer support them. Economists do not take into account the nostalgia that many people will feel, knowing that an old building is being demolished to make way for a new higher value use of the land. There are any number of cultural symbols associated in one way or another with changing states of the economy that have the capacity to move many people emotionally in powerful ways, making them feel happy or sad as economic forces work their way.

Economists do not incorporate such elements into their analysis for very good reasons. These types of costs, many having to do with individual perceptions about more or less desirable states of the world, would be virtually impossible for economists to measure. Such perceptions of the world can also be fragile, depending heavily on, for example, access to information. The degree of pain felt by Americans because of people suffering from AIDS in

---

★ This is much more than just a theoretical consideration. Indeed, much of American politics involves conflicting views concerning the social impacts and desirable pace of market change. The former Republican presidential candidate Patrick Buchanan attacked fellow Republican conservatives closer to the political mainstream precisely because of their unquestioning willingness to accept the full costs of the market process. Buchanan wrote:

> Unbridled capitalism is an awesome force that creates new factories, wealth and opportunities that go first to society's risk takers and holders of capital. But unbridled capitalism is also an awesome destructive force. It makes men and women obsolete as rapidly as it does the products they produce and the plants that employ them. And the people made obsolete and insecure are workers, employees, "Reagan Democrats," rooted people, conservative people who want to live their lives and raise their families in the same neighborhoods they grew up in.
>
> Unbridled capitalism tells them they cannot.

See Patrick Buchanan, "Schism Beyond Repair on the Right?" *Washington Times,* March 25, 1998, A19.

Africa, or dolphins being killed by fishermen off Mexico, may depend heavily on the number of TV cameras sent by the networks to cover the story—hardly the basis for the kinds of "hard" analysis traditionally sought by economists.[25]

Other institutions in society also do not recognize most forms of "psychic costs." This is so taken for granted in the law, for example, that the grounds are rarely even discussed in the legal literature. A recent exception is an article by Dan Tarlock, one of the few legal scholars to ask whether cultural environments should be given a formal legal standing as protected objects. His specific question was whether existing ranching and other "western communities" might be given any legal protection as "endangered cultural remnants"—in the spirit if not the precise manner of the protection afforded endangered animal and plant species by the Endangered Species Act.[26]

As Tarlock notes, the market is "an engine of perpetual change" that in many cases includes "the loss of traditional cultures" such as "small, stable communities, and the values they represent." A few local people in such communities have recently begun to make the novel legal claim that their cultural losses should be recognized in the law as legitimate third-party losses for which compensation or other redress should be provided—somewhat in the manner that a person is already protected against nuisance harm from, say, a smoky factory. Yet, as Tarlock notes, "many of the costs of growth are intangible and are not considered within traditional land use and water administration"; by long practice "growth management law gives little weight to the losers from growth." In the traditional attitude of the law, similar to the attitude found in economic analysis, "the long and the short of it is that the social consequences of market-driven change are considered *damnum absque injuria*"—that is to say, "a loss or injury which does not give rise to an action against the person causing it."[27]

Still, as Tarlock notes, Indian tribes in the United States and other native groups in other countries have received such legal protection. It is possible—radical as the broader social consequences might be—that a non-Indian group might be able to assert a similar social imperative and legal claim. Tarlock thus adventurously sets out to "examine the deeper question of whether at-risk [non-Indian] communities have, as they increasingly assert, a legitimate claim to be protected from the market because it threatens a unique culture." How might one think about the possibility of "special cultural rights for at-risk communities and the form that they might take?" Should small ranching communities in the rural West and other such communities elsewhere be taken at all seriously when they argue "that local control over landscape and resource use is essential to preserve distinctive behavioral patterns associated with the exploitation of land and water resources," and therefore the localities should be given formal legal protection from the market?[28]

Tarlock finds that the efforts of the pioneers in making these new legal claims often range "from the comic to the ineffective." Yet, he still concludes that "greater legitimacy" should be given to "the recognition of group cultural practices as a legitimate component of property rights." In many of his previous writings an advocate of market approaches to social problems, Tarlock nevertheless reaches this conclusion in full awareness of the fact that it would radically challenge the long-standing approach of "land use law [that] fundamentally seeks to ratify the market or to restrain it marginally rather than to impede its operation," partly out of a traditional concern that "protection of community interests creates high transaction costs" that would pose a major obstacle to the normal functioning of a market system, if they were given greater legal recognition.[29]

The legal complexities of offering formal protection to "endangered communities" would be great. Similarly, if economists did attempt to measure in a formal way these more subjective cultural elements, many of the principal policy recommendations on which economists rest their professional identity would no longer be defensible—or at least would no longer be defensible on value-neutral grounds, requiring that economists instead explicitly advocate these policies as a matter of making a particular social-value choice. Consider free trade, something on which most economists today agree. The loss of American industry and jobs, as production of clothing items, televisions, computers, and many other goods and services shifts overseas, is disruptive and painful to many of the people who lose their jobs or are otherwise adversely affected. Their personal feelings in this regard, however, are considered by economists to be outside the bounds of economic analysis for the purposes of assessing the real economic benefits of free trade. Economists ask only the narrower question: given that new foreign goods will come in as inexpensive imports, will American consumers benefit overall from the shifting patterns of economic production and consumption associated with foreign trade? The answer, as economists make the calculations (correctly), is almost always yes.

However, if the benefits and costs of free trade were extended to include full consideration of the pain and other psychic elements associated with resulting economic dislocations and disruptions in the process of change itself, it would be impossible to give any clear economic answer. Moreover, the decision of economists to exclude certain types of psychic and other "noneconomic" costs does not rest on any scientific grounds. Indeed, as a matter strictly of whether there is any effect on "utility," the individual feelings associated with transitional changes in the economy affecting personal lifestyles are often real and deep. They can have just as big an impact on an individual's sense of well-being as, say, the purchase of an automobile or some other major consumer item. They are excluded from economic analysis simply as an initial assumption, or as one might say in more religious terms, as "an act of faith."

"VALID" AND "INVALID" COSTS

Instead of being in the realm of science, the normal exclusion by economists of feelings of psychic transitional loss and gain—and many other such "soft" considerations—thus really represents a fundamental value choice made by the members of the economics profession.* It reflects a belief, not that these costs do not exist, or do not affect the perceptions of well-being of many people (economists are not that unaware), but that these particular costs should not be—do not deserve to be—counted. In deciding to incorporate some costs into their thinking while excluding others, economists have quietly and with little explicit recognition introduced a powerful set of value distinctions.

In economic practice, a "valid" cost is one that consumes resources that could be devoted to the advance of material progress on earth. In order to maximize the rate of economic progress, resources must be allocated with maximal efficiency, requiring that the "cost" of every such valid item be carefully measured, helping to ensure that a greater "opportunity cost" is not thereby lost. With "invalid" costs, they are defined by the fact that they have just the opposite character. To give any weight to the psychic pain or other stresses of transition and dislocation, as the economy moves from lower to

---

* Observers outside the economics profession tend to have a clearer understanding of the strong values implicit in economic methods than do most economists themselves. For example, with respect to the powerful values that can be harmed by the very process of change itself, one writer notes: "There was among the southern defenders of communitarianism, as there is among communitarians today, a willingness to accept lower mobility as a value and to express an active suspicion of it as an eroder of community stability. Thus Michael Walzer, who acknowledges more of the liberal project than many communitarians," writes [that]:

> [the old-fashioned] liberalism [of free markets] is, most simply, the theoretical endorsement and justification of . . . movement. . . . Nevertheless, this popularity has an underside of sadness and discontent that is intermittently articulated, and communitarianism is, most simply, the intermittent articulation of those feelings. It reflects a loss and this loss is real. . . . Social mobility, which carries people down as well as up [,] . . . requires adjustments that are never easy to manage.

See Philip Abbott, "The Lincoln Propositions and the Spirit of Secession," *Studies in American Political Development* 10 (Spring 1996): 121.

higher stages of economic productivity, is to stand in the way of economic progress. Legitimate costs for economists, in short, are those that consume actual resources that can be devoted to advancing the material productivity of society; illegitimate costs are those whose introduction into the economic calculus would stand in the way of economic progress.

Stated another way, for economists to take full account of every form of cost would be for them to impede the secular salvation of the world. In the implicit theology of *Economics* and many other economic writings, it would be to oppose the instructions of a modern god who, as it is now recently revealed, actually operates in history through the workings of the economic forces of production.[30] In the medieval era at the height of Christian faith, it was said that, as compared with salvation in the hereafter, the affairs of this world were nothing. No sensible Christian would jeopardize his or her eternal salvation for the benefit of a mere few earthly pleasures of the moment. In *Economics,* Samuelson implicitly reaches a similar conclusion. Compared with the attainment of a future heaven here on earth, the current transitional psychic burdens of progress, as borne by each citizen, are not important enough be to counted. Indeed, to count them might endanger the future economic salvation of the world.

It is instead the religious duty of all good citizens of our time to bear the sacrifices of economic progress without complaint. Hence, for example, if asked to move to another job in another city, to live away from their families, to see the character of their neighborhoods changed by development, to lose the remaining wild areas of the countryside, or to bear other burdens for progress, they should instead rejoice in the fact of their opportunity to participate in the achievement of a future heaven on earth. In this way, all of humankind will soon enough experience a transformation of the human condition, and the temporary burdens of the past will soon be forgotten.

Hence, Samuelson gives no weight in his implicit value system, as the image of the market mechanism developed in *Economics* powerfully communicates to its readers, to the complaints of those selfish people and other malingerers who might object that they are being asked to bear too great a burden of individual sacrifice in the name of economic progress. These people are listening to the voice of a modern devil, who roams the world tempting people to lose sight of the heavenly future that lies in store, hoping to lure them from a long-run economic salvation by the lesser prospect of short-term gains or pleasures of the moment. It is in "politics" especially that this devil is likely to be found working his evil ways, introducing impediments to market efficiency or other instruments of rapid economic progress.

Defense of the market mechanism requires a powerful religious blessing partly because most people—as recent economic research has been confirming in a more formal way—are normally resistant to change and averse to taking risks. Matthew Rabin summarized these findings in a recent review article in the *Journal of Economic Literature:* "In a wide variety of domains, people are significantly more averse to losses than they are attracted to same-sized gains." This phenomenon is closely related to the "endowment effect" also seen in studies of the reactions of people to changes in their circumstances. Economists who have actually studied individual psychological reactions in real-world situations find that "once a person comes to possess a good, she immediately values it more than before she possessed it." [31]

Such an attitude of ordinary people flies in the face of the workings of markets, which bring change at even the slightest chance for any increase of profit. People have to be educated and instructed to ignore the normal human resistance to change. Many religions and societies of the past have failed in this respect, condemning them to backwardness. If the citizenry cannot be taught to overcome this natural caution, the long-run economic progress of society and the future salvation of the world will be long delayed or perhaps permanently lost. Unlike economics, religion accepts that its basic function is to change the way people think about the world—to change their preference structure, as an economist would put it. The real task of Samuelson's *Economics* was of this kind; it was to provide an inspirational vision of human progress guided by science in order to motivate Americans and other people to the necessary religious dedication to the cause of progress.

Admittedly, the style of Samuelson's defense of the market system was not only a matter of providing a religious blessing. Martha Feldman and James March write that the manner in which a group aspiring to social leadership asserts its claim is closely tied to the "social norms of a society," including norms that often relate to "rational decision processes of a particular kind." In the Western world during the modern period, these norms have tended to be derived from the "rational traditions of the enlightenment," as they emerged with the spreading use of the scientific method in the eighteenth century. By showing capabilities in rational analysis in the Enlightenment mode, an aspiring leadership class can make its case for a prominent decision making role in society at the same time as it "symbolizes a commitment to rational choice." There is a benefit in two respects because "displaying the symbol [both] reaffirms the importance of this social value [of rational decision processes] and signals personal and organizational competence" in this very skill.[32]

That is to say, when Samuelson and other members of the American economics profession skillfully manipulate the scientific symbols of social decision making, they are both affirming the core value to American society of "Enlightenment" rationality in decision making and also staking a strong claim for economists to be the group that seeks to ensure the prominence of such rational considerations in the daily affairs of present-day society. The "signaling" component with respect to rational competence can be altogether independent of the actual usefulness to policy making of the analytical capabilities demonstrated in the acts of economic modeling.[33] These (genuinely skillful) analytical efforts serve merely to put economists in positions of authority in the broader society where they are then able to apply their pragmatic knowledge and general intellectual capabilities in more practical ways.

Based on his *Foundations of Economic Analysis* and many other technical writings for fellow economic professionals, and whatever their actual deficiencies as matters of high theory, Samuelson's "scientific" efforts at the time presented the appearance and were widely accepted in American society as the height of technical sophistication in the social sciences. In the framework of Feldman and March, Samuelson was succeeding through his "scientific" work in asserting a social leadership role for American economists by demonstrating exceptional skills in the formal methods of Enlightenment rationality. He may have had good pragmatic reasons—little related to his theorizing—for favoring a market system. Empirically, it was easy for anyone to see that market systems were delivering the goods around the world. However, if Samuelson were to succeed in gaining greater social influence for this view (if putting the market within the context of a mixed economy), it had to be presented in the scientific framework of a social physics and other "rational" models of Enlightenment thought. In this respect as in others, Samuelson was demonstrating a supreme pragmatism, skillfulness, resourcefulness, and political astuteness—even if it often seemingly had to come at the expense of the full economic "truth."

THE ETHICS OF USURY

This basic value system embedded in *Economics* is well illustrated by Samuelson's treatment of the age-old question of usury. In the past, and still to some extent today, many people have had strong negative feelings concerning the very act of charging interest on a money loan (or some are concerned more with interest rates that they regard as excessively high). Indeed, their personal "utility" can be genuinely affected merely by any awareness of the actual practice of "usury"—perhaps most of all if it affects them directly, but also for many people simply by the knowledge of a bank somewhere charging someone else "unfair" interest. There is no strictly scientific reason for excluding such strong feelings when an economist undertakes research concerning the overall net economic benefits associated with the conduct of bank loan activities.

Yet the Samuelson of *Economics,* as would virtually any economist today, dismisses out of hand the old thinking about usury. The very fact of charging a high interest rate cannot in and of itself be a valid cost—a valid economic consideration—for Samuelson. Indeed, as Samuelson writes in *Economics,* the attitudes of society about interest rates must not be controlled by such strange past practices as "considering the origin of the word in Latin" or by investigating "what Aristotle had to say about it" (482). Rather, charging interest performs an essential function in allocating capital efficiently in real-world economic systems, and must be incorporated into the workings of any modern economy committed to further rapid growth and development.

But why, as a strictly scientific matter? If I determine my attitudes toward interest from reading Aristotle, or from the condemnation of usury by a twelfth-century Lateran Council and subsequent Catholic Church rulings, or from Christian theology as developed by Thomas Aquinas, and consequently have a strong emotional aversion to high bank-interest rates, who is Samuelson to tell me that my strong feelings should not count? In ruling out my negative reaction as a valid economic cost, Samuelson is here again asserting a powerful value system of his own. He is rejecting my values in favor of a set of powerful convictions automatically incorporated into the standard belief system of professional economics. Charging interest rationalizes economic behavior and thus is a key instrument in advancing the cause of economic progress, the fundamental value system of *Economics.* Samuelson is, moreover, seeking to persuade the legions of students who would later study *Economics* of the superior merits of this set of social values. He is seeking to persuade them of the "irrationality" of the old Catholic, Islamic, Aristotelian, and other value systems that preached otherwise.

Indeed, Samuelson is on occasion explicit about the secular religion of *Economics* that rules out any concern for usury—or, for that matter, concern for virtually any other feature of the basic framework of economic institutions as an object of ultimate value in itself. Samuelson—like most other economists—thus would no doubt rule out any arguments about a "just wage," or more recently the "comparable worth" of a worker's salary, on much the same grounds that he rejects usury arguments. He would rule out government policies grounded in a simple preference—despite their "inefficiency"—for small businesses over large. As he says, "The primary purpose of economic activity is the provision of consumption goods and services"

(231). Hence, in the operation of the economic system, "objects are useful in the last analysis because of the services (or utilities) that they render," and the precise manner of their production should not be a matter of concern to society—as long as a final higher level of consumption is achieved. That is to say that the manner of organization of an economic system is for Samuelson not a matter capable of generating "utility" in and of itself. This is to say the least a heroic value judgment, all the more remarkable in light of the lack of any defense by the average economist of the grounds for making such a powerful assumption.

Economic policies or instruments for Samuelson (and for his entire generation of economists) are to be judged simply by their contribution to the goal of increasing the total amount of production and the resulting levels of goods and services available for consumptive use (properly measured over time with a discount rate).* The long-run amount of "discounted" consumption is the one and only measure of economic well-being for *Economics*. If John Calvin strongly disagreed, believing that people should work not for the pleasure of the consumption (which might in fact endanger their eternal souls) but primarily for the disciplining of their unruly natures through the very act of labor, so much for Calvin's belief system.

To be sure, Samuelson would no doubt acknowledge that the institution of slavery had to be abolished, even if it could have been shown that slavery produced more total economic product—for slaveholders and slaves combined—than the economic alternatives. He would probably concede the right of society to ban prostitution or drug use, even if it could be shown that the net willingness to pay minus the social costs of these activities was positive. However, for the vast majority of other cases involving social-value judgments about the manner of production and consumption, Samuelson reserves the right to apply his powerful (secular) religious lens. As a conse-

---

* Like other aspects of *Economics*, this feature of the standard neoclassical paradigm has been receiving growing criticism within the economics profession itself. In a recent issue of the *Journal of Economic Literature,* Samuel Bowles comments that "markets and other economic institutions do more than allocate goods and services; they also influence the evolutions of values, tastes, and personalities. Economists have long assumed otherwise; the axiom of exogenous preferences is as old as liberal political philosophy itself." As a result, an economics that ignores this factor—such as the economic system portrayed in *Economics*—will lack "explanatory power, policy relevance, and ethical coherence." A more realistic analysis that takes account of the impact of economic institutions themselves on individual preferences is yet another reason why "aspects of social life once thought to be the province of psychology or sociology are thus seen to be essential to the bread and butter of economics." Indeed, since religion in some broad sense is the study of how to change preferences (for the better, presumably), Bowles might have added theology to his list. See Samuel Bowles, "Endogenous Preferences: The Cultural Consequences of Markets and other Economic Institutions," *Journal of Economic Literature* 36 (March 1998): 75, 77.

quence, Samuelson must reject any suggestion that the framework itself of the economic system, the means by which prices are set, the legal definition of property rights, the institutions within which the market mechanism functions, the exact magnitudes of wage rates and interest rates, the degree of individual liberty maintained, the very existence of certain types of economic activities, are legitimate ultimate objects in themselves of the utility functions of the members of society.

THE "EVILS" OF MONOPOLY

Where do these deeply embedded values, admittedly still shared by and reflected in the analyses conducted by the great majority of the members of the economics profession today, come from? The answer can be seen on another occasion when Samuelson analyzes a different kind of high price, and reaches an altogether different conclusion from that in the example of a usurious interest rate. The high price in this instance results from firms employing "monopolistic devices." Such monopoly prices, as Samuelson declares, are in fact "too high"—indeed, a war must be waged against monopoly prices as genuine "economic evils." If others have long seen usurious interest rates as morally offensive, monopolistic prices are a genuine moral "evil" (the actual term used by Samuelson). The reason, Samuelson explains, is that they result in "wastage of resources and creation of monopoly profits" (127).

A monopolistic high price, in short, leads to the inefficient use of the economic resources of society. It thus stands in the way of material progress and the continuing advance of humankind toward a heaven on earth of complete abundance. Compounding the problem, it rewards this transgression against the secular religion of *Economics* with high profits to the evildoer. If a church should today declare that a usurious interest rate is a transgression against a command of God, as supported by passages found in the Bible, Samuelson would be scornful. However, when a monopolistic firm transgresses against economic efficiency, Samuelson feels deep moral outrage. If in an implicit fashion, Samuelson is thus saying in *Economics* that the place of the biblical word of God has been taken by the word of a newer and more modern deity, a god who delivers verdicts on human actions according to whether they are economically efficient and thus advance the cause of economic progress, the route of advance to heaven on earth.

In Christian theology, good and evil are distinguished by whether they promote God's plans for the world. Those who are saved, who will join the elect in heaven, should renounce evil in this world. The Christian turns to the Bible as a principle source of guidance in such matters. If the path to heaven takes an economic route in the modern age, however, there will have to be a new understanding of good and evil. That which is "good" will now be that which moves the human condition further along a modern path to salvation; that is to say, along the road of economic progress to the elimination of scarcity. That which is "evil" will be anything that obstructs such progress. Indeed, as described above, Samuelson in *Economics* recognizes precisely this moral distinction by excluding all costs that reflect unworthy motives—that serve to obstruct the rate of economic progress of society—as illegitimate. As a modern kind of evil temptation, often reflecting unworthy motives in "politics," these "psychic" costs will simply not be counted. Attempts to impose other kinds of barriers to the economic progress of society will similarly be dismissed.

For Samuelson, the traditional Christian concepts of good and evil thus take on a brand-new economic meaning. In the implicit theology of *Economics,* that which is good is now that which is efficient; conversely, evil is defined to be that which is inefficient. Samuelson is the heir to the progressive value system, often characterized by historians as the gospel of efficiency. George Stigler would once observe that when the time came to make policy judgments, the operative rule for an economist in the policy arena was "preaching efficiency." In the "economists' sermons" that had been preached over the past two hundred years, Stigler found that "the dominant theme has been that good policy favors, and bad policy interferes with, the maximizing of income of a society." In terms of value advocacy, the goal of "efficiency" has been, Stigler observed, "the main prescription of normative economics." [34]

Why is efficiency so important that it now defines the essential character of the value system of the economics profession? In *Economics,* Samuelson is hardly enthralled with the material benefits of high levels of consumption for their own sake. At various times he is scornful of the proliferation of frivolous products developed by American industry, pushed on consumers by Madison Avenue with its clever manipulations, even while there is little real difference among the items. Rather than ever higher consumption for its own sake, efficiency assumes such an exalted status in *Economics,* becomes the very means of distinguishing between good and evil, because efficiency is the best measure of the rate of movement along the path of economic progress. An efficient action will be one that moves mankind closer to the ultimate goal, the elimination of scarcity, the arrival at a full state of material abundance, the satisfaction of the preconditions for the attainment of a new heaven on earth.★

★ Samuelson, to be sure, seldom if ever put the matter as baldly as this. He was part of a generation, in contrast to that of the Progressive Era, in which the hopes for improving the human condition had been tempered. The message of redemption by material progress is to be drawn indirectly from the

The large body of research in the economics profession, designed to identify those specific actions that will advance the cause of a more efficient economic system, is designed to provide the practical knowledge in day-to-day situations to serve this transcendent goal. Like members of the priesthoods of old, American economists actually spend much of their time researching and pronouncing on the moral status of various actions in society, now assessed in terms of an economic morality in which efficient and inefficient have replaced the good and evil of old.

In various asides from the formal analytical apparatus, *Economics* is filled with normative references to the broader social importance of economic progress, transcending matters of material well-being. Samuelson thus comments at one point that the "political health of a democracy" depends in a "crucial way" on maintaining stable high employment (3). Historically, the fate of marriages "varied inversely with the price of bread" (4). The economic crisis of the depression years created social tensions that produced a "potentially revolutionary situation" that could have been disastrous in the United States—as it eventually proved disastrous in war, genocide, and other forms of destruction for many people in Europe (413). Past governmental interference with free trade had helped to create "the frictions that made war inevitable" (561). Indeed, if a society cannot assure high employment during peacetime, its people may be tempted by demagogues who suggest that war and prosperity have always been closely linked (394). In short, the most important benefits of economic progress do not lie in crass material satisfactions but in meeting the prerequisites for a healthy democratic society, one characterized by mutual respect and equality among its central features.

The future utopia anticipated in *Economics,* like most such visions based on scientific and economic progress, is expected to be an urban civilization. Samuelson complains at one point that the condition of chronic poverty and

---

method and logic of his economic reasoning in *Economics* and other writings. Without such an implicit assumption, the policy conclusions reached by the analysis will not follow from the premises.

Complicating the matter still further, Samuelson in his later years sometimes showed an increasing world-weariness, occasionally seeming to deny the power of economic progress to change the world for the better. In a 1979 *Newsweek* column, he suggested that there might not be an economic basis for "sociological behavior, power relations of government and . . . religious belief." Still more heretical for the economic gospel, it might even be true that in the long run we are no "happier than our fathers and grandfathers, even though we enjoy demonstrably higher real income than they did." If this were the case, however, there would be little reason for studying books such as *Economics.* If more goods and services do not yield higher welfare, if growth is not a central objective of society, why the overriding concern for economic efficiency in public policy? If stasis is as successful as growth in producing human happiness, it would seem to open possibilities for whole new economic systems, a conclusion that Samuelson never develops. Thus, his more pessimistic musings in instances such as the preceding seem to be little more than that, a temporary mood of the moment. See Paul Samuelson, *Economics from the Heart: A Samuelson Sampler* (Sun Lakes, Ariz.: Thomas Horton and Daughters, 1983), 48, 50.

deprivation found in many rural areas is often misleadingly portrayed as an "idyllic picture of the healthful happy countryside peopled by stout yoeman and happy peasantry." However, the incomes of the people there, and thus their real ability to participate in the full benefits of modern life, are low. The reality is that poverty is poverty, wherever it is found. While it may not be "so obvious" in many poor rural areas, the lack of income there leaves the people in fact living in conditions of true "squalor." In short, any alleged superior qualities of rural life, Samuelson says, are actually a "mirage" (67–68).

PRIESTS OF EFFICIENCY

Samuelson was, of course, reflecting a value system that was also widely shared by other economists of his generation. The winner of the 1999 Nobel Prize in economics, Robert Mundell, goes so far as to attribute the majority of the social and political ills of the twentieth century to economic misman-agement, often by the inexperienced U.S. Federal Reserve System in the first half of the century. He declared in his Nobel lecture in December 1999 that the international monetary system was severely mismanaged in the 1920s and 1930s and that it was this failure of economic policy that plunged the world into war and genocide. It is not merely that economic forces were a contributing factor—most economists would agree with this—but that "had the major central banks pursued policies of price stability instead of ad-hering to the gold standard, there would have been no Great Depression, no Nazi revolution, and no World War II." It is generally the case that "many of the political changes in the [twentieth] century have been caused by little-understood perturbations in the international monetary system." [35]

As a former director of the Bureau of the Budget and later chair of the Council of Economic Advisors, Charles Schultze has had ample opportunity to observe the functioning of economists in their professional roles in gov-ernment. Schultze long ago concluded that the "fact-value," "politics-administration," and other such distinctions characteristic of the thought of early American progressivism, and then incorporated in new forms by Samuelson into *Economics,* were not valid. He wrote in 1968: "Political values permeate every aspect of the decision-making process in the majority of federal domestic programs. There is no simple division of labor in which the 'politicians' achieve consensus on an agreed-upon set of objectives while the 'analysts' design and evaluate—from efficiency and effectiveness criteria—alternative means of achieving those objectives." [36]

Rather, as Schultze would later explain, any economist in government worth his or her salt should believe in something and be willing to fight for it. The proper role of an economist in governmental settings was to be the "partisan advocate for efficiency." [37] Efficiency was, Schultze in essence declared, the core measure of the desirability of taking a government action—in essence, the contemporary measure of its moral worth.* To fight for efficiency in society would for an economist be to fight for the forces of the good and against the forces of evil, much as the Christian priesthood of old had done. It would be to fight in a way now appropriate to a new religious understanding of the modern world, the salvation of humanity through eliminating the economic sources of fighting, cheating, and other human misbehavior.†

In a survey of leading American economists, William Baumol was asked a few years ago to explain why he had originally decided to enter the profession. Baumol replied, "I believe deeply, with [George Bernard] Shaw, that there are few crimes more heinous than poverty. Shaw, as usual, exaggerated when he told us that money is the root of all evil, but he did not exaggerate by much." [38] If poverty is the real source of evil in the world, then the battle

---

* In order to give legitimacy to a social idea or institution, current proponents typically find it necessary to appeal to efficiency. To take just one among any number of possible examples that could be given, in proposing a host of new worker "rights," the proponents were not satisfied simply to argue that these were necessary as a basic element of social justice. Rather, it was necessary to assert that they were also efficient: "far from reducing efficiency, we believe that collective bargaining rights, rights to advance notice and severance pay in layoffs, protection against unjust dismissal, and adequate unemployment benefits foster productivity because they give workers a stake in their companies." See Commission on the Future of Worker-Management Relations, "Employee Participation and Labor-Management Cooperation in American Workplaces," excerpts published in *Challenge,* September-October 1995, 36.

† It is the critics outside of economics who are often able to see its religious character more clearly—even while their proposals for alternative economic arrangements are frequently ill conceived. Thus one critic of the role of the World Bank in Africa states that economic "development theory and Christianity share one fundamental assumption: the inherent right and duty to change the world. The view presented here claims that the World Bank has become the predominant theological institution devoted to changing the world in the area of development." The author finds that

> the World Bank's major documents on sub-Saharan Africa over the 1980s encompass a variety of theological categories. One of the most prominent of these is the development of a theology of sin to describe Africa's failures. The sinfulness of Africa is characterized in all of the documents as economic inefficiency. The duality between the inefficient economies of Africa and the efficient economies of the industrialized countries is the central organizing feature of the World Bank's theology of sin. The redemptive call, issued by the World Bank, exhorts Africa to leave behind its sinful past [much as earlier Christian missionaries had so exhorted] to embrace the virtues now of the market.

See John Mihevc, *The Market Tells Them So: The World Bank and Economic Fundamentalism in Africa* (Atlantic Highlands, N.J.: Zed Books, 1995), 22, 25.

for ever more efficient use of resources is for the members of the economics profession nothing less than a heroic struggle to save the souls of fellow Americans.

It is not only economists who think this way; they are simply the leading experts and advocates of efficiency.[39] Their social legitimacy rests on the fact that such views were once almost universally shared and today are still widespread in American life. Protesting not long ago against a meeting investigating possible genetic links to criminal behavior, the demonstrators, according to *Science* magazine, complained that instead of being in genetics, "the roots of crime are in social causes—poverty, racism, unemployment."[40] A black activist complained that well-off Americans should stop criticizing black crime rates and other evidence of social dysfunction and instead do something constructive by focusing on "the [inner-city economic] conditions" that make some people "want to steal."[41] A white Protestant church activist stated that in rural areas of the United States it is "the harsh socioeconomic problems that push people to embrace hatred and violence."[42]

Indeed, the conviction that material causes explain lying, stealing, and other bad behavior has been characteristic of Samuelson's whole generation of American liberals. As Jerome Skolnick has recently commented, traditional twentieth-century liberalism of this stripe tends "to identify structural underpinnings, like work and opportunity," as the fundamental explanatory factors driving people to "murder, rob, rape, and steal." Their conservative political opponents, by contrast, have tended to dwell on such things as the success of "family and religion" in inculcating an adequate set of individual moral values.[43]

To be sure, the liberal consensus of Samuelson's generation has significantly eroded today on the left as well as the right. A recent Swedish analysis of that nation's welfare state noted that it had been built on an assumption that it was possible to cure "all ills of the psyche by means of material rewards." However, as Sweden has achieved many of its economic objectives, the perfection of Swedish society still seems far off, leading many Swedes "to wonder if their conception of the welfare state was not too materialistic."[44] A "neoliberal" publication recently described the ways of thinking of Samuelson's generation as the old "knee-jerk" liberalism, based on a standard understanding of human motivation that "the poor are just like the rest of us—all they need is more money."[45]

The economic journalist Robert Samuelson (no relation to Paul Samuelson) summarized a newer American view as it was emerging at the end of the twentieth century: "Prosperity is a necessary—but not sufficient—condition for solving most serious social problems."[46] This new realism had re-

placed the older optimism about the powers of economic progress by itself
to save the world. As (Robert) Samuelson now wrote from the perspective of
the 1990s:

> If you grew up in the 1950s, you were constantly treated to the mar-
> vels of the time. At school, you were vaccinated against polio, until
> then a dread disease. At home, you watched television. Every so
> often, you looked up into the sky and saw the white vapor trails of a
> new jet. You stared until the plane vanished. There was an endless
> array of new gadgets and machines. No problem seemed beyond so-
> lution. Good times and the power of American technology: these
> were not lessons learned, they were experiences absorbed. You took
> prosperity for granted, and so, increasingly, did other Americans.
> Thus quietly began the Age of Entitlement. We came to believe the
> prosperity was inevitable—and that it would automatically create the
> Good Society. On these two pillars of faith rested our national iden-
> tity and hopes for the future.
>
> Every age has its illusions. Ours has been this fervent belief in the
> power of prosperity. Our pillars of faith are now crashing about us.
> We are discovering that . . . even great amounts of prosperity won't
> solve all our social problems. Our Good Society is disfigured by huge
> blemishes: entrenched poverty, persistent racial tension, the break-
> down of the family. . . . The result is a deep crisis of spirit that fuels
> American's growing self-doubts, cynicism with politics and confu-
> sion about our global role.[47]

For the readers of *Economics* in the two or three decades following World
War II, however, material advance was the route of a secular salvation on
earth. God would not bring heaven to earth by means of some miraculous
transformation of the world in defiance of the laws of physics and in violation of other basic scientific verities. Rather, God had a new plan, as had
never been revealed in the old Christian Bible. According to this new word
of an economically oriented god, the divine plan would operate through the
economic forces in history, requiring the use of the productive resources of
society with ever growing economic efficiency, thereby achieving a state of
complete abundance that would bring on a whole new condition in the
world in the relationships of human beings with one another. Metaphori-
cally, this was also the message of *Economics,* the reason it was embraced so
enthusiastically by a whole generation that already shared its basic values.

TWO DEAD ENDS

At this point I would like to pause for a few pages to examine two issues of a more formal economic character that other economists might raise with respect to the themes developed above. As I have said, economic analysis in the neoclassical tradition seldom considered transitional costs. This is true as far as the efficiency analysis of production and consumption at the heart of economics. However, one form of transitional issue has received considerable attention in the area of social welfare analysis. The main economic result is the following: under the long-standing understanding of "Pareto optimality," it is possible to say unambiguously that a move from one position to a new economic outcome in society is desirable in a social welfare sense (both positions being perfectly "efficient" in the sense of being on the "production possibility curve") only if each person in society is equally or better off as a result. That is to say, the winners from change would have to be able to fully compensate the losers by a transfer of income, leaving everyone in society either equally well off or better off (and at least one person in the latter category).

This kind of formal discussion, however, is inadequate to address the broader transitional issues raised above in several respects. First, the Pareto analysis, like most economic analyses, compares equilibrium positions. The question asked is whether the winners at the new equilibrium position are sufficiently better off, compared with the old, that they can compensate the losers from the change. Little or nothing is said about the actual costs of the movement from one equilibrium position to another. Indeed, while generations of economics have perfected the methods of comparative statics, economics has no well-developed conceptual apparatus for evaluating the dynamic costs of transition.

Second, let us say that such methods were available, or could be readily developed. Economists thus far have made little effort to employ them. In reality, if such an analysis were undertaken, even some of the "winners" in the usual economic account would not necessarily be winners any more. They may have improved their individual position in shifting to the new equilibrium outcome, but it is quite possible in concept that the costs to them of the transitional movement could exceed their gains from the shift in relative equilibrium positions.

Then again, even if were possible to calculate transitional costs, there is no prospect that the winners would actually compensate the losers. As a result, any policy prescriptions in the neoclassical mode for reliance on the market would be based on a hypothetical assumption rather than any real-world practice of compensation. Indeed, while such compensation has occasionally been suggested for well-defined government programs that harm one or another group, it would make no sense to compensate the losers from the normal workings of the market process.★ It would in fact defeat a main point of the market. As Ronald Coase argued many years ago, the case for the market is that it is an efficient means of economizing on transaction costs. Any attempt to calculate necessary compensation for normal market change, and then to actually pay such compensation, would introduce an extraordinarily large burden of transactional costs. Moreover, the very act of paying compensation would introduce large new and counterproductive incentives into the economy. If an individual knew in advance that compensation would be paid, it would be rational for some people to cluster into precisely those areas of the economy that were about to be displaced by the workings of the market—an altogether perverse result.

The Pareto criterion is a political as well as an economic statement. Politically, it amounts to a requirement for social decision making by unanimous consent. The idea of unanimous consent has long had a strong appeal for political theorists as well. It has the great moral attraction that it avoids the necessity of any imposition of coercion to achieve the outcome. John Locke conceived of the institution of government as founded in an initial social contract by which all people living in an original state of nature agreed to create government as a more efficient way of enforcing their natural rights. Pareto optimality in economic theory has about as much relevance to actual economic policy making as Locke's social contract has to actual political decision making today. Indeed, Locke only posited one original unanimous agreement; after that, government would be free to proceed by majority or some other rule less than unanimity. In order to be able to say that the market process is Pareto optimal, there would (in concept) have to be the equivalent of a new original contract with unanimous consent achieved every time the market equilibrium shifted significantly.

The upshot of all this is that the literature of Pareto optimality has little to offer in terms of addressing the information and other transaction cost issues of dynamic change in any real-world market system.

★ If compensation of losers is actually proposed by government—for example, for people adversely affected by free trade—this is more likely to be the source of new inequities and inefficiencies. Out of the large number of transitional movements in a modern economy, why should a comparative handful be singled out for compensation, when no compensation is even considered in the great majority of instances?

EXISTENCE VALUE

If seldom applied to most economic issues, a new literature of "existence values" has been developed by economists in the past few decades in the environmental field. It sought to address the problem that many important environmental values could not be recognized within traditional economic methods. For example, many Americans who may know they will never visit the Grand Canyon in Arizona—they will never directly consume it—may still take considerable real pleasure in knowing about its existence and its protected status in the national park system. Similarly, they may very much enjoy knowing of the existence of the current one hundred million acres in the national wilderness system of the United States.

A substantial literature has by now developed that provides formal methods for estimating in dollar terms these existence values.[48] This literature has also begun to be applied to other kinds of cultural symbols, outside the environmental area, such as the existence of an old historic village or a farming community. Although existence values in practice have thus far mainly been employed to estimate the values of forms of environmental protection, they could also in concept be applied to such things as the existence of the Grand Coulee Dam, Hoover Dam and other symbols of progress in human control over nature (in fact, in the past such dams were regarded by many Americans who never visited them as virtual cathedrals of scientific progress).

The standard economic problem of maximizing the efficient use of resources in society could in concept be reformulated to include the full set of existence values in the "objective function," as well as ordinary consumption of goods and services. This could resolve the difficulty discussed in this chapter that standard economic analysis fails to take account of many potentially important psychic costs and other values associated with the process of economic transition. For example, economists could introduce into "gross national satisfaction"—now going well beyond "product"—an existence value for the real anger felt by many people when they know of a bank or other party charging a usurious interest rate. This would address the concern discussed earlier that Samuelson and virtually every other economic analyst currently would leave such feelings of anger with respect to usury out of their calculations.

One immediate consequence, however, would be to undermine most past conclusions of economic efficiency analyses of the market system. Because many existence values have no prices for most of the people who benefit from them, the market would provide the wrong signals. Government intervention on a large scale would be required to achieve the social optimum.

There would no longer be anything presumptively efficient about a market economy. That is to say, the normal objects of existence values have much of the character of a public good, and yet many potential objects of existence value (such the loss of a farm or a job) are now found in the private sector. The full incorporation of existence values into economic analysis thus could transform much of what is now considered private activity in the market into forms of public-sector activity requiring government management to achieve a socially efficient result.

Yet, as a matter of intellectual honesty, some economists and other people might argue that there is no choice. Since many people plainly do really feel strong emotional reactions to the very existence of objects such as wilderness, dams, farming communities, and factory workers employed in well-paying jobs (as well as usurious lending practices), perhaps those engaged in the fields of welfare economics and comparative economic studies have no real choice but to enter into comprehensive economic analysis of existence values in their full scope. If this should ultimately be the verdict, the routine practice of economics might well be dramatically transformed.

Consider, for example, a factory and associated jobs lost in Missouri in the electronics industry as a result of new competition in Mexico resulting from the North American Free Trade Agreement (NAFTA). Whatever the benefits of this event to American consumers, the economic analyst would also have to consider the transitional and psychic costs to the factory managers and workers of being put out of a job. This would depend on making estimates of their new job locations and of the existence value to fellow Americans of the loss of the factory and the impacts on the affected communities. If it were a small factory in Missouri, perhaps few people would know about it, and the resulting existence values across the United States might be very small. However, if a St. Louis TV station did a feature spot on the nightly news, tens of thousands of people in Missouri might find this factory entering their utility functions—having real affects on their sense of well-being for a few minutes at least while they are watching the program.

Then, if CBS national news chose to do a story about this community as a symbol of the economic dislocations of NAFTA, many Americans might feel real anguish at the sight of the "costs of progress" at this Missouri factory being shown right in front of them on their TV screens. For some individual Americans the sense of pain at that point (the impact on "utility") might be of a similar magnitude as say the pleasure of eating a sandwich for lunch.

Other Americans, however, might be indifferent to the visible problems of the factory managers and workers. Indeed, to the contrary, some might feel real pleasure at a sight of economic progress at work, and the expectation that in the future they would be facing lower electronics prices at Wal-Mart and other stores from lower-cost Mexican suppliers. Some people might think of the fact that the workers in Mexico might be poorer and need the jobs more than the factory employees in Missouri. Others might feel good through a greater sense of confidence that the government is working for their benefit and is resisting the pressures of special interests such as labor unions opposed to NAFTA. For such Americans their individual positive sense of pleasure at this sight on their TV screen might be of the magnitude of, say, drinking a Coke.

The feelings of people actually living in the Missouri community (but having no direct connection to the factory) would probably be different. On a daily basis they would see the factory closing up and the workers who had been put out of their jobs. Thus, different valuations would have to be made for them to reflect their stronger emotional reactions to all these events, probably much higher than for national observers seeing things on TV from a remote location.

If the economics profession should decide to incorporate such benefits and costs systematically into future efficiency calculations for economic systems, as measured formally by existence values, this Missouri factory may be a vision of the professional future in the United States. In a market economy as large as that of the United States there would be a very large number of events like the Missouri factory closing every year. If economists want to do a full economic analysis of the problem, they will have to develop probabilistic estimates of the chance that other Americans will come to know about the events. They will have to study how the feelings of such people may be affected by the medium in which the information is conveyed—by newspaper, magazine, radio, TV, or any other. Economists will have to consider the question of the impact of physical proximity to events on levels of psychic cost and associated existence values.

It may turn out that most psychic costs associated with economic events are small and do not much affect the usual economic conclusions of the past. It might turn out, however, that the results are dramatically altered—especially when the large number of potential forms of existence value associated with economic events are considered. In any case, there will be no way to know for sure without actually doing the analysis. Making an assumption here without a full analysis will be a mere act of (religious) faith.

The costs to society of doing all these economic analyses for a wide range of events in the economy could eventually become very large, when all the potential cultural symbols and psychic gains or losses associated with transitional and other events in the economy are entered into the social-efficiency

calculations. Indeed, one can imagine that the numbers of economists required in society could increase by orders of magnitudes. But another possibility is that a benefit-cost analysis would show the benefits of the economic
analysis of all these existence values to be less than the costs.[49]

And still another possibility is that the presence of all these economists
doing all these analyses might come in itself to have an existence value for
many members of society. There might be real irritation felt by many people
when economists claim to have the methods, for example, to be able to put
an existence value on such things as the right to perform abortions in society over the course of the coming year, versus the existence value of a
complete ban on abortions. Indeed, if the one particular existence value
associated with the very existence of so many economists in society were
sufficiently negative, relative to the benefits of doing all the economic analyses, the efficient outcome might be to abolish the economics profession. Presumably, the necessary economic calculations in this case would not be left
for economists to do.[50]

CONCLUSION

In his 1951 classic, *Social Choice and Individual Values,* the Nobel Prize-
winning economist Kenneth Arrow observed that there are three basic ways
for any society to allocate its resources and to make other basic "social
choices." In the most economically developed nations, social decisions are
either "political" in a democratic process or they are made through "the
market mechanism." In more-underdeveloped nations, however, Arrow
found that social choices were still often made through a "widely encompassing set of traditional rules," typically a "religious code."[51] It is only as a
nation enters more fully into the modern world that it substitutes democratic and market procedures for such old-fashioned systems of religious
belief.

There can be no doubt in reading Arrow's analysis that he both approves
of and is prepared to defend the triumph of the values of modern democracy
and the market. Arrow's implicit value position—widely shared among
economists—makes the market mechanism in part a religious subject. If the
rise of the market mechanism means the decline of religion in some of its
major traditional functions in society, this fact in itself indicates that the market mechanism and traditional religion are in some degree competitors with
each other. They are two alternative forms of religion. Samuelson's *Economics* appeared at about the same time that Arrow made his remarks, also re-

flecting the triumphalism of the secular religion of the American economics profession in the years after World War II.

Contrary to the views of most economists, the greatest significance of the main body of twentieth-century economics thus was not its new level of technical understanding of the workings of markets—which can now be seen to have often been deficient in fundamental ways. Rather, as Arrow noted, modern economics had displaced earlier religions that had often posed formidable obstacles to the market system and in fact to rapid economic growth and development of society by any economic system. Even today, religions such as Islam often continue to pose such an obstacle in other parts of the world.[52] Many of these older religions sanction an existing social order and condemn any efforts to make rapid changes. They condemn the individual pursuit of self-interest in almost every area of society, including the market. However, as preached in *Economics,* the rapid changes in society brought about by the workings of self-interest in the market was not only acceptable, but in effect divinely blessed.

At the same time, as *Economics* also preached, the motive of self-interest should be excluded from those key tasks that still remain for government to perform. Instead, here the motives of economic and other social science professionals—indeed of the entire governing class—should be the same higher ideals (admittedly not always realized then and now) of the priesthoods of old, involving a willingness to commit themselves for the common good of society. If self-interest dominated in the administrative apparatus of government, the government would surely fail in the goal to manage society in a scientific fashion. If voters behaved in a narrowly self-interested way, few would even bother to go to the polls, threatening the very democratic foundations of modern political systems.

It was a difficult religious combination to sustain—preaching a strong ethic of self-interest in the one arena of the market but a strong commitment to the common good in most other areas of society—but Samuelson pulled it off, at least until new doubts about science and progress appeared in American life, beginning with the social turmoil of the 1960s. For a time anyway, he had resolved the market paradox.

chapter FOUR

APOSTLE OF SCIENTIFIC MANAGEMENT

At one point in *Economics,* Samuelson comments in 1948
that "nations all over the world [are] moving increasingly towards a planned state." Following the positive results of the New Deal, the American people seem
willing to "adjust the minute hand of the clock of history" to fine-tune the role of government, but Americans are "unwilling to turn the hour hand back toward
laissez faire" (421). Samuelson thinks that this is in fact a
blessing and strongly endorses the developing American
"mixed system of government and private enterprise"
(36). It reflects a recognition that in many circumstances
"sensible men of good will [can] be expected to involve
the authority and creative activity of government" (153).
It should, moreover, be a centralized role for government
because "the present Federal government ranks far better than . . . the state and local levels" (158).

Hence, as *Economics* informs readers, it will be important to avoid any return to the old theories of Adam
Smith, who unfortunately still has many influential followers in American life who believe in the "mystical
principle of the 'invisible hand.' " Indeed, going out of
his way to disparage Adam Smith's economic theories,
Samuelson declares that they "have done almost as much
harm as good in the past century and a half" (36). By
comparison, the Soviet Union and other "collectivized
nations of the world," unless the United States learns to
better manage the market mechanism for its own overall
benefit, "will forge that much nearer or beyond us"
(394). In fact, at one point Samuelson—who elsewhere

deplores the dictatorial and antidemocratic tendencies of communist nations—declares that "Russia with its communistic government appears to be on the march" (584).

Samuelson, in short, follows very much in the old progressive tradition in his conviction that the trend of history is for government to undertake the scientific management of society.* However, drawing on the new economic understandings resulting from the macroeconomic theories formulated by Keynes, Samuelson departs in several important respects from the original tenets of American progressivism. The early true believers had expected that the goals of society would typically be realized by direct "scientific administration" within government; Samuelson now declares, however, that a better way for government to achieve the goals of society will be to manipulate the market mechanism.

Compared with direct government administration, the participants in the market will be more motivated to pursue economic opportunities and will have a greater flexibility to devise the most effective economic solutions. Earlier orthodox Progressives and socialists to the contrary, the time has not yet come to abolish self-interest from the ordinary affairs of the world. The private market, in short, for many purposes is likely to be much more efficient than a government bureaucracy. Hence, while the Progressives had originally looked to experts in administrative science, city planning, forest management, and other command-and-control systems, Samuelson's chief scientific planners of society will be the members of the economics profession. Economists compose the one professional class with the requisite technical knowledge to manage the overall coordinating instrument of the market mechanism in the broadest public interest.

In managing the market, the most important thing, in Samuelson's view, is

---

* The same basic mood and values of the post-World War II era were expressed by many others, if usually in less "scientific" language than Samuelson. Writing in the *New Republic* in 1964, "T. R. B." believed that

> we are just emerging into an era where the use of the federal budget to balance the economy by taxes and spending is being accepted. (The rest of the world accepted it long ago.) The arrival of medicare cannot be postponed very long. The task of government almost certainly will grow. There has been a slippage of business prestige in this century. Reporters used to dash to Henry Ford, Bernard Baruch, and J. P. Morgan to interview them on great events; now they are apt to go to some bespectacled college professor.
>
> I think the above trends will continue. I guess, too, that the ethics and perhaps even the calibre of men in Congress will improve. A century ago, Washington was a malarial, boarding-house capitol where Congressmen were corrupt and went armed. . . . Things have improved a lot since then.

See "T. R. B. from Washington," *The New Republic,* November 7, 1964, 12.

for the students studying *Economics,* and for the American public as a whole, to comprehend that the Keynesian scientific understanding of the problem of unemployment has now shown that this long-standing terrible economic disease can be readily cured. Samuelson presents the full macroeconomic panoply of consumption and investment functions, the multiplier, instruments of government fiscal policy, and other items in the standard macroeconomic bag of tools, as they have been familiar to students of introductory economics courses over the past fifty years.

A POETRY OF LARGE GOVERNMENT

Yet, in terms of the scientific details of his market plan for social engineering, Samuelson once again proved to have a great deal wrong.[1] His idea that government could easily manipulate aggregate national demand by controlling government and consumer spending, and thus determine precisely the overall outcome in terms of national income, proved to be almost as utopian as his microeconomic vision of the market mechanism in constant happy equilibrium where transaction costs do not exist (or do not matter). In the fifty years since *Economics* was first published, and much contrary to Samuelson's stated conviction, monetary policy has become the instrument of choice for overseeing the cyclical fluctuations of the American economy. The possibility of employing conventional fiscal policy for stabilization purposes is much less prominent in today's macroeconomic debates.

Indeed, the core of Samuelson's "scientific" treatment of macroeconomic issues in *Economics* would largely be invalidated by "post-Keynesian," "rational expectations," and other new thinking of the past twenty-five years.[2] In part, Samuelson anticipated some of the objections himself as long ago as his very first 1948 edition. In remarks tucked away in an appendix to one of the chapters, after presenting the simplified Keynesian imagery in the main body of the chapter—the poetic vision that most students would actually retain—Samuelson then notes that there are actually some significant qualifying factors. He comments, for example, that government borrowing actually reduces at the same time the wealth of consumers by "a present liability [equal to] the amount of *future* taxes" that these consumers—as some of them may now even recognize—will have to pay in order to cover the future greater government indebtedness (428).

As a result, long-run total consumer wealth, including expected future tax obligations, declines by just the amount of the added government borrowing. If consumers respond by behaving in a perfectly informed, rational way, fiscal policies implemented through government borrowing will increase total spending only to the extent that government has a higher propensity to spend from its marginal change in income, compared with the consumer marginal propensity to spend. If this is a small amount, as might well be the case, fiscal policy implemented through government borrowing simply will not work in the way that Samuelson has already promised in the earlier discussion.

Samuelson, to be sure, dismisses this as a mere theoretical possibility, with the glib observation that "he is a very rare man indeed" if he takes account of expected future tax obligations in his current consumption decisions. It may be irrational, but that will not stop consumers from still "feel[ing] richer" than they really are (428). It seems that the very success of the Keynesian scheme in *Economics* depends on making a psychological assumption of an element of consumer irrationality, hardly the secure foundation of "scientific knowledge" on which Samuelson has already said that the Keynesian prescriptions of economics are based. Indeed, as Kenneth Arrow has observed, it turns out on close inspection that "virtually every practical theory of macroeconomics" is based at least in part on the necessary assumption of one form or another of economic "hypotheses other than rationality."[3]

Samuelson also relegates to this same appendix the troublesome possibility that added government borrowing will raise interest rates, thus causing private investment to decline, and again perhaps undercutting much of the stimulative impacts of the government spending. Indeed, the only sure way of stimulating the economy through government spending may be to print the money or to borrow the funds from external sources—not attractive options, as Samuelson himself concedes.

Thus, like Samuelson's development of the vision of the market mechanism as religious imagery, the Keynesian technical apparatus of *Economics* is best understood as less a matter of science than another example of a powerful metaphor developed in the abstract symbolism of economic formalism. Samuelson's new form of economic "poetry," employing a Keynesian imagery of economics in the manner of physics, is designed to convey yet another strong value statement. The story Samuelson is telling in his macroeconomic discussions in *Economics* is that a powerful federal government is fully capable of doing many wonderful things for the American people, not only eliminating unemployment but also bringing about many other great benefits.

For example, at one point Samuelson declares that, given the critical importance of keeping the resources of American society fully employed, it may be worth pursuing Keynesian policies that involve a long-term inflation rate of as much as 5 percent per year (282). At another point, he suggests that there may be long-run tendencies in society towards excess savings relative to investment, which could justify a long-run government deficit maintained indefinitely at a level of as much as ten billion dollars per year (about seventy billion in 1998 dollars) (433). As Samuelson stated, "There is no technical financial reason why a nation fanatically addicted to deficit spending should not pursue such a policy for the rest of our lives, and even beyond" (433).

As Samuelson also informed the readers of *Economics,* "The primary cause of fluctuation in business activity is the fluctuation in *public and private investment."* Americans should "no longer hold out high hopes of effectively maintaining full employment and high production by means of Federal Reserve monetary policy" (338). Hence, whenever it might be necessary to give the economy a boost, still further government spending may be necessary (a tax cut is of course another possibility for fiscal policy). In such ways the macroeconomics of *Economics* provides all the rationale needed for a wide variety of ambitious government spending programs of all sorts in conformance with progressive design.

In writing a regular column in *Newsweek* magazine for fifteen years, Samuelson was free there to state his policy preferences in a more direct fashion. In a November 1967 column, he addressed the issue of looming inflation, stimulated by high Vietnam War expenditures, and the possible remedies of either cutting government domestic expenditures or raising taxes. The policy choice, as Samuelson declared, involved the making of some "value judgments." Samuelson himself was of the opinion that the federal government had many urgent programmatic responsibilities that were still unfulfilled. As he stated, "There is vast scope in the 1968 economy for expansion of *the public sector"* in a socially beneficial way. Indeed, the reality was that "America spends too little rather than too much on government." [4] Samuelson thus preferred a tax increase to cutting nondefense spending.

However, if raising taxes to cover the costs of the Vietnam War was politically infeasible, there was still a third alternative—simply accept the inflation that was likely to result, recognizing that inflation amounted to an indirect form of taxation. It was perhaps better to tax the assets of bondholders and holders of other forms of wealth denominated in current dollars than to cut government redistributive programs for the poor. That was in fact Samuelson's recommendation: before accepting any "deal to cripple important welfare programs, I would have to point out that a degree of open inflation is not the greatest evil." [5] Lyndon Johnson may have held a similar view, because he refused either to cut domestic spending or to raise taxes to cover war costs, resulting in an acceleration of inflation in the United States that lasted through the 1970s.★

★ In retrospect, to be sure, Samuelson would very probably have wished to reconsider his 1967 analysis and his expectation of the benign consequences of inflation. It proved impossible to bring the 1970s inflation under control until the early 1980s and might well have contributed significantly to the electoral success of Ronald Reagan in 1980. Indeed, few things did more to undermine Samuel-

Samuelson is the progressive heir to Keynes, of whom Milton Friedman has said that "his bequest to politics has had far more influence on the shape of today's world than his bequest to technical economics. [Keynesianism] has contributed greatly to the proliferation of over-grown governments increasingly concerned with every phase of their citizen's daily lives." Keynes led economists to believe, as Friedman puts it, that they "could best contribute to the improvement of society by investigating how to manipulate the levers actually or potentially under control of the political authorities so as to achieve desirable ends." As Friedman views the past fifty years, in actual fact "many economists have devoted their efforts to social engineering of the kind that Keynes engaged in and advised others to engage in."[6] In many cases, these economists were first inspired to such a Keynesian message of government activism as students poring over the pages of Samuelson's *Economics.*

"SOCIETY" AS "THE PUBLIC INTEREST"

Two generations of American college students have been told in *Economics* (and most other textbooks) that, every time the government pays some interest on the debt, one group of Americans will be paying the money to another group, balancing each other out. For purposes of public policy making, Samuelson was in effect saying in a metaphorical way that the American nation is a unified whole, that government can ignore differences of region, ethnic group, economic class, and so forth. To be sure, as a matter of technical economics, Samuelson's imagery here again was seriously flawed, a utopian statement like many other formal arguments he makes in *Economics.*

Indeed, in comments once again tucked away in an appendix, Samuelson himself acknowledges that there are major technical problems. For one thing, *"transferring tax money from Peter to pay bond interest to the same Peter will involve a heavy indirect burden on the economy!* This is because taxation always has some distorting effects on people's economic behavior" (429). This observation is hardly consistent with Samuelson's earlier unqualified pronouncement in the main body of the chapter—the part the students would remember—that large federal budget deficits into the indefinite future pose no "technical" problem whatsoever for the American economy.

Paying interest on the national debt could also in practice mean taxing lower- and middle-income groups to pay interest in the future to upper-

---

son's optimistic worldview of rationally managed progress by the federal government than the events of stagflation and other macroeconomic maladies of the decade of the 1970s. That an economist of Samuelson's stature could offer a policy recommendation with such unfortunate consequences (even in his own terms) provides one more illustration of the subjective elements in economic thinking and the failure of progressive aspirations for objective, "scientific" expertise in the public arena.

income holders of the bonds. In fact, as Samuelson admits, this outcome would amount to a future policy of "Robin Hood in reverse"—of "soaking the poor to pay the rich." Thus, payments on the debt, even when the money simply changes hands internally, are likely to be a "necessary evil" (429). Few students, however, would remember or even read such later qualifications in the appendix. Thus, most students were left with the simple idea that the national debt need be no concern because it is simply transferring money from one part of society to another—"we owe it to ourselves," as most readers of *Economics* heard Samuelson's message.

This vision again is best regarded, not as an economic argument of substance, but as an implicit value statement, another metaphor in the progressive poetry of *Economics*. Samuelson was implicitly saying that all Americans are united in one organic whole.* The relevant reference point for government policy making is all of "society." In practice, that means not the world, not state government, not local government, not private businesses, but the American nation-state. Samuelson elsewhere says that it is important for Americans "to learn the full significance of the fact that this is One Country" (183). "Society," Samuelson comments at another point, as manifested in "the collective conscience of the American people," must maintain certain "minimum standards of health, nutrition and security" for all (161).

Indeed, the very framework of public decision making portrayed by Samuelson throughout *Economics* rests on a core idea that "society" decides. It is society that must make the "what," "how," and "whom" choices that Samuelson regards as the essence of the economic problem. American society as a whole confronts the production possibility curve and the federal government, acting for all the members of society, must decide, in one way or another, where we want to be located along this curve, and then how to distribute its material bounties among the American people.

---

* While a shared belief in the redeeming power of economic progress is no longer such a strong bond holding Americans together, echoes of these themes are still an important part of the daily language of American politics. In his 1998 State of the Union address, President Bill Clinton appealed to such core values once again:

> We also should recognize that the greatest progress we can make toward building one America lies in the progress we make for all Americans. When we open the doors of college to all Americans, when we rid all of our streets of crime, when we make sure that all parents have the child care they need, we help to build one nation.
>
> On the forge of common enterprise Americans of all backgrounds can hammer out a common identity. . . . With shared values, honest communication, and citizen service, we can unite a diverse people in freedom and mutual respect. We are many. We must be one.

See "Clinton State of the Union Speech: A Trip We Can Only Make Together," *New York Times,* January 28, 1998, A20.

For Samuelson individual property rights may be useful insofar as they contribute to the workings of the market mechanism, but otherwise they have no special status. Indeed, while they may be necessary, they run the risk of promoting an unhealthy individualism and perhaps could become as much of a problem as a benefit. Private property rights are also suspect because they act to promote an unequal distribution of income. *Economics* thus declares that however important the maintenance of property rights may be to the workings of the American economy, it must always be kept in mind that "they are secondary to human rights and needs," and American society as a whole may be required to curb property rights in order to achieve more fundamental goals (72).

Throughout *Economics,* Samuelson's faith that all of "society" can act as one united body is his metaphorical way of reasserting the long-standing progressive conviction that government acts "in the public interest." From the depiction of social decision making along the production possibility curve to the portrayal of Americans together paying off the national debt "to themselves," *Economics* offers a progressive vision of Americans collectively making decisions to serve the common good. In practical terms, this would mean that Americans must put their faith in the federal government as the instrument to guide all of American society through the scientific management of its affairs.

While Samuelson's technical arguments in *Economics* never were very sound, the poetry of his progressive moral and political vision would have an inspirational influence on many people in the decades after World War II.*

---

* Another prominent American whose formative years, like Samuelson's, were in the 1930s and 1940s was President George Bush. Bush had perhaps less faith in the domestic regulation of business but overall shared many of the core values underlying the progressive imagery of *Economics.* In expressing these values Bush admittedly painted with a somewhat different brush, employing the more overtly proselytizing language of America's civic religion (and with powerful Christian overtones closer to the surface, as in his stated view that a good American should answer a "call" to which we are all "summoned"). In December, after he had already lost the 1992 election, Bush delivered a kind of valedictory speech celebrating the values that had informed his presidency (and indeed his life):

> From the days after World War II, when fragile European democracies were threatened by Stalin's expansionism, to the last days of the Cold War, as our foes became fragile democracies themselves, American leadership has been indispensable. No person deserves credit for this— America does. It has been achieved because of what we as a people stand for—and what we are made of.
>
> For the first time, turning the global vision into a new and better world is, indeed, a realistic possibility. It is a hope that embodies our country's tradition of idealism, which has made us unique among nations, and uniquely successful. And our vision is not mere utopianism; the advancement of democratic ideals reflects a hard-nosed sense of American self-interest.
>
> Each of these once seemed a dream. Today they're concrete realities, brought about by a

The activist federal government for which Samuelson was among the leading postwar advocates has become today an all-encompassing American welfare and regulatory state, including among its important responsibilities the correction of market failings, the maintenance of stable full employment, and the systematic redistribution of income.

FOR THE COMMON GOOD

Samuelson does not seem in 1948 in *Economics* to have had any concerns that the political allocation of resources on the scale he is contemplating might itself become a source of major inefficiencies in the American economy (although some of these doubts would start creeping in in later editions). Here again, *Economics* is faithful to the progressive vision that the scientific managers of society should be given the necessary power and can be counted on to act with it in "the public interest." The members of the new scientific elites will not be tempted to use the powers of government to serve their own purposes. They will not succumb to the pork barrel and other long-standing unsavory practices—including outright corruption in some instances—that have been found throughout the long history of government in America. Instead, more and bigger government will mean the widest application of economic, administrative, and other sciences to serve the broadest interests of all Americans collectively.

Yet, in the years following the original publication of *Economics,* economists and political scientists would increasingly find that the progressive view of government was more utopian than realistic. Twentieth-century American government, a new generation of social scientists would conclude, was still a product of the individual actions of the particular people (and interest groups) who typically acted in self-seeking—"rent-seeking," as some economists later described it—ways.[7] Indeed, as explained by political scientist Theodore Lowi in the late 1960s, the theories of "interest-group liberalism" had come to be accepted by much of the American political science profession. These theories suggested not only that American government was

---

common cause; the patient and judicious application of American leadership, American power and American—perhaps most of all—American moral force.

History is summoning us once again to lead. Proud of its past, America must once again look forward [to a future of progress]. And we must live up to the greatness of our forefather's ideals, and in doing so secure our grandchildren's futures.

See George Bush, "America—The Last Best Hope for Man on Earth," speech at Texas A&M University, December 15, 1992, reprinted in *Vital Speeches of the Day,* January 15, 1993, 195–97.

dominated in practice by the interactions of interest groups but also that this was the only realistic governing outcome in any democratic political system.[8]

Yet, as the "public choice" school of economics would soon demonstrate, any such conclusion raised profound problems for American democracy. It was not difficult to show that the interactions of interest groups in the political arena would result in violation of the basic American ideals of fairness and equality. As had happened often before in American history, the powers of government could easily be used to benefit narrow groups. Citizens might try to combat these parochial influences through collective actions, but their efforts would typically be defeated by the "free rider" problem.[9]

In *The Logic of Collective Action,* Mancur Olson in 1965 provided perhaps the most influential formulation of the problem, showing how many organizations—potentially including good government organizations—might never come into existence, even though it was possible that they could provide valuable services to society and to their members as well.[10] However, if the services were automatically available to each person, even if that person did not pay, everyone would have an individual incentive not to join the organization. Only collective efforts that could somehow overcome such free-rider incentives could manage to survive in the real world.

Led by James Buchanan (who later received a Nobel Prize in economics in 1986 for his efforts) and Gordon Tullock, the public choice school eventually documented all kinds of ways in which government could "fail," just as economists had often shown in the past that markets could fail.[11] The benevolent progressive view of government developed by Samuelson in *Economics,* in short, is difficult to reconcile with the traditional expectation of the economics profession that each person will act to maximize his or her own interest. If public officials do actually behave in an opportunistic way, the progressive formula for large government may even become a plan for the coercive extraction of benefits from the rest of the population by a dominant political class. The question then becomes merely how much can be extracted from the taxpayers without killing the golden goose.* In the for-

---

* The modern age has developed its own forms and nuances, but few of its discoveries are really new. A pattern of government behavior similar to that described by the public choice school today has characterized many governments from the beginning of recorded history. One history of Italy describes the behavior of "an ever more voracious" papal state headquartered at the Vatican in the fifteenth century: "Its mechanism was extremely simple: it amounted to guaranteeing the landowners and nobility of the various towns and provinces the peaceful enjoyment of their incomes and privileges, draining towards the Roman Curia the maximum possible amount of tax." Savonarola briefly rose to the leadership of Florence with his attacks on the wickedness of the Italian princes and their palaces and courts, which "had become the refuge of rascals and wretches who thought only of 'new taxes, to suck the blood of the people' " for their own benefit. See Giuliano Procacci, *History of the Italian People* (London: Penguin Books, 1991; 1st ed., 1968), 96, 120.

mer Soviet Union, the Communist Party, for example, assumed just such a predatory role. Many African states experienced similar outcomes in the years following their independence from colonial domination.

Why does Samuelson implicitly assume in *Economics* that things will be different under the progressive plan for government, as he proposes for the United States? Why does he assume that participants in the marketplace will behave in a self-interested way, while participants in government will behave in a public-spirited way? It is almost as though he is speaking of two species of human beings, one for the marketplace and one for the public sector. Clearly, there is nothing in the standard panoply of economic reasoning to sustain such an heroic assumption. It is instead another large leap of faith.

In religion, there are clearer precedents for Samuelson's dichotomous assumptions about the behavior of people in the commercial versus noncommercial realms. The Roman Catholic Church has long distinguished between the laity and the priesthood in a similar manner. Ordinary people cannot be expected to live most of their lives according to the same high standards as God's selected representatives on earth. Thus, although priests and nuns do not engage in sexual activity, ordinary people do. In the Catholic religion, and although it would never work for society in general, many possessions within the church are to be communally owned. Priests and nuns are not to be motivated in their work by self-interest. Yet, as Plato also had relegated commercial motives to the lowest ranks in society, in the theology of the Roman Catholic Church commercial motivations are the best that can be expected for most ordinary people in a fallen and sinful world.

Indeed, it was this strong distinction between ordinary people and the church priesthood that, among a number of other tenets of Catholic doctrine, incurred the wrath of Martin Luther. Luther saw the Roman Catholic Church as selling ordinary people short and thus declared a new Protestant "priesthood of all believers." The ministry of the Protestant churches would stand on an equal plane with the faithful—both, for example, would marry. The leadership of Protestant parishes would be elected by the ordinary members of the church, while the Roman Catholic Church would continue to select its own leaders in a hierarchical fashion, as when the pope designates the cardinals of the church.

In such matters Samuelson followed the Roman Catholic model. The members of the economics profession, and other scientific and professional elites, would be motivated by the higher considerations of a priesthood, as compared with businesspeople and other ordinary citizens in the commercial realm. There would be no popular votes held for the scientific leaders of society. Samuelson acknowledged the practical necessity to allow wide rein for the pursuit of self-interest in the marketplace. However, the professional economists and other scientific managers of the progressive state would function according to the ethical standard of the Roman Catholic priesthood. They would reject the commercial motive of self-interest and instead act in their professional and public capacity to serve the common good—"the public interest"—of all of society.

There are other surprisingly close parallels as well. The medieval Roman Catholic priesthood conducted its religious preaching and other discussions in Latin, a language no more understandable to ordinary people then are than the mathematical and statistical formulations of economists today. Latin served as a universal language that had the great practical advantage of allowing easy communication within a priestly class transcending national boundaries across Europe. Yet that was not the full story. The use of Latin also separated the priesthood from the ordinary people, one of a number of devices through which the Roman Catholic Church maintained such a separation in the medieval era. It all served to convey an aura of majesty and religious authority—as does the Supreme Court in the United States, still sitting in priestly robes. In employing an arcane language of mathematics and statistics, Samuelson and fellow economists today seek a similar authority in society.

When Martin Luther came to challenge the authority of the Roman Catholic Church, one of his most famous acts was to translate the Bible into ordinary German. Luther was determined to break the monopoly of the Roman priesthood in interpreting the plan of God to the world. As Luther saw matters, the church in Rome was making false claims to religious authority, based partly on keeping ordinary people in the dark. By contrast, the Protestant Reformers insisted that each member of the church must read the Bible and reach his or her own understanding of God's message. Current critics of the elite status of professionalism in American life—critics of the old progressive claims to pursue scientific management independent of democratic politics—now seek in a similar fashion to open public decision making, bringing the comments and opinions of ordinary people into the heart of the governing process.

Samuelson never explicitly said much in *Economics* about the social values of economists and others in the ruling professional classes. Yet much if not all of it was implicit in his grand plans in *Economics* for activist government management of American society—and the central role that the economics profession would play as scientific manager of the market mechanism.

The connections between American Progressivism and medieval Catholic religion in fact go deeper than what has been suggested thus far. It is too large a subject to explore in depth here, but a few of the more salient points can be mentioned. One can begin with the fact that historians of ideas commonly trace the origins of modern science to the medieval theology of natural law. It was a central conviction of medieval theology that God had designed a world that operated according to well-defined laws of nature.[12] If human beings wanted to know more about God, they might well seek a better understanding of these laws. The goal would in some sense be to gain access to the mind of God, to give further content to the biblical understanding that it was in the possession of reason and self-consciousness that human beings were made "in the image of God."

Thus, as the historian Lynn White notes, "before the 11th century, science scarcely existed in the Latin West. . . . From the 11th century onward, the scientific sector of Occidental culture has increased in a steady crescendo." Indeed, it is an historical fact that "both our technological and our scientific movements got their start, acquired their character, and achieved dominance in the Middle Ages."[13] Later on, medieval concepts of natural law would play a smaller role in the thinking of the Protestant than of the Roman Catholic clergy. Protestantism nevertheless gave a great boost to science in political and sociological respects, breaking many institutional constraints that had long limited the ability to think freely and independently in Europe, and permitting the destruction of the old Aristotelian orthodoxies.[14] However, theologically, in the sixteenth century the Protestant concept of fallen humanity mired in sin—a depraved condition that adversely affected human abilities to reason well or correctly, along with every other aspect of life—offered little encouragement for the belief that human beings would achieve great scientific breakthroughs in discovering the divine plan for the world.

All this changed again in the Enlightenment, which represented a return to natural-law conceptions in every realm. The American historian of thought Carl Becker would observe that the Enlightenment took Isaac Newton's demonstrations of the power of the scientific method as demonstrating that the "universe was rational and intelligible through and through," governed by laws of nature that could be discovered by the application of human reason.[15] The philosopher Isaiah Berlin would write that the Enlightenment took for granted that "what science had achieved in the sphere of the material world, it could surely achieve also in the sphere of the mind; and further, in the realm of social and political relations." Modern social science, including the efforts of Adam Smith, would emerge from the basic natural-law conviction, now recovered from medieval theology, that "laws governing human behavior" were there to be discovered by the use of the scientific method.[16]

John Bates Clark, a leading American economist of the Progressive Era, was often explicit about the connections to natural-law theology in his economic and other writings. As described by a current student of Clark's thought:

> [For Clark] in the early period, . . . an explictly specified deity, working through "moral force" is directing the economy toward an increasingly just state of affairs leading, eventually, to God's kingdom. Divine law prevails.
>
> In the mature period, overt references to a divine arbiter gradually disappear in his professional scholarship, though Clark continued to publish in religious periodicals wherein such references are continued. The emphasis came to be placed on "natural law" based on the marginal product and the forces of competition. However, this natural law is in reality the working out of God's plan. God is in nature, revealing His plan through the workings of a capitalist society. The concern for a divinely ordered, moral, just system of distribution first enunciated in his early period remains, but now capitalism itself becomes the "New Jerusalem," the culmination of God's evolutionary intent. It would certainly seem, given Clark's continued publications to this effect, that he himself saw no fundamental conflict between his natural-law theory and modern (progressive) religious doctrine.[17]

As a product of the progressive tradition, Samuelson's economic writings can be seen as yet another effort—if now buried still further below the surface—carrying on in this ancient natural-law tradition. Samuelson, like natural-law theologians going back two thousand years, is a believer in a rational world. A key to progress, whether in this world or in finding a path to a better world in the hereafter, is the rational discovery of the laws by which society is governed—in the context of a Judeo-Christian understanding, the laws set in place by God to rule the world.[18] If these laws can be discovered, then the government, the legal system, and other institutions of American society should be adapted to conform as closely as possible. The route to individual happiness, according to the long-standing view of natural-law thinking, is found in the rational apprehension of the laws of human action. As far as it can be achieved (always much less than perfectly in any real-world circumstance), individual conformance with these laws means to live according to the divine plan and thus to experience the grace of God. Except in those parts of the argument where the idea of God is introduced, there is little with which Samuelson could find any real reason to disagree.

In general, the American welfare and regulatory state of the twentieth century has much of the character of the universal Catholic Church in the medieval mode. It is not just the close parallels between the professionals and the priests. When Herbert Simon criticized neoclassical economics, one problem he found was that it resembled a modern form of "scholastic exercise."[19] Clever analyses of unimportant questions have substituted for deeper economic insights. Secession from the modern nation-state is not much more acceptable to the powers that be than founding a new religion in medieval Europe. The medieval Roman Catholic Church operated a far-reaching and comprehensive welfare system for the poor, another later point of difference with the Protestant Reformation (which argued that the Catholic Church was coddling and actually encouraging people to be poor). In general, and without my attempting to develop the argument in any great detail at this point, the modern continuities with medieval theology, as then embodied in secular forms in the Enlightenment grounded in natural-law assumptions, are much greater than most economists and other social scientists have realized.[20]★

Yet, historically, there have also been many critics of natural-law thinking who find that its world of human behavior governed by rational laws is an illusion. God is mysterious and his ways will always be beyond human comprehension. Human existence is by nature disorderly and unpredictable; much will necessarily have to be taken on faith—and this is a good thing, as

---

★ The institutional churches of Christianity are now relegated to the margins of modern public life, but in earlier times they assumed a central role in everything that was happening in society, much as the welfare and regulatory state today assumes such a role. As one student of those earlier periods writes,

> For centuries every European's vision of life was filled with Christian objects, Christian rituals, Christian laws. Christianity wasn't just a religion. For over a thousand years—from about 300 A.D. until after 1300 A.D.—it was the one universal government in Europe. It had a central bureaucracy in Rome, an organization with priests and churches spread to every village and hamlet in Europe, and its own universal language, Latin. The Church oversaw birth, education, marriage or holy orders, all professional activity, children, sickness, old age, death, burial, and of course, in general, society's morals. All the things that the State does today, the Church did then. Regardless of who was the local ruler, or what language he spoke, Europe's one enduring government was the Christian Church with its center at Rome.

See Richard Fremantle, *God and Money: Florence and the Medici in the Renaissance* (Florence: Leo S. Olschki Editore, 1992), 7–8.

many have said. What the theorists of natural law find to be "rational" may in fact be an illusory projection of their own values and convictions. Much the same criticism, as I have been contending in preceding pages, might be made of Samuelson and *Economics*. If Samuelson claimed to be a true modern scientist operating according to a standard of empirical testing and proof, it is apparent that this is mainly a rhetorical device. As Simon has said of economics more generally, the power of Samuelson's conclusions derives from the initial assumptions—the implicit value system for which *Economics* becomes a grand metaphor to inspire the people of America in the true progressive faith.

Increasingly, it appears that since the Enlightenment one of the great conceits of the modern age has been the conviction that it represents a fundamental break with the past in every area of society. A more correct understanding is that the outward forms of the study of society have changed greatly under the influence of the social sciences, but the actual level of insight and knowledge has shown much less advance. The social sciences over the past three hundred years of "modern" thought have been unable to replicate the extraordinary successes of the physical sciences. Rather than offering a great breakthrough into "enlightenment" as compared with the past, the "scientific" study of society has been notable for a frequent ignorance of history and for grand claims to final knowledge that repeatedly have proved later to be greatly exaggerated. Few bodies of thought have ever advertised as much and yet produced as little in comparison to the claims made as the social sciences in the modern era.

For those living through the Enlightenment, the mysticism and superstitions of the past had been banished. Here again, it is closer to the truth that the old habits persisted in new forms. The worship of the powers of science in social matters has been a mystical belief. The renaming in scientific terms of familiar objects and events in society has served to create a religious aura that functions to convey new forms of religious blessings. New sacred icons have arisen to symbolize the messages of modern secular religions of scientific progress. The transference of Christian aspirations for salvation in the hereafter now to be realized in a new heaven on earth has involved a new form of invocation of magical powers. Instead of believing that they would live on in the hereafter, modern men and women have believed that they will live forever in "history." Marxism and other secular religions have yielded new generations of martyrs, crusaders, and saints, all prepared to sacrifice their lives and fortunes for the cause.[21]

PROGRESS AS A COMMONS PROBLEM

Samuelson in *Economics* was implicitly addressing a question as old as the debates between Plato and Aristotle—when is self-interested behavior acceptable in society and when should individual behavior be directed to the realization of a broader good of society? Despite the assumption of self-interest in much of modern economic theory, no society has encouraged such behavior in every aspect of social interaction. In contemporary society, for example, if everyone acted strictly according to private incentives, the maintenance of a democratic political system would be impossible. For one thing, few people would ever bother to vote. Regarded "rationally," there is a cost to voting and essentially a zero chance as one individual of influencing the final result.

Many people also contribute to charitable causes of all kinds, even though the narrowly private incentive would seem to favor being a free rider. In warfare, some people knowingly sacrifice their lives for the cause, obviously not a self-interested action in any conventional economic understanding of the word. Elinor Ostrom in 1990 pointed out that many small groups facing free-rider problems in situations of common property resources do somehow manage to solve their problems without resort to government regulation or to the creation of a property right regime.[22] They talk to one another and manage to establish and enforce informally an allocation of the common property resource.

There are various circumstances likely to be found where such an informal solution to the tragedy of the commons is successful. For one thing, it is helpful when the users of the common resource have repeated interactions; such "patterns of reciprocity," as Ostrom calls them, ensure that violators of community agreements will be punished and thus will face direct incentives to comply.[23] She finds that a second element also contributes greatly to informal solutions to commons problems. It is very helpful to have a set of shared "norms."

If community values are held in common, it will be much easier to communicate expected behavior and to know when a person has deliberately violated these expectations and deserves punishment. Moreover, as in voting in modern societies, shared norms may induce people to follow behavioral patterns that are not strictly rational in the narrow self-interested sense of standard economic analysis. Shared norms of this kind can greatly reduce the potential for cheating on agreements, or other forms of opportunistic behavior, and thus promote trust and the success of sharing rules among groups of people. And shared norms, of course, are frequently sustained by the existence of a religion whose tenets are embraced in common by the members of a society.

Much of the study of the role of norms has focused on small communities, often with cultures formed before the beginning of the modern period. However, even in large nations such as the United States, it is necessary that some form of civic community should exist that is based on powerful shared beliefs—for example, a strong commitment to defend the status of property rights in the legal regime. The nation is in effect a modern church held together by the shared faith of a secular religion. Daniel Mahoney finds that "the nation was a secular substitute for the authority of religion and for a long time carried with it a sacred aura essential to the task of binding citizens in a common, human order." Writers such as Alexis de Tocqueville and his modern followers have denied "that human beings can subsist in a society without any public articulation of common values and without public-spirited virtues that transcend individual and communal particularities." A particular danger is the efforts of liberal theorists of the market who reduce "everything to the production and distribution of economic goods and the codification of ever expanding rights" and thus encourage "apolitical individualism or nihilism" that extends beyond the market domain and thereby "contributes to 'disenchanting' the political realm itself."[24]

The study of the role of norms in the functioning of political and economic systems is receiving new attention among social scientists. Political scientist Jon Elster comments:

> Much of the social choice and public choice literature, with its assumption of universally opportunistic behavior, simply seems out of touch with the real world, in which there is a great deal of honesty and sense of duty. If people always engaged in opportunistic behavior when they could get away with it, civilization as we know it would not exist. We should not assume that the only task of politics is to devise institutions that can harness opportunistic self-interest to socially useful purposes. An equally important task is to create institutions that embody a valid conception of justice. If people do not feel that they are being taken advantage of, the temptation to take advantage of society will be greatly reduced.[25]

Samuelson's performance in *Economics* can be understood in this light. He is seeking to persuade Americans that, if they will work together for progress in a grand cooperative effort, great economic advance can in fact be achieved. Stated another way, Samuelson faced a commons problem of a sort in that, if all people decided to resist economic change, whenever they were displaced or otherwise suffered local transitional disruptions, the workings of markets would soon grind to a halt. The functionaing of markets can hardly be a painless process; many people will in fact have a private incentive to resist the stresses and strains of market and other economic transitional processes. Even if such people believe devoutly in the great overall benefits to the nation from economic progress, it would still be individually in their own self-interest to be free riders—to oppose specific market outcomes and other economic actions that are directly harmful to themselves.

With few exceptions, the fate of any one project or business investment—even the largest and most efficient ones—will not have any noticeable overall effect on the rate of economic growth and development of a national economy as large as that of the United States. However, if all efficient projects succumb to such free-rider incentives, it must pose a severe obstacle to national economic progress. Samuelson thus faced the necessity not only of persuading fellow professionals in the governing elite to renounce self-interest, but also of persuading many individual Americans to bear significant burdens in the service of the cause of progress. He had to do his part in persuading the American people that if they accepted the principle of acting together in this pursuit, a glorious future would lie in store. It would be nothing less than the secular salvation of all Americans.* Like the small

---

* Samuelson was continuing in a long tradition. The vision of the nation as a substitute for the churches of old was explicit in the thinking of some of the founding figures of the modern nation-state. Italy did not become unified as a nation until the 1860s. A main leader in the drive to create the modern Italian nation, Guiseppe Mazzini, was motivated by "a religious intuition: a conviction that God had ordained nations to be the natural units of mankind." Mazzini wrote, "I saw regenerate Italy becoming at one bound the missionary of a new religion of progress and fraternity. . . . Why should not a new Rome, the Rome of the Italian people—portents of whose coming I felt I saw—arise . . . to link together and harmonize earth and heaven, right and duty." Historian Christopher Duggan comments that "the spiritual element was essential to Mazzini's vision of Italian unity." It was the aim of Mazzini's nationalist movement to persuade "the masses . . . that God no longer spoke through the pope but through 'the people' gathered together in nations, and that the cause of Italy was itself a divine mission requiring struggle, sacrifice, and if need be, martyrdom." See Christopher Duggan, *A Concise History of Italy* (New York: Cambridge University Press, 1994), 108–9.

Italy in this respect illustrates a broader pattern in Europe and around the world. In his inquiry into the historical origins of the nation-state in the eighteenth and nineteenth centuries, Benedict Anderson comments:

> The century of the Enlightenment, of rationalist secularism, brought with it its own modern darkness. With the ebbing of religious belief, the suffering which belief in part composed did not disappear. Disintegration of paradise: nothing makes fatality [fate] more arbitrary. Absurdity of salvation: nothing makes another style of continuity more necessary. What then was required was a secular transformation of fatality into continuity, contingency into meaning. . . . Few things were (are) better suited to this end than an idea of nation. If nation-states are widely

groups described by Ostrom, but now on the scale of an entire nation, Samuelson was engaged in seeking to lay a powerful foundation of social norms in the service of the attainment of a new heaven on earth.

In order for Samuelson to succeed, the readers of *Economics*—both among the general public and among prospective future members of the American economics profession—would have to be inspired to a religious dedication to economic efficiency and progress. If progressive values did not hold, if the necessary normative foundations could not be sustained, American government would likely degenerate into a beggar-thy-neighbor process of interest-group competition, waste of resources, and numerous other maladies—precisely the kind of rent seeking in fact later predicted by James Buchanan and his colleagues in the public choice school of economics.★

Indeed, in other economic writings directed to his professional colleagues, Samuelson could be more careful, more scientifically precise, than he was in developing the progressive poetry of *Economics*. If the very success of the gospel of economic Progressivism required that it had to be spread across the American nation as a message of religious inspiration, any necessary fixes in the technical details could later be resolved in conversations limited to the scientific elite among Samuelson's peers.

An observer who was there at the time, Albert Hirschman, recently testified to the considerable success of Samuelson and other economists in the postwar period. Samuelson's development of the Keynesian models in *Economics* did its part to create a new public confidence in the ability of government to manage and control the economy. To the extent that this claim to social engineering skills seemed credible, the belief in itself (whether true or not) was capable of inspiring a stronger sense of national community and greater citizen commitment to participation in government and civic life. As Hirschman comments:

---

conceded to be "new" and "historical," the nations to which they give political expression always loom out of an immemorial past, and, still more important, glide into a limitless future.

See Benedict Anderson, *Imagined Communities: Reflections on the Origin and Spread of Nationalism* (New York: Verso, 1991), 11–12.

★ It would seem that Buchanan was in effect saying that Samuelson was bound to fail either because any religion—no matter how true or how powerfully expressed—would ultimately be incapable of inspiring the necessary altruism on the scale of a whole nation of hundreds of millions of people. Or perhaps instead the problem was that Samuelson was preaching a false religion, and as Buchanan may have believed, this was bound to be recognized eventually. It might also be noted that, to the extent that Buchanan's arguments were widely believed, they became a self-fulfilling prophesy. Once people see government as a general domain of private interest, no one will want to be played for the sucker. Civic-mindedness will become an increasingly scarce commodity.

The political repercussions of the powerful recruitment effect of Keynesianism were notable. Large numbers of recruits were eventually drawn to Washington. . . . They came to their task often naively and arrogantly confident that they would solve the economic and social problems of their time, but at the same time infused into many areas of government . . . a spirit of dedication to public service and accomplishment.

One of the major unsolved problems of democratic political theory and practice is how to maintain a minimal degree of public-spiritedness among the citizenry in general and the bureaucracy in particular, of how to prevent what Machiavelli called *corruzione,* by which he mean not corruption or graft, but the loss of public spirit, the exclusive concentration of individual effort on personal or sectional interests. . . . We are now aware that in the public arena there is no invisible hand that will mysteriously produce the public good out of the clash of various types of self-seeking. . . . Pure exhortation in the name of morality or love of country is likely to fail. Hence we are reduced to looking around for sundry devices that can serve as occasional and temporary boosters of that precious public spirit. Via their recruitment effect, new ideas in economics and social science provide us with just such boosters. Keynesianism's most important political effect in the United States may well have been to have raised public-spiritedness in a crucial period of its recent history—the transition to superpower status [in the decades after World War II].[26]

Thus in this pragmatic sense, *Economics,* whatever its deficiencies as an exercise in the pursuit of economic "truth," was a major artistic and inspirational success. The utopianism of the market mechanism, the simplistic portrayal of the workings of the Keynesian model, the misleading treatment of the national debt as "owed to ourselves," all these and other imagery can best be understood once again as a form more of poetic metaphor than of rigorous scientific demonstration. In the medieval period, leading artists had inspired the faithful with paintings showing the annunciation of Christ's birth, the crucifixion of Christ, the resurrection, and the apostles' spreading the truths of the gospel. Until the 1500s, virtually all of Western art was formed around one Christian theme or another. If the manner of "painting" was now very different in a society in which Einstein commanded much more social prestige and authority than Picasso, Samuelson intended that his efforts in *Economics* nevertheless would to serve a similar function for the American people in the second half of the twentieth century.

In the last few pages of *Economics,* Samuelson puts his core belief in progress more directly in view. The real reason for maintaining a "free-enterprise" system, properly supervised by government, is that this system "has given the world a century of progress" (604). Economic progress is finally revealed here explicitly as the core value by which other matters must be judged. The basic purpose of *Economics* is to show the way to "the rich promise of America's future economic development" (606). Like other Progressives, Samuelson sees the greatest threat to this vision in the "special interests." Rejecting any willingness to concede the inevitability of a political system dominated by interest-group interactions—a view that was spreading among political scientists even at the time of the first 1948 edition—Samuelson declares that all the many parochial forces such as "agriculture, labor, and business" interests must be "kept from distorting the efficient response of the economic system to human wants" (606). The scientific managers must be free to manage scientifically.

Many years after the first edition of *Economics,* Samuelson was asked to describe how his economic vision would apply to the environment. He replied, "This is my credo: as science improves our potential for material living, it gives us the opportunity—if we are willing to use it—to employ some of the fruits of science in preserving and enhancing the beautiful garden mankind has inherited from the distant past." Protecting the environment is also a task that will depend on the advance of material progress, supported by an informed citizenry possessed of a strong community spirit—people who have the requisite "good will" for one another, as Samuelson says—to sustain and make the best use of this economic bounty.[27]

The goal of *Economics,* in short, is progress; the means is an efficient economic system; the sinners are the special interests; the greatest danger posed for the world is cyclical instability and unemployment of resources that will lead to demagoguery, dictatorship, and war. If the economy can instead be put on a track of rapid economic growth, poverty in the United States can soon be eliminated and with it the social ills of crime, drug abuse, suicide, and many others. As more and more people reach a high standard of living themselves, they will increasingly be willing to support government plans to redistribute resources to the less fortunate and otherwise take the collective actions needed for the further progress of American society. Growth can also provide the resources to build an environmentally beautiful world. Economic growth thus creates a "virtuous circle." Within a few generations, all the old wars and other ills of human existence can be abolished forever after.

This is the core value system of Samuelson's reinterpretation of the original gospel of efficiency of the Progressive Era. If enough Americans will subscribe to it, and act on its inspiring message, rejecting the temptations of the devil as found in various forms of opportunism and other diversions, the secular salvation of American society will soon enough be at hand.*

CONCLUSION

In such foundational matters, Samuelson's basic values changed little from 1948 to 1998. In the most recent, sixteenth, edition of *Economics,* published in 1998, Samuelson (now with his co-author, William Nordhaus) attached a two-page "Valediction" at the very end. Almost one-third of this brief ending commentary (perhaps Samuelson's last words for any edition of *Economics)* is devoted to a lengthy quote from Keynes's essay "Economic Possibilities for Our Grandchildren," already mentioned in the present book, in Chapter 1. The concluding two paragraphs from Keynes, as directly quoted by Samuelson, are as follows:

> There are changes in other spheres too which we must expect to come. When the accumulation of wealth is no longer of high social importance, there will be great changes in the code of morals. The love of money as a possession—as distinguished from the love of money as a means to the enjoyments and realities of life—will be recognized for what it is, a somewhat disgusting morbidity, one of these

---

* If Samuelson sought to unify Americans in their common interest, this task might be undertaken in various ways. Any failings of *Economics* were benign in comparison to the pathological approaches pursued by some other thinkers in Europe to the same end. In Italy at the end of the nineteenth century, many saw in the government a place of "venality, [which] brought parliament into growing disrepute." There was a wide lament of "the sordid feebleness of liberal Italy" where democratic institutions were "riven with factionalism." The solution, as many Italian intellectuals came to believe, might have to be a good war. A leading spokesman for the Nationalist movement early in the twentieth century declared that Italy "was 'a proletarian nation morally and materially': and just as the working classes had been spineless and divided before socialism taught them the value of conflict, so the Nationalists must now teach Italians the virtues of 'international struggle': 'What if that means war? Well, let there be war.' War . . . was the path to 'national redemption'; it was a 'moral order,' a way of creating 'the inexorable necessity of a reversion to the sentiment of duty' " among Italians.

Indeed, as Italy stood on the precipice of World War I, many felt an enthusiasm "that somehow or other war would be the making of the nation"; national armed struggle would "purify, with fire and steel" and in this manner offer "a chance to forge a national community." War would finally provide a solution to Italy's powerful tendencies towards fragmentation. By 1919, their wishes had been granted; six hundred thousand Italians had made the supreme sacrifice in the name of the bringing fellow Italians together in a single national community dedicated to a common good. Their sacrifice, to be sure, was largely in vain, as the rise of Benito Mussolini only a few years later would show. See Duggan, *A Concise History of Italy,* 164, 169, 186, 189.

semi-criminal, semi-pathological propensities which one hands over with a shudder to the specialists in mental disease. . . .

But beware! The time for all this is not yet. For at least another hundred years we must pretend to ourselves and to everyone that fair is foul and foul is fair; for foul is useful and fair is not. Avarice and usury and precaution must be our gods for a little longer still.[28]

One must assume that Samuelson is telling us that in some significant degree he has always shared this vision, as expressed by Keynes, the great hero of his early years. Yet Samuelson is honest enough to recognize that this prophesy has not yet been fully realized, that "great affluence has indeed not brought about a slackening of economic ambition in America." Indeed, Americans still find today, Samuelson says shortly after the preceding quote from Keynes, that they live in a "ruthless economy," in which "old-fashioned loyalty to firm or community counts for little." Instead of there being a diminishing role for private profit and market motives, as Keynes prophesied, Samuelson ruefully acknowledges that these ugly influences are "more pervasive, more intrusive." Instead of the realization of Samuelson's dream for a government rationally overseeing the progressive state in pursuit of the public interest, there has been a growing distrust of government, manifested in a "widespread desire for smaller government, less regulation, and lower taxes" on the part of the American people.[29]

Yet in the very last paragraph of this sixteenth edition of *Economics,* Samuelson reiterates his old desire that economic progress should lead to "that day [in the future] when everyone has the opportunity for a good job, an adequate income, and a safe environment." This is Samuelson's great hope, which he still believes can offer a set of "worthy goals for economics and for economists in the next 50 years," the goals that originally motivated Samuelson to write the first edition of *Economics* in 1948 and that are no less relevant today.

When Marx saw the proletariat leading the way to heaven on earth, he was yet another messiah proclaiming a message of salvation for yet another chosen people. The idea that the world can be perfected through human actions here on earth is at least as much a Jewish messianic as a Christian vision. Perhaps Samuelson as a modern secular Jew is nevertheless best understood as carrying on in this ancient Jewish tradition.

part **THREE**

THE GODS OF CHICAGO

The values at the heart of Samuelson's *Economics* reigned triumphant
in American life until the 1960s. In that decade, new doubts arose
concerning the core tenets of the progressive gospel. The Vietnam
War suggested to many that the abilities of professional elites to manage government might have been overrated. The environmental
movement warned that the great positive benefits of science might be
offset at least in part by unexpected harmful impacts. The power of
economic progress to transform the world for the better seemed at
odds with rapidly rising crime rates, drug use and other maladies in
the inner city even at a time of strong economic growth in the
United States.

In the 1960s, there was also a shift in the epicenter of economics
from Samuelson and his colleagues at (and connected to) Cambridge,
Massachusetts, to the school of economics associated with the University of Chicago. Consistent with other trends of the 1960s, the
Chicago school showed a much greater skepticism with respect to the

progressive plans for the scientific management of society. Chicago economics instead manifested a powerful new individualism and skepticism of authority that was taking shape during the 1960s in many areas of American life.

In the American intellectual world, the two most important agents for change in the past thirty years have been the environmental movement and a strong new libertarian trend of thought—both exhibiting an antagonism to many of the core assumptions of the progressive gospel.[1] As Samuelson did not create the progressive value system, the Chicago school of economics was not responsible for the new individualistic and libertarian directions in American society. The Chicago school was, nevertheless, an important influence in giving the newly libertarian value system a powerful symbolic representation (providing better "scientific" metaphors) and in seeking to translate the libertarian ethos into concrete plans for political and social change.

The story of the Chicago school begins with Frank Knight. Many people would say that John Maynard Keynes had more impact than any other economist on the history of the twentieth century. Yet it would not be far-fetched to argue that Frank Knight could be ranked with Keynes in this regard. The manner of their influence, to be sure, was altogether different. Besides writing *The General Theory,* Keynes circulated his policy advice at the highest levels of the British government and had a great ability to influence public opinion through his popular writings. Knight entirely lacked these qualities. His great impact on the world was, remarkably enough, as a teacher. It is quite possible that the University of Chicago school of economics would never have existed if Frank Knight had never taught in the economics department there. As Paul Samuelson declared, "Knight was the founder of the Chicago School in economics; if he was Abraham, Henry Simon was Isaac, and Milton Friedman was Jacob" to the Chicago gospel.[2]*
Given the subsequent extraordinary impact of Chicago economics on the

---

* Surprisingly, Samuelson is among the leading economists of the twentieth century who was significantly influenced by Knight. Samuelson attended the University of Chicago in the early 1930s and received his undergraduate degree there. He once reported of his economic studies at Chicago that "Frank Knight was the irresistable Pied Piper. For five years—from the time I was sixteen until I was twenty-one—I was bewitched by Knight." However, Samuelson more recently seems to have come to regard this as something of a youthful embarrassment. In 1998 he referred to his discipleship under Knight during his undergraduate years at Chicago as an "infantile infatuation." He now regards Knight with "measured respect for [being] a brilliant but erratic economist and theologian." See Paul A. Samuelson, "Jacob Viner," in Edward Shils, ed., *Remembering the University of Chicago: Teachers, Scientists, and Scholars* (Chicago: University of Chicago Press, 1991), 536; and Samuelson, "How *Foundations* Came to Be," *Journal of Economic Literature* 36 (September 1998): 1381.

world, it is fair to say that the source for this Chicago influence can in some real sense be traced back to Frank Knight.★

Yet Knight's greatness as a teacher was not as an inspirational lecturer or in instilling any specific body of knowledge in the students and younger faculty who passed through the Chicago department. Indeed, beyond the common antagonism of most leading members of the Chicago school to scientific management and other orthodox progressive themes, much of what Knight believed would later be rejected by his disciples in the Chicago school. Knight's greatest source of influence was in a spirit of radical questioning that he inculcated. Almost in the manner of Socrates, Knight was a doubter of every orthodoxy, often extending this attitude to his own arguments.[3] As George Stigler has commented, Knight was the original source of the Chicago tradition that "great reputation and high office deserve little respect." At Chicago, students were taught a "studied irreverence toward authority," which had a "special slant: contemporary ideas were to be treated even more skeptically than those of earlier periods."[4] Following after Knight, Chicago economists such as Friedman, Stigler, Coase, Becker, and others would all show a great independence of mind. Chicago economists have consistently exhibited a courage to advance ideas that at least initially might be offensive if not outrageous to much of conventional opinion—including in many cases the progressive mainstream of American society.

This irreverence was a trademark of the career of Milton Friedman. His 1962 book, *Capitalism and Freedom,* contained controversial policy recommendations for the negative income tax, school vouchers, the deregulation of transportation and other industries, the loosening of professional restrictions on entry, floating exchange rates, a flat-rate tax on income, reduced antitrust enforcement, the abolition of the military draft, and still others. Often met initially with rejection if not disbelief, in many cases they would be adopted over the following thirty years.[5] In the entire history of economics there may be only one other economist—Jeremy Bentham—who has had a comparable success in proposing a radical and controversial set of policy reforms and then seeing the bulk of these measures eventually accepted by the

---

★ According to Melvin Reder, " 'The personal affection and mutual esteem in which Knight and his protegés held one another facilitated the collaborative efforts of the latter. The informal, but very effective, promotional aspect of the Chicago School sprang from the affinity group of Knight's students and protegés that formed in the middle 1930s. The principal members of this group were Milton and Rose Director Friedman, George Stigler, Allen Wallis, and Henry Simons." As a result, "the 'baton passer' of the initial Chicago group . . . was Knight." See Melvin W. Reder, "Chicago Economics: Permanence and Change," *Journal of Economic Literature* 20 (March 1982): 6–7.

political leadership of his society (in Bentham's case, many of them after his death).★

Friedman had a lot of help, of course. In 1962 Stigler would begin the development of an influential set of Chicago arguments laying out an economic theory of government regulation of private industry.[6] The old progressive arguments that the government would act in "the public interest" were a mere rhetorical camouflage for regulatory actions that actually served private purposes.[7] Stigler's manner of studying government regulation was being systematized at the time to all areas of government by yet another product of Chicago, James Buchanan (who earned his doctorate at Chicago in 1948 as an admiring student of Frank Knight, although his teaching career has been spent elsewhere).[8]

As early as 1957, Gary Becker had shown how economic methods could be extended beyond their traditional bounds to examine the workings of racial discrimination. In the 1970s and 1980s, he applied an economic lens to the behavior of husbands and wives and other members of the family, and developed a systematic account of a new general "economic approach to human behavior," based on an assumption of maximization of individual advantage in all areas of society.[9] The Chicago way of thinking was increasingly exerting a powerful influence on sister disciplines in the social sciences such as political science and sociology. The law-and-economics movement—spawned at Chicago—would become the most important intellectual development in American law of the past thirty years.[10]

In the 1970s the development of rational expectations theory by Robert Lucas at Chicago contributed to a basic rethinking of the fundamental assumptions of Keynesian and other macroeconomic research, casting doubt on the ability of fiscal and other government macroeconomic interventions to have much stabilizing effect.[11] Chicago's influence thus was being felt almost everywhere. A recent study reported citations to economics articles published prior to 1990, as they appeared in economic journals over the period 1988–98.[12] Becker was far and away the leader, with 9,142 citations. Lucas was second (6,522 citations), and Robert Barro (5,939 citations)—who taught early in his career at Chicago—was third.[13] The fourth-ranking economist (5,230 citations) was yet another Chicago economist, James Heckman, whose work on econometric methods and the functioning of

★ Bentham was an advocate of public education, independence for British colonies, competitive admissions to the civil service, prison reforms, curbs on cruel treatment of animals, and an end to remaining legal discriminations against members of the Roman Catholic and other minority religions in England, among many reform proposals. For a discussion of the origins of such policy proposals in Bentham's utilitarian system of thought, see Nelson, *Reaching for Heaven on Earth,* 106–14.

labor markets has been widely influential. And the fifth-ranked economist, Zvi Griliches (3,059 citations), had spent most of his career at Harvard but had also taught early on at Chicago from 1960 to 1969.

All in all, the impact of the Chicago school not only on American economics but on all American social science and on government is nothing short of astonishing. The extraordinary impact of the Chicago school of economics was eventually bound to receive wider official recognition. Since 1975, there have been thirteen winners of the Nobel Prize in economics who have had some close connection, either as faculty members or recipients of doctoral degrees, with the University of Chicago. In the 1990s, seven out of the seventeen Nobel Prizes awarded in economics (some years there were multiple awards)—and including Ronald Coase (1991), Gary Becker (1992), and Robert Lucas (1995)—have been past or present (mostly) faculty members at Chicago.* Then, in 2000 yet another Chicago economist, James Heckman (jointly with Daniel McFadden of the University of California at Berkeley), became the first Nobel Prize winner in economics of the new millennium.

Chicago, like Samuelson and his fellow Progressives, has a secular economic religion—or as will be seen later, it is more accurate to say several secular religions united by some common themes. Paul Heyne, a rare member of the economics profession who had a doctorate in theology (in fact from the University of Chicago), argued at the 1996 annual meeting of the American Economic Association that the practice of economics can never be a value-neutral subject. It will always depend on some underlying "vision" that "provides the raw material for our analytical efforts, highlighting some features of reality and concealing others." As a result, Heyne declared, "any economist who is trying to understand the world of human interactions with the hope of making them more effective is very likely to be operating with a *theological* vision" of some sort.[14]

The Chicago school of economics encompasses three generations.[15] The first included Knight, Jacob Viner, and Henry Simons among its leaders, but Knight—as will be explored in Chapter 5—was the most influential figure. The leading figures in the second generation were Milton Friedman and George Stigler, whose economic values will be examined in Chapter 6. And the third generation, whose economic values will be described in Chapter 7, has been led by Gary Becker, Robert Lucas, and Richard Posner. (The work of yet another leading Chicago economist, Ronald Coase, will be examined in Part IV.)

---

* Other present or past Chicago economists who won Nobel Prizes in the 1990s were Merton Miller (1990), Robert Fogel (1993), Myron Scholes (1997), and Robert Mundell (1999).

If the professional classes of the American Progressive movement, as suggested earlier, bear a considerable resemblance to the priesthood of the Roman Catholic Church, the Chicago school might be said to represent in a number of respects a "Protestant" side of American economics. Like the Protestant Reformation itself, which spawned a host of religious denominations with widely varying beliefs, held together by antagonism to Roman Catholicism, the unifying feature of the Chicago school is its negative verdict on American progressive ideas. In that sense Chicago economics may be particularly instructive, as American society in the twenty-first century moves to construct a new governing vision, a replacement, as seems likely to be necessary, for the progressive vision of the twentieth-century welfare and regulatory state.[16]

chapter **FIVE**

FRANK KNIGHT AND ORIGINAL SIN

Frank Knight came to the Chicago economics department in 1928 and remained an active member well past
his retirement from full-time teaching duties in 1951
and until his death in 1972. George Stigler wrote his
doctoral dissertation under Knight, and Milton Friedman was a Knight student in the 1930s, later describing
him as "our great and revered teacher."[1] As the old saying went at Chicago, "There is no God, but Frank
Knight is his prophet."[2]

Ronald Coase once related that he could conceive of
himself matching the achievements of many of the leading members of the economics profession but that "I
simply cannot imagine myself to be like Frank Knight. I
guess that amounts to saying that Knight is a genius."[3] In
a reminiscence on his years as a graduate student taking
courses with Knight in the 1940s, Don Patinkin commented that Knight frequently spoke in a "rambling and
often obscure manner." Yet the demands he made of his
students and the range of his thought meant that he was
still "a great teacher," whose lessons would continue to
guide his students in their "thinking many years later."[4]
James Buchanan, who studied under Knight in the
1940s, would later observe that "I find myself confronted time and again with Knight's much earlier and
more sophisticated statement of the same thing [as I have
later said]. It is as if on rereading Knight I am retracing
the sources of my own thoughts, which themselves have
somehow emerged without conscious recognition that
they are derived from him."[5]

Knight did not consider himself a Christian—indeed, he was famous for his antagonism to traditional religion.[6] Yet he joined with a theologian to publish a book (each author wrote separate sections), *The Economic Order and Religion.*[7] When the time came to deliver his presidential address to the American Economic Association in 1950, Knight self-consciously labeled it his "sermon" to the profession.[8] In teaching his economics courses, as Patinkin observed, Knight was prone to engage in "long digressions on the nature of man and society—and God."[9] The core social and economic problem in Knight's view was one of "discovery and definition of values—a moral, not to say a religious, problem," which stood in great contrast to the progressive aspirations for "value-free" scientific management of society.[10]

Knight is best known to most economists today for his influential 1921 book, *Risk, Uncertainty, and Profit.*[11] He undertook there one of the first systematic explorations of a subject that has since become more central to economic theory, the impact of information uncertainties as a determining factor in the organization of industry.[12] However, Knight would soon move on to become more of a moral philosopher than a microeconomist.[13] Although current economists typically know less about this side of Knight, it was in this role that the key figures in the Chicago school of economics encountered him and in which he exerted his greatest influence on its future development.

If the ethics of self-interest is the core moral/religious problem for economics, Knight's way of thinking about the place of self-interest in society was in great contrast to that of Samuelson. Knight doubted that there could be any possibility of the scientific management of society, through the manipulation of self-interest in the market, or otherwise. Human reason, he believed, was a frail instrument, often corrupted by the baser elements in human nature. He thought, in contrast to the great majority of economists of his time, that the economic problem in society was in the end a religious problem. The defense of freedom—including the opportunity to express self-interest in the market—must rest not on a scientific demonstration but upon an adequate moral/philosophical foundation.

For Knight that foundation lay in the central moral importance he ascribed to individual liberty. Knight had a strong libertarian strain, the beginnings of a powerful libertarian influence that continues at Chicago to the present time. Yet he did not believe that individuals could exist independent of a grounding in some culture or society—human beings, he thought, were social by nature. Everyone had to be grounded in some cultural system, historically including religion as a main source of group identity. Nevertheless, given the inevitable wide range of religious views and the potential for strong disagreements, the market provided a place where people from different creeds could come together for voluntary exchange and mutual benefit, an alternative much preferable to the wars and other terrible conflicts of past human history, often the most destructive when fought in the name of religion.

If Knight's views were unusual for an economist of his time, they were less novel than it appeared to many of his professional contemporaries. Indeed, if now taking a secular form (as Samuelson had also secularized aspects of the Judeo-Christian tradition), Knight was expressing a classic Christian view of fallen human beings, beset by original sin. In a long-standing Christian tradition (if not the only such tradition), the existence of private property and the marketplace has been seen as an unfortunate but necessary concession to the pervasive presence of evil in the world. In the past in the Garden of Eden and in the future in heaven there will be no private property (or government either). In the current world infected by sin, it is simply that private property and the pursuit of profit are the best way to maintain a semblance of order in society. As Richard Schlatter explains, there has been a long-standing view in Christianity that "since the Fall [in the Garden] the natures of men, all of them depraved, make necessary instruments of social domination. The division of property, which gives some men a power over the lives of others, is one such instrument." [14]

For Knight, even a priesthood—of economists or otherwise—could not be exempt from the general human condition; the professional experts will be sinners as well. Knight marks the beginning of a fundamental break of the Chicago school with the Progressives of Samuelson's ilk, a new assumption that self-interest will be expressed not only in the marketplace but also in the actions of government and indeed perhaps in every area of society. It is a secular form of an old view, characteristic of Calvin and other Protestant Reformers, that sin has fundamentally invaded every aspect of human existence. While Roman Catholic theologians also recognized the centrality of sin in the world, they tended to show considerably greater faith in human reason and in the possibilities for rational striving toward improvement in the human condition.

DELUDED PROGRESSIVES

The key economist in the founding of the American Economic Association, Richard Ely, argued early in his career (he later would be more cautious in his rhetoric, although the core values would not change much) that the organizing principle of social behavior should be the biblical commandment: Thou shalt love thy neighbor as thyself. Thus, it was impossible to both "serve God and mammon; for the ruling motive of the one service—egotism, selfishness—is the opposite of the ruling motive of the other—altruism, devotion to others, consecration of heart, soul and intellect to the service of others." For Ely in the social gospel phase of his life, in the 1880s and 1890s, the chief motivating force in the world—even in labor and business—must be "love" of fellow human beings, rather than the "self-interest" long favored by most economists.[15]

Ely's attitudes in this respect were in fact representative of those of many leading progressive intellectuals, often associated with the social gospel movement.[16] For Knight, this was just one example of how progressive intellectuals had substituted "romantic" thinking for a realistic approach to the human condition.* It is impossible, he says, to conceive of the application of "the 'love' doctrine" as a guiding economic principle "over, say, the population of a modern nation—and, of course, it must ultimately be over the world since, for a world religion [like Christianity], national boundaries have no moral significance."[17]

Similarly, Knight strongly rejected the economic determinism characteristic of progressive thought and the resulting hopes for a radical improvement in the condition of the world (perhaps attaining a state of affairs where "love" would in fact rule), if the economic problem could ever be finally solved. As he stated, "There is no reason to believe that if all properly economic problems were solved once [and] for all through a fairy gift to every individual of the power to work physical miracles, the social struggle and strife would either be reduced in amount or intensity, or essentially changed in form, to say nothing of improvement—in the absence of some moral revolution which could by no means be assumed to follow in consequence of the change itself."[18] Thus, as Knight sees matters, a core assumption of the American progressive gospel—that economic events are the driving forces in history—is a serious misreading of the human condition. The presence of sin in the world cannot be abolished so easily as by the mere achievement of a state of great material abundance. As Knight once put the matter:

> The idea that the social problem is essentially or primarily economic, in the sense that social action may be concentrated on the economic

---

* This kind of thinking was still widespread in Christian social reform circles even into the late twentieth century. Max Stackhouse and Dennis McCann comment that "all too many religious leaders still cling to the belief that capitalism is greedy, individualistic, exploitative and failing; that socialism is generous, community-affirming, equitable and coming; and that the transition from the one to the other is what God is doing in the world." See Max L. Stackhouse and Dennis P. McCann, "A Postcommunist Manifesto: Public Theology After the Collapse of Socialism," *Christian Century*, January 16, 1991, 44.

aspect and other aspects left to take care of themselves, is a fallacy, and to outgrow this fallacy is one of the conditions of progress toward a real solution of the social problem as a whole, including the economic aspect itself. Examination will show that while many conflicts which seem to have a non-economic character are "really" economic, it is just as true that what is called "economic" conflict is "really" rooted in other interests and other forms of rivalry, and that these would remain unabated after any conceivable change in the sphere of economics alone.[19]

In the grand scheme of things, and if one motive had to be emphasized, rather than being love, this motive for Knight would be "power." The "solemn fact is that what people most commonly want for themselves is their 'own way,' as such, or especially *power.*"[20] Knight's sometimes chastised free-market economists, including his own Chicago colleagues, for putting too much emphasis on standard economic motives. In their thinking "the main argument for *laissez-faire* was instrumental, . . . it was intended to increase efficiency"—not so very different in this respect from the progressive gospel of efficiency. For Knight, freedom instead means a maximum of power for an individual to control his or her own actions, and this must be "an end or value in itself," not something merely "instrumental to efficiency."[21] It was closer to a libertarian than an economic way of thinking.

Indeed, clearly separating himself from the economic mainstream of his time, Knight believes that "men actually prefer freedom to efficiency, within limits; and both our highest ideals and our laws and institutions recognize that they ought to do so if they do not." Knight is even prepared to argue that people "may even rightly be forced to be free."[22] To submit to power is for Knight to succumb to the temptations of a modern devil—to chose sin over salvation. No one can be allowed, any more in modern times than in days of old, to make this choice.

For Knight—somewhat paradoxically, in light of the obvious powerful influence of Christianity on his own thinking—one of the main threats to freedom was found in the Christian religion.[23] Indeed, the "history of Christianity" shows that the role of its teachings "has been to sanction established morality, law, and authority, not reform, at least in any constructive or progressive sense." In the Middle Ages, the Roman Catholic "church became a theocracy" and demonstrated as much concern for preserving its own power as any kings or other secular authorities.[24] Once in power, Christianity forgot all its core messages of love of fellow human beings and became a "violently intolerant" religion, given to episodes of fierce persecution of heresy and oppression of perceived enemies. Knight noted the "familiar fact" that over many centuries "the Church never condemned or officially opposed slavery."[25]

If the progressive views of Samuelson and the mainstream of the economics profession followed in the natural-law tradition of emphasizing a rational world, Knight was particularly hostile to the ideas of natural law that have been central to much of the development of Catholic theology over the centuries. Knight never made any secret of his special dislike for the Catholic Church. Natural-law concepts, he argued, had been "bandied about since the earliest beginnings of the European intellectual tradition" but they had mainly served "to beg the question in favor of any position which a particular writer or school happened to wish to defend or promote." At one time or another, rigid social castes, rule by absolute authority, and various other forms of oppression had been declared by leading theologians of the time to be in conformance with the laws of nature. As Knight thus considered, "Natural law has served as a defense for any existing order against any change and as an argument for change in any direction."[26] The whole concept of natural law, in fact, was for Knight nothing short of an intellectual scandal—the perversion of reason rather than its reaching to the greatest heights.

SCIENTIFIC OPPRESSION

If the Christian religion had often been false to its own founding principles, in the modern age the Christian churches were no longer the greatest threat to human freedom. As Knight explained, even as Christianity was much weakened in our own time, we now confronted a new "milieu in which science as such is a religion."[27] Much as argued earlier in Parts I and II of the present book, Knight was already writing in 1947 that the newer forms of religion promoted a "gospel" that involved a kind of "salvation by science," following in the path of the old natural-law theories that promised a path to salvation by following God's laws.[28] The progressive follies of his day thus followed in a long tradition of religious pandering to power and oppression in the name of the human faculty of reason.[29]

The "plea of communism," Knight argues, with its claims to scientific authority, is much "like that of Christianity;" both asserting unique access to final truth and in this way justifying "absolute authority, ignoring freedom."[30] Communism is only one of the species of modern totalitarianisms, each of which offers "a priesthood as the custodian of [scientific] Truth, 'conditioning' each generation in helpless infancy to unquestioning belief." These new modern forms of scientific authoritarianism drew on "an inheritance" from earlier Christian traditions of "conformity to a sacred law and obedience to consecrated authority, Holy Mother Church and Holy Father King." [31]

Knight saw great danger in the tendency of most social scientists to believe that human behavior is rationally explainable in terms of behavioral laws and principles analogous to the laws discovered by the physical sciences. [32] It would serve merely to open the way to the expression of less exalted motives: "Any attempt at use of the unqualified procedures of natural science in solving problems of human relations is just another name for a struggle for power, ultimately a completely lawless one." [33] If the construction of a dam to control a raging river depended on knowledge of physical science, the advocates of the "scientific management" of society sought to employ social science to bring human actions under similar control. [34] Given the frailties of the political arrangements through which human beings governed themselves, and the unruly character of human nature, the end of human freedom was likely to be among the consequences. The grand schemes of progressive economists were based on an assumption that the world is a rational place, but they were bound to fail in the face of "human nature being as irrational as it is." [35]

Knight directed his barbs, for example, at a leading work of sociology published in 1947, one year before Samuelson's *Economics* first appeared, that reflected a value system similar to that of Samuelson's textbook. Much as Samuelson was seeking to convert economics to the methods of physics, the author of this bestselling work of popular sociology, George Lundberg, believed that "the problems of personal life, social relations, and political and economic organization are of the same kind as the prediction and control of events in (non-human) nature and so will similarly yield gradually to the same mode of attack." In order to solve social problems, as Knight characterized Lundberg's views, all that is needed "is that intellectual leaders . . . be converted to the scientific point of view," in order that "the social problem will be solved by the application of scientific method." [36]

Such thinking, however, as Knight labels it, is mere rationalist and "scientistic propaganda." [37] Indeed, the "fetish of 'scientific method' in the study of society is one of the two most pernicious forms of romantic folly that are current among the educated"—as bad as the natural-law follies of earlier Christian eras. The plain fact is that a fully rational "science of human behavior, in the literal sense, is impossible." Or again, as Knight writes, a "natural or positive science of human conduct" is "an absurdity." [38] A key reason that a science of society is impossible is that the scientific analysis is not independent of the object under scrutiny. The very ideas of social scientists can themselves change the conception of society and thus alter the very character of the object being studied.

Moreover, even if a true science of society were possible, it would not be desirable.[39] An individual whose behavior is perfectly and scientifically predictable is not a real human being. It is the element of self-consciousness and the ability to choose—the existence of "free will" in the classic Christian formulation—that distinguishes us from the animal world. If all is as determinate as in biology, what is to separate a man or woman in moral terms from a dog or an insect?* It may well be, Knight comments, "the idiot" who has the greatest amount of "happiness" among human beings, but the pursuit of this kind of pleasurable sensation "is not what makes human life worthwhile."[40] Many centuries earlier, Martin Luther had similarly complained that the Roman Catholic Church had diminished its followers and endangered human freedom by encouraging the faithful to believe that life—even in such fundamental matters as the attainment of salvation in the hereafter—could follow mechanical rules as set by the church hierarchy.

Rather, even if there is considerable truth to the idea that a human being is a biological entity governed by laws of physical nature, "we must [finally] understand ourselves and each other and act intelligently in relation to both, in other terms altogether." Hence, the rational methods of science—yielding the legalistic decrees of any church, Roman, scientific, or otherwise—can hold "no clue to the answer to the essential problems of free society," and the living of lives of genuine "spiritual freedom."[41] In opposition to Roman Catholic theology, the Protestant Reformation made as its watchword the concept that salvation is "by faith alone," and faith is ultimately a mystery fathomable only to God. Even in the modern age a "free society" must act to "find norms somewhere outside the factual space-time world" with which the rational scientific method is concerned.

In these regards Knight thus was following in the tradition of old-fashioned Protestant theology—so contrary to the rationalism of contemporary economics—with its tenet that original sin would inevitably undermine any human efforts to achieve a systematic rationality in the

---

* Among contemporary economists, one finds the clearest echo of Knight's thinking in the writings of his former student James Buchanan. Indeed, on many subjects Buchanan sounds remarkably similar to Knight. For example, Buchanan considers that a person who behaves strictly according to scientific laws "could not be concerned with choice at all." Indeed, it is "internally contradictory" to speak of individual "choice making under [scientific] certainty." If human dignity and freedom require the power to chose, if the ability to do either good or evil must be within the scope of individual decision making, then, Buchanan believes, human behavior cannot be strictly determined by scientific rules. The scientific view of a human being as mechanical instrument denies a person his or her basic humanity. See James M. Buchanan, *What Should Economists Do?* (Indianapolis, Ind.: Liberty Press, 1979), 281.

world. One of Luther's favorite sayings was the message of Saint Paul that "the flesh lusteth against the spirit and the spirit contrary to the flesh," and therefore "so that ye cannot do the things that ye would do." [42]

Knight's thinking thus adopts a characteristic Protestant skepticism of a world of beneficial human "works." He is opposed to the core ideas of American progressive thought—including those in Samuelson's *Economics*—and the optimistic faith that scientific management of society (a particular form of "works") is the path to a future perfection of human existence. Contrary to the rationalist theology of natural law, and now the mechanical prescriptions of science, no given set of rules will ever show the way to heaven, on earth or otherwise. As seen by Ross Emmett, a leading contemporary interpreter of Knight's moral philosophy, his thinking reflects an underlying theological view of the basic economic choices facing any society:

> In a society which has no recourse to the providential nature of a God who is present in human history, the provision of a justification for the way society works is a "theological" undertaking. Despite the fact that modern economists often forget it, their investigations of the universal problem of scarcity and its consequences for human behavior and social organization is a form of theological inquiry: in a world where there is no God, scarcity replaces moral evil as the central problem of theodicy, and the process of assigning value becomes the central problem of morality. Knight's (implicit) recognition of the theological nature of economic inquiry in this regard is one of the reasons for his rejection of positivism in economics and his insistence on the fundamentally normative and apologetic character of economics. In some sense, therefore, it is appropriate to say that Knight understood that his role in a society which did not or could not recognize the presence of God was similar to the role of a theologian in a society which explicitly acknowledged God's presence. As a student of society, he was obliged to contribute to society's discussion of the appropriate mechanisms for the coordination of individuals' actions, and to remind the members of society that their discussion could never be divorced from consideration of the type of society they wanted to create and the kind of people they wanted to become. [43]

REDISCOVERING ORIGINAL SIN

In the modern era in the Western world, there have been three main competing visions of the origins of human nature. First, there is the traditional Judeo-

Christian view of human nature at first innocent but then soon corrupted by sin since the Fall in the Garden of Eden, leading most men and women to lead lives of falsity, hatred, theft, lying, and other forms of distortion of their truer and better natures. Second, there is the Darwinian view in which human nature is determined by a genetic inheritance that is the product of many thousands (or millions) of years of biological evolution—and in which human nature is a form of behavior that has evolved to promote the long-run survival of the human species (any concepts in society of good and evil having no ultimate moral significance but representing merely instruments of the workings of the evolutionary process). In the third main view, human nature is shaped by the existing surrounding environment, predominantly the economic environment—making it possible that human beings might act on their own to abolish poverty and other causes of bad behavior, and in this fashion eventually to perfect the conditions of existence on this earth.

A great iconoclast (might we say modern "protester" in the spirit of Luther and Calvin?), Knight seemingly rejects all of these explanations for the existence of evil, which are grounded in a particular view of human nature. Yet he also does not offer any explicit alternative of his own. One must read behind the lines to find Knight's real views of the human condition. Indeed, despite all his outward hostility to Christianity, Knight's own theology—mainly expressed in an implicit fashion—follows surprisingly closely in the Calvinist understanding of Christian faith.★ While any notion of an actual Fall in the Garden of Eden might be a myth, human beings in Knight's view are in fact corrupt creatures whose actual behavior in the world corresponds closely to the biblical understanding of the consequences of original sin.†

Knight's system of thought is so far outside the assumptions of the economics mainstream that most economists have simply chosen to ignore his moral philosophy, concentrating on the technical arguments at which he was also skilled. His preaching is for many economists virtually incomprehensible, at times a seeming muddle of confused if not contradictory ideas, made

---

★ John Calvin was born in 1509 and followed soon after Martin Luther as a leading figure of the Protestant Reformation. Calvinists adopted a yet more radical version of Luther's complaints against the Roman Catholic Church. The Puritans in England were among the leading branches of Calvinism in Europe. Calvin died in 1564, a pivotal figure in the history of Western religion. See William Bouwsma, *John Calvin: A Sixteenth-Century Portrait* (New York: Oxford University Press, 1988).

† The Protestantism of the Reformation saw human behavior as especially corrupted by original sin—thus precluding any prospect of rationally directed action to achieve salvation. A typical Protestant expression was found in the writings of Richard Hooker (1553–1600), who wrote of "the shame of our defiled natures," which would surely "shut us out from the kingdom of heaven," if not simply for the great mercy of God. Quoted in John Kent, "Christianity: Protestantism," in R. C. Zaehner, ed., *Encyclopedia of the World's Religions* (New York: Barnes and Noble, 1997), 102.

all the more puzzling by the obvious fact of Knight's central role in the development of the Chicago school of economics. This failure of so many economists to better understand the direction of Knight's thought is powerful evidence—if any should be needed—of the secularization of American society and the lack of knowledge of old-fashioned Protestant theology. Once it is recognized that Knight's supposed antagonism to Christianity exists only on the surface, his thinking is easily seen as a secular version of Protestant Christianity, grounded in a conception of the ever present and powerful workings of sin in the world.

His student and disciple James Buchanan comments: "Why was Knight so different from his peers? My hypothesis is that he can be explained, phenomenologically, only through recalling his roots in evangelical Christianity." Knight was "a product of middle America, of the agricultural economy of Illinois, of the late nineteenth century, of evangelical Christianity." Buchanan attributes Knight's "intense critical spirit" to his having been forced to wrestle with conflicts and doubts about Christianity in his youth.[44] Here I think Buchanan goes wrong. A better explanation is that this critical spirit was a direct manifestation—if now taking a secular form—of a characteristic Protestant outlook on the world. The Calvinist and Puritan mentality in particular has been characterized by deep introspection and a harshly critical attitude toward all claims to authority, worldly or otherwise. It is an outgrowth of the Calvinist conviction that all human beings are deeply infected by original sin and that our best efforts are not likely to be worth much—and especially among those who make the grandest claims.[45]

Thus, one might say that Knight's real religion was a secular Calvinism—his own distinctive brand of "Calvinism minus God." As is the case with so many other leading intellectuals of the modern age, brilliant insights in many areas have been accompanied by a blindness with respect to the Judeo-Christian roots of the underlying value system being expressed. For example, like Calvin—and the English and American Puritans who later followed in the tradition of Calvinist theology—Knight saw a "positive moral value of pain and suffering. . . . The need for this emphasis is indubitable; human nature proverbially appears finer in adversity than in prosperity."[46] Much as Puritan theology had preached that excessive wealth was a temptation to sin and thus a danger to one's eternal soul, Knight would remark on another occasion that "it is human nature to be more dissatisfied the better off one is." The motive for providing one's labor was often as much a pride of "workmanship" as any desire for more income to obtain greater consumption. Knight found that humankind was in general a "contrary critter" prone to present a "false exterior."[47]

Knight was developing in a secular fashion a set of attitudes that were in fact common in American life in his formative years.[48] Paula Baker, in a study of rural life in upstate New York near the end of the nineteenth century, finds a common belief that "virtue inhered in hard work." Work was not a burden, but a source of "contentment," she writes. In this perspective there were large "moral and economic benefits" to the very act of labor itself. Indeed, it was no overstatement that hard labor "provided the basis for virtue in the producer's republic."[49] These attitudes were far removed from—virtually incompatible with—the narrow utilitarianism of mainstream economic thought, but manifested themselves in the thinking of Knight. As Knight had argued as early as 1923, it was necessary to reject "the assumption that human wants are objective and measurable magnitudes and that the satisfaction of such wants is the essence and criterion of value, and . . . on the basis of this assumption to [then] reduce ethics to a sort of glorified economics."[50]

An American student of the Puritan influence on American history, Paul Conkin, finds that the Puritan view of the human condition as derived from Calvinist theology has had great staying power in American life. As he explains:

> Briefly characterized, the typical Puritan, in 1630 or 1930, reflected ideological assurance but was, at least in most areas and when at his best, open to new ideas. He was very much a moralist, a political activist. . . . He venerated the rule of objective laws or principles, but he just as insistently believed in congregation and local democracy. He usually reflected a sense of mission, even of a peculiar destiny, and an atmosphere of seriousness and self-importance. Yet he was, or wanted to be, pious, ever mindful of his dependence upon an overarching but never quite fathomable reality, which he loved even without full understanding. Although he sought redemption above all else, he had a wholesome respect for the instrumentality of both material goods and scientific knowledge, trying always to keep either from becoming usurping ends. He demanded a conscientious stewardship of all men and wanted all to have a useful and fulfilling calling or vocation.[51]

While Knight does not fit every aspect of this description, on the whole it is close. In their own lives, he thinks, few people are likely to achieve a goal of happiness. The utilitarian philosophy of life is empirically in error and metaphysically shallow. The modern Calvinist must as always recognize the inevitability of pain and suffering, an outcome that perversely is likely to be aggravated by an excessive emphasis on the pursuit of happiness as the central goal in life. Indeed, an excess of utilitarianism is one of the many snares of the devil. Since the Fall in the Garden of Eden, the rational faculties of human beings have been undermined by their unruly emotions and their easy susceptibility to various hatreds, jealousies, biases, and other psychological maladies.★

Hence, as Luther and Calvin both preached, and Knight also believes, projects for self-improvement are often likely to achieve consequences that are the very opposite to the intended effect, owing to the frailties of the human condition. Ascetic discipline rather than the pursuit of happiness should guide human conduct. Patinkin recalled from his classroom lectures "Knight's commenting that from the long-run viewpoint, . . . denial of wants was the only way that a definitive adjustment of wants to resources could be achieved; for history had shown that Western society created new wants just as fast (if not faster than!) it expanded the means of satisfying them." [52]

In a recent commentary on Knight's economic philosophy, Richard Boyd notes that Knight's thinking has "much more in common with Augustine Christianity than it does with the [rationalism and utilitarianism of the] Enlightenment." [53] Martin Luther had originally been an Augustinian monk who despised the rational and mechanical (as Luther saw it) medieval theology of natural law constructed by Thomas Aquinas, instead looking—and followed in this respect by many other Protestant Reformers—to the earlier and more pessimistic (with respect to sinful life in this fallen world) theology of Augustine. [54] As Boyd adds, Knight thus exhibits a fundamentally different worldview from that of Adam Smith, Friedrich Hayek, and Milton Friedman, all of whom believed more optimistically in the great "benefits of progress, development and economic efficiency." [55]

★ George Stigler comments with respect to Knight:

> Economic theory prescribes the efficient ways of achieving given ends: this to Knight was a pathetically small part of human activity. The effects of acts often diverge grotesquely from the desires which led to them. Wants themselves are highly unstable, and it is their essential nature to change and grow. "The Chief thing which the common-sense individual wants is not satisfactions for the wants he had, but more, and *better* wants." So man is an explorer and experimenter, a seeker for unknown and perhaps unknowable truths, a creature better understood through the study of literature than by the scientific method.

See George J. Stigler, "Frank Hyneman Knight," in John Eatwell, Murray Milgate, and Peter Newman, *The New Palgrave: A Dictionary of Economics* (New York: Stockton Press, 1987), 58.

The Augustinian and Calvinist view stands in great contrast to the progressive view of the economic mainstream of a rational utilitarian choosing how to maximize his or her own happiness, or the view of a society acting through a rational process of scientific management to perfect the human condition here on earth. In such matters, and in coming down on the Calvinist rather than the progressive and rationalist side, Knight was a secular kind of Protestant fundamentalist, reacting against the thinking of virtually the entire economics profession of his time.

Knight makes his Calvinist proclivities clear in his unique manner of justifying a classical liberal outlook on the world.[56] Knight painted the following picture, so different from other economists' aspirations to the scientific management of society:

> While effort is justified by good results, these are not expected ever to be satisfying. The experienced reward is more the joy of pursuit than of possession. It is recognized that the solution of any problem will raise more questions than it answers, so that man is committed— "doomed" . . . —to strive toward goals which recede more rapidly than he as an individual, or even society, advances towards them. Thus life is finally, if one chooses, or if one's temperament so dictates, a sort of labor of Sisyphus.[57]

In the broadest view, one might say that, intellectually and theologically speaking, much of American history has reflected a struggle between the pessimistic Puritan view of fallen, sinful humankind and the optimistic Enlightenment view of rational, utilitarian humankind. If the great majority of American economists have fallen on the Enlightenment and progressive side of this divide, Knight was one of the rare exceptions.

If economics were truly a value-neutral undertaking, one would expect that members of the economics profession would have developed a full body of economic thought—and with a significant investment of resources and depth of technical analysis—based on Calvinist and Puritan assumptions. If economists had wanted to avoid taking any sides on fundamental value questions, they should have thoroughly explored the workings of Calvinist economic models of the world. An economics that conformed to Calvinist assumptions would have to be very different from Samuelson's *Economics,* or other mainstream economic models of individual behavior.

Efficiency could not be the highest value, because wealth would have to be treated not as a benefit but a temptation to sin—and thus to depravity on this earth and a danger to one's eternal soul. The benefits of work would not lie in the goods and services obtained for consumptive purposes; rather, in a true Calvinist economics a person would labor not for the benefit of the consumption obtained but for the disciplining by hard work of unruly minds and souls that are always in danger of succumbing to the temptations of the devil. Technically speaking, "utility" would be derived from the labor and the other inputs. A potential excess of consumption resulting from such labor would be a constraint (a threat to one's eternal soul, potentially with disastrous consequences, if constant vigilance were not maintained), rather than a desired outcome in itself. The real economic problem would be to serve a calling, to work long and hard, without producing so much wealth in the process as to fall inevitably into temptation and sin. Furthermore, pain and suffering in Calvinist theology (and a valid accompanying Calvinist economics), as Knight commented of his own thinking, can often be a benefit rather than a cost.

All this would amount to almost a complete inversion of the foundational assumptions of mainstream economics. That is to say, progressive benefits would systematically be Calvinist costs, and vice versa. To be sure, economics is not a value-neutral subject and few microeconomists have ever shown any interest in developing the technical details of a "countermicroeconomics" grounded in Calvinist and Puritan assumptions. With respect specifically to American society, where the value grounds have always been fiercely contested, economists have never sought to conduct an empirical test of the predictive capacities (or other usefulness) of economic models grounded in Calvinist and Knightian assumptions about the basic character of human motivation, as compared with the predictive powers of conventional economic models that are grounded in individualistic, rational, and utilitarian assumptions about human nature.

Scientifically, all this is indefensible; instead of being value neutral, the economics profession has actually been defending a strong value position. In building from only one view of human nature, mainstream economists have in effect been asserting that this is the one and only correct view.

COMMUNITIES OF BELIEVERS

For Samuelson and most other mainstream economists the issue of preference formation has been considered to lie outside the bounds of economic analysis. The structure of preferences—the utility function—is simply assumed to exist, wherever it may have come from (and it could have come directly from God, it matters little). Knight, however, argues that it is a "fundamental error" to regard "the individual as given, and . . . the social problem as one of right relations between given individuals."[58] Rather, the problem of ordering society should be conceived in the following terms:

> The social problem in the strict sense . . . is purely intellectual-moral. All physical activity involved in social-legal process is carried out by individuals who act as the agents of society, in so far as they are true to the trust confided to them. Social action, which is social decision, uses as data both facts and cause-and-effect relations, pertaining both to nature and to man. But the social problem is not one of fact—except as values are also facts—nor is it one of means and end. It is a problem of values.[59]

Such views led Knight to embrace a democratic politics of widespread "discussion," a theme that is found over and over again in his writings. Calvin and other Protestant Reformers had much earlier denounced the attempts of the Roman Catholic priesthood to impose authoritative and binding interpretations of faith on all the members of the church; instead, as the early Protestant Reformers declared, each person must come to his or her own understanding of religious truth, worked out in processes of discussion with fellow parishioners. Calvinism introduced a powerful commitment to local democracy in the church. For Knight as well, the citizenry will simply have to find a way to some common value basis for social actions through internal political processes of deliberation, however lengthy and cumbersome this social process of discussion may turn out to be. New communities of believers—perhaps now often believers in secular religions—are no less necessary today.

Whether organized on a market basis or any other, Knight declares that "society depends upon—we may almost say that it *is*—moral like-mindedness."[60] It is essential for Knight that this like-mindedness must not be dictated by any modern equivalent of the Roman bureaucracy of old, in the current era most likely to be acting in the name of the authoritative decrees of science. The truths of modern religion as well must be reached from the bottom up, from the interactions of free citizens in a democratic polity.[61]

A process of democratic discussion requires, to be sure, a whole host of intermediate institutions between the individual and the wider society. The process of discussion must yield "superindividual norms." It is no help in finding agreement on these norms to hear from each person the "mere expression of individual desires." Indeed, the carrying over of the individualism of the free market into the realm of democratic discussion would "intensify the problem" of bringing the discussion to any fruitful outcome.[62]

With a few rare exceptions, Knight finds, the individual never exists independent of some surrounding institutional and cultural context from which he or she derives basic values and an identity. For Knight the term *individual* as used in economic theory should in fact be regarded as shorthand for *family*.★ Mainstream economics has misconceived the social problem for American society because it has taken its individualistic and utilitarian models of human behavior too literally. We are all products of our time and place, Knight says. The idea of the lone individual creating (or obtaining in some manner) his or her own tastes and wants as an independent act is truly a heroic fiction. Rather, we all live within a specific "culture" that teaches common "taste and appreciation" that are "more important than means of gratification" in determining our sense of ourselves as a person and of our individual well-being.[63]

Hence, for Knight discussion in society is not about bargaining from fixed individual-preference positions to divide up the economic pie. Rather, the whole point of political discussion is to change minds; as a result of democratic deliberation, individual preferences should be constantly revised, leading to the necessary convergence ("like-mindedness") of values in the community. If much of the theoretical apparatus of economics is of little use in a world of constantly shifting preference structures, so much for the mainstream economics of the progressive gospel.

As a strong defender of market liberties, Knight partly blamed the current advocates of the free market, including some of his own Chicago colleagues, for the erosion of market freedoms and the wholesale turn to European socialism and American progressive principles that he saw taking place in his time. For a while in the nineteenth century there had been a "religion of liberalism [that] had a positive social-moral content."[64] But the value foundation for free markets had somewhere been lost. "One of the main factors in the present crisis is that the public has lost faith, such faith as it ever had, in the moral validity of market values."[65] Or as Knight similarly stated in another context, "The real breakdown of *bourgeois* society is only superficially economic; . . . it is rather political, since indisputably it is the business of the political system to make the economic system function; fundamentally, however, the breakdown is not structural at all, but moral." Classical liberalism had made a basic "intellectual mistake" in that it "failed to see that the social problem is not at bottom intellectual, but moral."[66] And no adequate moral

---

★ Gary Becker follows closely in the tradition of Knight and the Chicago school in that he directs an attitude of radical questioning toward many of the conventional values of society. However, if Knight still held to his many statements in his writings, he would have to be severely critical of Becker's recent economic approach to the study of the workings of family life as an arrangement among autonomous individuals each acting within the family for their own benefit.

defense of the free market had been forthcoming at Chicago, or among any other group of economists in the twentieth century.

Knight argues that the typical economist's description of the market as a "competitive" system has been "calamitous for understanding" of the true merits of a market system.★ In his own thinking about the market, it is ultimately desirable not because competition drives costs and prices down to the lowest feasible levels—thus putting the case for the free market in conventional progressive and instrumental terms of efficiency—but because the market provides the one practical mechanism for resolving in a more satisfactory way (one that preserves individual freedom) the value tensions that will permeate any large and diverse society. Rather than seeing competition as a benefit, Knight argues that the advantages of the market should be understood in terms of promoting a "pattern of cooperation" among people who come together on a non-coercive basis for mutual advantage.[67] In this way, even people in a pluralist society who have fundamentally different belief systems are able to work together without first having to reconcile their values to some common set of norms.

Hence, as Knight puts it, the market minimizes the role of power in human interactions because in a market "there are no power relations." The market enables each person "to be the judge of his own values and of the use of his own means to achieve them." In grounding actions on mutual consent, the market leaves out any moral judgments of "selfishness" or other factors of "moral quality or artistic taste" in determining social interactions. A Christian can as easily trade in a market with a Muslim as with a fellow Christian; if they had first been required to agree on value subjects such as religion, no exchanges might ever have taken place.

Here again, Knight's views hark back to Christian origins. In Christian theology, the existence of private property—and the necessity of markets as well—is a product of original sin. In an ideal world, neither would exist. In the cur-rent fallen world, property and markets give outlets to human striv-

---

★ According to Stigler, Knight had an explicitly normative vision of the case for the market, in contrast to most of his fellow economists:

> For most present-day economists, the primary purpose of their study is to increase our knowledge of the workings of the enterprise and other economic systems. For Knight, the primary role of economic theory is rather different: it is to contribute to the understanding of how by consensus based upon rational discussion we can fashion liberal society in which individual freedom is preserved and a satisfactory economic performance achieved. This vast social undertaking allows only a small role for the economist, and that role requires only a correct understanding of the central core of value theory.

See Stigler, "Frank Hyneman Knight," 58.

ings for power and advantage. It may be an imperfect solution but it is better than the alternatives.

If Knight strongly favored the free market over central state control, here again he was manifesting a Calvinist quality in his thinking. Compared with the Roman Catholic Church, Protestantism was fundamentally an individualistic religion in making each of the Protestant faithful responsible for his or her relationship with God, where salvation was a matter of individual "faith alone." This strong individualism eventually had profound social consequences outside the realm of theology. The religious beliefs of the English Puritans laid the basis for modern freedoms in the realms of both government (the democratic system) and the economy (the free market). As the distinguished German theologian Ernst Troeltsch would explain with respect to the great impact of the Puritans in shaping the basic values and social institutions of the modern age:

> The great ideas of the separation of Church and State, toleration of different Church societies alongside of one another, the principle of Voluntaryism in the formation of these Church-bodies, the (at first, no doubt, only relative) liberty of conviction and opinion in all matters of world-view and religion. Here are the roots of the old liberal theory of the inviolability of the inner personal life by the State, which was subsequently extended to more outward things; here is brought about the end of the medieval idea of civilisation, and coercive Church-and-State civilisation gives place to individual civilisation free of Church direction. The idea is at first religious. Later, it becomes secularized. . . . But its real foundations are laid in the English Puritan Revolution. The momentum of its religious impulse opened the way for modern freedom.[68]

CONCLUSION

Yet the Boston Puritans were also capable of hanging Quakers in the village square for religious heresy. Even as Protestants were oppressed elsewhere in Europe, Calvin's Geneva put limits on the tolerance for diversity of religious expression. Protestantism encouraged each small sect to fervently believe that it had found the one true faith and that dissenters were not only threats to civic harmony but also virtual (or actual) agents of the devil. Persecution of sinners proved easy to justify among the Protestant elect. The Protestant Reformation plunged Europe into many disastrous wars that went on for

150 years and with individual freedom often a casualty. If Knight was ultimately unable to fully resolve the tension between individual rights and freedoms (including the pursuit of self-interest) and the claims to the common good of the community, it must be said that he has had a lot of company in Protestant theology over the centuries.

Gradually, the Calvinist elements in Knight's economic thought would be recast by later members of the Chicago school in a more clearly libertarian direction. As one authority on Puritan thought comments, "The preponderance of modern libertarian theory—from French Huguenots, the Netherlands, Scotland and England—came from Calvinists."[69] Libertarianism may not have all the answers—libertarians also experience a tension in resolving the claims of individualism versus the demands of community—but in clearly and explicitly rejecting the orthodoxies of the progressive gospel and the prescription for the scientific management of society, contemporary libertarian thought opens the way to discussion of whole new governing philosophies.

chapter **SIX**

KNIGHT VERSUS FRIEDMAN VERSUS STIGLER

Subsequent to the prominent example set by Frank Knight, the encouragement at Chicago of an attitude of constant questioning has extended to the products of Chicago economics itself. Over the years, there has not been one Chicago view but many, held together to constitute a recognizable school by a tradition of irreverence toward intellectual authority and especially toward the follies of the progressive mainstream. In the second generation of the Chicago school, Milton Friedman and George Stigler were the two leading figures.★ Both Friedman and Stigler had studied under Knight and held him in the highest personal regard. Yet both departed significantly from his vision. In surveying the development of Chicago economics up to the early 1960s, Laurence Miller commented that Knight and others in the first Chicago generation "would not necessarily regard its direction of evolution over time as desirable in all respects."[1] In the last two decades of his career, Stigler not only rejected many of Knight's views but also disagreed in key areas with Friedman.

Friedman made heavy use of the same mathematical and statistical methods that Samuelson and his Cambridge colleagues were making standard operating pro-

---

★ Another leading figure in the second generation at Chicago was Aaron Director who had a large influence on the Chicago oral tradition in industrial organization and law and economics. However, he wrote little, thus limiting the broader impact of his ideas. As a result, he tends to be less remembered today.

cedure throughout the economics profession.★ Chicago in the second generation aided rather than resisted the methodological revolution in economics that is Samuelson's greatest claim to fame. Also in disagreement with Knight, both Friedman and Stigler regarded the efficiency of an economic system as the basic criterion of its success. Both accepted the utilitarian characterization that human beings pursue the maximization of individual happiness. The Calvinist sense of a fallen humanity in the iron grip of original sin appears in watered-down forms, if at all, in their thinking.

As his student Don Patinkin commented, Knight was "skeptical about the extent to which man could by deliberate policy-actions improve" government and other social institutions.[2] In contrast, William Niskanen would comment of Friedman's *Capitalism and Freedom* that on reading the book "one is struck by the sense of optimism about the ultimate power of ideas—a faith that closely reasoned argument, an accumulation of evidence, and a leavening of wit will persuade most people and that our governmental processes will be responsive to their preferences"—an outlook on the world closer in fact to Samuelson in this respect than to Knight.[3]

Knight may have laid the original foundation, but it was Friedman and Stigler (with Coase) who led the way for the policy and intellectual triumphs of the Chicago school in the later part of the twentieth century. A true follower of Knight would never have achieved such impact on the economics profession. (The one prominent economist who did follow more closely in Knight's path, James Buchanan—now at George Mason University in northern Virginia—did win a Nobel Prize in 1986 but has never been as fully accepted in the economics mainstream as other key figures at Chicago.) Most economists are simply too wedded to the progressive value system to embrace any such a degree of heresy as found in Knight.

Friedman's writings could receive much greater acceptance among economists because his work is best regarded as a synthesis of Samuelson and Knight—with perhaps the Samuelson element even more important in terms of both methodology and basic value assumptions. The affinity is suggested by the views of a leading current product of the Cambridge tradition in economics, Lawrence Summers.† He recounted, "As for Milton Friedman, he was the devil figure in my youth. Only with time have I come to have

---

★ In sharp contrast to Knight, Friedman stated in 1991 that he regarded "the change in the character of economic literature," requiring a much greater "command of mathematical and econometric techniques," as being "on the whole a good thing." See Milton Friedman, "Old Wine in New Bottles," *Economic Journal* 101 (January 1991): 35.

† The connection to Cambridge is more than intellectual. One of Summer's uncles (on his father's side) is Paul Samuelson. Another uncle (on his mother's side) is Kenneth Arrow.

large amounts of grudging respect. And with time, increasingly ungrudging respect."[4] As will be argued below, Friedman shared many of the basic progressive values—the tenets of the religion—but had a deeper insight into the policy actions necessary to realize these values. As an economic technician, Friedman was the most brilliant American economist of the twentieth century—and many would not limit this to the ranks of Americans.* As a moral philosopher, his efforts perhaps suffer from his peculiar mixture of progressive and libertarian values; it is a difficult combination to sustain.

A BELIEVER IN PROGRESS

Friedman's enthusiasm for the wonderful consequences for the world resulting from economic progress is evident throughout his policy writings. In the United States over its history, Friedman believes, there has been a political and economic "miracle." Immigrants to this nation achieved "rewards that were not even imaginable in the Old World," as the economy constantly "grew more prosperous and more productive." This has been the result of the free-market system "under which people make their own choices." Friedman acknowledges that in terms of impacts on individual businesses the workings of the market may have produced "more losers than winners." However, the pain of all these individual losses is not a great cause for concern, because "society as a whole benefited." Like Samuelson, Friedman never demonstrates scientifically, but simply takes as an article of faith that the "the resulting [great] addition to the wealth of the community as a whole" counts for much more than any transitional costs to individuals of the trial-and-error workings of the market along the road of progress.[5]

Friedman thus is in full agreement with a central value judgment of Samuelson's *Economics*—if he also seldom makes it explicit. The many short-run transitional costs of moving from one economic state of affairs to another, higher state can literally be ignored in the conduct of economic analysis. (Or, more formally, one might say that by initial assumption they are taken to equal zero.) They represent a minor price to be paid compared with the prospect of following down a road of economic growth and development to the gradual perfection of the human condition here on earth.

---

* Alan Walters would declare of Friedman that "the success of his advocacy has by any objective standard been enormous." Indeed, "in effectiveness, breadth and scope, his only rival among the economists of the 20th century is Keynes." See Alan Walters, "Milton Friedman," in John Eatwell, Murray Milgate, and Peter Newman, *The New Palgrave: A Dictionary of Economics* (New York: Stockton Press, 1987), 427.

Friedman also sets the same measure as Samuelson for determining the benefits of government actions—whether they will contribute to the increased material well-being of society. In Japan, he says, the economy fared much bet-ter than in India because the presence of a freer market imposed the "harsh test of efficiency."[6] In comparing the economic system of (then) West Germany with the centrally planned system of East Germany, the relevant consideration for Friedman is: "Which has prospered?" In the United States, our free-market system is a great blessing because the masses of ordinary people have achieved "levels of living" that have surpassed all previous historical experience of humankind. Indeed, the levels of "industrial progress" and "mechanical improvement" in the United States and other economically advanced nations are the "great wonders of the modern era." As a result, we in the United States have been able to "transform our society," to the enormous benefit of the citizenry as a whole.[7] In Friedman's writings there is no hint to be found of the Calvinist (and Knight) view that a high level of consumption might be a danger to one's soul, of the biblical message given by Jesus of "how hard it is for the rich to enter the kingdom of God. Indeed, it is easier for a camel to go through the eye of a needle than for a rich man to enter the kingdom of God."[8]

George Stigler on the whole exhibits a greater sense of irony than Friedman, seeing more paradox in life. If Friedman had the personal manner of a messiah, Stigler seemed to share with Knight a view that life was less scrutable and predictable; it was partly a game in which a spirit of "play" should be maintained. Yet at one point, Stigler—uncharacteristically for him—did decide to put his personal value system directly on the table, and this turned out to follow closely after Friedman's beliefs. The market is the best way of organizing society, because it both offers a maximum of freedom and is the best route to economic progress. Freedom and progress in turn can make the world a much richer and better place in which to live. As Stigler would put it,

> Important as the moral influences of the marketplace are, they have not been subjected to any real study. [Yet we can say that] the immense proliferation of general education, of scientific progress and of democracy are all coincidental in time and place with the emergence of the free enterprise system of organizing the marketplace. I believe this coincidence was not accidental: the economic progress of the past three centuries was both cause and effect of this general growth of freedom. The dominant era of the free marketplace was the nineteenth century. I believe, but with less confidence, that the absence of

major wars in that century—the only peaceable century in history—
was related to that reign of [economic] liberty. I believe, again with
less confidence, that the contemporary transformation of the British
public from a violent and unruly people into a population of almost
painful Victorian rectitude was related to this reign of liberty [and
the prosperity it brought].[9]

THE THREAT OF INTEREST-GROUP LIBERALISM

If Friedman and Stigler ultimately shared much the same faith in economic
progress with Samuelson, the Chicago school of economics was more at-
tuned to new threats to the success of progressive values emerging in American life in the years after World War II. Indeed, as noted in Chapter 4, a large
body of political science writing was already recording the failures of the
original progressive plan for American government.[10] As described by David
Truman, Robert Dahl, Charles Lindblom, Grant McConnell, Norton Long,
and a host of political scientists, the basic workings of pluralist democratic
politics in the United States were often yielding outcomes well removed
from progressive ideals of scientific management. Instead of "the public interest," the actions of the American government often seemed to be driven
by interest groups at virtually every step of the process.[11]

In the economics profession at the time, John Kenneth Galbraith was
writing—if with a more enthusiastic view—of a system of "countervailing
powers."[12] Such thinking had also extended to international arenas, where
Gunnar Myrdal commented in 1960 that "in the fully realized welfare state"
of Sweden, "resource allocation would be accomplished through a process of
bargaining among the leading social interests."[13] Reflecting the new political science consensus as it was rapidly taking shape in the United States by
the 1950s, David Truman explained in *The Governmental Process* that it was a
myth to think that American government was capable in any manner or
form of articulating a set of social goals and then pursuing these goals in a rational or scientific fashion. In the real world of American government, when
someone spoke of the public interest, it was likely to be in the form of a
rhetorical device designed to camouflage some special-interest use of the
government. As Truman would explain in 1951:

> Many . . . assume explicitly or implicitly that there is an interest of
> the nation as a whole, universally and invariably held and standing
> apart from and superior to those of the various groups included

within it. This assumption is close to the popular [progressive] dogmas of democratic government based on the familiar notion that if only people are free and have access to "the facts," they will all want the same thing in any political situation. . . . Such an assertion flies in the face of all that we know of the behavior of men in a complex society. Were it in fact true, not only the interest group but even the political party should properly be viewed as an abnormality. The differing experiences and perceptions of men not only encourage individuality but also . . . inevitably result in differing attitudes and conflicting group aspirations.

   Assertions of an inclusive "national" or "public interest" is an effective device in many . . . situations. . . . In themselves, these claims are part of the data of politics. However, they do not describe any actual or possible political situation within a complex modern nation.[14]

There was also a growing recognition by the 1950s that the progressive scheme for governing was failing in other respects as well. As things had turned out, the scientific capabilities of the field of public administration, as Herbert Simon complained as early as 1946, were much less than the progressive theorists earlier in the century had advertised.[15] In another key matter, there could be no separation of government into two distinct realms of value-laden and value-free functions, a concept asserted in the old progressive dichotomy of politics and administration. Instead, as Charles Lindblom famously wrote in 1959, the two functions of goal setting and implementation in the normal situation were inextricably interwoven in a governing process that moved only in small incremental changes; this meant among other things that any aspirations for comprehensive social and economic planning were likely to be more utopian than realistic.[16]

   The fact that progressive ideology continued to bless the workings of American government but that the interest-group realities were so different had resulted in a series of myths and fictions that were ritualistically invoked in the political process. However, few well-informed observers really believed them any longer. One prominent political scientist would write in 1961: "There is much in the democratic credo that cannot be taken literally. . . . Citizen participation, responsible government, the public interest, the democratic consensus, rule by public opinion—the operating significance of such sounds and symbols is acquired only by long habituation. We grow to learn which of the letters are silent."[17] Another leading political scientist, Theodore Lowi, would famously declare in the late 1960s that the acceptance of the central role for interest groups had become so widespread within American political science that it amounted in effect to a new public philosophy of "interest-group liberalism." ★

Yet in Lowi's opinion the workings of interest-group politics could not provide a satisfactory basis for governing; the growing acceptance of the pursuit of private advantage was creating a "crisis of public authority." † Interest-group government would "tend to cut out that part of the mass" of the people who were not represented by any powerful lobbying or other advocacy group. It would "create privilege" for certain groups skilled in politics or otherwise favored and "it is a type of privilege particularly hard to bear or combat because it is touched with the [progressive] symbolism of the state." And interest-group government would be "conservative in almost every sense of the term," because interest groups would block any changes that threatened their governmental prerogatives—as Mancur Olson would also argue a few years later in explaining why American society seemed so often to face administrative and policy gridlock.[18]

The Keynesian and Samuelsonian response to these developments was to

---

★ Lowi defined interest-group liberalism as having the following key tenets of belief:

(1) Since groups are the rule in markets and elsewhere, imperfect competition is the rule of social relations. (2) The method of imperfect competition is not really competition at all but a variant of it called bargaining—where the number of participants is small, where the relationship is face-to-face, and/or where the bargainers have "market power" which means that they have some control over the terms of their agreements and can administer rather than merely respond to their environment. (3) Without class solidarity, bargaining becomes the single alternative to violence and coercion in industrial society. (4) By definition, if the system is stable and peaceful it proves the self-regulative character of pluralism. It is, therefore, the way the system works and the way it ought to work.

See Theodore J. Lowi, *The End of Liberalism: Ideology, Politics, and the Crisis of Public Authority* (New York: W. W. Norton, 1969), 46.

† Lowi's fears of a loss of governing legitimacy in a world of interest-group liberalism proved in many ways to be correct. By the early 1990s, public opinion surveys were finding that

many Americans, as reported by the Public Agenda Foundation, [believe] that their country has been trending toward a psychology of self-interest so all-embracing that no room is left for commitment to national and community interests. They sense that we risk losing something precious to the meaning of the American experience. They fear that in the pursuit of their organizational goals, the politicians and the businessmen and the unions and the professions (not to mention the universities) have lost sight of any larger obligation to the public and are indifferent or worse to anything that does not benefit them immediately or directly—themselves or their institutions. They fear that the very meaning of the public good is disappearing in a sea of self-seeking.

Survey results quoted in Bill Moyers, "America's Vision of the Future" (keynote address to the National Legislative Education Foundation, "Democratic Issues" conference, March 8, 1991), 9.

turn to the market mechanism as the leading instrument of economic progress. The reliance on the use of the market might limit or forestall many opportunities for interest-group favoritism. However, as examined in Chapter 4, Samuelson's progressive vision still left wide latitude for an expansive role for American government. Samuelson, for example, had proposed in *Economics* that government should engage in widespread redistribution of income. The workings of interest-group liberalism suggested, however, that any such government role on a large scale was likely to end up redistributing income toward the middle and upper classes, the ones with the political power to secure the benefits of government actions.

THE "SAMUELSON VICE"

In practice, moreover, Samuelson mainly preached the virtues of the progressive value system; when it came time to challenge the interest groups that were pressing strong demands to serve their own purposes, Samuelson often seemingly lacked the courage of his own convictions. He did not have much heart for tough fights against teachers unions, welfare workers, farmers, defense firms, electric utility companies, medical and legal professional groups, and the many other beneficiaries of the welfare and regulatory state of the twentieth century. Many old Progressives had discovered that progressive plans for government offered numerous opportunities for private gain. Hence, the supposed defenders of progressive plans for government too often could now be found subverting them. In the former Soviet Union and other communist countries, a similar phenomenon had yielded a "new class" of communists who benefited greatly from positions of special privilege, even as they claimed to act in the name of the old socialist and Marxist ideals of equality. In short, if too many of the old progressive supporters had betrayed the revolution, in the United States and elsewhere, these were often Samuelson's erstwhile "liberal" political allies, and he was apparently unable or unwilling to forcefully and publicly break with them.

In *Economics,* Samuelson thus preached a gospel of economic progress as an ideal, but in a certain sense he accepted—like so many other leading intellectuals of his generation—the interest-group realities of American government. In his scientific work, the effect of his methodological revolution within the economics profession was to divert the profession from the practical problem solving in government that might have contributed to the actual advance of progressive principles. Instead, immersed in intellectually challenging scientific puzzles, the brightest members of the American economics profession avoided the nasty political disputes and other controversies that would have resulted from challenging the prerogatives of the many private beneficiaries of government actions. (Their fellow professional economists also often took this safer course in such places as the Soviet Union, but it could at least be said of the Soviet economists that they faced much greater dangers in abandoning mathematical games for genuine political engagement.)

Instead of making government work better, Samuelson concentrated on what amounted to inspirational poetry in *Economics*—and he was hardly alone. Following the publication of his *Foundations of Economic Analysis* in 1947, much of the economics profession would follow in his path.[19] The extensive mathematical symbolism has amounted to a special way of painting an inspiring picture of economic science at work, in the same way that space travel may have few practical benefits but seeks to uplift people's spirits with a vision of the power of the human mind and the awesome ability given by scientific knowledge to manipulate natural forces for human purposes. D. McCloskey describes this tendency in modern economics as a new "Samuelson vice" (following the "Ricardian vice")—the tendency "in economics over the career of Paul Samuelson . . . [to] drift away from scientific values and towards mathematical ones" for their own sake.[20] An economist can paint with a mathematical brush no less than a Van Gogh can use a brush of another kind.

NEO-NEO-PROGRESSIVISM

Rather than Samuelson, it was actually Friedman (and to a lesser extent Stigler, who was characteristically more conflicted about this role) who took on the burden of pushing the use of the market mechanism much further than Samuelson was willing to go. Ultimately, Friedman's career is best understood as seeking to uphold the viability of progressive values in the face of an intellectual crisis not only of the orthodox progressive but also of the Keynesian and Samuelson neoprogressive designs.

Admittedly, there are some passages in Friedman's most influential statement of his political and economic philosophy, *Capitalism and Freedom,* that might easily be taken for the writings of Frank Knight. "Government," Friedman declares as a "believer in liberty," is a major "threat to freedom." A main reason for "limiting and decentralizing government power" is to protect individual property and other private rights. The market offers a means of achieving "co-operation . . . without coercion."[21] All in all, the rise of big government has not only promoted widespread inefficiencies in the use of society's resources but also posed a major threat to the liberties of the citizenry.[22]

But such passages, which would be altogether out of character for Samuelson, have camouflaged the essentially progressive purposes of Friedman. If Samuelson was the most influential economist from 1945 to 1965, *Capitalism and Freedom* and other writings, in the judgment of Robert Heibroner, made Friedman "by far the most influential economist of the period" from 1965 to 1985.[23] In these writings Friedman is proposing yet another modification of the progressive plan for government—to adopt a plan for "neo–neo-Progressivism," as one might say—in the following ways.

First, while declaring once again that the market should be the primary instrument for organizing economic activity in society, Friedman is also prepared to acknowledge that there are "areas . . . that cannot be handled through the market at all, or can be handled only at so great a cost that the use of political channels may be preferable."[24] Friedman went on, however, to find that most economic Progressives—such economists as Samuelson—had left much too much responsibility in the hands of government. There were a host of areas in which these Progressives had declared that the market was "failing"—and government had stepped in to solve such alleged market failings—but Friedman now found the economic justifications faulty. Indeed, the government was typically making matters worse, an outcome all the more likely in light of the growing recognition that interest-group decision making was the norm for government allocation of the resources of society.

Hence, Friedman proposed that the government should step aside from its current efforts in a number of important areas. It would be desirable to deregulate the airline, railroad, trucking, and other transportation industries. The government should remove its support for various medical, legal, and other professional curbs on competition. Government should be more cautious about antitrust enforcement, because the actual extent of market competition was a more subtle matter than the typical economic theories of antitrust enforcement had supposed. Internationally, governments should cease trying to maintain fixed exchange rates and instead let the market determine the price of foreign currency. Using the military draft to obtain personnel for the army tended to yield a less skilled and less motivated body of soldiers and should be replaced by an all-volunteer army.[25]

Yet Friedman did not rule out the necessity of government interventions in a variety of areas. For example, the federal government would still need large revenues for national defense. Friedman was among the first to propose that rather than the current hodgepodge of federal income tax rates and loopholes, a flat tax would be both more efficient and more equitable. Fried-man also accepted a significant redistributive role for government. However, rather than suggesting a complex blend of income and in-kind transfers to poor people as under the existing welfare system, Friedman proposed to simplify matters with the negative income tax, involving the transfer of money directly to the poor by a much simpler formula with fewer adverse effects on work incentives.* Friedman objected strongly to the past conduct seen in monetary policy but proposed a better governmental strategy here as well—government monetary interventions should be based on more-predictable and less discretionary rules of monetary management.

In a number of areas government might have to provide goods and services to the citizenry. Rather than employing direct government efforts, it would be more efficient, Friedman suggested, to leave this provision to private suppliers. Friedman's most famous proposal along these lines was for education vouchers, an idea that has since been extended to housing vouchers, medical expense accounts, and other forms of social service. In the case of other government functions such as garbage collection, street cleaning, park management, and so forth, it would often make sense—assuming that these functions should not be privatized outright—for government to contract directly for their provision with private companies (perhaps selected by competitive bid).

Here again, the result was not a rejection of progressive values, but a better way of realizing them. The President's Commission on Privatization would report in 1988 that "contracting out . . . represents a revival in a new form of the old Progressive distinction between politics and administration, with the private contractor now taking the former place of the expert government administrator" in the earlier progressive thinking.[26] As Friedman was proposing, the role of democratic decision making should be limited to the tasks of setting overall contract objectives and the selection of a suitable private contractor, excluding day-to-day politics from the actual private performance of the service delivery. Privatization was a new and superior way of achieving the old progressive goal of separating the politics from the administration.

By the end of the twentieth century many of Friedman's proposals had been accepted by governments all over the world.[27] In many cases, reflecting the essentially progressive values served, Friedman's policy designs had been taken up by old socialist and labor parties. In New Zealand the Labour Party, abandoning its former socialist beliefs, implemented a comprehensive set of

---

* This idea, like many of Friedman's most important policy proposals, had previously surfaced (often at Chicago) but Friedman advocated them with a new energy and effectiveness. Indeed, Stigler had suggested a negative income tax many years before.

privatization initiatives in the 1980s and 1990s, based in many cases on market principles similar to those Friedman had long advocated.[28] China had embarked on extensive privatization programs within its economy, as had India to a lesser extent. The earned income tax credit (a version of Friedman's negative income tax proposal) was backed strongly in the 1990s by the Clinton administration. Charter schools, also a Clinton initiative, represented an adaptation of the voucher idea that could provide a new element of competition in the school environment.

If Samuelson had been timid in confronting the interest-group threats to the viability of the progressive cause, Friedman showed no hesitations about plunging into the political fray. He seemingly relished the chance to criticize interest groups and others who put their own private benefits and prerogatives in the way of better—more truly dedicated to economic progress—government. Friedman showed a general zest for political combat in the service of the cause that was seemingly alien to Samuelson's temperament. (The one exception might be macroeconomics, where Samuelson did become politically involved in support of Keynesian solutions, but this area of policy also posed no great threat to any powerful welfare-state clientele.) In a lecture celebrating his Nobel Prize, Friedman told the story of how he had first learned in 1976 of winning the award. In an event typical of his active involvement throughout his career, he had encountered an unexpected horde of reporters at a Michigan airport where he was traveling to begin a speaking tour in favor of a state constitutional amendment to require a balanced budget and to limit state spending.[29]

Besides having a greater zeal for political combat, Friedman had also thought more deeply than Samuelson about many of the practical problems of governing. If Samuelson was the leading preacher of neoprogressive values in his textbook *Economics* and in other writings, Friedman was the master technician. In terms of doing concrete, practical things to make the system work, as opposed to making symbolic statements of ideals, in the end it was Friedman, not Samuelson, who was the truer progressive. Norman Pearlstine, the former managing editor of the *Wall Street Journal* and now editor in chief of *Time,* commented in 1998 that John Maynard Keynes "had tremendous influence over economic policy through the Depression and in the years after World War II." However, Pearlstine considered that looking back from the end of the twentieth century, the impact of Friedman's ideas had proved more important than those of Keynes: "My own vote for economist of the century goes to Milton Friedman, whose books . . . articulate the importance of free markets and the dangers of undue government intervention."[30]

STIGLER VERSUS FRIEDMAN

Despite his devout belief in the benefits of economic progress and the progressive character of much of his writing, Friedman is sometimes described as a libertarian who has fought valiantly for the cause of freedom in American life. His efforts to curb the role of government undoubtedly did serve this cause. Yet the wide acceptance of his policy proposals in American government has not reflected any great impact in persuading the majority of American economists or the American people that their government poses a serious threat to personal liberty. Indeed, among those who did not take Friedman's professed worries in this regard all that seriously was Friedman's own Chicago colleague George Stigler.

Empirically, as Stigler stated in 1988, "the American citizen of today is regulated much more" than in the late 1940s, yet "his range of economic choices has become wider . . . and his main political rights . . . have not been seriously impaired."[31] On another occasion, Stigler declared that "on the subject of liberty the conservative should either become silent or find something useful to say"—in contrast to past "incantations" about losses of freedom typically made by many conservative thinkers in the absence of real "evidence." Stigler virtually seemed to be admonishing Friedman (and Hayek) when he indicated that others have been prone to "preach the imminent disappearance of freedom" even when they did not really know what they were "talking about."[32]

At the heart of their differences is a broader tension that arose between Friedman and Stigler concerning the motivating role of ideas (shall we say religion) versus the role of self-interest in American life (although it must also be said that neither was entirely consistent over the years). Friedman's career makes sense only as the expression of a deeply held belief in the power of ideas to change the world. According to Friedman, the current problem is that American progressive government in the past has had the wrong ideas (socialist, Keynesian, Samuelsonian, and so on) and this has many had harmful consequences. Friedman's lifetime mission has been to persuade the American public of the correct ideas, and thus the correct form of government, a task to which he devoted great energy, in writing *Newsweek* columns, appearing on television shows, writing popular books, and other efforts to publicize his views.[33] Friedman in a sense acknowledged the powerful impact of the progressive ideas of scientific management by the very amount of effort he devoted to opposing them.

Yet Friedman never seemed to feel the need to explain why he believed so strongly that ideas can move the world; he apparently simply took it for granted as an article of faith. However, as Frank Knight had suggested, original sin (or some modern equivalent) might have infected every area of life. A devotion to personal gain might reign not only in the marketplace and in the governing realm but also in the intellectual realm, making any appeals to higher ideals unlikely to succeed. Friedman clearly regarded himself as acting out of and appealing to higher values than simple self-interest (if he made a large amount of money from his books, that was not the main purpose).

Stigler at one point in his career seemed to agree with Friedman that the public acceptance of good or bad ideas could be important. In 1959 he would write that if "leading economists of the period" had been more diligent in exposing the failings of socialist thinkers of the late nineteenth and early twentieth centuries, they could have averted at least some of the mistakes of "modern English socialism."[34] Eventually, however, Stigler's thinking changed in this regard. He pushed the assumption of self-interest further than Friedman had, extending it to arenas such as the motives of university professors and other intellectuals. He saw government as exclusively a realm for self-interest, where ideas (presumably including Friedman's or his own as well) could never be much more than tools of political combat utilized in the service of particular private interests. As Stigler pressed forward with such views, he came to see government as in essence little more than a new arena for the economic exchange of goods and services. Exchange in the market reflected individual calculations in response to market prices; in government similar kinds of exchanges took place but less formally in response to implicit political prices.

The political system would seem, admittedly, to be a more cumbersome means of exchange because it is in essence a barter system. The market has the great advantage that the use of money and prices acts powerfully to rationalize the overall processes of economic exchange. Once government is conceived in these terms, a smaller role for it would seem to be a virtually inevitable conclusion—why substitute the clumsy processes of political barter for the efficiency of a market process? Yet, among political scientists in the 1950s and 1960s, the message of interest-group liberalism was that American government was in fact becoming a large national bazaar for a vast range of trading activities. By the 1960s, the public choice school in economics was affirming essentially the same vision, if now stated in a more formal economic language.[35]

However, if the transaction costs of political exchange can be reduced, the difference in efficiency may not be so great. Indeed, Stigler gradually came to believe that this was the case. By 1979 he would be saying that many political "conservatives" (presumably including Stigler himself in earlier incarnations) had been led astray by "mistake" theories in which it is alleged that in the activities of government "a misinformed populace has acted against its own interests."[36] Frank Knight, for example, Stigler wrote, "had often expressed the belief that many economists still share, that the actors (and especially the voters) in political life are ignorant, emotional, and usually irrational."[37] Friedman and Hayek also belonged to the category of "mistake" theorists of public opinion, as Stigler now characterized such misguided understandings that attributed a large role to ideas (if mistaken) in the workings of government.

Yet as Stigler realized, any assumption of widespread error in decision making was uncongenial to the Chicago school of economics. Another long-standing part of the Chicago tradition—one reason that it believes markets work so well—is an assumption of full rationality in individual behavior. Consumers, for example, understand their own preferences exactly, know price options precisely, and respond perfectly to maximize their individual welfare. For the amount of income they have to spend, no one could possibly do any better. Stigler now pushed this kind of thinking in a radically new direction for Chicago. If people can see their way to behave so rationally in the marketplace, might similar rationality perhaps characterize behavior in the political arena as well? Perhaps there as well they can see the available tradeoffs precisely, and make political deals carefully calculated to maximize their welfare. Why should rational behavior not extend to finding ways to reduce the transaction costs of political bargaining, thus perhaps even approaching the efficiency of a market system (if with a different starting point in the distribution of assets)?

As Stigler gradually pushed forward with such a way of thinking about government, one upshot was that he became less troubled than Friedman by the rise of government power. Even if it was less efficient (which now appeared much less obvious than many Chicago economists including Stigler himself in his earlier years had been saying), government did not represent any actual threat of a "leviathan." Thus, from Stigler's evolving perspective Friedman's incessant preaching in *Capitalism and Freedom* and other writings is largely a waste of time. If Friedman believed in the power of a (secular) religion of progress to move the world, Stigler was inclined to dismiss the real influence not only of this but also of any such set of ideological convictions to drive the actions of government.

RATIONAL POLITICS

Indeed, Stigler would eventually argue that the businesses, labor unions, and other economic interests involved in the affairs of government are fully capable of successful efforts to make progressive government serve their own purposes. Government powers can in fact prove very useful. The unique legal ability of government to make use of powers of coercion can sometimes be used to reduce transaction costs significantly.[38] It can force a minority of dissenting members of a workforce, for example, to join a labor union that most of their fellow workers support. The government can impose a degree of coordination on separate and independent firms that otherwise might have to be accomplished by horizontal and vertical integration within a single firm. Government can enforce cartel agreements otherwise impossible to sustain privately among a set of atomistic firms. All in all, Stigler would write, even in a world of big government, "political systems are rationally devised and rationally employed, which is to say that they are instruments for the fulfillment of desires of members of the society."[39] The powers of government could in essence be privatized and in that capacity they could serve usefully almost in the manner of a new kind of system of de facto private rights.

In the case of government regulation of industry, Stigler's ideas in this regard—a main factor for his winning the Nobel Prize in economics in 1982—had a significant influence on the broader thinking of the economics profession. In most cases, Stigler wrote in 1971, "regulation is acquired by the industry and is designed and operated primarily for its benefit" with the aim "to increase its profitability." Resembling a market transaction, "the industry which seeks political power must go to the appropriate seller, the political party." The regulated industry in effect makes a payment to the party in terms of "the two things a party needs: votes and resources."[40] In return, regulation might be described as creating new industry-wide rights of exclusion and control over entry and other matters.[41]

In later writings Stigler would extend such thinking to many—perhaps most—of the traditional activities of government. In general, he came increasingly to believe that fully rational individuals will take into account the likely behavior of government and will act to make use of the possibilities created. The concept of Robert Lucas and other developers of "rational expectations" theory—that individuals anticipate government fiscal and monetary policies and then determine their own actions in response to such expectations—has wider implications than for macroeconomic policy alone. Indeed, Stigler wrote extensively on what might be described as a rational expectations model of politics and government in general. It was a theory where Stigler now saw "rational political processes" constantly acting in all areas of government.[42]

Moreover, the longer the time period for adjustment and learning, the smaller the likelihood of any government errors in the allocation of resources. For example, tariffs and usury laws had existed for centuries in many societies. The attribution of such policies—in the manner of Milton Friedman, for example—to intellectual "confusion," Stigler suggests, is "singularly obfuscatory." When a government policy has been in place for a long time, the only proper conclusion is that the results serve an important practical purpose in society. By 1980, toward the end of his career (he died in 1991), Stigler would state that "we economists have traditionally made innumerable criticisms of the inefficiency of various policies, criticisms which have often been to their own (and my own) utter satisfaction. The meager success of these criticisms in changing these policies, I am [now] convinced, stems from the fact that more than narrow efficiency has been involved in almost every case—that inexplicit or incomprehensible goals were served by these policies and served tolerably efficiently."[43]

Even though Stigler is a great admirer of Adam Smith, he criticizes even Smith's policy views on these grounds:

> I wish to recur for a moment to the policy of mercantilism, which Smith attributed to the clever machinations of the merchants and traders against the simple, honorable landowners who still constituted the government class of Great Britain in his time. Smith and his followers should have asked themselves whether simple error could persist, to the large and centuries-long cost of a class intelligent enough to hire the likes of Edmund Burke. I say, with great fear and trembling, that it is more probable that Smith, not the nobility of England, was mistaken as to the cost and benefits of the mercantile system.[44]

In his 1982 review of the history of the Chicago school, Melvin Reder commented on this "serious intellectual disagreement . . . between Friedman and Stigler." The Stigler analysis was yielding the strong policy conclusion that "from Smith to Keynes to Friedman, reformers have all been deluded." Or if reformer behavior is seen to be rational in any sense (as a good Chicago economist must assume it to be), it will be rational only in serving the private needs of the reformer. It will consist of nothing more than individuals "agitating for their own amusement or private advantage," such as earning higher consulting incomes and appearance fees for speeches. Hence, the two domains of "economic science" and of "influencing public policy" can and should have little intersection: "there is no reason for individuals interested in the former to be engaged in the latter."[45]

Reder comments that the close personal friendship between Friedman and Stigler served to inhibit a no-holds-barred public airing of their basic disagreements.★ Yet "despite the lack of public debate the fact of the disagreement has been well-known at Chicago for the last decade."[46]

IDEAS DO MATTER

This disagreement between Friedman and Stigler reflected an element of intellectual confusion at Chicago that has never been adequately resolved. Given the traditional framework of Chicago analysis—to which Friedman himself had often contributed in his many oral and written expositions of price theory—Stigler was more correct than Friedman. The role of transaction costs tended to be minimized in the style of Chicago analysis (with Coase as a conspicuous exception, one reason he will be discussed later, in Part IV). People could behave as rationally as Chicago assumed because they could obtain all the necessary information and make all the necessary calculations to maximize their well-being. Indeed, for the purposes of analysis, price theory at Chicago in those days typically assumed—explicitly or implicitly—perfect information and perfect equilibrium. Yet if transaction costs were reduced to zero, government and the market would be equally (indeed both perfectly) efficient. While he might have expressed it somewhat differently, that was in essence what Stigler was saying when he described a world of rational political outcomes to match the rational outcomes of the market.

However, if Stigler was correct theoretically in terms of the Chicago tradition, he was wrong empirically. Stigler to the contrary, ideas do matter. The career of Ronald Coase has been characterized by a dispassionate observation of the facts and a dedication to describing the world however he found it. Coase took Stigler to task for his views: "As I watch people who are engaged in political activities, whether through voting in a parliamentary system or by taking part in political, including revolutionary, movements, supporting with enthusiasm policies which seem likely to greatly harm or

---

★ Friedman and Stigler remained close throughout their careers. They shared an office at the University of Minnesota before either had come to the University of Chicago. In 1946, the economics department at Chicago sought to appoint Stigler to a position on the faculty. When the university president turned Stigler down, following what Stigler later deemed must have been an unsatisfactory interview, Friedman received the appointment instead. Stigler went to Columbia and did not come to Chicago until 1958. This 1946 episode did not seem to have any negative consequences for their long-standing friendship.

even destroy the countries and perhaps themselves, I find it difficult to be-lieve that such behavior is best described as rational utility-maximizing." [47]

Ironically, some of the most powerful evidence of the impact of ideas on government is provided by the Chicago school of economics itself. Consis-tent with his broader viewpoint, Stigler was pessimistic that Chicago think-ing could ever have much impact on the design of American economic institutions and American government more broadly. The decades of the 1980s and 1990s, however, turned out to be a period of great triumph for Chicago. Friedman's and other Chicago ideas for privatization and other steps towards smaller government would in fact have a major influence on government decisions, not only in the United States (in the form of the deregulation movement) but also in many other nations around the world. James Tobin would comment in the 1980s that Friedman's 1967 presidential address to the American Economic Association, addressing matters of the natural rate of unemployment and of inflation, was "very likely the most in-fluential article ever published in an economics journal." [48] And if it was not this article, many of the other leading contenders would be pieces written either by Friedman or others in the Chicago school (ironically sometimes including Stigler). The ideas of the Chicago school have not only won many intellectual victories in the past quarter of a century but have moved the world of government and policy in the most practical of terms.

At the same time, however, this outcome poses a problem for Chicago economics. According to Stigler's way of thinking—and he was logically ex-tending the Chicago framework—Friedman never should have had the pol-icy successes that he achieved. Friedman's own career has in some sense been a one-man refutation of much that Chicago stood for, a delicate subject that neither Friedman nor Stigler, nor most others at Chicago, seemingly have ever fully confronted.

In another paradox, Friedman's triumph raised the stakes higher with re-spect to future threats of big government. If government once grew too large because of bad progressive ideas, had now shrunk in the 1980s and 1990s be-cause of good Chicago ideas, it could grow again under a new misguided set of ideas in the future. Friedman's views suggested that government is likely always to have immense power to do good or evil, that there will always be a war of ideas to influence government for better or for worse. Stigler's think-ing ultimately suggested that there might be a virtual indifference toward the relative roles of government and the market.

To be sure, the reality is that people are not, and can never be, as rational as many economists have long assumed, and Chicago economists in their as-sumptions and mode of analysis have been inclined to take to the extreme.

As will be examined in Chapter 8, a new institutional school is emerging today within the American economics profession based in part on this view. In a world where large uncertainties are the norm, where transaction costs will often be high, and for a host of other real-world reasons, there is abundant evidence that ideas (good and bad) can have a major impact on government—and business—outcomes. Broad ideas, if nothing else, might be viewed as a necessary way of economizing on information gathering. In the real world it will often be necessary to apply broad principles based on previous experience and to take other such heroic measures as a means simply to limit transaction costs.

AN ECONOMICS OF PUBLIC OPINION

Traditionally, there has been little effort made by economists to explore the development of ideas and their application to policy as a subject of legitimate economic inquiry in itself. However, in a 1995 book Timur Kuran seeks to develop such an analysis. In emphasizing the importance of "public opinion" in shaping events in the world, his book departs in this respect from a traditional Chicago way of thinking. Nevertheless, in other respects Kuran's analysis is very much in the spirit of Chicago economics. His overall plan is to analyze how individual incentives to maximize benefits minus costs may combine to produce different outcomes in public opinion—and consequently in public policy as well. Indeed, Kuran's analysis may shed some useful light on how Friedman and a few fellow economists in the Chicago school might have had such extraordinary worldwide influence on public opinion and then on government policy over the past quarter of a century.

Kuran begins with the observation that there are two kinds of opinion, private and public. Then, if each person considers whether to express his or her private opinion as his or her public opinion, there will be many occasions where such an action is likely to involve costs to the individual. Pressures of social conformity, and the fear of being labeled an "eccentric," for example, could make the public statement of an unconventional viewpoint a cause of considerable anxiety, and in some cases a direct economic burden (an angry employer might fire a "troublemaker" employee). In many circumstances, the private costs are likely to exceed the private benefits of "being honest," and the person will refrain—as Kuran develops his analysis—from revealing his or her private opinion in the public arena. The overall result will be that people will commonly tell "public lies" that in fact differ considerably from their "private truths."[49]

Kuran also thinks, like Friedman, that the content of public opinion plays a major role in deciding public policy. Yet his model of the manner of formation of public opinion suggests that it will often be difficult to change public opinion, and that unpopular governments may persist over long periods with much disliked policies, even though many citizens actually want a new government (but are unwilling to say so in public).[50] Kuran's model can also help to explain why at some moments there may be surprisingly rapid shifts in public opinion and then in government policy.[51] Once some people start to speak out, and thus the private costs of being honest in public begin to fall, more people will speak out, creating further new private incentives for public truthfulness, and all in all a "virtuous circle" may ensue.

Indeed, it may be just such a set of forces that can explain why Chicago economics has had so much impact on public opinion. The crucial element here is the strong tradition of public outspokenness at Chicago in the face of conventional wisdom, manifested since the days when Frank Knight made it a trademark of Chicago. Friedman and many other Chicago economists have seemed almost to enjoy expressing in public ideas that could provoke outrage and anger among many of their fellow citizens, and sometimes many of their professional colleagues as well. Even in 1976 when he was receiving the Nobel Prize, Niels Thygesen commented that it was surprising that Friedman "has not to a greater extent earned the gratitude of the profession. To a large degree this is due to the sharply critical form in which he has presented his ideas," even though "it is doubtful that any other economist has had a comparable impact on the public debate."[52]

Tobin on one occasion in the 1960s noted that "many controversies on monetary theory and policy pit Friedman and his followers against the rest of the profession."[53] Most economists would have lacked the courage or force of will to stand up to the pressures of a virtual professional consensus in opposition to their views. Rose Friedman recently related how her husband required special security guards and otherwise was partly sheltered from normal public exposure when he received his Nobel Prize in economics in Stockholm in 1976—owing partly to the controversy created by a 1970s visit to give policy advice to the government of Chile (advising Chile to follow policies, it might be noted, widely attacked at the time but not so much later followed by many Latin American countries).[54]

The manner in which Friedman's policy proposals have come to be adopted has often followed the general pattern described by Kuran for rapid shifts of public opinion. There is an initial strong negative reaction to Friedman's ideas that may persist for some time. Friedman and his Chicago colleagues are likely to be derided for their unrealism and dismissed as out of touch. Other economists and policy makers are likely to keep any private agreement with Friedman to themselves. However, when the tide of public opinion begins to shift, aided by the presence of Friedman and other Chicago economists who have absorbed the heaviest blows at the forefront of controversy, large shifts can seemingly occur almost overnight. Friedman relates the example of how in 1969 top officials from the International Monetary Fund (IMF) "dismissed my proposal for floating exchange rates as utterly impractical, as visionary theorizing by an academic who did not understand the real world." Only two years later in 1971 the Bretton Woods system of fixed exchange rates would collapse. The secretary general of the IMF was then describing "floating exchange rates as the only practicable system, and dismissed fixed exchange rates as having been completely discredited by recent experience." [55]

Not all Friedman's many public policy proposals have made the transition to conventional wisdom in such a short period. One that did was abolition of the military draft in the United States, which came with sudden swiftness in the early 1970s. The deregulation of the U.S. transportation industry seemed implausible in 1976, but the deed was mostly done by new laws enacted in 1978 and 1980. [56] Even where matters have proceeded more gradually—as in, say, the debate over education vouchers—Friedman's willingness to take a controversial stand in the face of wide public (and often professional) hostility has had a significant impact on the development of public opinion. Friedman, by endorsing a policy idea and then when joined by other Chicago economists, can significantly reduce the private costs of speaking truthfully in public for other economists, policy analysts, and eventually politicians as well.

Chicago economists may or may not be smarter than other economists. It is in fact implausible that their sheer intellectual capabilities could have been so much greater that it would explain how they have had so much larger an influence on government policy than most other economists. Indeed, the specific policy proposals of Friedman and other Chicago economists are often derivable from the unflinching application of one big idea—that the free market can do many things—an idea that it has seemed initially heretical (and bad form in public) to propose.

A CHICAGO ANALYSIS OF CHICAGO

Still, this explanation for the policy successes of the Chicago school leaves out one key question: why has the Chicago school been so willing to tolerate heresy, perhaps even value it for its own sake, when other economics departments have shown many fewer proclivities of this kind? Indeed, the role of the heretic seems to violate the very principle of maximizing benefits minus costs that has been central to Chicago thinking. The role of the person willing to stand up to all the forces of institutional authority historically has been more characteristic of the religious zealot than the utilitarian maximizer of self-interest.

The fact that Chicago economists show little introspection about their own behavioral motives is perhaps not in itself a major practical concern. Yet in other fields a professional practitioner is expected to understand his or her own behavior before offering advice to others. A psychoanalyst, for example, is limited in treating patients until that person has undergone a full professional analysis conducted by a qualified fellow psychoanalyst.

In the case of Chicago economics, however, there has been no similar requirement. If a Chicago (or other) economist were to undertake such an analysis, he or she would have to ask first what the individual benefits and costs are of being a controversialist in the typical manner of Chicago. The benefits potentially might include winning tenure, future consulting income, getting a better office, having more secretarial and other support, and so forth. To be sure, this begs the question of how the Chicago economics department decides tenure, salary, and other benefits.

In a heroic simplification—ignoring some significant collective action problems—one might assume that maximization of individual faculty welfare at Chicago is consistent with maximization of Chicago school resources as a whole. Yet there is also no good empirical or theoretical work that relates resources received by the Chicago department (or economics departments at other universities) to the set of activities going on there. It would be altogether contrary to the spirit of Chicago economics to assume that rewards to Chicago economists would be determined in any systematic and precise way by objective intellectual merit. In the Chicago spirit, Chicago economists must be presumed, like everyone else, to pursue their individual advantage, and truthfulness and individual advantage need not necessarily have any close correlation.

At best one might think that rewards to an individual Chicago economist could somehow be related to the prevailing departmental opinion at Chicago concerning his or her merit, and similarly for the rewards to the whole Chicago economics department depending on perceptions of merit within the larger profession. In short, it would seem that thinking about the behavior of individual Chicago economists—in terms of a framework of Chicago analysis—would require a theory of how professional opinion is formed within economics, and thus professional rewards might be handed out.

For this purpose, it is helpful again to turn to Kuran's model of the formation of public opinion. It requires only modest adjustments to apply essentially the same thinking to the dynamic processes by which professional expert opinion (economic or otherwise) is formed. There is likely to be a conventional wisdom among professional economists about various economic subjects—including the merits of individual economists and of specific economic ideas—and any economist who violates this professional understanding is likely to incur significant personal costs. For a young economist, for example, any demonstration of significant tendencies toward economic heresy is likely to significantly diminish the prospect of winning tenure.

Thus, one can expect, as Kuran describes for public opinion in general, that most economists—especially younger ones—will stay well within the existing conventional wisdom of the profession and will keep any divergent opinions private. But what about Chicago? Kuran does find that public opinion can have multiple equilibria, dependent on chance historical events relating to the benefits and costs of public expression of private opinions. It is possible that, if one or a few people are willing to speak out, the overall costs of speaking one's true private views will be less, and a more honest public discussion (or professional viewpoint) will result.

Perhaps, as has been noted, Frank Knight was the chance historical event in the case of the Chicago school of economics, the reason why he is still today held in such high esteem there. Perhaps the greatest benefits at Chicago were bestowed on precisely those economists who showed the greatest independence of mind, including an eagerness to offend the conventional wisdom if it can be at all justified.* Still, this attempt to model the behavior of the Chicago school remains incomplete, because it does not have an answer to the question of why outside funding for the Chicago department remains available. It is not as though the University of Chicago, or Chicago economics on its own, has a much larger endowment—and thus can offer much greater freedom of expression—compared with that of, say, Harvard or Yale, where views have tended to stay closer to the mainstream of professional opinion. Indeed, assuming that outside funders pursue their own private interests, one would assume that funds would be available to the

---

* As James Buchanan relates, "To Frank Knight nothing was sacrosanct, not the dogmas of religion, not the laws and institutions of the social order, not the prevailing moral norms, not the accepted interpretations of sacred or profane texts. Anything and everything was a potential subject for critical scrutiny." Knight was in fact a "radical critic" who believed that "we should, indeed, pay attention to those whose ideas have been influential, but our objective is to learn from their errors, not to celebrate their final achievement of truth." See James M. Buchanan, "Frank H. Knight," in Edward Shils, ed., *Remembering the University of Chicago* (Chicago: University of Chicago Press, 1991), 245, 246.

Chicago economics department only to the extent that the department serves these outside private interests.

ECONOMIC MISSIONARIES

Within the standard framework of thought of the Chicago school of economics, it thus seems difficult to understand its own existence. It is another example of a certain degree of intellectual confusion at Chicago, despite its great intellectual triumphs in other respects. Indeed, there may be little alternative but to turn to ideas and motives outside the normal framework of Chicago thinking in order to find a way of explaining the behavior of Chicago economists. Many of them may not be responding to price and other economic incentives but may simply believe in what they are doing. They may be willing to sacrifice to continue doing it, even when such efforts may come at some professional cost, and perhaps at some personal loss (as in a life in which some normal pleasures are foregone in an ascetic dedication to scholarly pursuits). The many economic heretics at Chicago may be like most of the other heretics of history, in essence possessed of a certain amount of religious zeal and who simply feel "compelled to do it."

Outside the economics profession, most people assume that such motivations are commonplace in the world, in the most extreme cases producing people such as Mother Teresa and other candidates for sainthood. Indeed, this hypothesis does an adequate job of predicting many features of the behavior of Friedman, Stigler, and other Chicago economists. It is quite obvious to most people that, temperamentally, Friedman is a born proselytizer. As Gary Becker would write in a personal tribute, Friedman has "a missionary's zeal in the worship of truth"; he has shown a deep commitment to the "appreciation of markets and free enterprise, frank and blunt discussion, and enormous zeal to convince the heathen."[57]

Although he died young (not yet fifty-five years old), another Chicago economist, Harry Johnson, produced twenty books and 525 articles. Nothing has been said of Johnson thus far, partly because he did not have any one or two large ideas that had a major impact on the profession, and partly because he died so young that he did not achieve all the awards and honors that otherwise might have been expected. In many ways, his greatest capacities were critical and his greatest successes were in helping others, including during a period as an editor of the *Journal of Political Economy*. These factors notwithstanding, Edward Shils includes Johnson as one of the great figures in the history of the University of Chicago. As Shils states in his remembrance,

Johnson had an astonishing capacity for work. Lying in a hospital bed in Italy after suffering a stroke, Johnson was determined that "I still have to work." Shils comments that "he believed in economic analysis." He thought that "intellectual integrity in the discussion of public policy would be impossible without the mastery and advancement of economic analysis." Shils considered that Johnson, dying at a young age, "gave his life" to this cause. It was, as Johnson declared of his own efforts, his "missionary" role in life.[58]

What Friedman or other Chicago economists would say about the actual motives of economists for doing economics—and whether they would acknowledge an element of the religious crusader in their own motives—is hard to know. Friedman is not inclined toward introspective analysis. Stigler on occasion playfully suggested that members of the American economics profession might be as much preachers or priests as scientists. When asked to deliver the Tanner lectures at Harvard in 1980, he gave them the title "Economics or Ethics?"[59] In his 1988 memoirs, three years before his death, Stigler captioned one of the pictures included in the book as "Prophet Frank Knight and three of his disciples"—showing Stigler as one of the three disciples.[60] A university community, Stigler suggested elsewhere, bears many similarities to a "medieval monastery."[61]

Ultimately, however, these religious terms would seem to be mere figures of speech—although perhaps also Stigler's way of hinting at some complicated matters that he preferred not to delve into much further. In any case, Stigler in most cases says that he agrees with Friedman that economics is genuinely a positive science. In his 1964 presidential address to the members of the American Economic Association, Stigler went so far as to suggest that the economics profession was "finally at the threshold of its golden age." A "scientific revolution of the very first magnitude" had taken place, making it possible to achieve much more precise "empirical estimation of economic relationships." Indeed, seemingly endorsing the broad agenda of the Samuelson project for economics, Stigler declared that "the age of quantification is now full upon us. We are now armed with a bulging arsenal of techniques of quantitative analysis, and of a power—as compared to untrained common sense—comparable to the displacement of archers by cannon."[62]

CONCLUSION

Stigler's declared commitment to the scientific practice of economics matched Friedman's crusading zeal to promote the free market in American society. Yet the ethos of science is also outside the normal Chicago framework of maximization of individual interest; in the scientific ideal one should pursue truth, whatever personal cost may be incurred. Stigler at times himself seemed to regard his own scientific motives in such a light.

From this perspective, Friedman and Stigler are perhaps best seen as co-religionists with Samuelson in seeking—if each in a somewhat different way—to advance economic progress in the world. Such a view, however, is inconsistent with the basic precepts of Chicago economics, as applied to analyze the behavior of just about everyone else in the world but fellow members of the Chicago school. Perhaps the error lies in Chicago's possible failure to understand some central element of the human experience—the role of religion (now frequently found in secular forms) in shaping events of the world, including the activities of the economists of the Chicago school.

In the end it is easy to see Friedman as a follower in the Jewish messianic tradition, offering a new message of salvation for the world. If seldom showing the same crusading zeal, Stigler for much of his career joined in this effort with Friedman. The shifts in his thinking in his last two decades might be regarded as a return to closer to the spirit of his old teacher Frank Knight. In a world where men (and women, too) are all infected by sin, crusading to perfect government will do little good. Life is a paradox; as Knight often said, the best attitude is a spirit of play; enjoy it if you can and don't expect too much. Stigler seemed to take particular delight in his later years in puncturing every orthodoxy, including some of his own. Whether he realized it or not, it was Stigler the old-fashioned Protestant skeptic of human nature reemerging in the secular guise of an economist.

chapter **SEVEN**

CHICAGO VERSUS THE TEN COMMANDMENTS

A third generation of Chicago economists has now won its Nobel Prizes, including Gary Becker in 1992 and Robert Lucas in 1995. Richard Posner, trained as a lawyer (first in his class at Harvard Law School), taught at the University of Chicago Law School from 1969 until being appointed in 1981 to the federal appeals court for the seventh circuit (where he is now chief judge). He has continued to write prolifically and for the past thirty years has been a leading participant in the development of the law-and-economics literature—the application of economic ways of thinking to traditional legal questions. Although Posner's legal background and style of scholarship make it unlikely that he will win the Nobel Prize in economics, one survey of economics journal articles that were published in 1990 found more citations to Posner's writings than to those of any other authority, economic or otherwise.[1]

The third generation has followed closely in the Chicago tradition in a number of respects. A fellow economist at Chicago, Sherwin Rosen, notes that Becker has been "one of the greatest risk takers in all the social sciences" and that initially his work has been "viewed skeptically and often with disdain by the economics establishment." Yet, like others at Chicago he would eventually be vindicated; by the 1990s it was apparent to all that "Becker has had an immense intellectual impact and influence in the economics profession."[2] Victor Fuchs has described Becker as "one of the most influential social scientists of the second half of the twentieth century."

He notes that "now, throughout the United States and in other countries, there are research programs in law and economics, health, fertility, and the family; they are all, in part, a tribute to Becker's influence."[3] Becker is rare for an economist in that his writings have been as influential in fields such as sociology and demography as they have been among economists (he holds an appointment in the department of sociology at Chicago as well).[4]

The more recent economists of the Chicago school have continued to promote a policy agenda of smaller government, as Becker has regularly done in his columns for *Business Week* magazine that began in 1985 (the year after Friedman stopped writing his *Newsweek* column).[5] It is illuminating, however, that in Becker's most famous work, *A Treatise on the Family*, among a large number of economists mentioned, there is only one citation to Friedman (dating back to 1955) and none to Stigler (other than an article co-authored by Becker with Stigler).[*] The Chicago tradition of disdain for established authority would now take a new direction in the economics of Becker and Posner. In turning to such subjects as racial discrimination, marriage, criminal behavior, the family, or other "sociological" matters, a main object of Chicago irreverence would now be the traditional moral outlooks of ordinary Americans.[6]

Biblical teachings of the Ten Commandments and other long-standing Judeo-Christian messages had sought to instill higher ideals in human behavior.[†] The message of Becker and Posner was that much of this was illusion. The mechanisms of individual exchange and other economic forces grounded in self-interest, not the teachings of the church, drive the world. Men and women marry because for each it maximizes their individual utilities, not because God or society has decreed that marriage is the proper outlet for sexual and other energies among male and female adults living intimately. Much as Buchanan and others in the public choice school saw the assertion of higher ideals in government as commonly a rhetorical mask for private gain, Becker and Posner now applied a similar perspective to the role of conventional morality throughout all aspects of personal behavior.

---

[*] The most cited economist is Jacob Mincer. It might be noted that Stigler was a great enthusiast for the more recent efforts to extend Chicago thinking into virtually every aspect of life. He would declare that "the prospect that economic logic may pervade the study of all branches of human behavior is as exciting as any development in the history of economics, or, for that matter, in the history of science." See George J. Stigler, *Memoirs of an Unregulated Economist* (New York: Basic Books, 1988), 203.

[†] It is not that Becker, Posner, and most other members of the current Chicago school are actively hostile to Judaism and Christianity (they are different in this regard from Knight). They may even look favorably on the role of religion in society. It is simply that the intellectual content of their analyses is not readily compatible with traditional Jewish and Christian teachings about marriage, divorce, children, crime, and many other subjects.

It put them in some surprising if very prominent company: Karl Marx, Sigmund Freud, and Friedrich Nietzsche also regarded traditional Jewish and Christian teachings as a grand illusion.★ This is not to deny that these teachings were accepted by or influenced the actions of believers. However, even though Christianity may have had a very large influence over the course of history, it had been in the service of other, more fundamental forces such as the workings of the class struggle or the tensions between the id and the ego in the mind. Becker has apparently heard comparisons in this vein—at least with respect to Marx—because at the very beginning of his Nobel lecture in 1992 he was at pains to assert otherwise: "Unlike Marxian analysis, the approach I refer to does not assume that individuals are motivated solely by selfishness or material gain. It is a *method* of analysis, not an assumption about particular motivations. Along with others, I have tried to pry economists away from narrow assumptions about self-interest. Behavior is driven by a much richer set of values and preferences."[7]

If Becker means by this that individual advantage or utility is derived from much more than things that involve the direct spending of money, or that social costs also can take many forms, he is obviously correct about the content of his life's work. However, for the most part his comments are disingenuous. Chicago school economics, like Marxist economics—and American progressive and European socialist economics as well—is fundamentally an economic interpretation of history. The drive for individual advantage—if now often expressed in broader terms outside a market context—moves the world in every respect. Reflecting a typical Chicago approach, Robert Tollison and several co-authors analyze the medieval Roman Catholic Church as a standard business enterprise, operating in the name of a church but actually acting to maximize the gain to the members of the priesthood itself.[8]

If something cannot be explained today in a narrowly individualistic framework of economic analysis, it is the belief of the "Chicago project" that in the future there will be a smarter graduate student, a more insightful theory, a better statistical method that will permit us to show the full workings of the forces of self-interest in more and more areas of life. As Becker believes, the goal for an economist should be that "one never reaches this impasse" where it is necessary to resort to changes in values or preferences (to

---

★ Marx and Nietzsche are well known for their antagonism to religion, seeing it as a grand self-deception. Freud similarly described religion as a "universal obsessional neurosis." Quoted in Reuben Fine, *A History of Psychoanalysis* (New York: Columbia University Press, 1979), 401. All of them regarded religion as real enough in the mind of the true believer but as making false claims to truth. Instead, religion served the workings of more fundamental forces in world history and personal mental development.

things like religion) to explain changes in human behavior. Rather, in all areas of human activity it is objective economic factors such as "differences in prices or incomes" that will fully explain—when economists have successful done their job—all "changes in behavior." For someone to resort to an appeal to "differences in tastes" from one observation point to another as a causal explanation is a mere "convenient crutch" that amounts to a confession of one's "analytical failures" as an economist.[9]

If love or altruism are taken to mean that one person's individual well-being can be increased by witnessing the good fortune of another person, Becker and other Chicago economists often seek to incorporate this element of regard for others in their analysis. However, if altruism or other noneconomic motives are taken to mean things such as a deliberate action that actually reduces the well-being of a person—or causes one to forgo an opportunity for individual gain—in the pursuit of some higher social ideal, Chicago cannot incorporate such motives in its framework of thought. It would be a virtual contradiction in terms from the Chicago perspective for a person to sacrifice their own advantage—to intentionally reduce their own level of utility—in the service of others. Indeed, many at Chicago might deny in principle that a person could ever deliberately choose to be less well off. Instead, maximization of individual welfare—recognizing that individual gain can be achieved in many ways that are sometimes difficult to see—drives the world in every respect. It is the denial of any social reality and authority—any role in the world for God to change the way people think, for example—that transcends individual motives and actions that is the identifying trademark of the Chicago school in the third generation. It is in contrast, for example, to the theories of Frank Knight, who believed—despite his great dedication to individual liberty—in the importance for individual behavior of social influences that transcended any individual advantage.

At present, admittedly, theories grounded in models of rational pursuit of individual well-being may be able to explain, say, only 60 percent of the variance in the dependent variable (technically, the "R-square" of a regression analysis) with respect to some aspect of human behavior, leaving 40 percent seemingly in the realm of "religion," "social influences," "culture," or other noneconomic motivations. However, the participants in the Chicago project are confident—they have a faith—that it is not likely to be very long before the unexplained residual can be reduced to, say, 35 percent. Then, with more time and economic research, it perhaps can be reduced to, say, 30 percent, to 25 percent, to 20 percent, and so forth. In the long run—possibly taking as long as fifty to one hundred years, maybe more, it is hard to say—it is the firm belief of the Chicago project, the noneconomic residual will gradually tend toward (if perhaps never fully reaching) zero.

From the Chicago perspective, any assertion otherwise, any claim that, say, 40 percent of human behavior in some realm is irreduceably noneconomic, would be virtually to say that science is in principle restricted in its scope— that in some domains of life perhaps god has simply reserved them for his understanding alone. Or, it would be as though Newton had discovered the laws of the solar system, but it was nevertheless asserted that 10 percent of the behavior of the sun and planets necessarily rested outside explanation by the methods of physics. Clearly, there can be no such "stopping points" within the value system—the moral philosophy—of the Chicago project today.

THE WORLD OF GARY BECKER

In Becker's first important work, his 1957 *The Economics of Discrimination,* he disavowed conventional morality and adopted what many people in American life would consider an offensive if not outrageous assumption. Becker argued that a "taste for discrimination" against black people (and potentially women, Jews, Arabs, and other groups as well) exists.[10] Some people simply do not like to work or live near blacks, just like other people prefer apples to bananas. The role of the economist as scientist is not to pass any moral judgments on this but to analyze its economic consequences.

The way to think about discrimination, Becker thus says, is that it introduces a nonpecuniary wedge in every transaction—equal to a monetary equivalent of the taste for discrimination. A white employer therefore must pay a black worker the money wage plus effectively a second amount reflecting the extent of the employer's distaste at having to be in contact with a black person. By making this specific assumption, and assuming that these wedge amounts stay constant, a "discrimination coefficient" becomes the equivalent to a tariff interposed in trading between firms located in two nations (here it is between two racial groups). The economics of discrimination then closely mirror the economics of an international trading regime with tariffs on a wide variety of transactions.

A further feature of Becker's thinking is that, starting from assumptions offensive to conventional opinion, he then goes on to test the degree to which the actual behavior in the world corresponds to the predictions he derives—predictions that are frequently counterintuitive. Thus, he comments with respect to racial discrimination that it reduces the total welfare of society as a whole (for the same reasons that the presence of tariffs reduces world welfare). However, he finds that the returns to white labor and, surprisingly, black-owned capital are increased. The losers include black labor and white capitalists—the latter directly contrary to the common view (especially among "progressive" thinkers) that it is always powerful businesspeople who are the ones exploiting the poor and oppressed.[11]

The *Economics of Discrimination* set the stage for Becker's career. Again and again, he has taken a subject considered to lie outside conventional economic analysis—to be a part of sociology, anthropology, or some other field—and sought to show that it can be successfully analyzed in economic terms. Even when others have assumed that noneconomic motives such as racial hatred or bias may be the true driving factors, Becker has sought to develop an analytical apparatus to show that the expression of these motives can be seen as actually taking a more conventional and rational economic form. In so doing, he has extended into many brand-new domains the traditional Chicago view that rejects a role for culture, religion, or any other social influences that transcend the Chicago rational actor model.

Not all the precedents set by *The Economics of Discrimination,* to be sure, were favorable. Jon Elster recently commented with respect to another of his writings that "Becker's model is incoherent."[12] Becker's analysis is often more interesting for the novelty of its assumptions than for the precise working out of the analytical details. He has more than once left out key factors that would significantly alter the conclusions of his analysis (see the later discussion of marriage in this chapter).

With respect to the impacts of discrimination, his broader conclusions in *The Economics of Discrimination* are doubtful. It would not require many employers who lacked a taste for discrimination (they might come from the North to the South, for example, attracted by the prospect of high profits) to undermine most of his results. Even a modest number of white-owned firms that did not feel any reluctance to hire black workers at subnormal wages would rapidly expand their business, and soon would undermine the competitive position of those white capitalists with typical southern attitudes, including a distaste for association with blacks. The wages of black labor would thereby be bid up, and they would end up being paid the same amounts as whites (for equal levels of marginal productivity), although worker segregation would still be maintained.

In essence, a freely competitive market would thus soon tend to eliminate wage discrimination against blacks. Southerners were in fact quite well aware of the danger and took nonmarket means to prevent this outcome. Starting in the 1890s, they adopted Jim Crow and other racially discriminatory laws and enforced powerful informal social sanctions on a widespread basis, preventing market incentives from advancing an equality of wages among segregated firms. Much of racial discrimination in the South, contrary to Becker's strictly economic approach, and from which he derives his analytical conclusions, was ultimately a political phenomenon that would have been defeated by ordinary economic forces if the market had been allowed to work.

THOU SHALT STEAL (IF IT PAYS)

It says in the Ten Commandments in the Bible, Thou shalt not steal (Exodus 20:15). For Becker, however, understanding (and preventing) crime is explained not by such Christian homilies, but by hard economic motives.[13] Indeed, stealing is simply another form of rational maximization of individual income and utility. Most people refrain from stealing because it would not be profitable for them; for some people it happens to be profitable and they become thieves. Economically, a theft is a "redistribution" of resources, in much the same broad category, technically speaking, as a government welfare program.[14]

Of course, most people would naively object that stealing is morally wrong, but that the welfare form of redistribution of income is legitimate because it has been approved by a democratic political process. However, the Chicago school also finds that official rationales in politics often cannot be taken at face value. Welfare programs really involve coercively taking money from some people to give it to others. If collective "theft" by government can be analyzed without one's feeling a need to interject extensive moral commentary, why not put theft by ordinary criminals in the same economic category? ★ As Becker argues, the "basic motivation" of criminals is the same as that of "other persons." Criminals are distinguished not by their lack of moral character, but by the fact that "their benefits and costs differ," perhaps in part a consequence of their having different physical and mental endowments for crime.[15]

★ The great Christian theologian Saint Augustine once developed a similar analogy to illustrate the point that all people—the government official and the criminal alike—are afflicted by original sin, leading most human beings to behave in evil ways. Government, Augustine suggests, is merely an act of piracy on a grand scale. He comments that an actual pirate, if apprehended by a head of state, might appropriately remark: "What thou meanest by seizing the whole earth; but because I do it with a petty ship, I am called the robber, whilst thou who dost it with a great fleet are styled emperor." See Augustine, *The City of God,* in Whitney J. Oates, ed., *Basic Writings of Saint Augustine,* vol. 2 (New York: Random House, 1948), 51–52.

Becker at one point comments that stealing per se is not inefficient. In a real sense, "frauds, thefts, etc., do not involve true social costs but are simply transfers, with the loss to victims being compensated by equal gains to criminals." [16] However, responding to their private incentives, people will steal up to the point where the objects gained (stolen) have a money value equal to the work effort in doing the stealing. It is only in this sense that it is possible to judge criminal actions as inefficient ("wrong" in the morality of economics) because acts of stealing produce no useful outputs, and yet can absorb considerable productive resources of society (the time and effort of the criminals themselves).★

In considering how society should deal with crime, Becker argues that the total social welfare function must also include "the social value of the gain to offenders" from crime. Criminal activities should be treated in the same way as building cars and engaging in other economic activities, although they have certain special economic characteristics—they are, for example, "an important subset of the class of activities that cause diseconomies" to others (i.e, to the victims of crime), a class which also include such things as factories that emit smoke and other public nuisances. [17]

In this framework, the optimal social allocation of criminal activity is obtained in much the same manner as nuisance activities that have "externalities," or as Becker calls them, "diseconomies." [18] If a pig farm creates smells offensive to its neighbors, market theory tells us that a correct allocation of resources can be achieved if the pig farmer is required to compensate the neighbors for their losses. For Becker, criminal activities should be treated much like pig farming. Given a requirement for criminals to pay a penalty equal to full compensation of victims and other people adversely affected by crime, this will serve to achieve a socially appropriate amount of crime. Realities such as people violating the law by driving cars over the speed limit will always be present in society; it would be altogether foolish, Becker thinks, for any society to seek to create sufficient punishments that all speeding or other criminal activity would cease. The solution would do much more damage than the problem. The real scientific issue is thus the "optimal" amount of crime a society should plan to tolerate.

Becker's treatment of crime highlights the absence of any absolute social concepts such as "justice" or "morality" in the framework of thought that he applies to human behavior. Individuals may constrain their behavior of their own accord (based on some concept of "justice" in their mind) but there is

---

★ Another source of inefficiency is that there is also a large social cost when people feel compelled to spend large amounts of time and money in trying to protect themselves against crime.

no place where "society" meaningfully says, "this is not allowed because it is 'wrong.' " Only those who may allow themselves to be affected by individual sentiments such as "guilt" will be significantly influenced in their behavior. A superman as Nietzsche envisioned would be entirely immune.

Becker at one point suggested that his approach to economics could be applied to the social treatment of "women, Jews, individuals with the same personality type, members of the same caste or social class, etc."[19] As Becker therefore would seemingly have to analyze the matter if he remained consistent to the logic of his approach applied everywhere else, even Nazi actions in Germany could be analyzed as yet another variant on economically rational behavior by ordinary people—if with very unusual "tastes," "capabilities," or other Nazi features affecting their calculations of benefits and costs. The various acts of persecution of the Jews could be condemned only if they were shown to diminish the aggregate utility of all the people in Germany (including the Jews, but who were a small number and whose preferences might be swamped by the majority Germans) or to be otherwise inefficient.* The morality of the Ten Commandments is replaced for Becker by a morality of advancing or impeding economic productivity in the broadest sense.

To be sure, economic analysis in general has this characteristic—as discussed in Chapter 3, good and evil are transformed to become efficient and inefficient in Samuelson's *Economics* as well. Most economists in the past, however, limited its application to the commercial sectors of society. They agreed that behavior in other areas of life might be driven by considerations

---

* Given that many Germans found the near presence of a Jew distasteful, as Becker would presumably want to analyze the matter (following the same approach applied earlier to discrimination against blacks), this presence would create "diseconomies" for these Germans, thus putting the close presence of a Jew in the same technical economic category to which Becker has already said ordinary criminal actions belong. Hence, it would seem to follow from Becker's uniquely economic approach to the analysis of crime that the Jews as special types of "criminals" (recall, this is just in the "scientific" economic sense that Becker seeks always to apply) might be required to pay compensation to other Germans for causing this diseconomy. In fact, the Nazis initially imposed "fines" by taking money and property from Jews. However, as the presence of Jews seemingly became even more distasteful (caused more disutility to other Germans), many individual Jews could no longer pay enough compensation and had to be imprisoned—as Becker suggests at one point that poor thieves today may have to go to jail for lack of enough money to fully compensate their victims (in contrast to rich criminals, whom Becker would allow to simply make financial payments to cover their fines). In the framework of Becker's general analysis of the economics of crime (encompassing, one must presume, also Nazi crime), this would all have advanced the cause of economic efficiency in Germany in the late 1930s. If the behavior of the Nazis might seem to be so morally repugnant that it should be excluded from any such economic treatment, Becker has already warned his readers elsewhere that they must learn to squelch their knee-jerk moral reactions; they should not "be repelled by the apparent novelty of an 'economic' framework for illegal behavior." See Gary S. Becker, *The Economic Approach to Human Behavior* (Chicago: University of Chicago Press, 1976), 79.

that are difficult or impossible to incorporate into the standard economic framework of analysis. Implicitly, most economists took for granted that there could exist a dichotomous morality. The pursuit of individual gain might dominate in the marketplace but other value systems transcending the individual would exert a powerful influence in other aspects of life. The great novelty of Becker's analysis is that he in essence denies this dichotomy. The real influence—the meaningful existence—of any collective "values," "religion," "culture," or "justice" that go beyond maximization of individual benefits and costs does not exist anywhere. Culture and religion do admittedly act to shape individual preferences for Becker, but his analysis is distinguished by the assumption that they do not have an explanatory power beyond that initial role; any subsequent changes in behavior reflect new calculations of individual utility maximization (or profit making) in response to changes in objective external events, not an inernal process of simply adopting new social values—in an important case historically, for example, of being visited by God and being "born again."

As discussed in the Introduction in the present book, the standard economic attitude in fact reflects an awkward dichotomy—why should ordinary economic forces and explanations reign in some places such as the market, and not others? Even the defense of a market system as a desirable institution that should be maintained by society requires a certain willingness to forgo "corruption" and other opportunistic gains that could well serve the self-interest of many individuals involved. Economists have never given a good explanation for their dichotomous framework of morality with respect to the role of self-interest in the world. It is a very large intellectual gap. Becker thus has performed an important intellectual service by bringing the whole issue to a much greater prominence. He does this simply by asking: What happens if the traditional individualism of the market is assumed to extend systematically into every area of life without exception? The very asking of the question, as is often the case in economics, is more important than the subsequent analysis—where Becker's efforts are often flawed.

Richard Posner—who considers himself a follower in Becker's footsteps—was asked not long ago to lecture on the meaning of another of the Ten Commandments, Thou shalt not kill, in light of the growing cost burdens being created by the efforts of modern medicine. The New Testament in fact prohibits suicide as an abandonment of hope in God's saving grace in this world. Posner's Tanner lectures on euthanasia and health care were delivered at Yale University in 1994.[20] Posner there felt the need to distinguish clearly between "involuntary euthanasia," as practiced for instance by the Nazis, and the much different subject of his own inquiry, "voluntary euthanasia."[21]

Applying a standard economic framework of individual utility maximization, Posner argues that euthanasia involves calculations such as "[If] ten years of life each of which would confer 100 utiles [units of utility] would yield a lower expected utility than eight years of life each of which would confer 150 utiles, . . . [then] the shorter life expectancy will be preferred" and the individual should be free to act on this preference—and presumably can be assisted by a doctor when and where mutually agreeable.[22] The appropriate criterion, in short, for an act of euthanasia is much like a business decision on profit and loss, but in this case involves whether it increases the expected lifetime utility of the individual.[23] If the overall utility should happen to be negative from today forward, euthanasia is just another legitimate exercise (if with unusual finality) in rational consumer choice, like buying a car or a refrigerator. The traditional Judeo-Christian attitude that suicide involves an absolute moral imperative—no issues of individual utility calculation should ever arise—is treated as in effect a baseless superstition of the past that impedes the maximization of individual well-being.*

PRIVATIZING MARRIAGE

Becker first took up decision making in the family in a widely influential 1960 paper on the economics of having children.[24] The current birthrate might be seen as reflecting the intersection of a demand curve for children and supply curve, yielding at this point both an equilibrium cost of a child and the number of children born. This paper in fact helped to bring a new analytical rigor to the field of demography. Then, in the 1970s Becker published several articles analyzing the internal dynamics of decision making within families.[25] He brought this material together along with many additional subjects in his 1981 *A Treatise on the Family* (with a revised edition in 1991).[26]

---

* Posner, to be sure, is also capable of subtle arguments outside the narrowly economic framework. For example, in the Tanner lecture he also makes arguments to try to persuade people who may not share his absolute individualism and utilitarianism. As he points out, if total years of life lived is the relevant criterion for setting policy (among its advantages, it is easier to measure than "utility"), then the availability of euthanasia by itself may result in more total "life-years" lived overall. A person with Alzheimer's disease, for example, may strongly prefer suicide to the last stages of the disease. If that person could make a reliable contract for termination of life when a stage of negative utility sets in in the future, he or she could continue living with peace of mind in the present. However, since the stage of negative utility may also be past the point at which the individual is capable of committing suicide on his or her own, it may be necessary to kill oneself much earlier while an act of suicide is still possible. In short, as Posner finds, the provision for future contracted euthanasia (involving some modest assistance by another party) may paradoxically extend considerably the desired length of life of current Alzheimer's sufferers.

As he states in his 1992 Nobel lecture, Becker considers this work on the family to be his greatest achievement. Besides looking at relationships in marriage, Becker had sought to examine the broader "personal relations within families between husbands and wives, parents and children, and among more distant relatives." The true explanation for the character of these relationships, he finds, is not a matter of familial duty and responsibility; rather, the conduct of family affairs is driven by "the [individual] incentives to invest in *creating* closer relations" with other family members.[27] A person may actually in his or her own mind perceive a "moral obligation" to another, but underneath all this obfuscatory language of duty is a deeper reality that Becker will now probe. The sense of mutual devotion, as found in the way many ordinary people think about marriage, is in fact just a disguised way of achieving a higher rate of return on individual investment.

Becker thus is again concerned to show that decisions about marriage, divorce, children, and others made in families are in essence acts of consumer choice. People will marry when their individual "utility from marriage exceeds their utility from remaining single."[28] Marriage works as a social institution because the sum of individual gains of the married couple exceeds what they can do on their own. It extends into family life the same point that Adam Smith was making in saying that the productive success of the marketplace lies in the division of labor—as in the much greater output of a pin factory when compared with that of the same number of people attempting to produce pins individually. As Becker writes, "The difference between married output and the sum of single outputs is the gain from marriage, and is measured [in some circumstances] . . . by the vertical distance between the infinitely elastic sections of the derived demand curve for wives and the supply curve of wives."[29]

Historically, the most important products of a marriage have been the various forms of economic output that put bread on the table, provided shelter from rain and cold, paid the doctor's bills, and created the means to obtain other goods and services for as comfortable a life as possible (in fact, not very comfortable for most people until very recently). The modern idea of "love" does not have deep roots in the history of marriage. Becker quotes one authority to the effect that in sixteenth-century England "romantic love and lust were strongly condemned as ephemeral and irrational grounds for marriage." In France in the fourteenth century, "concubines could be loved, and discreet affairs overlooked, but families had too great a stake in the marriages of members to allow love to thwart family objectives."[30]

Nevertheless, in light of the modern association of marriage with love, Becker is concerned to introduce this element into the economic analysis of family decision making. "Love," defined in scientific terms, means for Becker the deriving of utility from the utility of another. Becker puts it in the formal language of consumer choice:

> It can be said said that Mi [Man i] loves Fj [Female j] if her welfare enters his utility function, and perhaps also if Mi values emotional and physical contact with Fj. Clearly, Mi can benefit from a match with Fj, because he could then have a more favorable effect on her welfare—and thereby on his own utility—and because the commodities measuring "contact" with Fj can be produced more cheaply when they are matched than when Mi has to seek an "illicit" relationship with Fj. Even if Fj were "selfish" and did not return Mi's love, she would benefit from a match with someone who loves her, because he would transfer resources to her to increase his own utility. Moreover, a marriage involving love is more efficient than other marriages, even when one of the mates is selfish, and increased efficiency benefits the selfish mate also. . . . Marriages involving love are likely to be part of the equilibrium sorting [among potential partners] because in market terms they are more productive than other marriages.[31]

Overall, however, Becker regards love as a secondary consideration in the marriage market, even in contemporary society. He derives a number of significant findings relating to the character of economic exchange in marriage, taking pains to point out that "these results do not assume that men value wives for their own sake, but only consider the value of the [total] output produced by husbands and wives," and the ability of each of the participants in a marriage to negotiate for as large an individual share as possible of the collective marriage products.[32]

Offering yet another of the paradoxical results that Becker so much enjoys presenting, he finds that social prohibitions on polygamy are mainly harmful to women (and the existence of such prohibitions perhaps reflects the greater political power of men). Allowing polygamy would increase the total demands for the marriage services of wives, by allowing some rich or otherwise advantaged men to enter the marriage market to obtain a second (or still further) wives, while there is no corresponding increase (under the normal arrangements of polygamy) in the total aggregate demand for the services of male partners (one woman cannot have two husbands). It follows as an elementary application of the workings of supply and demand that the price of women (their ability to extract income from potential husbands) will rise under polygamy.* In short, in economic terms the outlawing of polygamy represents an inefficient restriction on trade that (like other such restrictions) harms the group whose opportunity to sell their services is being arbitrarily curtailed by government—in this case unmarried women who are precluded from contracting with already married men.

In another form of paradox, Becker frequently brings up what he regards as one of his most important scientific findings, the " 'rotten kid' theorem." [33] In essence, in the rotten kid theorem he seeks to demonstrate that in many circumstances it will pay you to make someone else better off, if you know that that person (who must be an actual altruist) will then transfer parts of his or her improved welfare back to you. Becker almost seems to celebrate the existence of rotten-kid motives because they reduce the total amount of real (as opposed to feigned) altruism necessary in the world. A world in which all motives are individual gain is a much simpler world in terms of not only the clarity of expectations with respect to the behavior of other people but also the ability to conduct economic analysis. If many people would lament rotten-kid behavior as conniving and manipulative, perhaps it is worth recalling in support of Becker that Machiavelli is perhaps the greatest political analyst in history, and Machiavelli's prince would share much common ground with Becker's rotten kid.

THE ECONOMICS OF SEX

Surprising for one who generally so much seems to enjoy shocking the moral values of ordinary people, there is about Becker an element of prud-

---

* In a Judeo-Christian culture, Becker's analysis of polygamy is of academic interest, or may be regarded as merely a symbolic way of expressing a general set of values. In a culture such as that of Zimbabwe today, however, where polygamy is still legal and commonly practiced, Becker's approach proves to have some practical relevance as well. In a proposed new constitution for Zimbabwe, one option under discussion in 1999 was to impose a ban on polygamy. It is a tribute to the generality of Becker's analysis that it encompassed some prominent elements of the public debate in Zimbabwe on this issue. As one newspaper reported:

> Some women in Hwange [in western Zimbabwe], including ladies of the night, want polygamy to be legalised, in spite of calls by activists to discourage the practice.
> The women, desperate to be married, said the new democratic constitution draft . . . should encourage polygamy so that most women could have access to marriage.
> Some unmarried women here complained that the introduction of monogamy violated their rights to marriage, as some men now stick to one wife.

See "Polygamy Is Our Democratic Right," *Herald* (Harare), August 9, 1999, 1.

ishness. His definition of love, for example, is so broad that it would encompasses my concern that the people of Africa should not starve (their utility affects my utility)—people whom I cannot by any reasonable definition be said to "love." Becker never gets down to brass tacks to discuss with any conviction something on the minds of many people entering into marriage—sex. It is as though sexual pleasure and the broader sense of personal identify of each marriage partner as a sexual being is just another "commodity," like bread on the table, that comes from marriage and requires no further special elaboration.

Posner in this respect, as in many others, is more worldly than Becker. This may partly reflect his career since 1981 as a federal judge, in which the events of the world are continually impressed upon him in his courtroom. When it comes to sex, Posner at least talks about the real thing, even as he employed the same individualistic framework of economic analysis as Becker. A remarkably prolific author, Posner has applied an economic perspective to a wide range of social institutions, including in *Sex and Reason,* to the implicit contracts of marriages and many other sexual forms of interrelationships. For Posner, one of the most important ways in which each party to a marriage in effect pays the other party is by performing sexual services.

Becker had earlier found that ordinary economic activities and crime fall in the same "scientific" framework of analysis. In *Sex and Reason* Posner similarly finds that marriage belongs to the same basic economic category as prostitution. Or, as Posner explains,

> In describing prostitution as a substitute for marriage in a society that has a surplus of bachelors, I may seem to be overlooking a fundamental difference: the "mercenary" character of the prostitute's relationship with her customer. The difference is not fundamental. In a long-term relationship such as marriage, the participants can compensate each other for services performed by performing reciprocal services, so they need not bother with pricing each service, keeping books of account, and so forth. But in a spot-market relationship such as a transaction with a prostitute, arranging for reciprocal services is difficult. It is more efficient for the customer to pay in a medium [of money] that the prostitute can use to purchase services from others.[34]

In other words, just as a power plant might purchase its necessary coal supply through a series of short-term purchases in the coal "spot market," or might instead choose to sign a long-term contract for many years of supply with one coal company, a man seeking sex has the same kind of economic options—either turn to the sexual marketplace for a short-term series of "spot-market" sexual alliances (frequently with prostitutes in order to minimize search costs) or enter into a long-term contract for sex by finding a wife.

While Becker has frequently developed his arguments in mathematical form and otherwise written in the formal language of current economics, Posner operates more within the literary traditions of legal scholarship.[35] Posner's intellectual authority derives in part from the sheer scope and brilliance of his writings. Posner is no less committed than Becker to applying the framework of individual maximization of advantage to every event in society. However, Posner is often able to summon a greater wealth of historical, institutional, political, and other detail that must impress any reader. If every book or article is in some sense a performance, Posner's high literary quality and general intellectual brilliance has been a leading contributor to putting a blessing on his libertarian outlook on the world.★

WOMEN AS PROPERTY

Even winning a Nobel Prize in economics is no assurance of economic analysis that is free of unexamined assumptions that reflect strong value positions that are never explicitly defended. These elements are so prominent in Samuelson's *Economics* that it is appropriate to regard his introductory textbook more as a work of religious symbolism in defense of the progressive gospel of efficiency than as a scientific exposition. Much of Becker's work also is best regarded as the creation of a particularly effective imagery and symbolism for communicating an implicit value system.

Consider the analysis of marriage described previously in which Becker has invested such a great amount of time and effort. Becker's starting point that a marriage should be conceived as an economic exchange is no doubt correct up to a point. However, Becker sees nothing else; he argues that the full workings of the institution of marriage can be analyzed in the manner of a typical exchange relationship in the marketplace. The overall concept is of potential husbands and wives bargaining over the terms of exchange that will be spelled out in a long-term marriage contract, including the services each party will perform and the price each will charge the other.

★ Robert Anderson distinguishes between "natural rights" libertarians and "empirical" libertarians. The latter believe that "the consistent application of libertarian principles will maximize collective utility; thus they rely on utilitarian arguments." Anderson notes further that "Posner describes himself as a libertarian; if so, he is of the 'empirical' school." This is true insofar as the explicit content of Posner's economic analysis. However, contrary to the views of Anderson, the underlying—and usually only implicit—presuppositions of Posner's analysis also contain a large dose of the "natural rights" element of libertarianism. See Robert M. Anderson, "EP Seeks EP: A Review of *Sex and Reason* by Richard A. Posner," *Journal of Economic Literature* 31 (March 1993): 194.

However, Becker's analysis is flawed as a matter of the actual history of marriage. What firm—outside Japan—has ever hired a workforce for life? To be sure, the marriage contract can now easily be broken by divorce. However, Becker himself comments that until the 1850s obtaining a divorce in England required an act of Parliament and the total number of divorces in the nation averaged fewer than two per year.[36] Becker never adequately addresses why anyone would be willing to make such a long-term commitment, so outside any normal exchange or contracting practice in the market.

Then, given the extraordinarily long-term character, a next logical question would be the provisions for dispute resolution. This has an actual historical answer. Subject to certain church or government supervision, the terms of marriage historically were determined unilaterally by the husband. The wife did have the potential recourse to run away, or to appeal to other members of the community to pressure her husband to behave more responsibly. But she had virtually no legal rights within marriage. Contrary to Becker, a more accurate way of describing the relationship of marriage until quite recently has been to say that the new wife would become the property of her husband. That was in fact the basic legal status of a married woman in the Western world until the twentieth century. In some other parts of the world, women today are still in this legal status, in places where it is still possible for a man literally to buy a wife from the parents of the "bride."

If a wife is property, then marriage might most accurately be described as a property relationship in which a woman is bound to a man for a lifetime. There is a special term for this. In a certain sense the historic practice of marriage—in the scientific framework that Becker is always concerned to follow—is in the same general economic category as slavery. One human being who belongs to another human being as property for life is technically defined as a kind of slave. Indeed, when the American suffrage movement began in the United States in the 1840s and 1850s, some of the women who were early leaders were abolitionists who had started off by working to free black slaves in the South. Women were obviously not slaves in the same sense as blacks—a married woman could not be sold to a new husband, and husbands were subject to criminal prosecution for murder or other severe offenses against wives. Yet it had not escaped the attention of women members of the abolition movement that some of the same property relationships that characterized southern slavery seemed to be replicated in the institution of marriage at the time.

In their history of the movement, the suffragists Elizabeth Cady Stanton and Susan B. Anthony thus note that "the immediate origin of the woman's rights movement of the midcentury was in the anti-slavery crusade" and in the recognition of women participants in this movement that "the cause of emancipation affected them as well as slaves."[37] One of the founding documents of the suffage movement, the Seneca Falls Declaration of 1848, declares the necessity of abolishing the "absolute tyranny" and the "social and religious degradation" that men had long maintained over women. On entering into marriage, a woman was "compelled to promise obedience to her husband, he becoming, to all intents and purposes, her master—the law giving him power to deprive her of her liberty, and to administer chastisement." Her husband had "taken from her all right in property, even to wages she earns"—indeed, the wife was "in the eye of the law, civilly dead."[38]

Becker's burden, if he had been more concerned to formulate his task in an historically accurate way, would then have been to ask why a system of female entry into a relationship of lifetime property ownership has typically been the prevailing form of the marriage relationship in history. One answer may be that the economic model of marriage is—or more precisely used to be, since the character of marriage has recently been changing rapidly—an inappropriate model. Men and women may have often entered into marriage for reasons of expected lifelong love or other emotional sustenance, rather than of economics. There was in any case little choice but to enter into the terms of marriage as defined by the church—as revealed in the absolute truths of the Ten Commandments handed down by God and that included marriage among their subjects.

Yet, simply from an economic view, it is also possible that there may be some practical benefits to be gained from women being owned by husbands as property. The incentive of the owner (husband) to invest in the human capital of the wife may be much greater when the wife is not free to leave to take a better offer—just as owned cars are often treated much better than rented cars. The wife in turn is likely to be much more devoted to the welfare of the owner (husband) when she knows she has no place else to go. One must then also factor in the consideration that there would be large transaction costs for a man in having to go into a spot market to rent a woman temporarily for the one specific and short-term purpose of bearing him a child. An analysis of this kind would have been very much in the spirit of Becker's other work—and would have satisfied Becker's own obvious personal "taste" for being provocative—but he never develops it. It is another example of his surprising tendency to neglect key elements of historical fact and analytical detail.

Indeed, much like that of Samuelson, Becker's economic scholarship is not his main achievement here or elsewhere. Becker's characterization of the marriage relationship is most important as a symbolic affirmation of powerful new value trends that were emerging in American society just as he was writing. However historically in error, Becker's analysis does much more accurately describe the emerging state of marriage since the 1970s with no-fault divorce, prenuptial contracts, and other changes in American marriage law.* One can actually speak of the contemporary institution of marriage as offering a reasonable approximation of an ordinary contractual relationship in a system of market exchange.[39] As Ramon Febrero and Pedro Schwartz comment, in Becker's thinking (and in the new world of marriage today) "decisions about their marital status (remaining single, marrying, or divorcing) [are] no longer taken as a given" by those involved, but are subject to regular reconsideration of the prospective net future benefits on the part of each individual involved in the marriage.[40]

It is not only that Becker was describing an evolving trend in society. He was also giving it greater social legitimacy. He was presenting the new world of marriage in the language of economic exchange, efficiency, and productivity. † In the progressive gospels of the twentieth century, maximizing efficiency in the use of the productive resources of society is the path to heaven on earth. If the older patterns of marriage had been blessed by God (or his representatives in the church), the newer forms of marriage would now be blessed by a more contemporary god who would save the world by eliminating scarcity and bringing on a state of complete material abundance. Reminiscent of Samuelson's *Economics*, the technical content of Becker's economics is secondary to the preaching of a powerful underlying value system. It defends a new set of values that manifest a strong individualistic and libertarian trend not only in marriage but in almost every area of society as it has been spreading in American life from the 1960s onward.

---

* One commentator writes of the new "cult of expressive divorce" that emerged in the 1970s and 1980s, promoted by "therapists, self-help books, and other vehicles of popular culture." The result was to shift "the normative image of marriage from that of an enduring covenant to that of a limited contract—and later, under no-fault divorce, to a contract that could be dissolved by either partner for any (or even no) reason whatever." See Mary Stewart Van Leeuwen, "Deconstructing the Culture of Divorce," *The Christian Century,* July 30-August 6, 1997, 691.

† To be sure, even with respect to the more-recent understandings of marriage, Becker again leaves out critical elements, which results in an incomplete if not faulty theory. According to one legal scholar, "Gary Becker's original economic theory of marriage focussed centrally on specialization as the economic foundation of, and motivation for, household formation. However, . . . this may explain the formation of households but does not explain the institution of marriage." The gains from specialization alone could be achieved by many contractual mechanisms that would not necessarily require all the features of the marriage arrangement. It is necessary to appeal to "lock-in" effects, "signaling," and other transaction cost and information considerations to explain contemporary marriage in its full dimensions as an economic act. One must thus go well beyond Becker's economic analysis to develop any kind of adequate economic explanation for alimony, child custody rules, divorce procedures, and other elements of modern marriage. See Michael J. Trebilcock, "Marriage as Signal," in F. H. Buckley, ed., *The Fall and Rise of Freedom of Contract* (Durham: Duke University Press, 1999), 249.

THE CHICAGO GOD

In pushing the motive of pursuit of individual advantage to its logical extreme, Becker, Posner, and other Chicago school economists of their ilk are in effect preaching a new secular religion. In Christian religion—and it has sometimes proven difficult for the faithful to understand how it can be reconciled with the simultaneous assertion of free will—everything that happens in the world is said to be controlled by God. Now in the Chicago project of the third generation, everything is controlled by economic forces of self-interest. The place of the Christian God in explaining the workings of the world has been taken by the workings of the economic drive for individual gain (broadly conceived). Instead of looking at the Christian Bible, it will be necessary to turn to the writings of Becker, Posner, and other co-workers located at (or operating elsewhere in the spirit of) Chicago, where the full scope of such individually self-interested behavior, controlling everything that happens everywhere in society, will be revealed for all to see.

As some people may find surprising, and as suggested earlier, the Chicago project in its economic determinism follows closely in the footsteps of Karl Marx. In their particulars, Chicago economics and Marxism have of course altogether different technical understandings of economic reality. Chicago goes beyond Marx to conceive of the determinants of individual welfare more broadly than the extent of material possessions alone. For Chicago, it is individual persons acting for their own gain who are the agents in history, while it is the individual economic class that serves this role in Marxism. However, as a matter of a basic assumption about the role of economic forces in driving the world, the participants in the Chicago project share with Marxism the underlying conviction that everything that happens in life and society is ultimately driven by individual or class advantage. If an event should seem to have a character outside economic explanation, it simply reflects a failure of analytical understanding up to that point.

In his 1992 Nobel lecture, Becker comments that there have been some times in his life when his full faith in the Chicago god has faltered. As he says, "Many economists, including me, have excessively relied on altruism to tie together the interests of family members." However, he has by now come to understand that even this past limited reliance on altruism was merely due to a failure of analytical insight on his part. Becker should have known better then, but he has at least now come to see in a clearer light that "the [implicit contractual] connection between childhood experiences and future behavior reduces the need to rely on altruism in families" and ideally (in terms of hopes for the future advance of economic science) will eventually eliminate the need altogether.[41]

Chicago thus is also like Marxism in regarding altruism, love, political ideology, and other such ideas in the mind as part of a grand social illusion—a social "superstructure" of "false consciousness," as Marx would label it—that is secondary to the more fundamental workings of underlying economic forces in society. Marxism competed directly with and, for many people, led to an abandonment of Christianity. The Chicago project has no desire to force acceptance of its belief system through government coercion, as Marxists so often sought to do in the twentieth century. In many cases, Chicago lacks the deep hostility of Marxism toward traditional religion. Yet, if its claims are taken literally and in all seriousness, the Chicago project in the third generation of Becker and Posner has much the same implications for Christianity.

Or, as some might say, Chicago has now taken us past the revelations of the Bible by showing how the one and only god in the universe actually operates exclusively through economic forces. The Chicago project in this perspective may not have transcended God per se—the Chicago religion need not be a form of atheism—but rather the Chicago project has perhaps found a new divinely inspired tablet. God may have sent Jesus to earth two thousand years ago but perhaps he now has thought it desirable after so many years to update his message. In a virtual miracle, the Chicago school may just happen to be— among all the many messengers on earth that would have been available to God—the chosen vessel for a new revelation to humankind. It has supplanted the outmoded (in language and substance) instructions of the Ten Commandments and other messages of the Christian Bible. In every area of life, men and women do—and should, as is also the implicit message—these things that will serve to maximize their individual well-being.

A CHRISTIAN VIEW OF CHICAGO

Outside the economics profession over the years there have been a large number of critics of the "materialistic" philosophy of economics and of its broader moral consequences. In many cases the critics have shown a weak understanding of the actual workings of markets and other economic phenomena, tending to detract from any other merits of their criticisms. A recent critic, however, is economist Donald Hay, who is both a highly qualified economist, well regarded in the profession, and a devout Christian (one of the very few by his own account among his sixty or so economist colleagues at Oxford).[42] Hay has been bothered enough by the tensions he sees between the economic way of thinking and his Christian religion that, almost alone among economists in such high standing in the profession, he has written a book on the subject.[43]

At the end of the day, Hay is of the opinion that there is a basic conflict between Christianity and the free-market views of the Chicago school (and indeed much of economic thinking more broadly that Chicago merely takes to an extreme). The implicit ethics of the economic way of thinking "have no basis in Christian ethics and are indeed incompatible with them in substantive respects." Conflicts arise at the most fundamental level; the values of economics are at odds with the "Christian conception of creation, providence in history and revelation of God's will for mankind."[44] Economics fundamentally sees each person as an individual acting to maximize personal welfare; Christianity fundamentally sees each person as seeking a union with God in which individual motives have no place—even if this goal frequently must be deferred in the present world due to the effects of original sin.*

If the market were merely a place for channeling less harmfully the unruly impulses of sinful men (and women), if it were merely a setting for voluntary exchange among members of diverse religious and other groups, there would be little or no problem. However, the economic value system, as Hay says, exalts the goals of "efficiency, growth and progress"—as Samuelson did, for example, in *Economics* and as Becker has done in making efficiency the ultimate criterion in his treatment of various sociological subjects. The result is an alternative religion whose tenets stand in marked "contrast [to] the biblical framework" of salvation based on the teachings of Jesus. It is difficult to see how to incorporate in the economic framework a concept such as the Christian commitment to membership in a community of fellow believers—the members of the church who are all God's children together, all created in common in the image of God, despite all their real-world flaws.†

---

* Harvard theologian Harvey Cox comments that "the latest trend in economic theory is the attempt to apply market calculations to areas that once appeared to be exempt, such as dating, family life, marital relations, and child rearing." This has merely exacerbated a fundamental tension that preexisted this newest development in economics: "Disagreements among the traditional religions become picayune in comparison with the fundamental differences they all have with the religion of The Market. . . . I am usually a keen supporter of ecumenism. But the contradictions between the world views of the traditional religions on the one hand and the world view of the Market religion on the other are so basic that no compromise seems possible, and I am secretly hoping for a rebirth of polemics." See Harvey Cox, "The Market as God: Living in the New Dispensation," *Atlantic Monthly,* March 1999, 23.

† The degree of tension between Christianity and mainstream economics is a perennial subject of discussion among the members of the Association of Christian Economists. While many Christian economists disagree (in my mind mistakenly), others share Hay's overall assessment. Arnold McKee recently declared:

Those who sincerely confess and place their reliance on God and Jesus Christ clearly acquire an outlook on all life and knowledge different from that of the secular humanism characteriz-

Even a goal as basic to the methods of economic analysis as the necessity of a high rate of economic growth is questionable in a Christian framework, Hays says, because "materialism is closely related to idolatry in Christian thought," that is to say, to the worship of a false god.[45] Or as another devout Christian academic put it elsewhere, "according to Christianity wealth is a snare, and its continual increase even worse."[46]

Seen from Hay's perspective, the claims of Chicago (and many other) economists to be value neutral reflect a great lack of self-awareness.[47] Hay writes that "it is generally true that a pure positive economics, without reference to any value system, is simply not available." ★ Doing benefit-cost studies when protection of human lives is involved, for example, in itself expresses a value judgment that "in some fundamental sense . . . a fellow human being [is] . . . an object like an expensive car." Indeed, calculations of benefits and costs therefore should not be used routinely for social decision

---

ing the modern university. This is the effect of Grace (God within us, in an old phrase) that results from a certain indwelling of Father, Son and Spirit promised by Jesus. Consequently, Christian academics are confronted by a choice, increasingly acute in today's society, either to accept the conventional standards of knowledge and research agreed on in a given discipline, or to introduce the ill-understood and widely rejected criteria of the Christian mind which combine faith with academic work. Jews, Moslems and others face the same choice and compromises. . . . In my view Christian economic thought cannot really progress without offering alternatives to the conventional positive theories it rightly criticizes.

See Arnold McKee, "The Christian Mind and Economic Welfare" *Bulletin of the Association of Christian Economists*, no. 33 (Spring 1999): 5.

★ In a later paper, Hay comments that, unlike Becker's assumption of individual utility maximization in every aspect of behavior,

the rational economic man model is incomplete: it does not encompass the human capacity to show love to a neighbor, the importance of human relationships which transcend market contracting, and the undoubted fact that for many people work is a good in itself, and not just an unfortunate necessity.

The Biblical material would suggest a much richer agenda [for a Christian economist] than the trinity of efficiency, growth and distribution of utilitarian welfare economics. The Biblical analysis . . . suggests the following criteria for our research agenda: (i) How far do economic institutions allow human beings to exercise responsible stewardship? (ii) Is the use of natural resources characterized by care for the created order? (iii) Does the economy create opportunities for satisfying work? (iv) What are the causes of poverty? and are there societal mechanisms to prevent destitution? (v) Has the pursuit of wealth, for its own sake, become detrimental to other values in society, e.g. family life? (vi) How effective are the authorities in promoting justice in the economic sphere?

See Donald Hay, "On Being a Christian Economist" (paper presented at the conference "Christian Economists Doing Economics: A View from the Trenches," sponsored by the business and economics department of Wheaton College, Chicago, Ill., January 6, 1998), 2.

making.* Hay in fact perceives a direct conflict between Christian morality and economic morality, found in its purest form at Chicago: "The Christian conception of the good is that man should love God with all his heart and mind, and that he should love his neighbour as himself. Whatever *content* is given to these commands to love, one thing is clear: the good is defined in terms of persons *other* than the individual himself, although a proper self-love is not excluded." [48] Christian thought may be fuzzy about how much "self-love" is to be allowed but the answer cannot be to dismiss any real place for a concept of the "common good" that transcends individual gain (and where the common good means more than just the inclusion of the welfare of others in maximizing an individual "utility function").

In the past many others have agreed with Hay that Christianity cannot successfully coexist with the values that often prevail in the modern state. For some of them, however, the appropriate conclusion is that Christianity must be abandoned (or rendered practically impotent). As long ago as the mid-eighteenth century, Jean-Jacques Rousseau declared that Christianity could not coexist with the *religion civile* on which his new secular society of the Contrat Social would be based—that the two represented "two legislations, two sovereigns, two native lands" that imposed "antithetical obligations." [49] If that were the case, it would be Christianity that would have to go. Becker and others at Chicago are not so blunt (or perhaps so aware of the full implications of their analysis), but the final outcome of their work is little different.

CHICAGO AS NATURAL LAW

Another accomplished and also devout professional economist who has addressed a topic similar to Hay's is Jennifer Roback Morse. As a longtime libertarian, she finds that having a child, among other things, altered her perspective. Perhaps there is an essential truth to the feeling of many ordinary mothers, as they commonly express it themselves, that a child is not supposed to be an economic asset paying a return on investment but an outlet for love—an "opportunity to give" that is deliberately sought for this very purpose of giving of oneself. [50] It is a maternal sentiment very much at odds with

---

* As Hay thus writes, "Does this mean that an economist who is a Christian must abandon welfare economics? In terms of using it as a tool for policy recommendations, I believe it does." Similarly, because benefit-cost analysis is a form of efficiency analysis, Hay finds that "it is evident that a Christian should not be applying the same criterion for efficiency as is applied in economic analysis." See Donald A. Hay, *Economics Today: A Christian Critique* (Leicester, U.K., Inter-Varsity Press, 1989), 201.

the standard framework of economic thinking.* Indeed, as individualistic values spread in a society this trend is commonly manifested in increasing numbers of couples who choose to have only one child or to remain childless altogether, and more broadly a declining birthrate.

Morse does not seem any more sure than Hay of her ability to reconcile her Christian morals and her lifetime professional role as economist. Brought up in a Roman Catholic family, she suggests that perhaps the long-standing tradition of natural-law thinking in Catholic thought can help to reconcile the expression of self-interest and ideas of the common good. Among other things, "economists, like natural law thinkers, affirm that human nature is universal and enduring." Indeed, for Morse the best "hope" for economists may well lie in a turn back to concepts of "Christian natural law."[51]

From a natural-law perspective in Christianity, a perspective that has always put a high premium on the role of reason in human affairs, perhaps one might take a more favorable view of the Chicago project.† Indeed, the Chicago project does hold out the prospect of a more rational world. Human actions will become more predictable, as people are more capable of behaving rationally according to the pursuit of their own advantage. Wars and other disasters may be averted as the pursuit of individual self-interest is more widely accepted and is channeled in more-individualistic forms of activity such as the market. People will be less likely to fight, they will be less bothered by seeming emotional departures from rational thought, once they understand that universal economic forces common to all human beings have actually been working below the surface everywhere at every time, however difficult it may sometimes have been in the past to recognize them.††

---

* Economics often tries to incorporate every action within its utility-maximizing framework. However, to take an extreme example, a mother might step in front of a bullet to save the live of her child, giving up her own life in the process. There is no plausible way that any such action could be described as the mother "acting to maximize her utility" over the long run. Economists need to accept and learn to deal with the fact that there are simply social concepts such as "duty," "honor," and "obligation" that are real motivations in human existence and that lie altogether outside the normal economic framework of utility maximization.

† As I have suggested, the Chicago school of economics represents a Protestant side of American economics. However, to the extent that it preaches a perfectly rational world that operates strictly according to natural economic laws, it is more in the Roman tradition. Most great thinkers and schools, as I contend, have a preponderant emphasis but nevertheless it is also true that they usually do involve some mixture of elements both from the Roman and Protestant traditions in Western thought.

†† Pope John Paul II, to be sure, would almost certainly strongly disagree with any such interpretation that the economic logic of the Chicago project can be regarded as a modern reinterpretation of the traditional natural-law thinking of the Catholic Church. The pope instead is concerned that there exist "broad sectors of public opinion [that] justify certain crimes against life in the name of the rights of individual freedom." People falling into such ways of thinking have a diminished sense of "conscience" to the extent that they find "it increasingly difficult to distinguish between good and evil"—

The Chicago gospel in this respect is actually at least as old as Adam Smith, who also believed in the harmony of the natural order, grounded in the operation of the law of self-interest. The theologian Paul Tillich once explained that it was characteristic of the thinking of the entire eighteenth century that the "principle of a presupposed harmony . . . produces indirectly what [in an earlier era] was supposed to be produced directly by a divine interference." Well before the Enlightenment, the natural-law theology of the Roman Catholic Church had sought an improved understanding of a harmonious world operating according to rational laws put in place by God. In the Enlightenment, the secular idea of the "harmony" of nature replaced the earlier transcendent role of "supernatural authority." Indeed, Tillich found, "the first clear expression . . . can be seen in the area of economics. It was expressed by Adam Smith . . . in his idea of harmony" as yielded by the workings of the natural forces of self-interest in society.[52]

As a modern and secular form of natural-law theology, Chicago economics thus might "work" for its true believers, not in a scientific but in the old-fashioned manner of a religious belief. Chicago preaches individual pursuit of self-interest as making for a rational world but this faith in a rational world grounded in natural law may in fact be a comforting gospel for the members of the Chicago "church." Initiates into the Chicago school of economics do in fact commonly exhibit the behavior of the true believer; they are a small band who profess to have unique access to the fundamental truths of the world. Despite their methodological individualism, Chicago economists— more than most other economists—are socialized to a powerful common value system. Chicago proselytizes a set of values that it believes should be common to all, even as these very same values seemingly deny the existence of any common truth that transcends individual motives. It is not the first time in history that a powerful religious commitment and sense of deep personal satisfaction in the lives of the followers in a set of church dogmas have been derived from a confused—if not internally contradictory—theology.

---

as Becker's economics finds that crime is simply another variant on ordinary human behavior, springing from the same human sources and with no moral judgment implied. If economic thinking seeks maximum personal happiness, Pope John Paul II laments a current "cultural climate which fails to perceive any meaning or value in suffering, but rather considers suffering the epitome of evil, to be eliminated at all costs." If Posner considers the morality of euthanasia to be a question of benefits minus costs, the pope condemns a way of thinking that regards "euthanasia [as] sometimes justified by the utilitarian motive of avoiding costs which bring no return and which weigh heavily on society." In short, as Hay suggests of Christianity more broadly, any reconciliation of the pope's thinking and the moral framework of Chicago analysis in the third generation is likely to be problematic at best. They are simply two clashing outlooks on the world—whatever the difficulties this might create for any people who might today regard themselves as both Chicago economists and devout Catholics. See John Paul II, "Encyclical—Evangelium Vitae," *Origins,* April 6, 1995, 692, 695.

In the basic individualism of its moral outlook, the Chicago school of economics is not alone among the social sciences; indeed, there is a particular affinity with Freudian and other twentieth-century psychology. As James Davison Hunter observes, the basic way of thinking of psychology reflects a set of "utilitarian formulae" that focus on the well being of the "autonomous individual." The psychological emphasis is on the use of self-knowledge to promote "self-esteem," thereby enabling a person to achieve a higher level of satisfaction in life. The details of psychological analysis are much less important than this very framework of thought, which, Hunter thinks, defines "the height, length and breadth of moral hope and possibility" for individual behavior over much of American society today. It has not only invaded the mainstream Protestant churches, but surprisingly has extended its reach as well into evangelical Christianity, where there is "little to distinguish" the moral teachings of leading evangelical preachers from the lessons of "secular family therapists."[53]

The inclusion of psychotherapeutic categories of thought does not merely supplement the traditional Christian theology. In the therapeutic way of thinking, for example, there is little place for "shame-based morality" and "the problem of sin is all but absent. "The central goals for the individual become such things as "reducing harmful stress," "overcoming negative emotions," and "building self-confidence." When these individualistic messages become part of the core teachings of the church, the result is that "the Christian worldview . . . undergoes a peculiar reworking." Indeed, compared with historical messages such as the fundamental corruption of human nature since the Fall in the Garden, or the possibility of salvation only "in faith alone," the theological departure is so great as to be "breathtaking."[54]

Hence, despite the Christian trappings sometimes present, the actual result is the elevation of modern psychology, like Chicago economics, to the status of a new religious truth. For the many people who may then come to dispense with the Christian elements altogether, it represents a secular form of religion—a faith that also parallels closely in its basic values the utilitarian and individualistic messages of the Chicago school, as developed by writers such as Becker and Posner. Hunter describes the place of psychology today in American society:

> When it comes to the moral life of children, the vocabulary of the psychologist frames virtually all public discussion. For decades now, contributions from philosophers and theologians have been muted or nonexistent. . . . Rather, it is the psychologists, and in particular the developmental and educational psychologists, who have owned this

field—in theory and in practice. All of the major players in the last half of the twentieth century have been psychologists, Erik Erikson, B. F. Skinner, Benjamin Spock, Havighurst, Carl Rodgers, Jean Piaget, Abraham Maslow [and others] . . . —their assumptions, concepts, and paradigms have largely determined how all of us think about the moral lives of children, and, indeed, about moral life generally.

Why has psychology become so dominant—even . . . infiltrating religion? The discipline itself has maintained over the years that, as the science of human motive and behavior, it comes closest to a rational understanding of that difficult and elusive phenomenon, human nature. As such, psychology is supposedly in a position to specify the conditions that permit or impede the full realization of a person's natural creativity, productivity, and well-being.[55]

To understand human nature is to answer a central question of traditional religion. Yet, if the Chicago school has now improved upon psychology in developing a yet more rational understanding of human behavior in matters of family, marriage, birth, death, children and other domains from which economic analysis had previously been excluded, it will then have laid a superior base of rational understanding for a still higher level of well-being— of "individual utility," in the language of economics. If Becker has not supplanted Dr. Spock (or his successors) in *Redbook, Family Circle,* and other popular magazines, popular religion has seldom incorporated the highest levels of theological reasoning. Over the centuries few ordinary Roman Catholics read or understood the full logic of Thomas Aquinas. Perhaps Becker, Posner, and others of their Chicago ilk have now laid the groundwork for a new modern *Summa* that for the instructed will move past the lesser truths not only of Christianity but also of psychological bedfellows in the social sciences to provide the most fundamental understanding of all, grounded in the economic teachings of the Chicago school.

POSTMATERIAL VALUES

As the Chicago school triumphed in American economics from the 1960s onward, Becker, Posner, and others at Chicago thus had a lot of company in challenging the traditional claims to authority of family, country, church, government, and other institutions. Indeed, their efforts served to create a new economic imagery and poetry that would bless with a modern economic and scientific symbolism a powerful rethinking of social values taking shape in American society. The University of Michigan political scientist Ronald Inglehart, in commenting on the "erosion of institutional authority" in American life in recent years, attributes it to the emergence of "postmaterialist values." As attested to by survey data and various other forms of evidence, there has been, Inglehart says, a "massive erosion of trust in government" since the 1960s. Indeed, this is the case not only for government; "we are witnessing a long-term trend that is weakening the authority of established institutions" in all walks of American life.[56]

According to Inglehart, it is the very success of economic growth and progress in the United States that has laid the basis for the new skepticism of authority. The progressive agenda of Paul Samuelson and many others has been so successful as to undermine its own foundations. The economic successes of the United States and Europe since World War II have encouraged a widespread public sense of "security" that basic material needs will be met. As a result, "the public gradually sees less need for the discipline and self-denial demanded" by previous institutional arrangements and social values.[57] Because "postmaterialists take prosperity for granted," Inglehart thinks, they end up focusing on "other aspects of life, such as politics and the quality of the physical and social environment." There is also a "postmaterialist emphasis on self-expression and self-realization."[58] This postmaterialism first exerted a significant influence in the 1960s and gathered momentum in the 1970s.[59] In popular music, the Beatles, Bob Dylan, the Rolling Stones, and other performers challenged long-standing conventions. In universities, students protested against traditional patterns of paternal supervision of their lives. Urban ghettos across the United States erupted into riots. Distrust of the federal government expanded with each new draftee sent to fight an increasingly unpopular war in Vietnam. The Watergate scandal led to the first forced resignation of a president in American history.

Becker, Posner, and other Chicago economics of the third generation were first achieving their professional reputations at about the same time as this period of remarkable changes in American values. There were powerful trends toward the erosion of traditional authority, a decline in social trust, eroding moral restrains, and a new focus on individual self-expression in American life. As recently described in polling results done for the *Washington Post*,

> Over the last 30 years, polling shows the proportion of people saying they think their fellow citizens generally are as honest and moral as they used to be has fallen significantly. In a 1952 survey, as many answered yes as said no. In 1965, there were three yeses for every four

noes. But this year there were almost three noes (71 percent) for every yes (26 percent).

In the same period, trust in government has also declined radically. In 1968, 61 percent said they trusted the government in Washington to do the right thing most or all the time; in 1998, only 33 percent felt that way.

Pollster Dan Yankelovich wrote that "the transformation of values from the mid-'60s to the late-'70s confronts us with one of the sharpest discontinuities in our cultural history." In that period's "radical extension of individualism . . . from the political domain to personal lifestyle," he notes, the concepts of duty, social conformity, respectability and sexual morality were devalued, in favor of expressiveness and pleasure seeking.[60]

The Chicago project as seen in the work of Becker and Posner is not so much an explanation of this phenomenon as an affirmation of it.★ A modern priesthood is giving its approval in a new artistic imagery of economic "science." Chicago economists blessed the new changes in the technical language of economic efficiency, still the leading moral arbiter of good and evil,

---

★ By the 1990s, many of the young rebels of the 1960s against authority had become the new elite in American life. David Brooks wonderfully describes their convoluted and often comic efforts to reconcile a youthful worldview that rejected most forms of social authority with their new status of power and influence in American society. The new establishment was based on intelligence and merit, rather than the inherited position and proper social manner of the old Protestant elites, but it was an establishment nonetheless. The occupants of the highest ranks of American society still sought to maintain their 1960s attitudes of irreverence and rebellion, showing at times an almost willful blindness to the contradictions involved. Even as they were lawyers and doctors making hundreds of thousand of dollars per year and sending their children to Harvard and Princeton, they still professed to believe that

> the [1960s'] move from home and religion toward autonomy and psychology . . . was the way of progress.
>
> Most social critics [then] were calling for a more individualistic form of spiritual life. . . . Freudians, theologians, or Beat poets—[they] were telling the young to break loose from their communities, groups, and religious orders. Spiritual fulfillment is found when you go your own way.
>
> Among the intellectual class, mores had changed. Writers and academics sought to instill a more individualistic ethos in their children. One that would encourage self-exploration over obedience.
>
> The dominant trend of through of those years [of the 1960s] was . . . away from the group loyalty and deference that were the ideals in communities like St. Nick's parish. Each person can and must find his or her own course to spiritual fulfillment.

See David Brooks, *BOBOS in Paradise: The New Upper Class and How They Got There* (New York: Simon and Schuster, 2000), 232–33.

the most powerful source of social legitimacy in American life today.* Chicago might be said to have been a professional economic equivalent in the 1960s and 1970s to the counterculture and its manifestations of disrespect for traditional authority and the promotion of a new individualism and libertarianism in many areas of American life. The challenge posed by Becker to the implicit social values previously embedded both in progressive economic analysis and Judeo-Christian morality was as great as the challenge posed by the Dylan song "Mr. Tambourine Man," with its nasal twang, for pre-1960s music-listening habits.

In the end, all this admittedly involved a certain intellectual incoherence, although that seemingly has not detracted from its wide impact. Becker was in effect employing the economic framework of efficiency maximization to justify a new libertarian value system. Yet achieving a high degree of economic efficiency in society is a collective undertaking, as Samuelson had earlier portrayed matters in *Economics*. One might say that Becker was employing a (progressive) analytical apparatus developed for a framework of rational social action—the working together for ultimately the achievement of heaven on earth for all humankind—to defend a libertarian value system that fundamentally rejects most forms of rationally directed collective action. In its deep-seated individualism, the libertarian value system is necessarily at odds with the progressive values of the gospel of efficiency that had provided the grounds for the American development of the welfare and regulatory state of the twentieth century.

---

* Besides the Chicago school of economics, another leading source of social legitimacy for the new libertarian individualism in American society has been Freudian psychology. The moral implications of Freudian thinking were laid out by Philip Rieff many years ago in *Freud: The Mind of the Moralist*. A more recent commentator, inspired in part by Rieff's analysis, observes:

> For Freud, psychopathological habits of mind were not exceptional; they were, rather, ordinary and commonplace. In moral terms, the exception did not subvert the rule so much as expose its arbitrariness.
>
> The visit down to these more disturbing realms of the mind . . . has produced a fascinating range of public excuses for behavior once judged morally wrong. Freud stands behind the modern movement to abolish culpability generally. . . . He was . . . unwilling to advocate the moral judgments of any established order in society.
>
> Therapy attempts to establish a certainty about who one is. Freud's rejection of the religious bases of this certainty necessitated a search for another way to secure self-affirmation. The new basis is an intense and continuous study of self, which has spawned a therapeutic elite that has developed a "science" of self-concern. Priests were once responsible for the cure of souls. Today therapists transform selves by offering exercises in self-awareness and self-improvement.

See Jonathan B. Imber, "American Therapies and Pieties," *The American Enterprise* 4 (May/June 1993): 18.

As an illustration of the conflicting strains in Becker's thinking, it might seem, for example, that Becker's libertarian values could be applied to the United States' "war on drugs"—the long-standing crusade against the use of illegal drugs such as heroin, cocaine, and marijuana. It is now costing American society on the order of twenty-five billion dollars per year in direct government expenditures as well as other substantial burdens in other countries (including frequent corruption of the political process). The lives of millions of Americans have been adversely affected by the war on drugs, many people being simply caught up in government enforcement efforts even though they have had no involvement themselves with illegal drugs (in being required to take drug tests in the workplace, for example). Yet the war on drugs seems to have had little impact on the price and availability of illegal drugs in American life or on levels of drug use (which have gone up and down but have not shown much clear correlation with enforcement efforts).

If Becker were a policy activist in, say, the manner of Milton Friedman, one might well have expected him to become a prominent crusader in American life for the abolition of the war on drugs. Becker may somewhere have made some criticisms of U.S. drug policy, but he has not followed Friedman's crusading example. Perhaps Becker simply lacks Friedman's taste for public controversy, finds active political involvement distasteful, or fears the negative consequences for himself of taking such an unpopular stand against the mainstream of American public opinion.

However, another consideration may be that a full-fledged application of Becker's economic approach to decision making in society can also provide some powerful justifications for the war on drugs that lie outside any official explanations. The war on drugs has a significant external benefit that may significantly exceed the direct benefits (themselves seemingly rather small) to society of its effects in reducing consumption of illegal drugs. The prisons of the United States now hold the extraordinary number of about two million people, many of them sent there for violations of drug laws. Young males in particular are likely to be apprended for drug offenses and sent to prison. These same males (especially the ones caught using drugs) also have much higher propensities to commit violent crimes, as compared with most other population subgroups in American society. By sending many young males (disproportionately black) to prison for illegal drug offenses, one might say, American society (without ever saying so explicitly) has adopted a de facto policy of "preventive detention." Before someone with a high-risk profile can commit a more serious crime, it may be more "efficient" simply to put him in prison, given the opportunity created by a drug-law offense. The crime rate in American society has in fact been declining rapidly as the number of people in prison for drug offenses has climbed (there have obviously been other factors such as the economic boom of the 1990s and demographic shifts).

Given the very same level of illegal drug use, a young and potentially dangerous male is much more likely to end up in prison than another drug abuser in American society. The economic explanation may be that other types of drug users—older people living in the suburbs, for example—have much lower propensities to commit violent crimes in the future, and thus there is little "external" economic benefit to society from putting these kinds of drug users in prison.

A civil libertarian, to be sure, would strongly object to the very idea of putting large numbers of people in prison under a system of virtual preventive detention—simply because they have a much higher future likelihood of committing an armed robbery, personal assault, or other violent crime. Hence, following Becker, the "distaste" for violating the personal liberties of so many Americans would have to be factored into overall calculations of benefits and costs in society. However, there would also be a large countering benefit in terms of satisfying a strong public "taste" for a reduced level of anxiety about crime.

Considered as a matter of overall benefits and costs, an economic approach as Becker might apply it to the war on drugs thus might in fact suggest that a policy effectively of preventive detention of many young males is in fact a successful government policy. If it would seem a radical assault on individual freedom, it is a distinguishing characteristic of the Becker approach to exclude such abstract social ideals in favor of more-real underlying economic calculations.

There is thus a basic tension in Becker's thinking. On the one hand, his emphasis on individual motives as the driving force in the world tends to affirm a libertarian outlook on the world. On the other hand, his emphasis on achieving economic efficiency through comprehensive calculation of benefits and costs of all kinds may serve to undermine those very same libertarian values.

AN ULTIMATE CALVINISM

For those who might object to the social values advanced by the Chicago project (even as it seemingly denies the existence of such collectively powerful values), it might be suggested that perhaps they should try to protect their community by banning Chicago economists from their own circles—as a community might seek to exclude, for example, movies with high pornographic content. At a minimum, they might attempt to ban the application of the morally corrosive Chicago way of thinking in matters outside conventional marketplace contexts.★

However, any such approach would put defenders of traditional moral systems, including some devoutly religious economists, in an unduly defensive posture. If the economic model of a world of rational individual maximizers of their utility, as developed and applied by the Chicago project, should actually turn out to be valid in every area of life, it will be impossible to deny the correctness of the Chicago vision. If the scientific explanatory power of Chicago theories (as shown by regression analyses and other valid statistical methods and confirmed by long and rigorous testing) keeps steadily improving, there will be no way to deny this reality. It would simply be necessary to face the fact of a new religious truth for the world. The Christian religion bases its authority on its claims to ultimate and absolute truth. God is inseparable, as many Christian theologians have long said, from the basic laws of the universe giving a direction and meaning to history.

If the Chicago assessment of the human condition were ever genuinely confirmed, the new religion that would result would be grounded, in some respects, in strong Protestant tendencies. Becker and Posner, in this regard following in the path of Frank Knight, exhibit powerful Calvinist tendencies of a secular sort. The theology of Calvin and other sixteenth-century Protestant reformers put particular emphasis on the sinful condition of fallen humankind in this altogether depraved world. Becker and Posner's view of crime, family life, and other social matters is in fact consistent with a Calvinist sense of a gravely fallen condition of humanity. Self-interest and calculation of personal gain—among the results of original sin in the classic Christian formulation—will rule everywhere without exception. In the past only the most extreme Calvinist could ever have believed that the corruption of human behavior in this world is total, that true devotion and sacrifice for others, or other such motives outside ordinary individual advantage, are nowhere present in human affairs.

★ For example, Arnold S. Relman, a former editor in chief of the *New England Journal of Medicine*, argues that the intrusion of a market ethic is undermining the practice of American medicine. Instead, it will be essential to establish a clear moral distinction, he contends, between the ethics of the marketplace and the ethics of the practice of medicine: "If this description of a contract between society and the medical profession is even approximately correct, then clearly there are important distinctions to be made between what society has a right to expect of practicing physicians and what it expects of people in business." See Arnold S. Relman, "What Market Values Are Doing to Medicine," *Atlantic Monthly,* March 1992, 100.

If its message should turn out to be true, the Chicago school of economics thus might be regarded as the bearer of a new ultra-Calvinist revelation from God. Alternatively, the economics of the Chicago project may provide the foundation for a brand-new secular religion that leaves God out of the picture.[61] It would be an all-encompassing form of libertarian religion—not the only form of libertarianism possible—in which the only loyalty, the only frame of reference in which anything can have meaning, is the act of individual consumer choice for individual benefit. Even "altruism" in such a Chicago frame of reference is not really altruism as people ordinarily understand it; it is merely a different way of going about maximizing one's own individual well-being. No members of the Chicago project can ever intentionally reduce or limit their own utility—it would be a virtual contradiction of the basic tenets of Chicago faith—because they are simply doing something that is "the right thing to do" or because "God has told them so."

CONCLUSION

In preaching the social benefits of a free-market system, Milton Friedman had to believe that someone was listening and might be inspired to act to defend the market. Yet such a market defense would have to be provided for social benefit, as a statement of the true believer's commitment to economic progress and other social ideals. Other than possibly Friedman himself, no one individual (economist or otherwise) could reasonably expect that his or her efforts could have a perceptible impact on the future role of the market, the achievement of economic progress in the world, or the future preservation of economic freedom. If his efforts were less obvious than Friedman's missionary zeal to improve the human condition, Stigler also showed a strong commitment to the cause of economic science as a collective undertaking in search of genuine truth.

None of this behavior would make much sense in the framework of economic thought presented by the most prominent members of the third-generation Chicago school of Becker and others—as Stigler himself also seemingly came to realize, if only later in his career and coincident with the rise of this third generation at Chicago. Within the framework of this most recent Chicago outlook on the world, collective arrangements of most kinds would be difficult or impossible to sustain. The market system probably would not survive, because its existence requires an element of commitment to the defense of property rights and other market sustenance that transcends individual benefit. Many other social institutions on any large scale probably would not exist. The nation-state as we know it might well disappear because it would lack the social bonds necessary to sustain it.

This is not to say that the motives of individual gain are not widespread in all areas of life, including family, religion, marriage, charitable activities, and other places where high ideals are often professed and then set aside in practice. Becker and his followers have contributed valuably by taking the assumptions of the marketplace to their furthest possible reach to see the analytical outcomes. However, while there is genuine intellectual interest in such an exercise, the results are not real life but a caricature of real life.⋆ The Chicago school and its followers do not always seem to be aware of this.

Becker, Posner, and others in the Chicago project can also be given a large amount of credit for, if not their precise intent, bringing a new clarity to a central issue for economics. Where does the boundary for the pursuit of individual interest lie? Is there any boundary at all, despite what most economists (implicitly if seldom explicitly) assumed in the past, even while they offered few if any reasons for locating it? How can the institution of the market be defended—seemingly requiring collective action of some sort—in a world limited to actions based on the market ethic of self-interest alone? In short, for those who may find markets to be a desirable form for organizing the economic activities of society, how might they resolve the market paradox?

The old answers such as were found in Samuelson's *Economics* no longer seem satisfactory at the beginning of the twenty-first century. Moreover, the standard framework of analysis of contemporary economics seems unable to provide persuasive new answers. If any answers are to be found within the economics profession, it seems that economists will have to turn their attention in new directions, toward things such as the motivating force of religion and the possible roles of "economic theology" and other secular belief systems in sustaining the economic systems of modern (or postmodern) society.

⋆ Economist Glenn Loury has recently commented on the limitations of the analytical approach generally taken by all the social sciences in the current era, elements that Chicago has taken to an extreme:

> [I am] impressed with the limited utility of the social sciences in the management and conduct of human affairs. . . . We tend to take only a piece of the person as the venue for our study. There is something that is reductive about our process. . . . [In reality] human beings are not defined by their personal desires at a point in time, and they are not even defined by their biological limitations. . . . We have a free will, we are spiritual creatures, we have souls. So what we are in the fullness of our humanity transcends what it is that can be understood through the particular window that an economist or psychologist or sociologist might bring to it.

See interview with Glenn C. Loury, "Economics Raises Profoundly Moral Questions," *Religion and Liberty* (November and December 1996): 2.

part **FOUR**

RELIGION AND THE NEW INSTITUTIONAL ECONOMICS

The Chicago school produced yet another great economist, who was mostly left out of the account in Part III. Winner of the the Nobel Prize in economics in 1991, Ronald Coase was born and educated in England, moved early in his career to the United States, and taught at the University of Chicago law school from 1964 to 1981 (where he still has emeritus status). More than most economists, Coase comes close to the scientific ideal of the detached observer interested mainly in achieving an accurate understanding of the world as it actually works.[1] The world that Coase found sometimes did not conform very closely with the thinking of his fellow Chicago economists—one reason for not including him in Part III.

Coase's influence on economics is mainly derived from two articles, "The Nature of the Firm," published in 1937; and "The Problem of Social Cost," published in 1960.[2] The influence of these two publications has been such that Eirik Furubotn and Rudolf Richter describe Coase as "the 'father' of the New Institutional Economics," which is today having a major impact on much of the work of the economics profession.★ Douglass North, who received the Nobel Prize in economics in 1993 for his contributions to institutional economics, declares that Coase "provided the link to connect neoclassical theory to institutional analysis."[3]

After Coase, the leading figure in reviving institutional economics has been Oliver Williamson (whose teaching career has been spent mainly at the University of Pennsylvania and the University of California at Berkeley). He acknowledges four people as the "key academic figures in my research": Kenneth Arrow, Alfred D. Chandler, Jr., Ronald Coase, and Herbert Simon.[4] In books such as *Markets and Hierarchies* in 1975 and *The Economic Institutions of Capitalism* in 1985, Williamson provided new kinds of explanations for a wide range of economic phenomena that a standard neoclassical analysis could not do much to illuminate.[5] As Coase had pointed out as long ago as 1937, neoclassical economics was of little help in understanding a fundamental economic question: why some industries are organized as a few large corporations, while others are configured as a much larger number of atomistic firms.

The role of information in an economic system has been central to the thinking of the new institutional economics. It was not until George Stigler's 1961 article "The Economics of Information" that economists began to pay significant attention to this subject. By the 1970s the literature was growing rapidly and included leading contributors such as George Akerlof, Joseph Stiglitz, and Michael Spence. Spence would comment in 1975 that there was already "an impressive and growing body of literature that suggests [that] the firm, in large part, consists of nonmarket institutions whose function is to deal with resource allocation in the presence of informational constraints that markets handle poorly or do not handle at all."[6]

In the early part of the twentieth century, historical and institutional research had been a thriving enterprise in American economics. John R. Commons, Thorstein Veblen, and Wesley Clair Mitchell were part of the institutional school. In the years after World War II, however, the members of the economics profession mostly directed their efforts to neoclassical analyses of static "equilibrium" systems. The literary style of institutional economics

---

★ From the mid-1980s to at least the mid-1990s, Furubotn and Richter organized an international seminar to discuss new developments in institutional economics, attracting many leading economists who were participants in this effort to reconstruct economic theory. The papers from the conference were then published each year in the first issue of the *Journal of Institutional and Theoretical Economics* (a journal more than one hundred years old, formerly published as the *Zeitschrift für die gesamte Staatswissenschaft*). They have authored the most comprehensive survey available of this important new field of economic research. See Eirik G. Furubotn and Rudolf Richter, *Institutions and Economic Theory: The Contribution of the New Institutional Economics* (Ann Arbor: University of Michigan Press, 1997).

lost out to mathematical, statistical and other formal methods—regarded by most economists as analytically more scientific and more sophisticated.

The revival of institutional economics in recent years has not yet meant a return to the older literary forms.★ Indeed, as Furubotn and Richter comment, the more recent institutional economists "have been at pains to disassociate themselves" from their predecessors, showing no inclination to return to the style of "massive historical-descriptive studies" that had often included, for example, lengthy historical explorations of the role of cultural and religious influences on economic behavior (as undertaken, for instance, by Max Weber in Germany).[7] As Viktor Vanberg has recently commented (although he is somewhat skeptical himself), the new institutionalists have believed that "their research program can be easily based on the core of conventional neo-classical theory and that it is not necessary to turn as radically away from it as had been demanded by some of the old institutionalists."[8] Still employing high-powered quantitative methods, the new institutional economists have introduced a new vocabulary of "asymetric information," "information signaling," "principal-agent problems," "opportunism," "implicit contracting," and various other terms of art.[9]

In the 1990s, however, some economists would suggest that the new directions taken by institutional economics might yet lead to more radical changes in economic methods. Those employing the formal apparatus of quantitative economics were still finding it difficult to shed light on many central economic questions. There has been a growing movement to recognize a larger role for cultural influences in economic performance.† Some

---

★ A small band of American economists did attempt to maintain the old institutional tradition through the Association for Evolutionary Economics and its publication, the *Journal of Economic Issues*. However, their efforts went largely ignored by the economic mainstream after the 1940s. For examples of more recent writings of this school of "evolutionary economics," see Philip A. Klein, ed., *Beyond Dissent: Essays in Institutional Economics* (Armonk, N.Y.: M. E. Sharpe, 1994).

† Economic journalist Robert Samuelson recently commented on a new trend in economic thinking that he was witnessing:

> Globalization's boosters claim it's been stymied: Too many countries abstained from reforms—or botched them. True. Africa largely missed the process. In Russia, the dismantling of the command-and-control economy enriched local elites through corrupt "privatization" programs. The overall economy slumped even as a blessed few profited. But these facts beg the basic questions. Why did some countries reject reforms? Why did they fail elsewhere? Much of Latin America, for example, abandoned longstanding policies of trade protectionism and favoritism for local companies. Between 1985 and 1996, the average tariff in Latin America fell from 50 percent to 10 percent. The results so far have been modest.
> What explains the contrasts [with places like East Asia]?
> Perhaps culture. The gospel of capitalism presumes that human nature is constant. Given the proper incentives—the ability to profit from hard work and risk taking—people will thrive. Maybe not.

economists are now saying that the modern business firm is shaped not only by its formal wage, salary and other incentive systems but also by the contents of its belief system. The internal structure of informal incentives created by a business culture may have a major impact on the ability of the firm to make efficient use of its resources. Top business managers may be selected as much for their "leadership" and "inspirational" qualities as for their ability to precisely calculate profit and loss.

Similar things are now also being said of whole national economic systems. Besides relying on the inputs of capital and labor and the structure of property rights and other legal arrangements, the functioning of a national economy may depend on a host of less well defined factors involving elements of culture. Then, once a national culture comes into the picture, it is a short distance to religion. Economists today are being pushed to accept that they may have to take up the role of religion if they want to understand the full workings of economic systems.* From one newly influential perspective, religion is often a decisive influence on the form of "social capital" of a society. A number of economists and other social scientists are now suggest-

---

[Some] scholars from the United States, Africa and Latin America argue that strong social or moral values predispose some peoples for and against economic growth. Among some, corruption is an accepted way of advancement. Culture affects politics, and some societies—as a result of history, tradition, religion—can't easily adopt capitalist attitudes, institutions, and policies. Even when they try, they often fail because it's so unnatural.

No one likes to talk about culture, because it raises two contradictory objections. The first is that the West (mainly the United States) is foisting its values on others in the name of economic growth. The second is that some cultures perpetuate economic inferiority or poverty. But culture will not vanish because its inconvenient. It's constantly colliding with rampant global capitalism. This is a defining conflict of the new century.

See Robert J. Samuelson, "Persistent Poverty," *Washington Post,* September 20, 2000, A33.

* In non-Western cultures, many dramatic examples can be found of the direct practical impact of local beliefs on economic actions. In Zimbabwe and Zambia, one researcher relates that at Lake Kariba (a huge body of water between the two countries created by the completion of the Kariba Dam on the Zambesi River):

> The majority of the Tonga who became wealthy from fishing were viewed by their kin as using magic which required the sacrifice of their relatives. They were viewed as having "invested in medicine which required the sacrifice of kinsmen through magical means." As a way of avoiding such pressures, the majority of the Tonga quit fishing and re-invested their capital in agricultural implements and livestock.

See Isaac Malasha, *In Search of a New Management Regime on the Northern Shores of Lake Kariba,* Occasional Paper Series of the Center for Applied Social Sciences (Harare: University of Zimbabwe, February 1996), 16.

ing that social capital can be a key explanatory factor along with physical and human capital in determining national economic outcomes.

In Part IV, I will examine the rise of the new institutional economics over the past thirty years within the American economics profession and the potential implications for the greater study of religious influences as part of the accepted subject matter of professional economics. A wide range of changes in economic methods might be required, if religion were to be taken more seriously as a key "factor of production."

chapter EIGHT

A NEW ECONOMIC WORLD

Unlike those working in the physical sciences, economists typically make heroic assumptions and then work out the logical implications, recognizing full well that the models depart radically from the real world. The process of going from the assumptions and models to insights about actual economic events thus necessarily involves considerable exercise in judgment. Although Milton Friedman and other economists have sometimes asserted that the usefulness of economic models can be determined strictly by their predictive powers, few working economists actually function that way. Economics is too much a historical subject, limited in its ability to create replicable experiments. Indeed, judging the usefulness of an economic model is more like saying whether a painting by Picasso tells us something interesting or important about the world. Because there is such a large degree of subjective judgment involved, fashion and fad play a larger role in the daily practice of economics than in the physical sciences.

This is one of many differences, despite the outward attempt of the social sciences to model themselves on the methods and forms of the physical sciences. For example, the "definition of the problem" plays a much greater role in economics than in physics. When Einstein reached the outcome that $E = mc^2$, the initial question he had posed was startling and novel but would have attracted little interest among physicists without the bottom-line result. Because of the complexity and interconnectedness of the social world, it is often the case that the best economists can do is to suggest a new and perhaps better way of thinking about possible causes in the real world. When it is so seldom possible to achieve the equivalent of $E = mc^2$, a different working approach is necessary.[1]

In one of the most important economic articles of the past forty years, George Akerlof's discussion of the used-car market and the problem of "lemons," Akerlof did not establish any precise laws or reach any definitive conclusions about used-car versus new-car markets.[2] Rather, for the very starting point for the article, he pointed to the fact that economists had left out of past theorizing a key element of consumer decision making, the difficulties experienced in efforts to verify product quality. This is typical of economic advance. It is the interest of the economic question raised, and then the way of thinking about the economic world as seen in the development of the model, that is the critical element in achieving professional interest and recognition. Indeed, Akerlof's article was initially rejected by several leading economics journals, not because it contained any scientific errors, but because the reviewers did not think it was "interesting" enough.

Moreover, it had not taken any rare insight on Akerlof's part to understand that the problem of verifying product quality existed—any ordinary consumer had to deal with it all the time. Akerlof's article also did not do anything to make the problem of ensuring product quality any simpler or easier for consumers to resolve in the future. Its contribution to economics was that product-quality issues and the consequences for the workings of markets had not been part of the standard economic imagery. Akerlof made the argument that they should be and that a more accurate and realistic portrayal—including elements traditionally neglected by economists—would result. After it was given some thought for a while, and in light of subsequent writings by other economists, his point was accepted and he went on to become a famous economist who one day may win the Nobel Prize (for other important writings as well). Akerlof had shifted the manner by which economists "painted" the market system; again, in his method, we see a way of illuminating an important economic issue that is closer to Picasso than to Einstein.

If economics resembles any of the traditional sciences, it bears the closest resemblance to the biological method of Darwin in the development of his theory of evolution. Darwin's theories were not directly testable; in his method he was closer to a historian than a physicist in the manner of Newton. Before DNA, much of the discipline of biology consisted of field studies for the purpose of developing various classificatory schemes. The objective was to put plants and animals and other components of the natural world into categories that helped to satisfy an intellectual curiosity about the workings of nature. It was never an "exact science," however, and few new powers of control over nature ever resulted. Even today, when it is important to know the precise definition of a species for the purposes of administering the Endangered Species Act, biologists are not sure they have a very clear idea.

Although many working biologists now employ the more exact methods of biochemistry, the old biology lives on in the field of ecology. It is telling that ecology has suffered along with economics from some of the same tendencies toward exaggerated claims to a scientific status.[3] Ecological writings have often been more important intellectually for a powerful set of metaphors that have been used by "scientific poets" such as Aldo Leopold.[4] They have employed the language of ecological systems to communicate powerful value systems concerning the true relationship of human beings and nature—becoming in this respect, and like economics, closer to a branch of theology than to most other forms of intellectual inquiry.[5]★

INSTITUTIONS AND TRANSACTION COSTS

These features of economics are illustrated by the history of Ronald Coase's 1937 article "The Nature of the Firm," which was cited by the Nobel committee as a main reason for his winning the prize. In a 1994 lecture, Coase described the contents of the article:

> Economists [in the 1930s] talked about the economic system as being coordinated by the pricing mechanism (or the market) but had ignored the fact that using the market involved costs. From this it followed that means of coordination other than through use of the market could not be ruled out as inefficient—it all depended on what they cost as compared with the cost of using the market. I realized [then] that this way of looking at things could affect one's views

★ The idea that management of ecological systems involves a spiritual purpose has been gaining ground even in official scientific reports. In its 1999 report on management planning for the national forest system under the management of the U.S. Forest Service, a Committee of Scientists (assembled by the Forest Service and the Department of Agriculture) defined "effective management of National Forest System lands" as management that "provides important material, aesthetic and spiritual contributions to society." The committee similarly stated that the national forests are "places where people work, live, worship, and play." If management of public ecological systems includes a prominent function of providing a place for "spiritual" activities and for "worship," many analyses of these systems are bound to include a large theological as well as scientific dimension. See Committee of Scientists, *Sustaining the People's Lands: Recommendations for Stewardship of the National Forests and Grasslands into the Next Century,* a report to the secretary of agriculture and the chief of the Forest Service (Washington, D.C.: Department of Agriculture, March 15, 1999), 44. See also Robert H. Nelson, *A Burning Issue: A Case for Abolishing the U.S. Forest Service* (Lanham, Md.: Rowman and Littlefield, 2000).

on centralized planning. But, and this was what really mattered to me, it also meant that we could understand why there were firms in which the employment of the factors of production was coordinated by the management of the firm while at the same time there was also coordination conducted through the market. Whether a transaction would be organized within a firm or whether it would be carried out on the market depended on a comparison of the costs of organizing such a transaction within the firm with the costs of a market transaction that would accomplish the same result.[6]

As Coase was modest enough to say in this 1994 lecture, all this was actually very "simple and obvious," although it had taken Coase a while in the 1930s to come to this recognition.[7] The point he was making—if not the specific vocabulary he was using to make it—would have been known to many successful businesspeople of the time. When Alfred Sloan consolidated major parts of the automobile industry into the single firm of General Motors, he was making on a grand scale the kinds of calculations described by Coase.[8] It is unlikely that if Sloan had actually had access to Coase's specific terminology of "transaction costs," it would have made any practical difference to his efforts. The potential interest of Coase's work was thus as a form of descriptive classification of economic events for the use of other economists. However, at the time, the members of the economics profession did not regard it as intellectually interesting enough or useful enough to pursue further. That is to say, Coase's 1937 article did not meet the "Picasso test" at the time and it was largely ignored for that reason for the following thirty years.

His 1960 article "The Problem of Social Cost" made much the same point about the workings of the economy but met an altogether different reception. The time was simply ripe and Coase by then was a more visible figure within the economics profession.[9] Coase pointed out that in a world without transaction costs it did not make much (or any) difference how legal or other economic institutions were structured; the same economic outcomes would be achieved. It was the resulting corollary that was revolutionary for economics in its consequences. If the structure of institutions was irrelevant in an abstract world of zero transaction costs, then the existence and character of economic institutions must somehow depend on the nature of transaction costs as found in the real world.

Indeed, that is precisely what Coase in his 1937 article had said about industrial organization. Whether economic activity was organized into many small firms bound together by formal market contracts, or organized within one large corporation centrally administered, would depend on the relative magnitudes of transaction costs. Yet because of the suppositions of perfect information and a state of perfectly competitive equilibrium, as had long been the common initial assumption in economic modeling, this amounted to assuming zero transaction costs. The result, it could be seen clearly after Coase, was a neo-classical economics of surprisingly little interest or relevance. It could say little about the institutional structure of the economy, including such fundamental questions as whether a capitalist or a socialist economy would be more efficient (in a world of zero transaction costs both would be equally and perfectly efficient).

It is also in the nature of transaction costs that they arise in actual or potential disequilibrium situations. The study of transaction costs points to the dynamic aspects of the workings of an economic system. However, the traditional neoclassical analysis focused on comparative statics; its methods offered little help in understanding many dynamic phenomena. The neoclassical methods were in fact ill suited to many circumstances where significant transaction costs might arise. Brand-new methods of economic analysis might be required, if the role of transaction costs in the economic system was to be explored systematically.

Once the radical implications of Coase's 1960 article were fully digested (and his 1937 article would also now be recalled), the basic task of the economics profession was redefined: the efficiency of an economic system would depend on its specific institutional forms and the resulting levels of transaction costs.* The emergence of the law-and-economics movement in the 1960s at the University of Chicago reflected a recognition that the structure of property rights and other legal rules were among the most important institutional factors influencing the level of transaction costs. In 1986, John Wallis and Douglass North would estimate that in 1970 the costs associated with economic transactions in all forms had absorbed more than 50 percent of the total output of the U.S. economy (an increase from an estimated 26 percent in 1870, reflecting the greater role of information transactions and the generally greater institutional complexity of the late twentieth century).[10]

THE NEW ECONOMICS OF INFORMATION

In the specific example explored in Coase's 1960 article, the largest part of transaction costs seemed likely to be the time and other expenses of direct

---

* It is a fact still little appreciated by most current economists that John R. Commons made the analysis of the workings of "transactions" the centerpiece of his institutional economics. It is an interesting exercise to speculate on why Coase's 1937 article—of about the same vintage—has become a modern classic and Commons is still largely ignored. See John R. Commons, *Institutional Economics: Its Place in Political Economy,* vol. 1 (New Brunswick, N.J.: Transaction, 1990; 1st ed., 1934).

negotiation between the two involved parties. However, in a modern economy where many participants start off with minimal knowledge of available options, another form of transaction cost will typically be more important. Before entering into a negotiation or a contract, a considerable investment in gathering information will be needed.

One might think that, just as with any other product, the amount of information produced and distributed could be left to the workings of the market. However, as an economic good, information has some peculiar properties. It is difficult to assert a property right to information per se—unless I work for the Central Intelligence Agency society has no reliable way to control the information I can pass on to you. (Indeed, freedom of speech in many cases makes the contrary assertion a part of the U.S. Constitution.) Property rights to information can be asserted indirectly, as in the copyrighting of a book. However, in the end many of the most important forms of information amount to "public goods"—once they are available to one party, it will be difficult or impossible to exclude others from gaining access to the same information.

Hence, lacking property rights, the institutional structure of an economy will have to find ways of providing socially useful information in other than the standard market ways. The success of a Sears, Roebuck or more recently a Wal-Mart can be understood in this light. These companies solve the search problem for consumers who want to be assured of finding reasonably low prices and also avoid being "ripped off." With Wal-Mart stocking most items, and knowing that Wal-Mart adheres fairly consistently to a policy of charging prices in the lower range for its items for sale, the consumer can simply go directly to a Wal-Mart store whenever a new type of purchase need arises.

Even more important than price uncertainty is often product-quality uncertainty.[11] A main attraction of McDonalds is that it can offer a standard hamburger of acceptable quality at thousands of outlets around the United States. If I live in New Jersey and am traveling in New York, I solve my information problem—I obtain the quality assurance I need—by going to McDonalds, or to some other national franchise outlet. Economists for many years had attributed the high degree of industry concentration in the United States mainly to physical economies of scale in production. Yet, as the new institutional economics now suggested, information needs relating to product quality could be just as important. Many other organizational features of the economy could be significantly affected as well. As Akerlof had pointed out, the fear of purchasing a "lemon" could result in a smaller number of transactions in the used-car market—and more purchases in the new-car market—than would have occurred if it had been easier to be sure about used-car quality.[12]

There was a long tradition within economics of scornful treatment of the practice of advertising—commonly seen as "manipulating" consumers for "unproductive" purposes. Admittedly, much of the advertising in newspapers and other places is useful in spreading information about prices and the availability of products and brands. The new institutional economics, however, now made a radically new argument; even advertising that is altogether empty of content (as is often the case for, say, television ads) may still "signal" important information.[13] A true fly-by-night firm would never be able to afford the investment of a large payment for advertising on a television station or other expensive outlet. It would lose its customers before it would be able to sell enough goods to recover such a large investment cost. For a reputable firm the very act of "throwing away" a substantial amount of money (it could be wasted on anything, but advertising works best because it serves another need as well—to make the consumer aware of the money being spent) can in effect offer a financial "hostage" that provides an effective assurance of future product quality.[14]

Similarly, why might a business hire people who have invested heavily in an education, even when the specific contents of the education might often seem to be only tangentially related to the needs of the business? As the new institutional economics now analyzed this question, the very fact of making an investment in education—like the spending of money on advertising—could in itself provide a useful signal.[15] The fact that a potential employee had invested, for example, seventy thousand dollars to get a master's degree in business administration is an effective indication that this person intends to stay in the business world for a considerable period of time. A good business school will also serve as an effective filter of talent through the selection process to gain admissions.

Furthermore, as Michael Spence found, the very fact of going to a business school can "signal" real talent—it can induce the student to honestly reveal some important things about himself or herself—in yet another way.[16] The time and effort to complete business school will be lower for people with higher levels of business ability (for the same results they will be able to devote less time to studying and other business school requirements). Prospective students with more business talent thus will face a lower "price" of attending business school and therefore will be more likely to attend (and the business school can also contribute to the effectiveness of this filter through the proper design of its courses, making them difficult to pass for people who lack the kinds of abilities that will later be required in the practice of business).

All in all, as the new institutional economics was finding, in concept, businesses might rationally hire graduates of business schools without the business schools ever having taught anything of value with respect to the actual practice of business.* It could also explain why the grades of students graduating from business schools might often weigh less in hiring decisions than one would naively have expected. (And similar arguments could be made with respect to other many areas of education besides business.)†

THE NEW INDUSTRIAL ORGANIZATION

In 1972, Coase would comment that "we are, in fact, [still] appallingly ignorant about the forces which determine the organization of industry." [17] In the following twenty-five years, however, there would be a great renewal of interest, partly in response to Oliver Williamson's 1975 publication of *Markets and Hierarchies* and his subsequent contributions in this area. [18] The large business firm, in essence, could be explained as a superior institutional re-

---

* It might be noted that it also follows from this line of thinking that the social investment in business schools could be in large part a social waste, if there were any other better way of directly or indirectly signaling the same information at less cost. Another "hostage" strategy that might be more efficient in some respects would be to offer a large company pension as part of the overall compensation package. If this pension only became vested after a certain number of years, it would similarly act to filter out those potential employees who might not actually be planning to stay very long or those who did not really think that they would make the grade at a given company. Without such an indirect method of information generation, simply asking potential employees about their future work plans and the quality of their business talents would not be of much use.

† The role of investment commitments as a "signal" also plays a large role in the dating game and the rituals of courtship and marriage. In social encounters with a new potential partner, a woman may require several dates before showing any willingness to enter into an intimate sexual relationship. She may calculate that a man interested only in a "one-night stand" would be unwilling to make such a large investment of his time—much in the way that the spending by a business of large up-front sums of money in advertising can rule out the possibility of a "fly-by-night" business firm. Similar considerations apply in marriage decisions. Spending a year or two in courtship, several thousand dollars for a diamond wedding ring, perhaps considerably more for a formal wedding ceremony, and other investments signal assurances to each other that the partners are serious about maintaining a long-term relationship. Legal requirements for alimony in the case of divorce also have this function, in addition to the direct-support benefits to the party receiving the alimony payments. Indeed, much as a large part of advertising might be described as "conspicuous waste," the signaling function of alimony—making it unlikely that anyone will enter into marriage without a serious long-term intent—could be served equally well by other forms of monetary sacrifice in the event of divorce. For example, as Eric Posner comments, rather than a direct payment of alimony to one of the partners in a dissolving marriage, it would be equally effective as a signaling device to require "that upon divorce each party had to pay half his or her future lifetime wages to the government or to a charity." If any such legal requirement existed, taking the marriage vows would surely be treated as a matter of the utmost seriousness, entered into only by those confidently expecting the marriage to last for a very long time. Indeed, if the penalty of divorce became too great, the problem then might become that too few marriages would then result. See Eric A. Posner, "Family Law and Social Norm," in F. H. Buckley, *The Fall and Rise of Freedom of Contract* (Durham: Duke University Press, 1999), 269.

sponse, when compared with the atomistic structure of a market, to a number of important information and other transaction cost problems.[19]

For one, as Armen Alchian and Harold Demsetz had already highlighted in a 1972 article, it was difficult for each small firm (or individual member of the workforce) to monitor the performance of other small firms.[20] In order for me to write a market contract with you, I need to know what you can add to my output and profit levels. But you will have an incentive to misrepresent yourself about your potential contributions in these regards. Moreover, if I have to contract with many other suppliers of inputs simultaneously, and they are all interacting with one another, it will be difficult to separate out the contributions of one source from another.

As Alchian and Demsetz argued, the consolidation of a number of potentially small independent producers (and workers) into a single business unit of "team production" could provide the answer.[21] Business management performed a "monitoring" function in overseeing the full production process and the actual contributions of the various inputs. The managers of the firm in effect earned profits (for themselves, their stockholders, or both) for undertaking the overall orchestrating and team monitoring tasks. As two later contributors, Paul Milgrom and John Roberts, described the new view of the business firm, it provided a team solution substituting "monitoring of inputs for standard, output-based, incentive schemes, thus moving away from traditional market forms of organization and creating a role for other, more formal, sorts of [larger integrated] organizations."[22] In essence, business production needed managers like football teams needed coaches; pickup games in the park—like atomistic markets—are not noted for the coordinated team efforts that they produce.*

Yet another Alchian article—co-authored in this case in 1978 with Benjamin Klein and Robert Crawford—offered reasons to expect considerable vertical as well as horizontal integration of American industry.[23] As Williamson had also emphasized, many exchanges among firms involve circumstances of "asset specificity" that eventually take on a "bilateral" character in the relationships among the participants.[24] Let us say I agree to build a manufacturing plant to your design specifications, and this plant has few other uses. Once the plant is actually built, your incentive will then be to cheat on paying me, and in complying with other provisions of the original contract. You may promise many things up front but it could all be an act of deception on your part.

---

* Yet there has been a growing tendency in American industry to obtain inputs from independent suppliers. The "temp" industry, for example, providing short term secretarial and office help, has been a rapid growth area of the economy. Throughout business, many firms that formerly produced their own inputs have now taken to contracting their production out to independent suppliers.

As Klein, Crawford, and Alchian put the matter, such behavior could create a "hold-up" situation. The only recourse of the original builder would then be to try to enforce the terms of the original contract in court. In a world of perfect information and zero transaction costs, this would not be much of a (or any) problem—the contract would have already covered all the possible future areas of dispute and a legal remedy would be readily at hand. However, in the real world it will normally be impossible to cover in advance every contingency in a contract. Moreover, given an ambiguous situation and the necessity to make subjective judgments, judges often behave unpredictably. Recognizing such problems beforehand, the builder may simply refuse to construct the plant—or perhaps will demand a very large risk premium. The solution in this situation, as the new institutional economics now explored in detail, might be various forms of consolidating vertically into a single business firm that would include the builder of the plant and other input suppliers within the same organization.*

Another important information problem falls in the category of "strategic intelligence." Proctor and Gamble might conduct extensive marketing surveys before committing to full production of a new brand of soap, but no small soap manufacturing firm could afford such comprehensive surveying (even though many small soap firms might collectively realize substantial economic benefits if they were somehow able to get together to generate the same information).[25] Information often yields significant "externalities" (benefits to others not captured in market relationships), and it will therefore often pay to internalize these benefits by consolidating the processes of information gathering under one large business ownership.[26] Efforts by separate firms to do the same thing through mutual contracting would often be defeated by the free-rider problem. Moreover, the range of types of strategic information that could be of significant value to businesses in an industry might be very wide.

Differential access to information is at the heart of the "principal-agent" problem, another new important area of inquiry for the new institutional

---

* The analysis of such circumstances has been elaborated and extended to more-complex circumstances by the "property-rights" approach to industry organization. As one of the developers of this approach, Oliver Hart, has written, in various circumstances "giving control of these assets to two different management teams is therefore bound to be detrimental to actors' incentives, since it increases the number of parties with hold-up power. The result confirms the [intuitive] notion that when lock-in effects are extreme, integration will dominate nonintegration." See Oliver Hart, "An Economist's Perspective on the Theory of the Firm," *Columbia Law Review* 89 (November 1989): 1770. The more technical and formal development of this theory is found in Sanford J. Grossman and Oliver D. Hart, "The Costs and Benefits of Ownership: A Theory of Vertical and Lateral Integration," *Journal of Political Economy* 94 (August 1986); and Oliver Hart and John Moore, "Property Rights and the Nature of the Firm," *Journal of Political Economy* 98 (December 1990).

economics.[27] Jean Tirole commented in 1988 that "in the last fifteen years the development of the principle-agent model has deeply modified the way theorists view organizations."[28] In essence, principal-agent theory seeks to take account of the fact that, contrary to the usual assumption of neoclassical analysis, the "agent" and the "principal" (the party who has obtained the services of the agent) are potentially in an adversarial relationship. They not only may have different incentives, but one or the other may choose to mis-represent current circumstances, future intentions, and any number of other matters pertinent to economic transactions. Principal-agent theory is closely linked with another large body of literature generated by the new institu-tional economics in the past two decades, research into the organizational and other consequences of "asymmetric information."[29]

A classic example of a principal-agent problem is the relationship between the managers of a large corporation and the stockholders.[30] The stockholders want the management to act in their interest but may lack the information to monitor managerial performance effectively—the two parties thus possess asymmetric information. One possible strategy—in fact increasingly adopted by corporate boards of directors in the past two decades—is to pay top man-agement in the form of stock options. In this fashion, the incentives facing top management will be more closely aligned with the goals of the stockhold-ers—both will benefit together from rising stock prices.

Williamson has emphasized throughout his writings that the problem of "opportunism" has a pervasive impact on the structure of economic institu-tions.[31] Rational economic actors cannot assume that another party is trust-worthy, absent an actual incentive for them to behave in a truthful way. Drawing on the writings of Herbert Simon, Williamson has also pointed to the importance of "bounded rationality," the limited capacity of any individ-ual or organization to receive and process information.[32] As noted earlier, another consideration emphasized by Williamson is the frequent "bilateral" character of exchange relationships among the firms interacting with one another within an industry. As a result of the efforts of Williamson and many other economists since the 1970s, as Furubotn and Richter have com-mented, the "traditional neoclassical theory of the firm" has been "in the process of being destroyed by modern institutional economics."[33]

As Williamson explained, significant progress was finally being made to provide an answer to the challenges that Coase had first posed many years earlier:

> The markets and hierarchies approach attempts to identify a set of *en-vironmental factors* which together with a related set of *human factors*

explain the circumstances under which complex contingent claims contracts will be costly to write, execute, and enforce. Faced with such difficulties, and considering the risks that simple (or incomplete) contingent claims contracts pose, the firm may decide to bypass the market and resort to hierarchical modes of organization. Transactions that might otherwise be handled in the market are thus performed internally, governed by administrative processes, instead.[34]

STIGLITZ VERSUS SAMUELSON

Although many economists have yet to recognize it fully, the fact is that very little has been left standing of neoclassic economics—including the core ideas presented by Samuelson in 1948 in *Economics*. As himself one of the leading contributors, Joseph Stiglitz believes that the "New Institutional economics will flourish" in the twenty-first century.[35] Stiglitz is a product of the MIT economics department and a former star pupil of Samuelson. Indeed, he was an editor of Samuelson's collected papers. For many years he has been one of the most prolific publishers in the most prestigious journals of American economics.

Much of Stiglitz's past work has served to show how "what is at issue in the analysis of how the economy allocates its resources is more than just the solution to a complicated maximization problem: economics is far more complicated, and more interesting, than the engineering approach that prevailed in the decades following Samuelson's *Foundations of Economic Analysis.*" For economists of that period, "the quality of decision making was of little relevance."[36] The main task of economics then was to explore the implications of rational consumer and firm behavior in response to price and other given incentives. Who might be the person (or economic entity) actually behaving rationally, or how they might obtain the information and the calculational ability, were all outside the scope of interest of the great majority of economists of that time.

As Stiglitz writes, "In Samuelson's classic textbook [*Economics*], the question about who decides or how decisions are made was not even included in the standard list of the basic questions of economics." The result, however, is "an incorrect understanding of how competitive markets work."[37] The fundamental problem with the neoclassical framework of analysis is its treatment of information.[38] A better starting assumption than that of perfect information might well have been that of perfect ignorance.[39] An entirely new and more useful approach to economic analysis might then have resulted: starting from very little knowledge, how can a decision maker assemble the information he or she needs to make even minimally adequate—rather than perfectly rational—decisions? For complex decisions being made for the first time, that is closer to what real life typically feels like for individuals as well as businesses.

For example, as noted earlier, dealing with opportunism—the problem of avoiding being cheated—requires a knowledge of the reputations of others for honesty and reliability. No market participant can feel comfortable in making a purchase (unless the quality of the product can accurately be determined at the point of making the purchase) without such knowledge. In order to cut down on information-gathering costs, the purchaser may simply eliminate many potential suppliers of a good or service from any consideration at all; it would be too costly to try to learn about most potential suppliers. For this and other reasons, as Stiglitz explains, "markets that work on the basis of reputation mechanisms are markedly different from standard competitive markets" of the neoclassical kind.[40] Or, "whenever information is imperfect and markets incomplete, actions by one individual (firm) give rise to [information] externalities, limiting the extent to which the economy could be efficiently decentralized." There is something important to be learned from the fact that in the real world "few firms make extensive use of the price system for the allocation of resources within the firm."[41]

Economists have been getting it wrong for a long time. As Stiglitz puts it, this has reflected the fact that "for the past half century a simple paradigm has dominated the economics profession—variously referred to as the *competitive paradigm,* or the neoclassical or Walrasian model. The most precise statement of that paradigm is provided by the [1954] model of Arrow and Debreu." Stiglitz summed up his fundamental objections to this way of thinking about economic issues as follows:

> The competitive paradigm not only did not provide much guidance on the vital question of the choice of economics systems but what "advice" it did provide was often misguided. The conceptions of the market that underlay that analysis mischaracterized it; the standard analyses underestimated the strengths—and weaknesses—of market economies, and accordingly provided wrong signals for the potential success of alternatives and for how the market might be improved upon.
>
> The fundamental problem with the neoclassical model and the corresponding model underlying market socialism is that they fail to take into account a variety of problems that arise from the absence of

perfect information and the costs of acquiring information, as well as the absence or imperfections in certain key risk and capital markets. The absence or imperfections in these markets can, in turn, to a large extent be explained by problems of information. During the past fifteen years, a new paradigm, sometimes referred to as the information-theoretic approach to economics (or, for short, *information paradigm)*, has developed. This paradigm is explicitly concerned with these issues. This paradigm has already provided us insights into development economics and macroeconomics. It has provided us a *new new welfare economics*, a *new theory of the firm*, and a new understanding of the role and functioning of financial markets. It has provided us new insights concerning traditional questions, such as the design of incentive structures.[42]

ANALYTICAL FORMALISM

For reasons explored also in Chapter 3 of this book, Stiglitz and many others in the new institutional economics have succeeded in demolishing much of the old theoretical framework of neoclassical economics. It is less clear, however, that they have provided a successful new alternative. The new institutional economists may have ended up with an awkward compromise—rejecting neoclassical assumptions but employing the same analytical formalism long favored by the neoclassicals.* In order to make the problems of a world of imperfect information analytically tractable with existing economic tools, it is often necessary to make an assumption of the precise degree of ignorance—the exact gaps in the state of knowledge, the precise probability of being right or wrong in various estimates to fill these gaps, the probability that this first set of probabilities is seriously wrong, and so on and so forth. It

---

* Deirdre McCloskey has recently commented:

> I have gradually come to understand that culture matters for economics and for the economy. It was hard to learn, because I am a "neoclassical economist," from the subschool of Chicago.
>
> We neoclassicals are taught early to sneer at sociologists and philosophers, anthropologists and English professors, who foolishly believe that culture matters. . . . When a management consultant talks about the "culture" of IBM the neoclassical economists sneers and says, "Don't you know that the market simply bypasses all that? IBM can have any culture it wants, but the tastes of consumers and the technology of computers will force IBM to behave the same way."

See Deirdre McCloskey, "Missing Ethics in Economics," in Arjo Klamer, ed., *The Value of Culture: On the Relationship Between Economics and Arts* (Amsterdam: Amsterdam University Press, 1996), 187.

seems to raise a conundrum for economic analysis in this mode: How could a person ever be expected to know exactly what knowledge they are missing, or the precise probabilities of various contingencies that are possible outcomes in an uncertain world, unless he or she already had a perfect knowledge of the overall situation? How can I know precisely what knowledge I am lacking, without already knowing perfectly the knowledge sought in the first place?

One description of this difficulty is that it poses an "infinite regress" problem. The attempt to precisely characterize one state of imperfect knowledge depends on being able to precisely characterize a prior state of still imperfect knowledge (often an even more difficult problem), and so on without end. As Mark Pingle has observed: "The decision-cost associated with solving the higher order problem is necessarily larger than that associated with the lower order problem. *It follows that decision-costs act to limit the extent to which rationality can be displaced to higher levels.* There must come a point where ... the 'rational thing to do is to be irrational' and simply choose a choice method without reason. Otherwise, all resources would be used in decision making." [43]

In continuing to use mathematical and other analytical methods that still depend on a form of perfect information (if now perfect knowledge of the exact elements of imperfection), the analytical formalists among the new institutional economists may be misconstruing the fundamental character of the economic problem. Indeed, members of the Austrian school of economics have long made this argument. Peter Boettke has commented recently that he and other "Austrians have traditionally rejected calculus, topology, and other mathematical methods on philosophical grounds," believing that the essence of the economic problem involves "individuals acting under the inescapably subjective conditions of time passage, ignorance, and genuine uncertainty." These are things that "cannot be meaningfully captured nor understood through mathematical technique." [44]

It is not only Austrians who are troubled by the continuing emphasis on formal quantification. Furubotn and Richter describe the approaches commonly employed by the new institutional economics as "hybrid" models. The modelers typically posit situations in which economic actors are "perfectly informed about some matter yet completely ignorant about others." For example, one finds economists commonly studying problems where "the basic situation envisioned is one in which the principal is 'blind' as a direct monitor of his agent but otherwise has full knowledge of his agent's characteristics (i.e., the preference function) as well as precise knowledge of the distribution function of the external disturbances of the system that affect economic performance." [45]

Furubotn and Richter note, however, that such assumptions lead to economic "structures that are *internally inconsistent.*" In order to analyze the multiple information, opportunism, principal-agent, bilateral negotiation, and other transaction cost issues appropriately raised by the new institutional economics, it may be necessary to assume imperfect information in most respects, including an initial inability to specify what knowledge would be most helpful (to know what information is missing). It would seem that this might require radically new approaches to economic analysis; it may be necessary to explore an "economic universe that is *strikingly different*" from any that most economists in the new institutional school have yet been willing to contemplate.[46]

In a world of significant uncertainties about almost everything, "transaction costs must appear *everywhere* in the system because of the nature of the individuals making decisions." Information must be consistently and systematically imperfect, decision making capabilities must always be strictly limited. Admittedly, such a world might lead outside any familiar economic territory: "Thus, once we reject the notion of the omniscient decision maker who is 'completely rational,' the economic model undergoes a basic transformation and a change in paradigm appears to be unavoidable."[47] The focus of economic analysis in the future might have to be on things such as "information shortcuts," "culture as information," "'irrational' decisions made rationally," "ideology as knowledge," "deciding in the dark (or perhaps twilight)," "learning from history," "framing the problem efficiently," and so forth. If a few economists such as Herbert Simon and James March have already ventured to delve into such matters in the past, there may have to be many more in the future and they may have to devise whole new economic ways of thinking about the task.[48]

Delivering the Richard T. Ely lecture at the annual meeting of the American Economic Association in 1994, Kenneth Arrow raised one possibility of such a redirection. The very framework of assumptions of rational individual behavior—"methodological individualism," as Arrow called it—might have to be jettisoned in many situations. Arrow commented that "economic theories require social elements," and therefore "I do conclude that social variables, not attached to particular individuals, are essential in studying the economy."[49] Social variables play a number of crucial roles, including the legitimizing of economic activities and institutions, but also serving as a shorthand way of providing information to people who may in general be operating in a high degree of ignorance. For one thing, people who share a common culture will be able to more accurately predict the behavior of one another. Being part of a culture might in this sense also be described as an informal method of contracting with other members of the culture; in that case one should be bound to obey the rules of the culture even when they might not strictly maximize individual well-being. The issue of how to design an "efficient" culture—a collective, not an individual, task—may have to become a central economic problem in the future.*

If Arrow's and other similar suggestions are taken seriously, it thus would seem that economists may need to incorporate elements of social belief into their analyses. Changes in belief systems—in many cases these will be forms of religion—also can significantly influence individual behavior along with the maximization of individual profit and utility. These social influences may not be confined to family and other "noneconomic" areas (which in any case have now been incorporated into the accepted subject matter of economics) but may extend throughout the economy and society. Cultural motives may provide a powerful independent incentive structure of their own, in some societies perhaps having as great an impact on economic outcomes as the price and other individual incentives of the marketplace.

Priesthoods and others in a leadership class are often the ones who define the culture of a society and thus the informal incentive structures. More narrowly, a business firm has its own leadership class that seeks to define a suitable company culture (a firm "religion," one might call it). As Furubotn and Richter comment, "One may say that the function of the manager in a hierarchical firm is not to shape the behavior of subordinates by designing an optimal system of [financial or other formal] incentives but rather to provide *leadership* so that individuals are induced to cooperate in achieving the firm's objectives." [50] In joining the firm, the employees implicitly agree to abide by

---

* Indeed, not only the conduct of business but also the very idea of the pursuit of happiness ("utility") may also have little meaning, independent of a social context. Despite the individualistic assumptions of modern utility theory, the achievement of happiness may in fact be a collective action problem. Charles Murray has reached such a conclusion after systematic exploration of the best paths to happiness:

> Our relationships with other human beings constitute the master resource that we use in the other ways of pursuing happiness, be they making money or achieving self-respect or doing fulfilling work. Human relationships constitute the master resource because, necessarily, *people pursue happiness by actions, and these actions are usually social.* Most of what an individual might find important to his happiness, whether a loving family or fame or riches or helping others, can be achieved only through social interactions with other human beings. The only exception I can think of is the person who finds happiness in being a hermit, and the number of such people is exceedingly small.

See Charles Murray, "The Pursuit of Happiness Under Socialism and Capitalism," *Cato Journal* 11 (Fall 1991): 242. See also Charles Murray, *In Pursuit of Happiness and Good Government* (New York: Simon and Schuster, 1988).

its cultural rules as part of their contract. It is the responsibility of top management to establish and make clear a set of cultural rules that then effectively serve the profit and other objectives of the firm.

All this is leading in some surprising directions. Coase may have let the genie out of the bottle. The introduction of transaction costs into mainstream economic calculations has led to a chain of events where it now may mean that economists must "pay more heed to the significance of such 'esoteric' [for an economist] factors as the moral rules of behavior, fairness, trust, human learning, and legal evolution. In this respect the New Institutional Economics can perhaps be said to be drawing closer to the old institutionalism" of Veblen, Commons, and others in the early twentieth century.[51] If economists for much of the twentieth century relegated "evolutionary" studies to the margins of the profession, a prominent mainstream economist, Avinash Dixit of Princeton University, now calls for the adoption of an "evolutionary perspective" in the study of economic policy making. This will require that the "framework for analysis must be more flexible. It must be more dynamic, or even evolutionary, in the way it treats policy rules and acts." Economists should begin "to take the history and the institutions of politics seriously."[52]

One of the founders of the new institutional economics, Michael Spence, already had commented in 1975 that "the sheer complexity of the decisions" that top corporate managers had to make was creating a daunting prospect for economists. It was probably unrealistic to hope, Spence thought, that "the process of generating strategic alternatives" in the business world would ever lend itself to formal economic models. The character of the "perceptual problem" as found in top-management decision making simply was not amenable to any kind of formal "economic tools." Even for the simpler aspects of corporate decision making, Spence seemed to have his doubts—although he remained optimistic that it might be possible to find "a practical and helpful middle ground between the unrealistic assumption of full optimization on the one hand, and totally random or unpredictable behavior on the other, at both the firm and industry levels."[53]

A TRANSITIONAL PHASE?

The new institutional economics has been attracting some of the most talented members of the profession for at least a quarter of a century, including leading economists today who hold tenured professorships at MIT, Harvard, Princeton, Stanford, the University of California at Berkeley, and other prominent departments.* Yet these new institutional economists are not themselves a confident group; Spence's 1975 concerns have yet to be resolved. In a 1988 survey article, Paul Milgrom and John Roberts comment that "all the theories reviewed above are incomplete in important ways." Given the extensive research into the new institutional economics, the results had been surprisingly barren: "the vast bulk of the research has been primarily deductive theorizing and where too often the questions that the latest paper seeks to answer arise not from consideration of puzzling aspects of observed practice or from present trends in business organization but from the desire to extend the analysis in an earlier paper that, in turn, may have been only tenuously connected to observation."[54] Another leading theorist of the new institutional school of economics commented in 1989 that "most formal models of the firm are extremely rudimentary, capable only of portraying hypothetical firms that bear little relation to the complex organizations we see in the real world. [However], theories that attempt to incorporate real world features of corporations, partnerships and the like often lack precision and rigor, and have therefore failed, by and large, to be accepted by the theoretical mainstream."[55]

Ten years later, in 1998, the *Journal of Economic Perspectives* included a set of articles from a symposium titled "The Firm and Its Boundaries." Robert Gibbons concluded that economists had successfully opened "up several new areas of inquiry" in the 1990s but that "the best economics on this subject is still to come." Gibbons suggested that further advance may require tapping "the large literature in organizational sociology" that has so far been little explored by economists. Or perhaps more powerful results could be obtained by incorporating "social psychology." Without help from somewhere outside formal economic methods, economists perhaps will always be facing seriously "incomplete (but perhaps still useful) descriptions of incentives in organizations."[56]

In the same symposium, Bengt Holmstrom and John Roberts found that typical analyses of the new institutional school "focus on one incentive problem that is solved by the use of a single instrument" but that they "give much too limited a view of the firm, and one that is potentially misleading." They observed at another point that there are "an assortment of conditions [that] have been adduced by Williamson and others to limit firm size—costs

---

* The roster of the new economics stars who have advanced along this path includes many of the names already mentioned earlier and a number of others. A partial listing would include people such as Oliver Williamson, Joseph Stiglitz, George Akerlof, Sanford Grossman, Michael Rothschild, Oliver Hart, John Roberts, Robert Wilson, Michael Jensen, Michael Spence, Paul Milgrom, Andrei Shleifer, Benjamin Klein, David Kreps, Bengt Holmstrom, and Drew Fudenberg; and there could be numerous others.

of bureaucracy, the weakening of individual incentives, the hazards of internal politicking, and so on—but none of these costs are easy to measure, and (perhaps for this reason) they have not played much of an empirical role" in the subsequent efforts of new institutional economists. Hoping to advance beyond such limitations, Holmstrom and Roberts suggested renewed attention to "agency problems, concerns for common assets, difficulties in transferring knowledge, and the benefits of market monitoring," all now to be blended together in forms of synthesis with which economists have not yet had much experience and thus "these suggestions are tentative, and we confess that they are mostly without a good theoretical foundation. They are offered in the hope of inspiring new theoretical research."[57]

One thus hears serious doubts among leading economists that existing formal methods will ever be up to the task of understanding business behavior in all its complexity. These economists are in fact reenacting yet another round in what has become by now an old ritual in the profession: past failures of the most analytically sophisticated methods to generate much real economic insight (as is now the verdict on neoclassical analysis) are candidly acknowledged, but then encouragement is offered for the economics profession to press forward to develop still more analytically advanced methods (often involving yet higher levels of abstraction and mathematics) in hopes that perhaps these newest methods will finally overcome the formidable hurdles of real-world complexity. At some point it may have to be admitted that the problem lies in the methods themselves, not the talents and skills of the economists who are seeking to apply and refine them. One hopes that the economics profession will not spend the whole twenty-first century waiting for a new Newton or Einstein of formal economics to emerge to shed a more powerful light in the current darkness.

CONCLUSION

If most current members of the economics profession have been resistant to drastic changes in method, Stiglitz addressed some of the concerns in commenting that it would be hard to turn back to the old historical and institutional approaches, because they had been used to promote "doctrinaire ideologies."* Marxism and social Darwinism were extreme cases of "evolu-

---

* To be sure, there is also a less idealistic side to the resistance to change within economics, described recently by James Buchanan as the large "social wastage in intellectual rent seeking" within the economics profession. As economists pursue their own amusements (even while being supported at high expense by the rest of society), they have been "producing massive investment in empirical inquiry that has yielded few genuinely new insights into the workings of the institutions of human in-

tionary" economics, but there had been many others in the late nineteenth and early twentieth centuries. The historical and institutional studies of American progressive economists had often been infused by the spirit of Protestant Christianity. As Stiglitz put it, the old economic ideologies had "replaced the religious doctrines that had so long held sway over humankind but were [now] held with the same emotional fervor; indeed the fervor was reinforced by the false sense that the [new economic] ideologies rested on scientific premises." [58] The later turn by economists to mathematical and other analytically more rigorous methods in the twentieth century was in part a counterreaction to the perceived failures of economists in the older historical and institutional school to live up to their professed scientific ideals.

Any proposal that economists today should again do economics in, say, the manner of John R. Commons (if hopefully with considerably greater grace and clarity of expression) thus encounters strong resistance. In the minds of contemporary economists, it would be to abandon the goal for a value-free scientific economics that has characterized professional economics for the greater part of the past seventy-five years.* There is, however, a large problem here. The perception that the methods of the older historical and institutional school were heavily value laden is no doubt accurate. But there is not much to distinguish them in this regard from those of Samuelson's *Economics,* Becker's economic treatment of marriage and the family, and indeed most of the economics of the second half of the twentieth century. These newer economic writings are also filled with heroic value assumptions and implicit strong value advocacy. The manner of incorporating the subjective element, to be sure, is different. Contemporary economists have been assert-

---

teraction." But many economists with attractive university positions, small teaching loads, research assistants, sabbaticals, and other perquisites of the academic life have been doing a good job of successfully maximizing their own individual welfare. See James M. Buchanan, *Has Economics Lost Its Way? Reflections on the Economists' Enterprise at Century's End* (Fairfax, Va.: Institute for Humane Studies, George Mason University, 1997), 1.

   * And these hopes for a positive economics—despite the numerous philosophical and other doubters that this positivism is possible even in concept—still represent an important part of the self-image and value system of many current economists. Harvard economist H. Gregory Mankiw recently declared that economists as professionals "make a distinction between positive or descriptive statements that are scientifically verifiable and normative statements that reflect values and judgments. The question is, can you do positive economics without normative economics. I think so." Stanford's Paul Roemer suggests that economists should be like medical doctors: "You can let the pastor, the legislator, the family and the philosopher struggle with the moral question of whether to actually stop the treatment but what you want from a doctor [like an economist] is correct scientific statements about what will happen if." Quoted in Louis Uchitelle, "A Challenge to Scientific Economics," *New York Times,* January 23, 1999, A19, A21.

ing a claim to be doing economics in the manner of physics. Their predecessors in the late nineteenth and early twentieth century also claimed that they were genuine scientists. In their case, they said they were doing historical and institutional research into the "evolutionary" workings of society that was following closely in the great scientific tradition of Darwin's studies of biological evolution.

In the three hundred years since modern economics first emerged in a secular mode in the Enlightenment, no one has yet developed a value-neutral economics of any great interest or social usefulness. Whatever the choice of economic method selected, it seems that there is bound to be a powerful set of value assumptions—sometimes more up-front and explicit, sometimes more hidden.[59] Then, it is not just that the assumptions shape the form of analysis, but the very act of making them on the part of the economic analyst amounts to an assertion of their special merit. The economist is saying, in effect, that these values accurately describe the human condition. The truth of the human condition is, of course, the subject matter of theology.

In short, economists would not have much to lose in turning back in their methods of inquiry to the approaches of the old historical and institutional school. They may think they would be losing their scientific virtue, but it would be more correct to say that they would be abandoning their scientific hypocrisy.

chapter **NINE**

EFFICIENT RELIGION

If people always behaved truthfully, if they lived up to their agreements, if they represented themselves and their intentions honestly, much of the research agenda of the new institutional economics would be of little interest. Almost by definition, there would be little further problem of "opportunism." The "principal-agent" problem would be much less if principals only had to worry about honest mistakes of agents (such as agents who in good faith overestimate their own abilities). There would be many fewer circumstances of "asymmetric information" in the world, if all information conveyed was done so in a truthful fashion. It would not be necessary to discover as many indirect "signaling" devices if people could be routinely expected to give their honest opinion of their skills, plans, and abilities.

The possibility that economic actors might behave with less than complete honesty obviously could not have come as a great surprise to economists—as it would not to anyone else living in the real world. Rather, the wide range of possibilities for opportunistic behavior was simply one of the many things that economists chose to ignore; it was part of the process of heroic abstraction characteristic of the economic method. If dishonesty and misrepresentation were lesser factors, mere "frictions" in the basic workings of the economic system, why complicate the analysis unnecessarily? Implicitly, economists were assuming that the economy rested on a foundation of moral values that kept "unethical" behavior to an acceptable minimum. The portrayal of an economy where no one ever cheated or lied can be seen as also in part an attempt to uphold this ideal.

Occasionally, these ethical dimensions became explicit, as when Frank Knight once remarked that standard-price theory actually depended on an assumption by economists of honest behavior on the part of the participants in the market.[1] Then, to the extent that the maintenance of high standards of ethical behavior depended on a grounding in religious conviction, there was already an important link to religion as well, even in the neoclassical economics that generally disavowed any such connections. Economic analysts of markets were thus in a position similar to that of progressive advocates of scientific management of society, who had implicitly assumed that professional experts and other civil servants in government would behave according to certain ethical standards—that the governing classes in society would act of their own accord "in the public interest." If government actors were the "agents," and citizens and voters were the "principals," one could say that the progressive theories of government, like the economists' theories of the workings of markets, simply regarded principal-agent problems as a lesser or nonexistent concern.

However, beginning in the 1960s, all this began to change. It was part of the wave of cultural change and questioning of old assumptions and traditions that swept over American society at large. The long-term trends of Gallup polling have found that "the '60s and '70s were the time when our country fell apart and the bonds began to dissolve. You had a war between the generations, a war between the genders, you had Vietnam, break-ins, resignations, pardons. You had a huge dissolution of trust. And we have gone from a time when we presumed good intentions on the part of our leaders to the presumption of bad intentions."[2]

In matters of government, the public choice school of economists (along with many political scientists adopting similar approaches) showed how many aspects of government behavior would be greatly altered if professionals and other participants were assumed—contrary to the prevailing view up to the 1960s—to act opportunistically in their own interest (and thus felt free to "cheat" on their explicit or implicit contract to serve the public interest). At almost the same time the new institutional school of economists undertook what might be described as a public choice analysis of private business. This analysis assumed that business managers and other individual actors in private profit-making organizations behaved as well according to their own interests—and these personal interests in many cases could diverge significantly from those of the stockholders or even the top leadership of the organization. In many other situations in business, as in government, an assumption of opportunistic motives by the players involved could radically alter the expected workings of the system.

Again at almost the very same time, new assumptions about the presence of opportunistic motives were also being extended into other areas of social behavior. As examined in Chapter 7, Becker, Posner, and others in the Chicago school of economics were bringing a new economic approach to the study of crime, children, marriage, law, sex, and many other subjects. The beginning point for this third-generation Chicago project was that love, altruism, and other ethical ideals commonly assumed in the past might not actually be such powerful influences. Instead, Chicago economists developed their analysis on the basis of the assumption that the full-fledged pursuit of individual advantage—necessarily including opportunistic calculations— was motivating virtually every actor in virtually every area of society.

The public choice school in matters of government, the new institutional school in matters of private business, and the new third-generation Chicago school in matters of "sociology" thus were closely linked. They all were carrying over into the methods of social science a broader phenomenon taking place in American life. There was a simultaneous loss of respect for the old ideals and values and a new assumption that the individual can be expected to act to serve his or her own wishes and desires. This new emphasis on uninhibited self-expression for individual gain meant that traditional ethical commitments to honesty, personal sacrifice, duty to country, civic participation, political involvement, and so forth would have a declining role in society. Increasingly, it seemed, the economic individual of economic theory was in fact the appropriate model for the behavior of Americans in all walks of life.

As the American baby-boomer generation had reached adulthood in the 1960s and 1970s, it had in fact rebelled against many forms of institutional authority. Now, the values of the baby-boomer generation were in effect being carried over into the social sciences with the rejection of the historic assumptions that had reflected past normative foundations in many areas of American society.* A new and more individualistic (or as some would say

* This new individualistic ethos involving an attitude of "do your own thing" has been increasingly manifested since the 1960s in the character of American religious beliefs—among churchgoers and nonchurchgoers alike. Indeed, it is a force today shaping all areas of American life. Based on a comprehensive survey of religious attitudes among five hundred people who had been confirmed in Presbyterian churches across the United States, a 1994 article in *Theology Today* described the rise of a powerful "lay liberalism" since the 1970s:

> This reluctance to insist on absolute standards of faithful participation is part of a larger pattern of beliefs that we detected among our Baby Boomers. We have labeled this pattern "lay liberalism." It is an "almost theology" that is held by more than half of our Baby Boomers.
>
> It does not strictly conform to any of the prevailing systematic theologies. It evokes no resonances with process, feminist, liberation or contextual theology. Indeed, when we asked our

self-centered) American outlook would now have to be the starting point, requiring in some cases the development of whole new approaches to social science analysis.

When the term "new institutionalism" is used in economics, it most often refers to the new approach to the study of business organizations and the resulting implications for the workings of markets and businesses. However, it is also appropriate to include the new political science of the public choice school and the new sociology of Becker and Posner as part of a broader new institutionalism in all of American social science. If one considers that the founding figures are Coase in business, Buchanan in government, and Becker in sociology, it would not be much of an exaggeration to say that a few Chicago economists have been transforming the study of the institutions of American society (and having considerable worldwide impact as well).★

Yet it is a paradox that this influence would be difficult to explain in terms of the methodological individualism that is at the core of this new institutionalism. Chicago's great influence is astonishing testimony to the power of ideas, even as the content of the new Chicago analysis of economic, political, and social life suggests that ideas have less importance. Clearly, there is a problem here.

The old saying is Watch what I do, not what I say. Chicago is saying that people behave according to individual advantage and are not much swayed by appeals to ideology, religion, culture, altruism, or other ideas in the mind (beyond individual utility). What Chicago is doing is spreading this particular idea with all the power of a modern religious movement.†

---

respondents about these more formal articulations of contemporary Christianity, we were generally greeted with incomprehension. Lay liberals have pieced together their beliefs in the manner of all folk religions.

Lay liberalism is "liberal" in its stress on acceptance of differences, its tolerance of uncertainty, its strong commitment to individualism, and its generally liberal position on social and moral issues. The defining quality of lay liberalism is its wide-open tolerance of diversity in matters of belief and practice.

Few would agree that salvation is only through Jesus Christ or that Christ is the only source of absolute truth. . . . Many Baby Boomers go so far as to say that they would be content if their children adopted non-Western religions "as long as they are happy" and as long as they are moral citizens.

See Donald A Luidens, Dean R. Hoge, and Benton Johnson, "The Emergence of Lay Liberalism Among Baby Boomers," *Theology Today* 51 (July 1994): 252–53.

★ The only real debates here might be whether Williamson should be included with or substituted in place of Coase, and Gordon Tullock included along with Buchanan.

† One might argue, to be sure, that the new institutionalism in political science, economics, and sociology was in fact a latecomer to a new individualistic pursuit of individual desires pioneered earlier by Sigmund Freud and then various other schools of psychology. In the Freudian analysis, the Christian and other traditional religions had no objective validity, but did tend to create guilt and other problems for the individual trying to find a healthy balance between the id, ego, and other com-

A place of amazing intellectual fertility, the University of Chicago was also a leader in the old institutionalism. Thorstein Veblen taught in the economics department there, and Frank Knight could well be considered among the leading institutional economists of the twentieth century—although people usually have not put him in that category, partly because of a common association of early American institutionalism with progressive and other left-wing political views. As a professor at the University of Washington from 1950 to 1983, Douglass North says that he was "fortunate" in that he had for colleagues there people such as Steven Cheung and Yoram Barzel, both associated with the Chicago school. Because they "took Coase's work seriously," North was encouraged early on to study its implications closely as well.[3]★

Winner of the Nobel Prize in 1993, North has become the most prominent economist today advocating a radical change in economic methods.[4] North has incorporated into his thinking and puts a great deal of stock in the economic role of opportunism, principal-agent problems, asymmetric information, and others of the familiar concerns of the new institutional economics. However, he also emphasizes a new element, the central role of cultural influences for the workings of economic institutions and the performance of the economy in general.† Indeed, the lowest-cost way to deal

---

ponents of the mind. Indeed, all ethical and other social beliefs were in much the same category, outside constraints in the social environment that might complicate the task of achieving a satisfactory balance between the various psychological forces in the mind.

Such an analysis promoted an individualistic and utilitarian ethic very similar to Chicago economics. If you are happy, and it "works for you" (achieves a successful outcome in the mind), the psychological mindset tells you that you are free to go ahead. If getting divorced, if living together outside marriage, if living an openly gay lifestyle, if living in a new-age commune, if these or any other of a host of new lifestyles truly make you "feel good about yourself," the individualistic and utilitarian ethics of Freudian psychoanalysis and its therapeutic successors says that the old moralities should not stand in the way.

Indeed, the psychological mindset arguably has done as much or more to promote such an individualistic and libertarian ethic in popular culture as the arguments of the Chicago school or any other group of economists. However, the economic arguments have probably had a more powerful legitimizing influence in areas of elite opinion such as the legal system and the administrative apparatus of government.

★ In the 1960s and 1970s, the Chicago school had several outposts within American departments of economics, including the University of Virginia (where Coase had taught from 1958 to 1964), the University of Washington, and the University of California at Los Angeles (UCLA). Thus, North is also closely linked to the Chicago school, although he was never a graduate student or teacher there.

† North thus far is part of a small minority of economists, however. For most economists, the introduction of an element of "culture" into his or her research is still regarded as a concession of analytical failure. If an economist is good enough, culture ideally should never become part of the economic explanation. Such attitudes were reflected in a leading macroeconomic textbook in considering why it might be that the Japanese save more. The authors explain, "There are also some noneconomic explanations. As stated by Hayashi, 'If all else fails, there is a cultural explanation.' " See Robert E. Hall and John B. Taylor, *Macroeconomics,* 5th ed. (New York: W. W. Norton, 1997), 278.

with opportunism is to have a trustworthy citizenry. If you can count on other people being honest, there will be no need for elaborate signaling devices, honesty filters, and other institutional mechanisms to combat the threat of cheating, lying and other dishonest behavior. Because the level of transaction costs will be reduced correspondingly, a national economy will operate all the more efficiently.

A critical economic question thus may be the manner in which a society might be able to instill a belief system that ensures trustworthy behavior to the maximum degree possible.* A better moral environment, it seems, could be as important as an investment in physical capital in sustaining a strong performance of the economy. If the "cost" of the moral system is less than the cost of the physical capital, cultural innovation could be the more "efficient" way to achieve a more rapid economic growth and development. In other words, if economists hope to analyze economic efficiency in its full dimensions, it would seem that they will have to extend the range of their analyses to include consideration of the factors determining the level of trust and honesty in society. Slowly, a few economists—often encouraged by other social scientists—are coming around to this view.†

Yet why deny the obvious? The Japanese do (or at least they have in the past—things may be changing) behave differently. Consider that in 1948 the American occupation established daylight saving time, but once the Americans left, the Japanese abolished it, in 1952. The reason was that "too many people felt they couldn't possibly leave the office while it was still light outside," and Japanese officials did not want to further burden a workforce already putting in very long hours. See Mary Jordan, "Japan Looks to Daylight Time to Brighten Its Economy and Evenings," *Washington Post,* February 23, 1999, A13.

* The level of trust in society and what to do about it—including issues of how to assess trustworthy behavior—are today receiving more attention among practicing businesspeople as well. A cover story in *Business Week* asks, "Who Can You Trust?" in a time when "Companies Fudge Their Numbers"; when "Accountants Turn a Blind Eye"; and when "Analysts Have a Conflict of Interest." See cover of *Business Week,* October 5, 1998.

† Herbert Stein called for economists to "contribute to understanding and possibly solving the conflict of values problem." What will be required in the future is that economists "participate in a value-free study of values, because values affect many of the phenomena that economists have always considered part of their province." This will require, however, some significant changes in the culture—the values—of professional economists themselves. "If economics is to contribute to the study of values it will have to change in several ways. First, it will have to recognize the critical importance of the subject—the character, distribution, and determinants of values. Second, it will have to become more history-minded, recognizing that what has happened in the past changes what can happen in the future in a way that can be reversed only slowly if at all. Third, it will have to get used to collaborating with [other] social scientists." See Herbert Stein, "The Washington Economist: The End of Economics as We Know It," *American Enterprise* 5 (September/October 1994): 9.

TRUST AS AN ECONOMIC ASSET

While many of the rising stars in economics were abandoning the old normative ground rules in the 1960s and 1970s, other economists were still interested in a world where the traditional social restraints retained their significance. Kenneth Arrow observed in 1974 that the workings of the economic system depended on the existence of "invisible institutions." Whatever was happening at Chicago, most economists, Arrow noted, still typically assumed (if often implicitly) the acceptance in society of certain "principles of ethics and morality." These principles amounted to "agreements, conscious or, in many cases, unconscious, to supply mutual benefits."[5] Without the existence of social bonds grounded in shared ethical principles, and despite all the clever devices for detecting and precluding opportunism that Oliver Williamson and other new institutional economists were identifying, the functioning of the economy would be grievously impaired in the absence of strong internal restraints on dishonest behavior. As Arrow explained: "Societies in their evolution have developed implicit agreements to certain kinds of regard for others, agreements which are essential to the survival of society or at least contribute greatly to the efficiency of its working. . . . [One of the main] properties of many societies whose economic development is backward is a lack of mutual trust. . . . It [is] essential in the running of society that we have what might be called 'conscience,' a feeling of responsibility for the effect of one's actions on others."[6]

Williamson himself had recognized that the transaction cost advantages of markets versus corporate and other administrative hierarchies depended in part on considerations of "quasimoral involvements among the parties" involved in market and administrative arrangements. Economic organization internal to a firm could benefit from an "atmosphere" that served to stimulate the "sociological phenomenon of reciprocity." The very features of the organizational structure of a firm in themselves could be an important object of individual welfare because "differing exchange relations" may involve varying "nonpecuniary satisfactions" and thus the specific forms of "these relations themselves are valued." Moreover, as Williamson comments, "transactional attitudes," and thus the actual transaction costs associated with alternative economic institutions, "are greatly influenced by the sociopolitical system in which exchange takes place."[7]

In other words, in a culture—corporate, or extending to the whole society—where social norms of honesty and solidarity are powerful, and where people like the arrangements of their work and believe in what they are doing, the role of opportunism and other transaction cost problems may be much reduced.[8] A successful corporation might find that one of its most important tasks is to instill a suitable set of internal loyalties to the organiza-tion.[9] The success of top business leaders might depend as much on their "preaching" ability as on their skillfulness in making exact calculations of potential profit and loss.[10] In short, corporations and churches to a surprising degree might be engaged in the same social task, one focused on improving the values of a particular organization, the other on improving the values of society as a whole with consequent economic as well as other benefits.*

As most economists would, Williamson felt poorly equipped to conduct what might have seemed more an anthropological, sociological—or even theological—form of analysis. As he commented, a full discussion of the role of national and corporate values and their broader economic "ramifications raises a wider set of sociopolitical issues than can be addressed here."[11]

IMPLICIT MUTUAL CONTRACTS

Nevertheless, some economists have recently sought to move beyond the re-luctance of most economists to enter such domains. It has helped that it may be possible to study the culture of a corporation without abandoning the in-dividualistic outlook characteristic of economic methods. Indeed, it may be that the very idea of a corporation as a decision-making entity in itself is in some sense a fiction; a corporation may be more like an ecological system where the outcomes reflect the complex and formally uncoordinated inter-actions of the individual plants and animals that can be found there. Thus, as some economists have come to think of it, a corporate "ecology" is actually a complicated setting for many kinds of individual choice.† Michael Jensen

---

* Michael Novak writes, "The business corporation . . . is a relatively new organism in social his-tory. It is, perhaps, the best secular analogue to the church. It is a legal person, a unitary being, consti-tuted by voluntary contract, animated by social purposes and subject to pervasive disciplines. Churches themselves are often incorporated. The kinds of community and sociality which corporations make possible within corporations and in the social field around them deserve concrete description." See Michael Novak, "God and Man in the Corporation," *Policy Review*, no. 3 (Summer 1980): 23.

† This kind of thinking can be extended as well to more radical lines of thought. The individual "person," as some biologists now describe an individual human being, can be seen as really just a com-plicated setting for individual cell actions. Biologists have concluded that it is even possible for differ-ent kinds of cells within the same plant or animal organism to be in conflict with and to compete with one another for survival in an evolutionary sense at the expense of the host plant or animal—as eco-nomic "agents" may behave opportunistically relative to their "principals." To be sure, while this might be a scientifically correct way of characterizing the situation, it would probably be difficult to persuade "you" and "me" that "we" do not really exist as a genuine single being but merely represent the cumulative actions of our constituent cells. This example serves also to illustrate the limits of other kinds of reductionist approaches. In much the same way that "you" may think that your existence transcends the actions of your individual cells, a "corporation" may think that it has an existence that transcends the actions of its individual employees. See, for example, Richard Dawkins, *The Selfish Gene* (New York: Oxford University Press, 1989; 1st ed., 1976).

and William Meckling observed in 1976 that "most organizations are simply legal fictions, which serve as a nexus for a set of contracting relationships among individuals."[12] In an atomistic market the interactions among individual players are organized around a large set of explicit market contracts. In the corporation the employees are instead bound together in their sets of interrelationships by "implicit contracts"—formally unstated but nevertheless powerful sets of mutual expectations of future rewards and punishments within the firm. A market and a corporation can then be seen as simply two different institutional settings for creating systems of individual incentives that achieve the desired result of coordinating economic behavior. As Paul Milgrom and John Roberts put it,

> In the Arrow–Debreu theory of the private ownership economy, the distinction between firm and market is absolutely clear: a firm is a production set summarizing the possibilities for transforming one bundle of time-, event- and location-differentiated commodities into another; a market is the coming together of economic agents (firms and consumers) to exchange ownership of such commodity bundles. However, as our analysis of the firm deepens, the firm–market distinction blurs; for production itself involves exchange. The boundaries of firms are fuzzy: two legally separate firms may be more closely integrated in their planning and operations than are any pair of divisions in a conglomerate; and even though there is no commonality of ownership or explicit long-term contract linking them, they may continue their close relations over indefinitely extended periods. Moreover, decentralized firms may adopt market-like solutions to their organizational problems, using, for example, arms-length negotiations to determine transfer prices and evaluating employee and divisional performance on profit criteria.[13]

Within a business organization the implicit (and sometimes explicit) contractual expectations may be poorly understood, potentially resulting in organizational confusion. It would be like a formal market trying to function without any set of legal contracts. However, a market arrangement may not work well either, because of the large transaction costs in obtaining the necessary information on market participants and then negotiating and enforcing all the many separate contracts. Indeed, the key to economic efficiency may be to establish a corporate culture that succeeds in defining the implicit set of contracts within the corporation in an informal but nevertheless clear and effective way that promotes an efficient business outcome.

The corporate culture in this perspective can be seen as a kind of alternative to—an institutional substitute for—the legal contracts of the market-place. The corporate culture should address matters such as expected salary increases and other potential rewards for various forms of entrepreneurial successes within the corporation.[14] In part, individual expectations of reward and punishment are found in the "reputation" of the organization, in the "soul of a firm . . . in the eyes of its trading partners, in particular its employees. Corporate culture can then be identified as the main vehicle for sustaining and advancing reputation."[15]

Students of business practices in business schools have long recognized the importance of corporate culture.[16] It may be important to an economic understanding of business behavior, as Martha Feldman and James March find, to understand the mechanisms by which corporate "gossip" is exchanged.[17] The members of the economics profession, however, have almost always shied away from such inquiries. The only way to understand the informal incentive structures facing the individuals operating within a culture might actually be to spend time living and experiencing the corporate culture itself. For the ordinary economist, this kind of fieldwork sounds more like an anthropological or sociological than any traditional form of economic inquiry. It is all part of a general reluctance on the part of economists to analyze cultural elements and the behavioral impacts of social structures of internal expectation. Even if social values might be important motivating factors in individual behavior, it will have to be left to other people, as most mainstream economists still seem to think, to do such "soft" analyses.*

---

* Many businesspeople themselves, however, show no such reluctance to seek a better understanding of the central role of business culture in achieving business success. Consider the comments of Dexter Baker who started with a small-technology company with $2.5 million in sales in 1952, and rose to become CEO of Air Products and Chemicals, Inc., a corporation with more than fifteen thousand employees and three billion dollars in sales in 1992.

> I believe it is the responsibility of the chief executive of a corporation or any organization to set the moral and ethical tone of the organization. If he or she is firmly determined to conduct the business of the organization on the highest possible ethical standards, others will follow because that is what is expected of all employees.
>
> On the other hand, if half truths are tolerated, gift taking and giving accepted, less than top-quality products supplied, less than safe operations permitted, a sloppy environmental performance tolerated, then that will become the corporation style and standard.
>
> At every level in any organization, almost no day, certainly no week, passes free of the responsibility of thinking through and applying ethical judgments in ways that promote or protect the character of our company or the well being of our people and those we serve in the external world.

See Dexter F. Baker, "Ethical Issues and Decision Making in Business," *Vital Speeches of the Day,* January 15, 1993, 211.

The consequence of continuing to hold such attitudes, however, may be to maintain an ostrichlike posture for the economics profession. It may exclude the members of the profession from any real understanding of much of the economic action in society. Furubotn and Richter comment:

> The more general term *organizational culture* . . . applies to all kinds of organizations—among them markets, firms and states. In the case of markets, "culture" relates to the specifics of what "one does" in a sequential contract facing the unforeseeable. In other words, in cases of long-term customer relationships individual "cultures" can develop to supplement the purely legal clauses of contracts. Under certain conditions (e.g., long-term multilateral labor contracts), hierarchical transactions within the firm may be considered preferable to market transactions by one or both parties for the formation and cultivation of organizational culture. It can be concluded from this that incentives may exist to integrate in order to build up a more efficient and attractive organizational culture. Such improvement, of course, may bring about, in turn, an enhanced reputation for the firm and a more stable structure of (relational) employment contracts.
>
> It is well known, of course, that the efficiency and success of any business organization will be greater the more effectively the various members of the unit cooperate in the process of production. But wholehearted cooperation among the individuals who constitute the coalition of resource owners representing the firm is by no means assured. Rather, difficulties can be expected because individual firm members normally have private objectives that are in conflict with the collective or social interests of the coalition as a whole. A basic problem for organizational theory, then, is to explain how individuals can be motivated so that they will cooperate fully in trying to achieve the collective interests and ensure enterprise efficiency.[18]

As the analysis of the new institutional economics now finds, the "focus has to be shifted from incentive systems to the role of the manager as a leader and shaper of attitudes within the [business] organization"—in effect, as a definer and instiller of the comprehensive set of informal expectations that constitute the corporate business culture.[19] Robert Gibbons recently commented that economists may have to begin studying the "incentives in organizations" that are associated with, for example, the workings of corporate "politics." They may have to begin to study such things as the "troubling possibility" that a potential incentive structure of a firm, while it might narrowly encourage the correct forms of behavior (say a piece-rate system of paying workers), might thereby also damage overall corporate morale ("intrinsic motivation"), and thus be counterproductive to the corporation's long-run profit-making objectives.[20]

VALUES AS SELF-INTEREST

If it will be necessary in the future to analyze the determinants of an ethical climate of trust in business and in society, some economists now propose to treat the ethical system as an outgrowth of the normal expression of self-interest grounded in motives of individual profit or utility maximization.[21] The idea is to incorporate ethics and trust into economic analyses without having to abandon the methodological individualism characteristic of the economic method. Indeed, there is much to be said for this approach; a person will often find it in his or her own self-interest to be honest (or more precisely, to be perceived by others as honest). Investing in a good individual reputation can create a valuable personal and business asset. Economic interactions among people who trust one another, based on past experience, may greatly reduce the levels of transaction costs among them, and the levels of profits and utility realized individually and collectively.

However, while it can explain a great deal, it is doubtful that this approach can yield the full explanation for a culture in which honesty and trust have become ingrained social expectations.* A culture of honest dealings may ultimately need to encompass the old-fashioned kind of trust as well, not only the kind that results from individual incentives to create the appearance of honesty (leaving open the option to be dishonest whenever a person can "get away with it"—either no one will know or in any case the future net returns of dishonesty might turn positive for other reasons). Thus, as Howard Margolis of the University of Chicago relates, any realistic theory of "social

---

* Daniel Hausman and Michael McPherson, for example, address the question of whether there is "any *inconsistency* between economically rational action and morally motivated action." While concluding that there is no "inherent incompatibility," they also find that "it is questionable whether the full range of familiar moral phenomena can be accommodated within" a framework of individual utility maximizing. If people act rationally to maximize self-interest—which may include recognizing an economic advantage to being perceived as honest—their responses to "problems of moral backsliding, of weakness of will, and of doubt" will still not be in full accord with long-standing expectations of ethical motivations and behavior in Western society. See Daniel M. Hausman and Michael S. McPherson, "Taking Ethics Seriously: Economics and Contemporary Moral Philosophy," *Journal of Economic Literature* 31 (June 1993): 686. See also Daniel M. Hausman and Michael S. McPherson, *Economic Analysis and Moral Philosophy* (New York: Cambridge University Press, 1996).

life" involves the development of "respect for norms that goes beyond what can realistically be accounted for in terms of prudent pursuit of self-interest." In an entirely individualistic world, the usual assumptions of free-rider behavior made by economists might gradually yield "the erosion of all norms," which creates something of a mystery for conventional economic thinking because an absence of norms "is not what we routinely see." As a result, as Margolis observes, "no leading institutional economist believes that all economically significant behavior is strictly self-interested." [22]

Reaching a similar conclusion from a basis more in practical business experience, the *Business and Professional Ethics Journal* in 1997 published a symposium issue, "Trust and Business: Barriers and Bridges." Regarding attempts to model trust as an economic choice of self-interested rational actors, Fernando Flores and Robert Solomon comment:

> The new attentiveness to trust betrays the damage that results from all of those years of neglect. What caused the neglect of trust (in part) was the avoidance of the "softer" aspects of ethics, of ethics as feeling or "sentiment," of ethics as an essential function of relationships. Too much of the current attention to trust still tends or tries to avoid these "soft" areas. Trust is reduced to strategy and rational expectations. Trust is discussed as a risk to be justified instead of an existential stance in which such questions are put out of play. Trust is treated as an individual's attitude or a set of subjective probabilities and not as an essential ingredient in a relationship. . . . Accordingly, the phenomenon of trust is often distorted as much as it is clarified. . . . We are given a variety of much too "thin" accounts of a rich phenomenon which is actually quite varied and multi-dimensional. [23]

The idea of trust as a social commitment rather than an act of individual self-interest inevitably leads to the subject of religion as a possible factor in the formation of social beliefs that could sustain trust. Religion involves group value formation and, as Margolis notes, religion "is not only a vehicle of rituals that bind a community together . . . but also identifies who is committed to morally right behavior and who undermines that," thus helping to provide a basis for economic exchange. Margolis believes, agreeing with Arrow, that "the inferior status implicitly granted to social as against self-interested motivation" in the economics of the past will not be sustainable. [24] Indeed, the typical refusal of most current economists to go beyond self-interested motivations is itself a religious act within the framework of a powerful economic theology—or, as Margolis puts it, "it is an act of faith. . . . Or so its seems to me, though I realize hardly so to most of my [economist] readers." [25]

THE VOTING PROBLEM WRIT LARGE

An ethical system that promotes trust can be an immensely valuable economic asset for a society. It can go far to resolve in one fell swoop a whole host of opportunism, principal-agent, incomplete contracting, asymmetric information and other basic transaction cost problems. The question is how to create and sustain such an ethical system. It may help to consider previous economic attempts to analyze the act of voting because this involves a similar problem in economic explanation. Both the act of voting and the honoring of social commitments to honest behavior exhibit forms of collective action that are difficult to explain in terms of the standard economic models of rational choice in response to individual incentives.

Except in very small jurisdictions, a person can confidently expect to go a lifetime without ever casting a vote that makes a practical difference to an election outcome. Yet, most people, including most economists, do vote. From a framework of rational individual maximization of self-interest, most voting would seem to be a waste of time. Moreover, the average voter is more likely to vote in elections with national than with local offices at stake— given the much smaller likelihood of affecting the national outcome, seemingly just the opposite of a rational decision (assuming a person is going to vote at all). Why all this seemingly uneconomic behavior?

One attempt to reconcile rational self-interest with ordinary voting behavior starts by assuming that each individual is in fact rational but the same person believes (mistakenly) that most other people are not. Such a person therefore may think that his or her own individual actions—whether this person votes or not—will somehow influence the behavior of other people. In fact, many people do seem to say to themselves, "If I do not vote, then no one else will either." And then they vote because they know that a complete absence of voting would undermine the social basis for a democratic society—a very practical matter in which they do have a large individual interest.

In this way, it thus may become individually rational to vote. And having mistaken expectations—believing that others will be influenced by one's actions even when they are not—is not in itself a violation of the core rationality principle of economics. However, as Jon Elster comments with respect to this kind of salvage job for standard economic modes of analysis, behavioral models of this kind formally sustain the principle of individual rationality at the cost of assuming "a form of magical thinking"—that my individual behavior is somehow really influencing the actions of many other people.[26]

Admittedly, once it is granted that people feel some kind of social obligation to vote, it is easily enough seen to be in their rational self-interest to do so. If I do not vote, I will feel guilty, and avoiding the pain of the guilt will then rationally cause me to vote as a matter of individual self-interest. But this begs the question about the origin of the sense of social obligation. Why might a rational maximizer of individual self-interest ever internalize a social ideal that subjects his or her sense of well-being to such potentially powerful outside influences and feelings of guilt? Where does this ideal and the individual sense of commitment to honor it come from in the first place? It is the kind of question that does not lend itself to traditional forms of economic analysis.

And voting is merely the tip of the iceberg. In a whole host of situations in society, people behave according to expectations of ethical behavior and dedication to larger social ideals. They donate to charities or contribute their efforts to political campaigns without any expectation of individual reward. At the extreme some people die in war for their country, even volunteering for a particularly dangerous military operation that they know in advance could well yield this outcome. And many people do in fact behave in a trustworthy fashion in market settings, even when dealing with strangers whom they never expect to see again. Another part of the new institutional economics, the economic study of politics, has now shown how all kinds of "outcomes are contingent on complex group-level arrangements, norms, and expectations" that cannot be "predicted or described by reference to individual decisions alone." As Gary Miller has commented, "the evidence gathered in the confrontation of economic models with political reality" has exposed the difficulties of the typical individualistic assumptions in economic theory and thus "has the potential for transforming [the practice of] economics as well."[27]

The existence of voting and other such acts emphasizes that there is a powerful element in each person that is social rather than individual. People derive their identity and sense of themselves as persons from the groups with which they associate. They may not even know what they want individually (their "preference function") until the group helps them to decide. Indeed, the group may achieve a collective resolution through a process that Frank Knight commonly described as extended "discussion." The outcome of the discussions is a set of group values that the members implicitly agree to follow as part of their "culture"—even when it may not always serve the individual interest of one or another member, narrowly construed. Much of social life then consists of participation in group activities including frequent declarations of group solidarity and many symbolic affirmations of the common values of the culture.

Voting is not difficult to understand in this framework of thought; it is one of the many symbolic affirmations of membership in the democratic community of all the citizens of a nation-state, province, region, city, or other political entity.[28] People are more inclined to participate in American national elections—however irrational from the economic perspective, given the virtually zero chance of having any real impact on the national result—because for many of them their sense of identification with the national community is stronger than with state and local communities. The declines in voter-participation rates in elections in the United States in recent decades similarly are not based on rational economic explanations (the probably of affecting the outcome has stayed constant at essentially zero). Rather, this trend in voting reflects a declining sense of identification that many have with the national community and consequently their reduced interest in making symbolic statements of loyalty and commitment. In short, if a nation is in some sense a modern form of church, voting has little to do with consumer choice but is best understood as being in the same behavioral category as taking communion in church.

People outside the economics profession might well say: All of this is obvious, why belabor the point? By contrast, most economists themselves are socialized (they have their own group with its own special values to which they make their own frequent symbolic affirmations of commitment) to believe otherwise. It may take years of graduate school, but the end result is a profession (a priesthood) that is trained to see every action in society as an expression of an individual rather than a social motive. Indeed, the very concept of a "social motive" does not exist in the working vocabulary of most current economists.

CULTURE AS A DECISION "FRAME"

Nevertheless, traditional ideas of economic rationality are presently under challenge on many fronts even within the economics profession.[29] Another area of challenge comes from the actual empirical observation of individual exercises of consumer choice. Even individuals supposedly acting to maximize their own self-interest often do not conform to standard economic understandings, as is revealed when their decision making is closely observed. Consider the following two options. First, one group is given (in an experiment run by an economist, or in analogous situations that might arise in the real world) a sum of $300, and then required to choose between two possibilities: a certain additional payment of $100 or a one-half chance of receiving another $200. Then, another group is confronted with the following problem: its members are given $500 and required to choose between a certain loss of $100 or a one-half chance of losing $200.

In terms of the formal calculations of rational decision-making, the choices are analytically identical. They should thus produce identical outcomes by the normal assumptions of economic analysis. However, in practice it has been shown in many experimental studies that people instead make systematically different choices.[30] They are much more likely to take the one-half risk (of winning or losing $200) when told their initial endowment is $300, and much more likely to select the sure thing when told their initial endowment is $500. There is now a growing literature on how such "framing effects" can significantly affect the exercise by consumers (and other economic actors) of individual choice.[31]

The medical profession long ago discovered that placebos and other forms of patient expectations could have powerful effects—that patient outcomes often did not conform very well to the rational models of the mechanical ("engineering") approaches of the American health care system. If a witch doctor in a society was actually believed to have curative powers, the belief could be self-fulfilling. American economics is now finding that things such as placebos and other "nonrational" framing effects play a significant role in a much wider range of consumer decisions than health care alone.

In a recent survey of the new economics literature, Matthew Rabin finds that framing effects are not merely errors of calculation, but "the 'frames' may in fact partially *determine* a person's preferences." In one experiment, when required to choose between receiving six dollars or a Cross pen, 36 percent chose the pen when that was the only choice. However, 46 percent chose the Cross pen when a third option of an inferior pen was added in. Rabin comments that in experimental situations "subjects often required an order of magnitude more money to [be willing voluntarily to] expose themselves to the disease than they would pay for a cure." In actual consumer choice it is generally true that "even when people *do* seem aware of the shape of their global utility functions, they may not properly maximize those preferences because they take an overly 'piecemeal' approach."[32]

One way of thinking about the subject of culture is that culture itself serves to provide a particularly important kind of "frame." If framing effects are in fact pervasive in individual consumer choice, it is yet another reason to study the impact of culture on economic behavior. Then, to the extent that the "cultural frame" of a society proves important, history assumes a new economic significance. In the examples given above, the consumer decision is framed by reference to some prior set of events. That is to say, different histories leading up to the same rational consumer choice will often yield different consumer outcomes.

The most powerful cultural frames are likely to be associated with religion. Indeed, one might argue that religion is in some sense about learning new (and perhaps better) "frames," as when a person who is "born again" sees the world in an altogether different light—and perhaps learns to be much more "accepting" of outcomes that earlier might have caused anger or frustration. Such changes in the "cultural frame" in which an act of individual choice takes place can not only alter subjective perceptions of utility for individuals, but can also have broad implications for the degree of efficiency in the productive workings of an economic system as a whole. Economists, for example, have long studied the economic consequences of one particular framing effect, "money illusion" on the part of workers. It seems that workers often strenuously resist any decline in the nominal wage they are paid, but are much less upset when inflation erodes—if less explicitly and directly—the value of their wage by exactly the same amount in real terms. It would seem that whole new categories of "consumer illusion" exist that remain to be described and analyzed by economists.

REDISCOVERING HISTORY

Although a reorientation of economic research to study history and culture would be a large departure for most economists, it would not be altogether new.* As noted previously, American historical and institutional economics

---

* While economists have been slow to take up this charge, partly because their professional training leaves them poorly equipped to do so, other disciplines have begun to move forward. Property rights, for example, can be as much a matter of the culture in which they are found as the formal statements found in the law books. Yale law professor Carol Rose thus writes that an important element in the institution of property in the United States is "storytelling." When a person makes a "claim of [property] ownership," it amounts to "a kind of assertion or story, told within a culture that shapes the story's content and meaning." The successful defense of property rights thus depends on the ability of property owners to tell stories that other people "find persuasive as grounds for the [property] claim asserted." A formal legal regime of well-specified property rights imported wholesale from one country to another may work very poorly because the residents of the second country have little familiarity with the associated cultural framework and accompanying rhetoric of property persuasion. Indeed, this can be a problem even within contemporary American law of property rights:

> [The trouble is that] we sometimes seem to start out with perfectly clear, open-and-shut demarcations of entitlements—and then shift to fuzzy, ambiguous rules of decision. I call this the substitution of "mud" rules for "crystal" ones. . . . The straightforward common law crystalline rules [of property] have been muddied repeatedly by exceptions and equitable second-guessing, to the point that [for example] the various claimants under real estate contracts,

early in this century—following closely after models in Germany and other European nations—studied culture and history as a central element in determining basic economic change during the industrial revolution and the general processes of modernization around the world.[33] Indeed, economics was part of a broader trend. Much of the whole intellectual life of Europe over the course of the nineteenth century was dominated by a historical manner of understanding of society.

Early in the century, Hegel's philosophical system portrayed the evolution of human thought as moving from a primitive condition through various higher stages until finally reaching a culmination in the rational mind of the Enlightenment. A little later, the philosophical positivism of Auguste Comte offered another portrayal of the development of human intelligence from primitive beginnings to a current advanced stage of scientific knowledge, opening the way to the genuine scientific management of society. Darwin then shifted the workings of history from the mental to physical and biological realms. Darwin's theory of evolution was by far the most influential of the many new interpretations of history of the nineteenth century. In the second half of the century, Marx was only one of the many economists who regarded their purpose as extending the methods of Darwin into social and economic realms. Herbert Spencer also thought he had achieved this objective; his portrayal of the evolutionary processes of social Darwinism proved to be the most influential economic idea of the era in both England and the United States (where Yale economist William Graham Sumner was the leading proponent).[34]

As the intellectual historian J. L. Talmon has commented, throughout the course of the nineteenth century older religious energies were diverted to become new forms of "political Messianism" in which each new messiah preached the one and only true "religion of History," all part of a process that Talmon characterizes as the period's "idolization of History."[35] Eventually, however, there would be a counterreaction in the twentieth century; physics would replace biology as the dominant model of science, and the study of society would turn to a prevailing positivism that lasted until recently. In retrospect, the evolutionary economic histories of the nineteenth century (and some continuing into the twentieth) appeared as obvious scientific failures;

---

mortgages, or recorded deeds don't quite know what their rights and obligations really are.

See Carol M. Rose, *Property and Persuasion: Essays on the History, Theory, and Rhetoric of Ownership* (Boulder, Colo.: Westview Press, 1994), 25, 200. See also Lewis H. Larue, *Constitutional Law as Fiction: Narrative in the Rhetoric of Authority* (University Park: Penn State Press, 1995).

they had commonly made grand claims to an ultimate scientific truth of history, and yet time after time these claims would prove to be baseless. Marx is merely the extreme case and the one with the most unfortunate real-world consequences.

As noted above, economists today are legitimately concerned to avoid any repetition of this discrediting course of events. Yet Frank Hahn, for one, has argued that in the future "economics will become a 'softer' subject than it now is" and that "historical modes of [economic] analysis will eventually seem to be unavoidable."[36] Following a survey of the major economic developments of the past two hundred years, Richard Easterlin comments that "if economics were to return to the study of history, it might conceivably gain better insight into the factors that have shaped this remarkable new world of the 21st century."[37] Douglass North began his career as an economic historian but then moved to the study of history as part of a broader institutional analysis of economic phenomena. He now argues that research into the history of a society will normally be central to achieving any accurate understanding of its economic workings.

North systematically assembled his ideas in his 1990 treatise *Institutions, Institutional Change, and Economic Performance*. Harking back to Coase, he reminds us that in the standard neoclassical analysis, there is a radical assumption of "zero transaction costs." This amounts to assuming that every party knows everything there is to know about "the other party and [that] enforcement is perfect." The result, as Coase said long ago, and which North now reiterates from the perspective of economic history, is a form of economic analysis singularly lacking in interest because "no institutions are necessary in a world of complete information."[38] Yet, as Mancur Olson once observed, "the *main* reason, as far as my studies have been been able to determine, why a country is relatively prosperous or relatively poor, is the quality of the policies and institutions of that country."[39]

Similarly, in a 1997 review of the literature of economic growth, Robert Hall and Charles Jones find that "differences in levels of economic success across countries are driven primarily by the institutions and government policies (or *infrastructure*) that frame the economic environment in which people produce and transact."[40] In a survey of the failures of economic-development programs in Africa, the authors conclude that "domestic policies . . . may be the main obstacle to growth in much of Africa," in part because these policies contribute to an economic environment in which "transaction costs are unusually high."[41] North concludes that the institutional heart of the matter is the success or lack of success "of societies to develop effective, low-cost enforcement of contracts." Looking around the world, regions or nations that have remained poor simply lack an adequate institutional structure of secure contracting. Their contracting arrangements exaggerate rather than resolve problems of opportunism, bounded rationality, principal-agent, security of enforcement, and other familiar transaction cost problems. Poor nations, North writes, typically have saddled themselves with a set of misguided arrangements for "property rights that do not induce economic growth."[42]

In much of the less developed world today, it is not just that one property owner has difficulties in establishing relationships of predictability and reliability in contracts with other private owners, but that these private actors also face the significant possibility that the government will act unilaterally to alter previous contractual arrangements. Where such government uncertainty exists, it is the functional equivalent of a large tax on every form of economic transaction—much as money inflation can also be regarded as imposing a kind of tax on society.

North also emphasizes the critical role of trust—the economic benefits of "ideological commitments to integrity and honesty." Hence, "traditions of hard work, honesty and integrity simply lower the cost of transacting and make possible [many forms of] complex, productive exchange" that otherwise might not be feasible at all.[43] But granted that there are large efficiency and other direct economic gains from a climate of trust, how might a society act affirmatively to establish such a climate? North observes that historically a social environment of trustworthy behavior is "always reinforced by ideologies that undergird those attitudes." And if "ideology" tends to refer to a modern belief system, in earlier times much the same role was played by "religion." Even today, as North observes, the interrelated phenomena of powerful "ideas, organized ideologies, and even religious zealotry play major roles in shaping societies and economies."[44]

It would thus seem that the study of religious history should be added to a new list of important topics for contemporary economic research.* It would be following in the path of one of the great social scientists of the twentieth century, Max Weber, who employed a historical and institutional approach, including a heavy emphasis on the role of religion in economic behavior.[45] Weber's studies included systematic inquiries into the religions of China, India, and other societies, and the broader religious implications there for the full workings of their economic systems.[46] As one student of Weber

---

* It is interesting in this regard that in 1996 Eirik Furubotn and Rudolf Richter chose to hold their annual conference on issues in institutional economics—a leading vehicle for a decade or more for exploring developments in this field—on the subject "religion and economics." See the March 1997 issue of the *Journal of Institutional and Theoretical Economics* for the set of papers from the 1996 conference.

comments, he saw his goals as "documenting through systematic empirical findings the interlocking action of economic and spiritual factors in producing the great social transformations of the past."[47] His best-known work, *The Protestant Ethic and the Spirit of Capitalism,* traced a critical role to the precepts of Calvinist theology in the development of capitalism in Europe. The pursuit of a calling and other theological beliefs spurred motives of capital accumulation that continued to exert a powerful influence even long after the original religious impulse was gone.[48]

More recent scholars, to be sure, have suggested that many of the key institutions of capitalism were first developed in Italy or other Catholic areas, and that many Catholic businesspeople showed an equal enthusiasm for capital accumulation. Yet, in reviewing the economic development of the West, Nathan Rosenberg and L. E. Birdzell find that on any large geographic scale "private firms could conduct trade and investment only if there existed some basis, beyond kinship, for mutual trust." It was necessary to have confidence that others "were honest, diligent and could be trusted. Such trust presupposes a widely shared sense of business morality." If not for exactly the same reasons, Rosenberg and Birdzell thus agree with Weber that the Protestant Reformation was a decisive historical event in promoting a cultural environment in which long-range trust could exist across Europe.★ The new economic bonds were especially powerful among Calvinists, for whom "the sanctification of work . . . served to generate reliable patterns of behavior . . . of a kind which were wholly compatible with a smoothly functioning capitalism: an intense commitment to work, dependability, diligence, self-denial, austerity, thrift, punctuality, fulfillment of promises, fidelity to group interests."[49]

Even well before the Protestant Reformation, as North finds, "intellectual life during the Middle Ages in the West was dominated . . . by the church." Religion at that time shaped the ways in which people would "rationalize, explain, and justify" the world around them, matters that could have a major impact on practical economic considerations such as "the costs of contracting." Today, ideology, culture, secular religion, new forms of traditional religion— in whatever form one finds contemporary social belief systems—continue to

---

★ It is not only social capital in the form of longer-term and longer-distance trust that may have been advanced by Protestantism. It may also have been human capital in the form of education. Protestant religion taught that each person must reach his or her own understanding of the message of God as found in the Bible. As Richard Easterlin comments, differences in educational levels among European countries "reach as far back as the 16th century, well before the onset of modern economic growth, trends that are connected in part to the Protestant Reformation with its emphasis on the need for each individual to be able to read the Bible himself." As this example illustrates, potentially important influences on economic development may result from noneconomic motives having little or nothing to do with estimated return on investment. See Richard A. Easterlin, "The Worldwide Standard of Living Since 1800," *Journal of Economic Perspectives* 14 (Winter 2000): 19.

determine "the subjective mental constructs by which individuals process information and arrive at conclusions that shape their choices."[50]

The field of economics may therefore have to be extended to include systematic empirical investigation into such subjects. Yet, as North finds, economists' long-standing "preoccupation with rational choice and efficient market hypotheses has blinded us to the implications of incomplete information and the complexity of environments and subjective perceptions of the external world that individuals hold." Moreover, some belief systems and institutional forms succeed much better than others in providing "the freedom to individuals to incorporate their ideas and ideologies into the choices they make," and thus in minimizing transaction costs and other information burdens for an economic system.[51] Radical as it may sound to most economists, the logic of North's analysis leads to the conclusion that economists committed to promoting a more efficient economic system may also have to think about how they might act to promote a more "efficient" religion.

Although they would never put it in these terms, many economists have in fact already done this. As examined in Parts I and II in the present volume, Samuelson's *Economics* sought to instill such a secular religion in American society. Samuelson of course was not alone; he had a large number of disciples within the American economics profession.

PATH-DEPENDENT ECONOMICS

If a "cultural frame" for economic behavior can be derived from history, the beginnings of a historical interest among economists is seen in the new literature of "path dependence," associated with Brian Arthur and his colleagues.[52] Thus far, the focus of this literature has been on more-traditional economic subjects such as the history of the development of new products, evolution of individual firms in the market, changes in industry organization, and so forth. Arthur, for example, has addressed the topic of whether the current location of Silicon Valley in California is a product exclusively of proximity to skilled labor, nearby airports, and close access to academic research centers. Or, is Silicon Valley also partly a result of the "chance" historical event that "the Packards, the Varians, the Shockleys of the industry . . . happened to set up near Stanford University in the 1940s and 1950s"? He concludes that economic phenomena such as the great extent of increasing returns to scale (so that the first firm to enter a new industry could well stay first) and "lock-in" effects mean that "a mixture of economic determinism and historical chance—and not either alone—has formed the spatial patterns we observe."[53]

The literature of path dependence is helpful in redirecting the attention of economists to history and the role of unplanned events in economic outcomes.[54] In emphasizing the importance of history, the new literature makes the essential point that in the real world there are often "multiple equilibria," that the "butterfly effect" of chaos theory (the idea that a tiny movement of air created by a butterfly's wings at one place on earth could be a precipitating event setting off a major windstorm at other, distant places on earth) can apply to economic phenomena as well.[55] Yet, much like the new institutional economics, the path-dependence literature has often sought to retain much of the formal analytical method and technical vocabulary of neoclassical analysis. The tight limitations imposed by such methods restrict the potential scope of historical analysis in this mode. The very term "path dependence" employs a stiff formalism for saying something much older and less novel—the recognition that "history matters."

This literature thus may well prove to be a transitional phase itself, a part of the evolutionary history of social science (which has its own "path dependence"). The existing members of the economics profession may not yet be prepared for a full-fledged revival of historical methods—in the style of, say, Max Weber—within the scope of acceptable economic research. But they may be willing to explore new approaches, as long as they are sufficiently couched in mainstream economic language. The current efforts of Arthur and his colleagues may be somewhat like arguing in Latin that the use of Latin as a working language is fading. Such arguments are not likely to define the future, but they can serve a useful role in facilitating a moderate degree of present-day change.

NORTHERN VERSUS SOUTHERN ITALY

The disciplinary boundaries of the university world today pose a formidable obstacle to the forms of broader historical and cultural inquiry that seem to be needed. Members of different academic departments often do not talk with one another. There is little encouragement for the blending of political, economic, sociological, and other forms of research.* Some individual

---

* To some degree, the vacuum left in the university world is being filled by the growing importance of think tanks in American intellectual life. Think tanks are able to do several things that are seemingly more difficult for universities: (1) easily integrate thinking across multiple disciplinary boundaries, (2) abandon the false positivist claims to value neutrality and more honestly make intellectual arguments with a value position on the table, and (3) develop an institutional identity more clearly associated with a value position and the advocacy of these values in the formation of public policy and other activities in the public arena.

scholars, however, are making the effort within their own work.[56] It is perhaps in recognition of the fact that Harvard political scientist Robert Putnam is exploring important new ground that his studies of comparative economic performance among the regions of Italy have received such wide scholarly attention.[57]

Italy is almost two nations. Northern Italy has a vital economy, government works reasonably well, and there is a strong sense of civic pride. Southern Italy, by contrast, has long been an economic backwater of Europe. In the 1980s the per capita income of the South was not much more than half that of the North. These large regional differences have long attracted the attention of social scientists.[58] Some of the theories offered have attributed the greater success of the North to a more educated population, to a more urban economy, to greater social stability, and even to the more prominent political role played in the North by the Communist Party.

However, as Putnam concluded in his 1993 book, *Making Democracy Work: Civic Traditions in Modern Italy,* none of these explanations seems able to withstand close scrutiny.[59] Rather, differences in "civic community" provide the most convincing explanation of differing economic outcomes among the twenty regions of Italy. A high level of civic community was characterized by active citizen participation in public affairs; a strong commitment to equality of rights and obligations among the citizenry; the existence of powerful feelings of solidarity, trust, and tolerance; and wide participation in associations and other local institutions. Putnam concluded that "the least civic areas of Italy are precisely the traditional southern villages" where life was "marked by hierarchy and exploitation" and where the economy along with government administration (and most other things) also worked poorly.[60]

Traditionally, as discussed in previous chapters, economists have regarded culture as a manifestation of deeper economic events that were themselves the basic causal explanation. The forms of culture were shaped by the material realities of life, an economic determinism that prevailed in economics during most of the twentieth century. It was therefore startling—and difficult for many economists to accept—that Putnam's statistical analyses showed precisely the opposite. If his results were correct, cultural factors explained the relative economic levels of the regions of Italy, and not the other way around. The supposed egg was really the chicken in the social and economic development of Italy's regions.

Thus, as Putnam describes his findings, the statistical results showed that "such indicators of socioeconomic development as industrialization and public health have no impact whatsoever on civics. . . . There was no . . .

tendency for the civic traditions to be remolded to fit the 'objective conditions' " of their economic surroundings. Instead, "civic traditions turn out to be a uniformly powerful predictor of present levels of socioeconomic development." In short, the "contemporary [strong] correlation between civics and economics reflects primarily the impact of civics on economics, not the reverse."[61]

Moreover, these relationships had persisted over long periods of time. The differing "regional traditions of civic involvement" had already existed in the nineteenth century and were little changed today. It was possible to take patterns of civic life already seen centuries before and use them to predict reasonably well the current relative economic status of Italian regions. Acknowledging a debt to Douglass North and the new institutional economics, Putnam proposes that a strong sense of civic community has such a large economic impact because it plays a critical role in "overcoming dilemmas of collective action and the self-defeating opportunism that they spawn."[62] Effective government and other institutions in Italy have resulted where there was a social environment of strong mutual trust to sustain them.

As Putnam states, a strong sense of civic commitment will in general reflect the presence of "norms of generalized reciprocity and networks of civic engagement [that] encourage social trust and cooperation because they reduce incentives to defect, reduce uncertainty, and provide models for future cooperation." All this serves to inhibit "opportunism, cheating, and shirking," along with other factors that might increase transaction costs.[63] Sisela Bok wrote in 1978 that "trust is a social good to be protected just as much as the air we breathe or the water we drink."[64] Numerous economists have explored the role that physical and human capital play in economic growth and development. Now, however, borrowing from James Coleman, North, and others, Putnam concludes that "for political stability, for government effectiveness, and even for economic progress social capital may be more important than physical or human capital." * Without the proper cultural elements present, the regions of Italy were likely to manifest debilitating problems of "amoral familism, clientelism, lawlessness, ineffective government, and eco-

---

* As early as 1991, William Griffith and Robert Goldfarb were among the first economists to explicitly refer to the idea of "social capital." They wrote of the "moral norms or values" of a society which can "contribute significantly to Paretian social welfare." Hence, "economists should apply their analytical apparatus to studying the generation and maintenance of norms." See William B. Griffith and Robert S. Goldfarb, "Amending the Economist's 'Rational Egoist' Model to Include Values and Norms: Part I, The Problem," in Kenneth J. Koford and Jeffrey B. Miller, eds., *Social Norms and Economic Institutions* (Ann Arbor: University of Michigan Press, 1991), 50, 51.

nomic stagnation," thus imposing burdens of high transaction costs on everything going on in the region.[65]

Putnam could not offer any one simple explanatory model for why one region of Italy had a high level of trust and another region a low level. Unlike increasing physical capital or building human capital, creating social capital is not simply a matter of making appropriate investments, based on some estimate of an expected rate of return (and in this sense, the term social capital perhaps is best understood as a compelling metaphor, rather than an actual investment like other forms of capital). Indeed, much depended on history and the relevant regional histories in Italy could go as far back as one thousand years.[66] Putnam concluded that a high level of civic-mindedness and trust was not built by any rational processes of individual or social choice. The people living in a region had not acted to achieve a particular cultural environment advantageous to high economic performance.

If a particular culture happened to promote growth, perhaps the residents should simply count themselves lucky. As Putnam commented, "Voluntary cooperation can create value that no individual, no matter how wealthy, no matter how wily, could produce alone"—or even acting with others in the pursuit of a collective outcome. The subtle workings of history, involving complex interactions of economic, political, religious, and other forces, in some cases had simply yielded social environments in which "civic community associations proliferate, memberships overlap, and participation spills into multiple arenas of community life. The social contract that sustains such collaboration in the civic community is not legal but moral. The sanction for violating it is not penal, but exclusion from the network of solidarity and cooperation. Norms and expectations play an important role."[67] All this provided an illustration, within the Italian context, of a wider observation once made by Edward Banfield:

> A political system is an accident. It is an accumulation of habits, customs, prejudices, and principles that have survived a long process of trial and error and of ceaseless response to changing circumstances. If the system works well on the whole, it is a lucky accident—the luckiest, indeed, that can befall a society, for all of the institutions of the society, and thus its entire character and that of the human types formed within it, depend ultimately on the government and the political order.[68]

"CULTURE" AS INDEPENDENT VARIABLE

As long ago as 1980, although their study did not find much of an audience among economists, Alex Inkeles and Larry Diamond had discovered "a strong positive association between economic development and a psychological disposition to trust other people."[69] Francis Fukuyama has argued more recently that "the neoclassical economic perspective . . . is not sufficient to explain many aspects of economic life," in part because "not all economic action arises out of what are traditionally thought of as economic motives." Indeed, "culture shapes all aspects of human behavior," including the overall level of trust maintained in a society, which itself exerts a powerful influence on economic outcomes.[70]

In a 1997 econometric study, a team of four economists (three from Harvard and one from the University of Chicago) used survey data to measure levels of trust as found in nations around the world. They then sought to examine whether differences in levels of trust showed a strong explanatory power with respect to national administrative and economic performance. They concluded that "the effects of trust on performance are both statistically significant and quantitatively large. . . . Putnam's results for Italy appear to be confirmed worldwide."[71] In a follow-up 1998 study for the National Bureau of Economic Research, the same set of researchers found that, culturally, "countries that are poor, close to the equator, ethnolinguistically heterogeneous, use French or socialist laws, or have high proportions of Catholics or Muslims exhibit inferior government performance. . . . The importance of historical factors in explaining the variation in government performance across countries sheds light on the economic, political, and cultural theories of institutions."[72]

Admittedly, this new direction in the thinking of current economists again had to be couched in a formal technical language that is still a requirement for any serious attention from the economic mainstream. The econometric consideration of the impact of religion consisted of dividing countries into categories of historically "Catholic," "Protestant," and "Muslim" and then using the national religion as one of the explanatory variables in the regression analyses. Yet it is a heroic simplification to say the least to consider that the French history of Catholicism is essentially equivalent in economic consequences to the Spanish history, or then again to the Italian and the Irish history.

Overall, judged as an exercise in historical analysis, this effort should be regarded as mainly metaphorical, like so much in economics. However flawed as an exercise in historical research, its conclusions were more acceptable to other economists than a literary form of exposition, because it employed a recognized formal apparatus of quantitative analysis. Like the literature of path dependence, this may well be a transitional phase as economists move toward incorporating historical influences that do not lend themselves to any formal modeling or other quantification.*

MANAGING THE COMMONS RELIGIOUSLY

If sustaining an environment of trust, like many other collective action problems of modern society, has much the same character as a problem of the commons, here as well it took a social scientist outside economics to show that cultural influences may have an essential role in finding a solution. Elinor Ostrom undertook a comprehensive review of the results of many studies of the management of rangelands, forests, and other common property resources around the world.[73] She concluded with Putnam that "shared norms and patterns of reciprocity" are critical. When people have lived "for a substantial time" in mutual interaction with one another, they often build up a high level of "social capital with which they can build institutional arrangements for resolving CPR [common property resource] dilemmas." History is often critical because "past institutional choices open up some

---

* There are, to be sure, formidable obstacles to the development of a new historical and institutional school within the present-day economics profession. Perhaps the greatest obstacle is that most faculty members at current economics departments are neither interested in nor equipped to undertake such studies. Surveying the chairpeople at top-ranked economics departments, the Commission on Graduate Education of the American Economic Association found in 1991 that the goal of instilling "institutional-historical" knowledge ranked dead last in priority, far behind economic "theory." In the current economics profession there was, the commission found, a "systematic downplaying of economic institutions and history, economic literature, and economic applications-policy issues." Such tendencies, as even many economists expressed the concern, had acted to undermine "the capacity of economics and the economics profession to make useful connections to real world issues." It was currently quite possible to "obtain Ph.D.'s with little or no knowledge of economic problems and institutions." The emphasis on mathematical methods risked producing students with ample "tools" but without any similar capabilities in asking the right "questions." In the worst case, the commission expressed the "fear . . . that graduate programs may be turning out a generation with too many *idiots savants,* skilled in technique but innocent of real economic issues."

Academic tenure ensures that some of these same people will be teaching the next generation of graduate students as well. In the end, the commission was more effective at diagnosing the problem than identifying a solution. This should not be surprising; a genuine solution would require fundamental institutional changes in the current practice of professional economics, a daunting prospect for most members of the profession in existing university departments. See W. Lee Hansen, *The Education and Training of Economics Doctorates: Major Findings of the American Economic Association's Commission on Graduate Education in Economics* (Madison, Wisc.: American Economic Association, January 1991), 17, and table 25. A revised version was subsequently published in the *Journal of Economic Literature.* Other quotes are from "Report of the Commission on Graduate Education in Economics," *Journal of Economic Literature* 29 (September 1991): 1040, 1041, 1044–45.

paths and foreclose others to future development."[74] Cultural inhibitions to opportunistic behavior, Ostrom found, are particularly important:

> In a setting in which few individuals share norms about the impropriety of breaking promises, refusing to do one's share, shirking, or taking other opportunistic actions, each appropriator must expect all other appropriators to act opportunistically whenever they have the chance. In such a setting it is difficult to develop stable, long-term commitments. Expensive monitoring and sanctioning mechanisms may be needed. Some long-term arrangements that once were productive are no longer feasible, given their cost of enforcement. In a setting in which there are strong norms against opportunistic behavior, each appropriator will be less wary about the dangers of opportunism.[75]

For example, Torbel is a village of about six hundred people in Switzerland. It has written legal documents dating back to 1224 describing the local management of five types of communally owned property. In 1483 the residents signed formal articles establishing an association to manage their common grazing areas, forests, and wastelands. Access to common areas was restricted to citizens of the village. Each person was limited in the area available to them for grazing by the number of cows they could feed during the winter. Other lands in Torbel have been owned under a variety of tenures ranging from individual ownership to complex condominium-type agreements.

Ostrom reported that "for at least five centuries these Swiss villagers have been intimately familiar with the advantages and disadvantages of both private and communal tenure systems and have carefully matched particular types of land tenure to particular types of land use."[76] The key to the communal management regime was that the residents "keep their monitoring and other transaction costs relatively low and reduce the potential for conflict." An important element here is that village rules are considered "fair by all participants." Cheating on grazing allocations and other informal rules has been rare. In short, the strong bonds of community in this Swiss village have made it possible over centuries to manage a common property resource effectively, despite the absence of formal property rights.

CONCLUSION

The work of the new institutional economics is persuasively showing in both theoretical and empirical terms that norms of honesty, a sense of community, respect for the rules, and other elements of culture can have a major impact on economic growth and development. In many cases the old-fashioned methods of history will provide the most effective way of studying and understanding such influences, more effective than the quantitative and other formal analytical methods commonly employed by economists for the past half century.

Many economists are not content with understanding economic outcomes but also wish to have a significant policy influence on them. Economists typically are strong advocates of policy measures to promote a more efficient economy and more rapid economic development. As policy advocates, in most of their efforts in recent decades they have stressed the technical aspects of economic performance. However, if institutions and culture often represent powerful influences on economic outcomes, it may be unavoidable that economists become direct advocates of institutional and cultural change.

To the extent that culture is grounded in religion, any efforts by economists to promote cultural "improvement" might actually mean religious improvement. The possibility that economic policy advice might enter into the domain of religious advocacy is at odds with the self-image of virtually all current members of the economics profession. Nevertheless, in many less developed nations a new belief system that provides a value-foundation for a modern economy may be the single most important requirement for future economic advance. In practice, organizations such as the World Bank and International Monetary Fund are routinely engaged in proselytizing efforts of this kind, seeking to reach "modern" values.

The kind of religion most likely to promote economic development should encourage the expression of individual self-interest in the market. However, and here there is an obvious tension, it should also act to curb the various forms of self-interest (opportunism) that might otherwise act to undermine the workings of the market, the legal system, and other key institutions in society. In many nations, such a faith has proven elusive. Under socialism, the tendency was to try to ban self-interest over much of the production processes of society. As many developing nations have turned to the market in the past two decades, they have faced the problem that the encouragement to self-interest in the marketplace might yield increased corruption and other less desirable forms of expression of self-interest as well. It takes a special form of religion to resolve the market paradox.

part **FIVE**

ECONOMICS AS RELIGION

The analysis of the new institutional economics has brought us to the following point. A society with a culture that sustains firm "implicit contracts" among its members will be able to overcome collective action problems that might otherwise be costly or even impossible to deal with. Familiar examples include the implicit contract that if we all (or enough of us) agree to vote, we can maintain a democratic society, or if we all agree to fight in a war for our country, we will be able to provide for our collective defense when necessary. Another less obvious type of implicit contract—but of great significance to the workings of a market system—is that each person accepts as socially legitimate the verdict of the market, even when this verdict in particular instances may turn out to be quite negative for some of the individuals directly affected. The market in general must rest on a normative foundation that excludes or inhibits a host of economically "illicit" actions that have the potential to undermine the efficient workings of the market system.

Since they are not legally binding or otherwise enforceable in well defined ways, the willingness of individuals to abide by the implicit contracts within a large business firm or among the members of an entire society cannot easily be explained through a conventional economic account.[1] It is encompassed within a subject that contemporary economists find it difficult to address with their existing methods of analysis—the workings of "culture." The field of economics is thus unable to say much about why some societies have achieved—and continue to achieve—effective implicit contracting solutions to a host of potential tragedies of the commons, prisoner's dilemmas, free-rider problems, and other well-known obstacles to collective action. Yet it is the societies that are most successful in these respects that are often among the most successful in achieving a high level of national income and general economic well-being.

Hence, however ill equipped by professional training many economists may be, in the future they may have little choice. If the members of the American economics profession do not move to incorporate cultural elements, including religion, more directly into their thinking, they may simply have to concede that professional economics is unable to say anything of importance concerning some of the most vital determinants of the efficiency and other outcomes of economic systems.

Moreover, many economists seek to make public policy recommendations to raise the level of economic performance. If religion has a potentially powerful role in determining economic performance, it raises an even more delicate issue. A key factor in achieving a more efficient economy may be a religion that works better in promoting a system of low-cost implicit contracting—perhaps a belief system more like that of northern Italy than of southern Italy. It seems clear that the economic problems of many of the less developed parts of the world today stem in significant part from corruption, rent seeking in government, and other forms of opportunism that reflect the lack of such an "efficient" religion (or other equivalent element of culture).[2] The rise of modern economies in Europe and the United States coincides closely with the spread of "modern" values.

All this raises the possibility that if current religious leaders are not fulfilling the religious needs of the economy, it may be that economists themselves will have to move to fill the gap. Getting the religious aspects of an economy in working order may be too important to leave to the existing leaders of institutional churches. Indeed, many current professional economists working in Africa and other less developed parts of the world are engaged in efforts that in practice go well beyond teaching the technical aspects of economics. In order for these countries to develop economically, they will need not only a better banking system but also a "better" value system (where "better" means, for example, uniting the members of a country behind a set of values that curb market corruption and advance respect for property rights). The Peace Corps might well be regarded as a modern form of missionary society for modern values that would serve to advance the cause of economic progress. The processes of economic development may, in short, require proselytizing and religious conversion (leading to the creation of new forms of social capital) as much as increased investment in physical and human capital. Economists may have to be priests as much as engineers.[3]

In the United States, as I have been arguing in this book, economists have indeed long taken it upon themselves to help in achieving greater civic-mindedness and social solidarity, resolving implicit contracting problems, and dealing with other obstacles to effective collective action. In modern society, economists have themselves become the preachers, the proselytizers, of various forms of religious belief in economic progress that create social bonds in the service of greater economic efficiency and a higher national income. Stated so baldly, the role of economist as proselytizer admittedly seems a radical departure from conventional professional understandings of the responsibilities of economists. Yet it is not difficult to discover this underlying religious role in works such as Samuelson's *Economics*. Its greatest influence on American society was in delivering a scientific blessing for the American welfare and regulatory state.

Economics was in this regard a sociological and religious triumph in American life. The power of Samuelson's message, produced by a great American artist working with the images of "science," was fully capable of moving the world in real terms. Samuelson was an American master in the forms of "inspirational painting" of the economic progress of society. He proved to be supremely energetic, skillful, pragmatic, and successful in these respects, if not in the modes usually attributed to him. It is as the developer of an important American style of literary and artistic expression that Samuelson is properly ranked as a significant figure in American intellectual history.

In its actual economic content, however, as Stiglitz and many other new institutional economists have been saying in recent years, *Economics* contained much interesting and useful information of a practical nature, but the theoretical side of the book was founded on fundamental misconceptions. The theoretical apparatus served instead to make a claim to a scientific status for economics in American society and in this way to enable economists to put a religious blessing on the workings of various economic institutions. It also put many individual economists in government jobs and other positions of authority to influence social decisions through the application of more commonsense ways of thinking—in which economists are often quite skilled and effective once they set aside their formal models grounded in "high theory." In light of the usual opportunistic motives that prevail in politics, many economists have in fact been dedicated to making a contribution to the governing process as pragmatic advocates of a general public benefit.

The American theologian Michael Novak has commented that the American welfare and regulatory state might well be regarded as the "church" of a state secular religion:

> The religion of America is not Christianity. It is not Judaism. There are many theories about what it is. Professor Sidney Mead calls it "the religion of the Republic." It is, Robert Bellah says, "the civil religion"; or John Dewey, "the common faith"; Will Herberg, "the American way of life"; John E. Smylie, "the nation itself."
>
> No one church was allowed to become the official guardian of the central symbols of the United States. Instead, the nation itself began to fill the vacuum where in many cultures a church would be. The nation became its own unifying symbol system, the chief bestower of identity and purpose.
>
> A candidate running for the presidency of the United States does well to recognize that he is running for a religious office. The national religion is, to be sure, quite pragmatic and secular. His concerns will be power, vested interests, money, jobs, and other utterly mundane affairs. Still American conducts itself like a religion.[4]

It is not only successful candidates for the presidency who have had to keep this truth in mind; economists such as Samuelson have also shown that they understand it well.* Rather than being a technical analysis, "economic

---

* In recent years, there has been a growing recognition that American politics is often an (only slightly) disguised form of religious controversy—that issues of political debate are issues of the content of the American civil religion and that ultimately this faith is derived from Judeo-Christian sources. Writing of "the born-again Republicans" shortly after the 1992 Republican presidential convention in Houston, Gary Wills declared:

> The Democrats were excoriated as godless in Houston, yet . . . the Democrats must not be lacking in God but lacking in the *right* God. The religion of the Republicans in Houston is judgmental, punitive, and individualistic.
>
> It is true that an individualistic/predestinarian theology underlies much of American religious culture; but that is not, as the Houston Republicans would have it, the only religion of America. Abraham Lincoln was constantly invoked in Houston, and no one more eloquently expressed the vision of a mutually culpable and mutually forgiving "people of God" than he did. [It was Lincoln who] urged the whole nation to repent its historical sin of slavery. . . . It was not religion that was being defended in Houston, but authoritarian religion.

See Garry Wills, "The Born-Again Republicans," *New York Review of Books,* September 24, 1992, 14. See also Wills, *Under God: Religion and American Politics* (New York: Simon and Schuster, 1990).

science" has had more power to move the world as part of the secular religion of progress of American civil society, helping to provide a normative basis for the necessary implicit contracts of a modern economy. In the first half of the twentieth century, Marxism swept across the world with all the conquering force of early Christianity in the Roman Empire or of Islam in the seventh and eighth centuries elsewhere. Marxism did this, one might say, by establishing an extremely effective set of implicit contracts among the Marxist faithful. Held together by a secular religion of tremendous emotional appeal, the members of Marxist parties fought valiantly to take over nation after nation, eventually bringing approximately a third of the population of the world into the communist orbit. In one of the last such conquests, it was partly the inability of the United States—approaching the problem too "rationally"—to comprehend the power of the Marxist gospel (blended with strong nationalist elements) that led to the debacle for U.S. foreign policy in the jungles of Vietnam.

It is said that many old communists in Russia never lost the faith, even as Stalin sent them to the firing squad. The failure of the Soviet economy in the 1970s and 1980s may be attributable at least in part to the loss of idealism and increasing cynicism about Marxism in Soviet society at large. The implicit contracts maintained by a powerful religious faith can serve to overcome even major defects of institutional design—just as, conversely, a society that lacks strong normative barriers to opportunism may fail economically, even though it possesses an institutional framework otherwise well suited to the task. It has been said that Swedish society looks about and works about the same in Minnesota as in Sweden, despite the substantial differences in institutional setting.

In Chapter 10, I propose to take up briefly a particularly important topic of economic history—the past religious role that economists have played in Western society. From the Enlightenment to the present, a period that I will now refer to as the "modern age" (recognizing that "modern" can be used to apply to a wide range of time periods), economics has been the source of the most influential religions in public life (if still leaving traditional religions to answer such "private" questions as one's fate in the hereafter).⋆ My thesis, to put it succinctly in one place, will include the following main points.

⋆ The displacement of Christianity from the center of public life may have begun even well before the Enlightenment, although secular religion did not rise to preeminence until that era. Richard Fremantle comments that "by the late 18th and early 19th century Roman Catholic government had everywhere been reduced to a meagre part of its former power, and Roman Catholic Church law had been more or less completely displaced by commercial law and scientific law." This was a culmination of trends that had first appeared in the fifteenth century and throughout the Renaissance that was

1. By the modern age traditional religion in the Judeo-Christian sense had lost much of its earlier authority in public life, thus posing a large transaction cost problem for the functioning of economic (as well as other) institutions in society.

2. Following Isaac Newton, much of the authority of traditional religion was transferred to science. Science became the dispenser of valid truth claims, and in this respect scientific knowledge was now seen as having the greatest religious authority in modern society.

3. Since the physical sciences had little to say about human affairs, the social sciences moved to and were successful in assuming the mantle of science—and also acquired the religious authority of science in matters of the economy, politics, and other spheres of social action.

4. Social science thus became the religion of the modern age in regard to the conduct of affairs in this world (and also assumed a transcendent significance for many people in promising the arrival of a future heaven on earth), and in this capacity social science became responsible for resolving the collective action problems of the economic system that only a common religious bond (or some other similarly powerful set of normative beliefs) can resolve.

5. As religious hopes for a secular salvation increasingly turned to economic events in this world—and from the mid-nineteenth century onward many people sought a secular salvation through abolishing economic scarcity and arriving at a state of complete material abundance on earth—economists became the preeminent social scientists, the proselytizers of those forms of secular religion that in fact served as the main religious focus for efforts in the West to defeat opportunism, to establish strong implicit contracts, and to solve other transaction cost and collective action problems.

---

an attempt to see Christ and Christianity in a new, personal, humanistic way, an attempt on the part of Christians to be more spiritual in the face of a Christian Papacy which no longer acted very spiritually. With this [increasing displacement of Christianity from worldly affairs], came a deep study of history and literature, particularly that of ancient Greece and Rome, as well as the scientific study of every aspect of nature, of economics, of government, of the rights of man, and other facets of man's natural existence. All this developed and replaced the previous interest in Christianity.

See Richard Fremantle, *God and Money: Florence and the Medici in the Renaissance* (Florence: Leo S. Olschki Editore, 1992), 12, 8–9.

6. The success of economics in its religious function was to a significant extent independent of the degree of validity in the specific truth claims produced by economics as an analytical science—and in cases such as Marxism, the religious function was powerfully served despite an analytic framework that today appears to have been gravely flawed from the start. Other economic systems of thought frequently fare better than Marxism in their core analytical schemes, but it is probably true that almost all the leading schools of economics have had more impact on the world by virtue of their religious authority—and resulting contribution to the solution of collective action problems—than by the specific technical knowledge of economic systems that they have provided (which in other cases besides Marxism has in fact been rather limited).

7. While all this may have "worked" in some pragmatic sense, boosting economic performance and the status of economists, it has been bad for economics and religion alike in a more fundamental—a genuine "truth"—sense. Economists have been led to pose as scientists and to make claims for scientific knowledge in regard to the workings of economic systems that were much inflated from what they could actually deliver. With the most vital religions of the modern age taking the form of economics, the field of religion has also suffered from a theologically incomplete and inadequate development. Economics as religion has been incapable of answering in a satisfactory way many of the fundamental questions that religion historically has been asked to address.

chapter **TEN**

GOD BLESS THE MARKET

As I have described in this book, a core problem posed by
a private market as a system of economic organization is
the following. The market is based on the idea of individual pursuit of self-interest. At the same time, however, a
market system will work best if there is a clear limit to self-
interest. The pursuit of self-interest should not extend to
various forms of opportunism, such as cheating, lying, and
other types of deception, misrepresentation, and corruption within the marketplace. Self-interest should not
extend to "political opportunism," the attempt to use
government to coercively extract benefits from others or
to protect each business firm and each worker from any
negative consequences in the normal workings of market
competition (say, by demanding a tariff to protect against
job losses from international trade). Another key consideration is that property rights, contracts, and other legal
arrangements should be fairly and consistently enforced.
In short, the market must exist within an institutional
and civic-value context that transcends individual self-
interest and supports and encourages actions that have a
wider benefit for the common good.

Thus, upon observation of development experiences
in many nations around the world, Francis Fukuyama
comments that "the ability to cooperate socially is dependent on prior habits, traditions, and norms, which
themselves serve to structure the market." As a result, the
very ability of a society to maintain "a successful market
economy . . . is codetermined by the prior factor of social capital." Experience has shown that "a healthy capi-

talist economy is one in which there will be sufficient social capital in the underlying society to permit businesses, corporations, networks, and the like to be self-organizing." [1] This social capital is found in such things as attitudes of trust, commitments to honest behavior, respect for property rights, and—perhaps most important in many societies—the bonds of social cohesion that allow for effective collective action (including the maintenance of the market institution itself).

Drawing on more-formal methods of economic analysis, Eirik Furubotn and Rudolf Richter recently summarized the conclusions of economic theorists with respect to much the same issue in the following terms:

> Unfortunately, freedom of contract does not necessarily guarantee "voluntary exchange." To secure the latter, at least in general equilibrium theory, the principle of contract has to be *limited*. Individuals must not be permitted to contract in order to form coalitions whose purpose is predatory. That is, any coalition that is organized so as to improve the lot of its members at the expense of individuals outside the coalitions must be ruled out. . . . As a practical matter, there can be no pressure groups, no cartels, or, indeed, any coalition possessed of monopoly power. . . . Force is monopolized by the state, but the state's power of coercion is strictly limited by law—that is, by the state's constitution. Nevertheless, even if the state's powers are perfectly controlled, there remains the problem of the formation of pressure groups and the control of private coercive power.
>
> The principle of freedom of contract can destroy itself through the evolution (via contract) of pressure groups, monopolies, and so on—. . . therefore . . . the constitutional state must protect its citizens not only from the coercive power of government but also from arbitrary acts by other citizens. It follows that the formation of the institutional framework of the economy should not be left to itself. [2]

The development of a satisfactory constitutional framework and its enforcement thus may be critical to the effective functioning of a market system. Yet this may be a difficult requirement to meet. In some ways it depends on simultaneously encouraging and discouraging the expression of self-interest. The demands placed on the normative system, religious or otherwise, that will sustain the market are thus rather precise. It cannot be any old religion. There have in fact been few times and places in the history of the world where the market has been given wide freedom to function with minimal state interference. [3] The more normal circumstance—still true today in many nations—is a set of tight limitations that insulate much of the existing political and economic order from market pressures. In many feudal societies of the past in the Western world, the role of the market was considered to legitimately encompass only a small part of the activities of society.

Although scholars have criticized a number of the details of Max Weber's interpretation of the role of Calvinist religion in the development of capitalism, he was probably correct to argue that there was something "irrational" about the motivations that were required. A good capitalist should pursue the accumulation of capital beyond what would be rationally sensible; he thus forgoes hedonistic pleasures and may be serving society's interest more than his own. As suggested here, another element of "irrationality" may stem from the need, on the one hand, to very aggressively pursue one's private interest in the market and then, on the other hand, to turn around and to renounce the pursuit of private interest in many other areas of society, including preserving and protecting the market as a working institution.

Before the modern era, one approach to resolving this tension—if realized by only a small minority of religions—would be a decree by God that it should be so. However, since at least the Enlightenment the authority of traditional religion in the West has been much weakened. As will be further explored below, new "economic religions" have emerged that could provide secular religious blessings in place of the old Judeo-Christian theologies. Economists have been a modern priesthood, capable of establishing the social legitimacy of market institutions defined in religious terms more acceptable to the modern age, grounded in "scientific" truth. As worked out by economists, such teachings themselves necessarily transcended self-interest, but they had the curious property that the new secular religions simultaneously blessed the powerful expression of self-interest in one very important area of society, the marketplace.

PROPERTY AS A WAGE OF SIN

Many economists have the impression that the subjects currently studied in the field of economics are much newer than they actually are. The debate over property rights and markets, however, goes back at least as far as Plato and Aristotle. As Karl Popper once wrote, Marxism might be seen as merely a "theory revived" from the communism of Plato's *Republic*. Both Plato and Marx offered a vision of "apocalyptic revolution which will radically transfigure the whole social world."[4] By contrast, Aristotle was more concerned with satisfying the pragmatic requirements for living in the world as it exists—where property rights have the great advantage that "when everyone has a distinct interest, men will not complain of one another, and they will make more progress, because everyone is attending to his own business." Otherwise where things are held in common, "those who labor much and get little will necessarily complain of those who labor little and receive or consume much."[5] Aristotle did not specifically describe property rights as a solution to the "problem of the commons," but that is what he was effectively saying. The practical usefulness of property rights in organizing a society is not a recent insight.

When Christian theology moved into a stage of formal development, it borrowed heavily from Greek philosophy. Discussion of many of the same kinds of economic questions would now be played out among Christian theologians. Much as in Plato, the highest expressions of Christian ideals denied any place for expression of self-interest in society—and thus for property rights. A system of property rights meant the creation of a set of artificial barriers dividing one person from another—it is "my" property, and "not yours." There was no private property in the Garden of Eden before the fall, and there will be none in heaven in the hereafter. On this earth, the priests and nuns of the Roman Catholic Church have mostly lived communally, as good an approximation as could be obtained in the here and now to the ideals common to both Plato's *Republic* and the Christian heaven in the hereafter.★

The Catholic Church—eventually to incur the ire of the Protestant Reformation for this reason—decreed that the ordinary person, however, could not be expected to live according to the same ideals as the priesthood. Since the Fall of man in the Garden, human beings had been sinful—not to say depraved—creatures. Any attempt to require ordinary people to try to realize a standard of perfection would be beyond their capacity as fallen beings, and would surely prove disastrous in the end. Thus, in Christian theology, self-interested behavior and the need for private property rights have been regarded as an unfortunate but necessary concession to the fallen condition of humankind.[6]

The basic philosophical and religious foundations of Western civilization

---

★ Sexual ties also, as both Plato and the Roman Catholic Church full well recognized, could create powerful feelings of individual possessiveness, perhaps deeper even than the ownership of private property. Plato's solution in *The Republic* was to remove the possessive element by abolishing marriage and other limits on free sexual expression, further establishing common ownership of children (the mother should not know the identity of her child). More pragmatically, the Roman Catholic Church took the opposite tack, requiring its priests and nuns to be celibate, seeking to ensure that their highest loyalties were not to another person but to God and the Church.

can be traced back to a synthesis of ancient Greek philosophy with Jewish and early Christian religion. With respect to self-interest and private property, the common thinking can be summarized as follows. In a perfect world, divisions among people, the pursuit of self-interest, the existence of markets, the ownership of individual possessions, and thus private property rights should and would not exist. Since the world we live in is still in the grip of sin, it must inevitably fall far short of the ideal, and it will be necessary to make some major compromises to allow for the existence of property.★

Indeed, over the past 2,500 years, the great debates about the role of property in Western civilization might be seen, in one light, as a debate about the extent of the compromises that would be necessary. At one extreme, Plato and Marx argued that they should be minimal, and that the pursuit of self-interest in the world could in fact be substantially abolished (at least when an appropriate stage of history had been reached). The Roman Catholic Church, as noted, prescribed different degrees of communalism for its priest-hood and for ordinary people. Samuelson and other American Progressives in the twentieth century took a similar approach to the Catholic Church, expecting self-interest to reign in the actions of the ordinary people in the marketplace, but a communal dedication to the common good ("the public interest") to rule among the pro-fessional classes of society—these people responsible for the "scientific management" of the market mechanism and for administering other government actions.

Marxism, European socialism, and American Progressivism all in one degree or another reflected once again—if now in a secular form—the old Christian view that the pursuit of self-interest and the ownership of private property are the wages of sin. Given even any tenuous grounds to hope that it would no longer be necessary to accept the fallen condition of the past (that a "new man" might be possible, finally escaping the curse of Adam and Eve), people in the modern age flocked by the millions to join Marxist, so-

---

★ In the very earliest years of Christianity, even the necessity for compromise was denied. The first Christians professed a strong commitment to communal ownership of property as a central article of the faith. This ideal later made its way into the art of the medieval era and then the Renaissance, much of which consisted of images designed to illustrate and uphold the core messages of Christian history and theology.

For example, in the Brancacci Chapel of the Church of Santa Maria del Carmine in Florence, Italy, is one of the most famous set of paintings (renowned for the realism of the figures and the introduction of new techniques of perspective) in the history of Western art. In one of them the painter of these wall frescos, Masaccio, has chosen for his subject matter the image (drawn from Acts 4 and 5 of the Bible) of Ananias, who lies dead on the ground, struck down by God. Ananias's great sin for which he has paid such a large price is that he has broken the early Christian rule that ownership of property must be held in common.

cialist and other crusades to abolish the divisions in society created by self-interest and property. They came to believe that with the end of scarcity and the attainment to a state of total material abundance, it would actually be possible to reach a new heaven on earth in the here and now.

The Protestant tradition in religion as well would have to struggle with such issues and would often reach a different conclusion from that of the Roman Catholic Church. The Protestant Reformers of the sixteenth century generally sought to abolish the distinctions between the leadership and the members of the church—to create, as the Protestant Reformers described their project, a new "priesthood of all believers." Initially, among some of the new Protestant sects, that led to attempts to abolish property throughout society, in hopes that every member of the church might live together communally in the manner of the Roman priesthood of old. In the end and more pragmatically, the insistence on a single standard led to the Protestant ministry living under the same rules as other men and women, including those of marriage and the individual ownership of homes and other private property.

In the current period, the Chicago school of economics, following more in the Protestant tradition, rejects the Samuelson view and again denies any special ethical standard for professional groups in society. In now declaring that one standard of self-interested behavior will apply to all people, the public choice school of economics finds that self-interest will rule individual actions in government as well as in the ordinary commercial behavior of the marketplace. The effects of sin are all-pervasive, including the actions of the modern professional priesthoods of society and others in the governing classes. They extend as well into such areas as marriage and the family, where Judeo-Christian religion had traditionally said that "sacred bonds" should govern individual actions, but as Gary Becker suggests, this might in fact be impossible for most sinners in this fallen world.

In summary, Western history shows that even when the existence of markets and private property are defended, it is always to some degree regarded as a compromise. It means giving up on the highest ideals of humankind, if perhaps not permanently. Since theologians have defined these high ideals for most of the past two thousand years in the West, it has also usually fallen to theologians to say to what extent and in what manner such ideals could legitimately be compromised—when self-interested behavior in markets and the institutions of private property could be said to fit within God's plan for living in this world.

THE MARKET IN MEDIEVAL THEOLOGY

The question of the legitimate place for self-interest became more important in the late medieval period, as the pace of economic development increased significantly in Europe in the twelfth and thirteenth centuries. As more trading took place among parties who did not know each other well, and market processes thus increasingly replaced barter exchange in medieval society, the ethics of individual behavior in the market became a question of growing theological urgency.[7]

The theological outcome may be surprising to many economists today who have been led to believe that the medieval Roman Catholic Church regarded the workings of the market as morally suspect. It was, for example, widely believed among scholars for many years—and many economists still think this—that medieval religion sought to impose moral rules, such as the "just" wage, that were designed to override market outcomes. However, prompted in part by the twentieth-century scholarship of Joseph Schumpeter, and with further scholars such as Raymond de Roover confirming his findings in the decades to follow, such views have by now largely been discredited.[8]

Indeed, the scholarship of the second half of the twentieth century shows that the concept of the just price was typically interpreted by medieval theologians to be the competitive price in the market.* As Schumpeter wrote of Thomas Aquinas, the just price in his theological system "is simply normal competitive price."[9] Duns Scotus, another leading medieval theologian, made the further connection that the competitive price would tend toward the cost of production. Schumpeter explained, "If we identify the just price

* Catholic scholars themselves have typically been more aware of the traditional favorable attitude of the Catholic Church toward the market. They have known that

> for centuries, Catholic scholars who studied the ethics of economic affairs have recognized the importance of markets. They took the view that competition in the marketplace can protect consumers against excessive prices and exploitation. For example, Dominique Banez commented in the 16th century: Either the goods search for buyers, and this is one of the many reasons why prices sink, or else buyers search for goods and prices rise. In the writings of Konrad Summenhart from Wurttemberg (who died in 1502), we find the intimation that we should give preference to the economic system which (in the words of Oswald von Nell-Breuning) manages to operate with a "minimum of morality." As Summenhart notes: those who compete against each other have less brazenness and opportunity to sell their goods at usurious prices than the merchants who are in sole possession of such goods. If they did dare to demand excessive prices, people would flock to others who sell at lower prices.

See Joseph Cardinal Hoffner, "Economic Systems and Economic Ethics," *Catholicism in Crisis,* June 1986, 11.

of a good with its competitive common value, as Duns Scotus certainly did, and if we further equate that just price to the cost of the good (taking account of risk, as he did not fail to observe), then we have ipso facto, at least by implication, stated the law of cost not only as a normative but as an analytical proposition." [10]

Jacob Viner, another prominent economist of the twentieth century with a scholarly interest in the historical interaction of economics and religion, similarly explained that the generally prevailing view in scholastic writings of the medieval period was that "the just price was the 'common estimate' which was the price that would be reached under normal conditions in a competitive market as a result of the bids and offers by buyers and sellers." [11] This view of market ethics was not limited to Christian thinkers: Ephraim Kleiman finds that in Talmudic literature as well the just price "was none other than the going market price." There was a recognition in "the mainstream of Talmudic thought" that a key criterion in identifying a legitimate market price was the existence of sufficient "competition." [12]

However, the medieval theologians did not believe that self-interest should be left to operate without social limits. [13] Thus, in the scholastic literature of the period, there were three basic types of circumstances in which a price in the market could be said to be "unjust" and the intervention of the state or the church might be necessary. [14] The first circumstance was where a seller was charging different people a different price for the same good, what an economist today would call price discrimination. A second situation of injustice would be where there existed collusion among sellers or buyers that could inflate or deflate the price relative to the competitive outcome. And the third situation of potential injustice involved the taking advantage of supply shortages to charge very high prices in an emergency situation such as a famine.

What is remarkable is that these three conditions of medieval "injustice," as derived from the natural-law theological reasoning of the times, prescribe almost exactly the same sets of policies for curbing self-interest in the market that have been widely recommended by leading economic and other defenders of the welfare and regulatory state in the twentieth century. In the United States the Interstate Commerce Commission and other regulatory bodies were created in part to prevent the railroads from continuing their aggressive policies of price discrimination—charging different prices to different buyers for essentially the same railroad services. The Sherman Act and other antitrust legislation were designed to prevent monopolistic or other collusive pricing. And as recently as the 1970s, the U.S. government refused to allow oil prices to rise to their competitive market level in the wake of the severe oil shortages caused by the Organization of Oil-Producing Countries (OPEC) restrictions on supply. American Progressivism in this respect—and there are many others as well—might thus be described as a modern, secular manifestation of a powerful "Roman" tradition of thought at least one thousand years old.[15]

If the progressive economic ideas of the late nineteenth and the twentieth century seem very far removed from the religious beliefs of Thomas Aquinas and other medieval theologians, they reached a similar understanding of both the workings and the ethics of markets, despite the separation of many centuries and vast changes in economic circumstances. The market, it seems, can arouse fundamentally similar reactions across great distances in time and place—to the extent that people so far removed from one another have shared even a common ethical understanding of what are legitimate social practices in the functioning of private markets.

Indeed, as this example illustrates, a recurrent theme in twentieth-century historical scholarship shows a greater continuity of modern thought with the Judeo-Christian tradition than many people recognize. One authority has commented that the "major ideas" of the Enlightenment "are for the most part secularized religious concepts."[16] Indeed, it is not just Enlightenment thought, Arend van Leeuwen explains, but also "modern nationalism, democracy, liberalism, capitalism, and socialism, the concepts of modern science and the rise of modern technology" that are in significant respects "the 'secularized' products" of the Western religious heritage. If the Bible promised "a new Paradise . . . the good life and the true life at peace with him, for the whole earth," much the same promise in the nineteenth and twentieth centuries has been offered by the scientific and economic advances of modern "Western civilization."[17]

Indeed, one might even say that modern thought (with respect to society, not the laws of the physical universe, wherein radical new developments in fact did take place) is distinguished from previous thinking not so much by any pathbreaking or otherwise startling discoveries, but by a lack of historical awareness and introspection. Social science has commonly entailed a failure to understand even the most basic aspects of its own historical roots. In this respect, rather than it being a sharp improvement in intellectual quality as is typically supposed, modern thought with respect to the workings and values of society might be better regarded as a retrogression (even as the social sciences have served many legitimizing and other practical "signaling" and other useful but informal functions in society).

In a comprehensive survey of past research into the history of economic ethics, Murray Rothbard finds that Aquinas "was highly favorable towards the activities of the merchant." Merchants, Aquinas full well recognized, "perform the important function of bringing goods from where they are abundant to where they are scarce." Commenting on the long-standing view that had seen medieval theology as antagonistic to economic functions, Rothbard now attributes it to an anti-Catholic bias manifested in the leading economic histories of Europe since the Protestant Reformation. The most influential histories of medieval economic thought were often written in Protestant nations such as England, Germany, and the United States. As Rothbard comments, for people such as John Locke and many others who followed him, "the real enemy of civil and religious liberty, the great advocate of monarchical absolutism, during the late seventeenth century and into the eighteenth century, was the Catholic church."[18] It was not only Protestants but also leading secular figures of the Enlightenment who often saw its new truths about the world as a radical departure, in particular from the self-serving biases and errors of outdated Catholic belief and understanding. Such antagonistic attitudes, Rothbard suggests, then carried over to many historians in Protestant nations in the nineteenth and the first half of the twentieth century.

As a religious system for determining the place of self-interest in the world, medieval Roman Catholic theology could appeal to God for justification of its pronouncements. It was according to natural laws put in place by God that self-interest would work through the institution of the market to serve the common good. If there were other areas of society, or circumstances in the market, to which self-interested behavior should not extend, this would also be part of the divine plan. The priesthood of the Roman Catholic Church thus put a religious blessing—and thereby established a social legitimacy—on the workings of markets and other economic institutions, even while its members could act to limit the role for opportunistic behavior outside legitimate market circles.

Since the eighteenth century, however, the authority of God as a source of absolute truths of the world—the essence of the historic claim to authority of Jewish and Christian religion—has been superceded in many areas of society by the rise of science. Patrick Miller, the editor of the journal *Theology Today,* commented recently that there has been a long "conflict waged between religion and science" in the modern period over the possession of valid "truth claims."[19] Miller considers that theology is making somewhat of a comeback today (and he is seeking to encourage a new reconciliation of science and religion), partly because science in the twentieth century lost confidence in its full ability to comprehend the foundations of its own thinking. That said, for the past three hundred years the typical state of affairs has been as follows: "In Western cultures, public expectation relies predominantly on scientific procedures and not much, if at all, on theology in the endeavor to get close to truth and evaluate evidence as well as to gain certainty and reliability in difficult and critical issues. Despite the crisis in scientific epistemology, and a growing suspicion with respect to the benefits of much technological progress, common culture in the West still sees the measure and model for truth claims as lying in the sciences." [20]

Hence, in the modern age, instead of being determined by medieval theologians, as before, the proper role of self-interested behavior in markets and of property rights in society would have to be resolved by economic truths as discovered by scientific methods.

THE SECULARIZATION OF THE MARKET

Commenting on the history of political and economic thought in England, the American historian Joyce Appleby would observe:

> The idea that individuals when buying, selling, investing, and producing invariably sought to maximize their own profit appeared increasingly as a dependable theoretical element in these writings. The widespread acceptance of the naturalness of personal striving for private gain worked to legitimize and probably encourage this response. Acquisition . . . shared in the respectability that naturalness acquired. . . . Writers began to reason that legislators and policy makers should accommodate normal human drives by relying less upon coercive authority and more upon the manipulation of economic incentives. . . . English economic commentators were articulating a new social reality in which the self-seeking drive appeared more powerful than institutional efforts to mold people's action. [21]
>
> Economic writers imputed to human nature a constancy that permitted them to treat it as a dependable factor in analysis. Men might be charitable; they might be foolhardy or absent-minded, but for purposes of economic reasoning men were handled as rational calculators animated by a drive for personal gain. The pressure to understand economic relationships encouraged an emphasis on regularities and consistency. Moreover, the random responses of others in international commerce were hidden from view. Instead, only the conclusion of the bargain was transmitted, summarized in the impersonal price, the method of whose exact determination could not be re-

traced. This reality not only worked to minimize the importance of personal influence but also strengthened the idea that trade was an inexorable process beyond the reach of human interference—like nature itself. Included in this concept was the embryonic economic man whose natural propensities moved the whole.[22]

Many economists would probably think that Appleby was writing about economic thought in England around the time of Adam Smith or even somewhat later, perhaps the early nineteenth century. She was in fact describing the economic thinking of the mid-seventeenth century. Long before Adam Smith wrote *The Wealth of Nations,* his essential ideas had been fleshed out in many pamphlets and other popular publications of the time. As the economic sophistication of medieval writings also suggests, the basic workings of markets, and the many practical gains to society, have not been a great mystery in many times and places.

Indeed, if someone were to ask the question, How will a barter system for exchanging goods and services perform, as compared with a market system? the answer must be straightforward. The use of money and prices as an instrument of exchange greatly facilitates the organization of trading activity, in effect conveying information about trading opportunities to market participants in a much more convenient and accessible way. It does not take the use of any great scientific apparatus of economic analysis to appreciate this point. It has been well recognized for a very long time, and was explicitly acknowledged by many writers in Western society well before the modern period.

How is it, then, that much of the elaborate theoretical arsenal of modern economics has been deployed—at least as economists have frequently portrayed their own efforts—to explain something already so well understood in its basics long before? Economists in the modern era have argued that economic theory demonstrates scientifically the efficiency of the market system. Implicitly or explicitly, their benchmark of comparison is some kind of political allocation of resources—that is to say, one special form of a barter system of exchange. Deploying the full arsenal of the economic theories of the modern age to "prove" that market exchange will outperform barter exchange is, in scientific terms, like shooting a mosquito with a cannon.

The explanation for this otherwise surprising behavior of economists does not lie in science but in religion. The market has faced, as noted above, two obstacles: (1) the view of many people that self-interested behavior is morally inferior, a large compromise with the highest ideals of a society; and (2) the strong incentives to (as we would call it today) "rent seeking" and other forms of opportunism that can undercut market workings. Thus, as described above, it is essential for maintaining a market economy that it have a foundation of social legitimacy that encourages self-interested behavior in appropriate domains, yet prohibits it in others. As the authority of traditional Jewish and Christian religion declined, the possibility arose that the market would no longer have adequate ethical support. One might say that the field of modern economics emerged as a secular religious answer to this problem.

Economists provided the necessary legitimizing set of ideas by appropriating the rising social authority of science to deliver a new form of religious blessing for the workings of self-interest in the market. It would necessarily be a scientific blessing suited to the new age. Appleby comments that there was already in the mid-seventeenth century a "widely shared assumption that economic activities conformed to a determinable, natural order." The participants in this order understood that they "required . . . a theoretical explanation" for what they already knew less formally. For this purpose, and if the market was to have real social legitimacy, they turned to "the scientific mode of observation and analysis," then emerging in England as a powerful new way of thinking about the natural order. Adam Smith was not the beginning but the culmination of this trend. As Appleby puts it, "When Adam Smith freighted the full burden of automatic, self-sustaining economic laws upon the basic human qualities of a love to 'truck and barter' and a ceaseless urge to 'self-improvement,' he was standing in a long line of thinkers who had rested their theories upon these tendencies in human behavior"— including one author who already in 1601 had anticipated many of the practical benefits attributed to a market system of exchange in *The Wealth of Nations*.[23]

SOCIAL PHYSICS

What was new in Adam Smith, what set him clearly apart from most economic thinkers of the seventeenth century, was that he could shape his new science of economics to fit the scientific model of Isaac Newton.[24] Following the astonishingly powerful discoveries of Newton, many of the leading intellectuals of the Enlightenment concluded that science was capable of explaining the complete natural workings not only of the solar system and other elements of the physical universe but of the social universe as well. The laws of nature, previously known only to God, would in both physical and social realms become accessible to human understanding through the scientific method. It was an intoxicating possibility, holding out the prospect of perfecting the human condition—achieving a world in which all actions were in perfect conformity to the laws of nature as God had actually designed them, not according to the frail human understandings of the past that had always necessarily introduced large elements of error.[25]

This conviction was not simply a vague hope left to be realized at some point in the future. Indeed, the Enlightenment embraced the science found in Newtonian physics as its new religion. Newton was the new Moses who had come to show humankind a new set of laws in God's universe in much greater precision and detail than ever before. Newton's scientific discoveries resulted in a theological revolution in the Western world, a shift from an active God intervening routinely to manage human affairs to a distant God who perhaps had set the world in motion at the Creation through the laws of nature. The world now functioned according to these laws of nature, laws that the Enlightenment believed would soon be revealed by scientific methods for all people to know and to follow. Indeed, it would now be the responsibility of the field of economics to discover and make known the laws of nature over that wide range of social activities that in the eighteenth century were encompassed within the growing domain of industry and commerce.

In claiming (whether the claim was explicit or implicit was of no great moment, because an implicit claim would have almost equal influence in an age when the virtual worship of Newton was widespread) to wear the mantle of physics, modern economics in its early development was thus effectively asserting a religious authority.[26] If economics was revealing the natural laws of the economic order as put in place by God, scientific economic truths would have the power to bestow religious blessings, including the determination of the legitimate role for the pursuit of self-interest in society. In the modern age economic "science," instead of pronouncements of priests and theologians based on the Bible and other traditional sources of Judeo-Christian truth, would become the new source of an ethical foundation for the market system and other economic institutions.

It also seemed reasonable to economists and other social scientists that God might well have designed the social universe in a manner similar to the physical universe. To discover a science of society, it would therefore be appropriate to look for models similar to those already found in Newtonian physics. For the moon, the sun, and the planets, the relevant units of a Newtonian social physics would apparently be individual people functioning with the same kind of autonomy. The driving force in the social world that corresponded to gravity in the physical world would then evidently be the individual pursuit of self-interest—not only in the marketplace but in all areas of the social order. To understand the full workings of self-interest in society would be to achieve a comprehensive social knowledge equivalent to the wondrous discoveries then being made by physicists studying the work of gravity and other forces.

Hence, as the intellectual historian J. L. Talmon comments, all manner of social thinkers throughout the eighteenth century regarded self-interest as "the most real and most vital element in man and human relations."[27] Or, as Louis Bredvold explained, for the Enlightenment self-interest was the "moral law of gravitation."[28] Francis Hutcheson, a teacher and mentor to Adam Smith, had declared that the force of "self-love" was as central "to the regular State of the Whole as Gravitation" was to the harmonious workings of the physical universe.[29]

A DISCIPLE OF NEWTON

The elements were now all in place for a new Newtonian science of society. Adam Smith became the founder of modern economics by putting it all together effectively in one grand picture, supported by a great wealth of practical detail. The free market portrayed by Smith showed a Newtonian mechanism operating in perfect harmony according to the natural laws of the force of self-interest. For "Smith, if something is truly natural," in effect "it is right because it conforms to the will of the Deity."[30] All that is necessary to achieve the wonderful prospect of living in strict conformance with the laws of the universe is that governments, churches, and other social institutions cease to interfere with individual actions in pursuit of self-interest in the market. The result in the late eighteenth century was "the spiritualization of economic life."[31]

In these regards, Smith was carrying on the mantle of the Scottish Enlightenment whose later members had sought to find "the Newton of the moral sciences."[32] Indeed, one present-day student of Adam Smith's thought finds that "Newton's system has so carried Smith's imagination that his mind has almost literally tried to make it a stand-in for nature itself."[33] A leading contemporary authority on Smith's writings, Andrew Skinner, reports that Smith's grand design in his work over the years was that "each separate component of the system represents scientific work in the style of Newton, contributing to a greater whole which was conceived in the same image."[34] Reflecting a typical Enlightenment view, Smith himself stated that science is "the great antidote to the poison of enthusiasm and superstition."[35] Skinner writes that Smith consciously drew upon analogies from the natural sciences, where Newton's example was of course paramount:

[Smith] drew attention to the importance of analogy in suggesting that philosophers often attempt to explain the unusual by reference to knowledge gained in unrelated fields, noting that in some cases the analogy chosen could become not just a source of "ingenious similitude" but "the great hinge upon which everything turned."

Smith made extensive use of mechanistic analogies, derived from Newton, seeing in the universe "a great machine" wherein we may observe means adjusted with the nicest artifice to the ends which they are intended to produce. In the same way he noted that "Human society, when we contemplate it in a certain abstract and philosophical light, appears like a great, an immense machine," a position which leads quite naturally to a distinction between efficient and final causes, which is not inconsistent with the form of Deism associated with Newton himself. It is also striking that so systematic a thinker as Smith should have extended the mechanistic analogy to systems of thought: "Systems in many respects resemble machines."[36]

It was not only in the economic realm that such mechanistic, Newtonian ideas were acting to shape the basic institutional forms of society in the late eighteenth century. A recent commentary on the United States Constitution notes that it "reflects two concrete, vivid and mechanistic images prevalent in writings at the time of the Framing—a clock and a solar system." The eighteenth-century authors of the American Constitution sought to "set in motion a [Newtonian] machine with internal mechanisms that would ensure its efficient operation." For example, in creating distinct executive, legislative, and judicial branches that would thereby achieve a balance of powers, the eighteenth-century Framers were consciously following the model of the solar system where "each planet [had] its own path." In the Madisonian scheme of the U.S. Constitution, "the disparate elements work in conjunction toward the same goal," although each pursues separately its own political interests—to do otherwise would lead to the ruin of "the entire operation [just as] no planet may leave its path without throwing the others' paths into disarray."[37]

In the free market of Adam Smith, the new modern science of economics had thus shown how to achieve a natural harmony in society by obeying the natural laws of the universe. Like Newton in the physical world, Smith had uncovered God's true plan in society. Smith commonly described his overall economic design as a "system of natural liberty," thus effectively portraying it as a new and properly scientific understanding of the natural-law thinking that had long played such a central role in Western philosophy and theology. Hence, as Istvan Hont and Michael Ignatief write, "Smith himself left no doubt that in crafting his argument for a 'system of natural liberty,' he was deploying terms whose provenance had to be traced to Grotius, the founder of modern natural jurisprudence, and to his reformulation of the heritage of Aristotle and the [medieval] Schoolmen" such as Aquinas. Smith had developed an "analytical demonstration of how markets . . . balance themselves out in a manner consistent with strict justice and the natural law of humanity."[38]

SMITH THE CALVINIST

Besides these elements, there was yet another important feature that contributed to the immense influence of the *Wealth of Nations*—a free market was also congenial to certain long-standing tenets of Calvinist thought.[39] Free-market ideas have been received with particular favor in nations such as England and the United States, where Calvinist and Puritan traditions have maintained a long and influential existence.* The Protestant Reformation had introduced a new individualism into the relationship of human beings and God, abolishing the large intermediary church role as found in Roman Catholicism. Salvation was "by faith alone" and only God could know what was really in the heart of a man or woman. In the free market of Adam

---

* Murray Rothbard comments on the Calvinist origins of much that would be found in Adam Smith as follows:

> The British tradition, . . . beginning with Smith himself, was Calvinist, and reflected the Calvinist emphasis on hard work and labour toil as not only good but a great good in itself, whereas consumer enjoyment [as often looked upon more favorably in Roman Catholic economic writings] is at best a necessary evil, a mere requisite to continuing labour and production.
>
> Even though Smith was a "moderate" Calvinist, he was a staunch one nevertheless, and I came to the conclusion that the Calvinist emphasis could account, for example, for Smith's otherwise puzzling championing of usury laws, as well as his shift in emphasis from the capricious, luxury-loving consumer as the determinant of value, to the virtuous labourer embedding his hours of toil into the value of his material product.

See Murray N. Rothbard, *Economic Thought Before Adam Smith: An Austrian Perspective on the History of Economic Thought* (Brookfield, Vt.: Edward Elgar, 1995), xii.

The extent to which Adam Smith actually followed a labor theory of value, it might be noted, is a matter of some scholarly disagreement. But there is little doubt of a significant Calvinist element in his overall body of thought.

Smith, conformance to the natural laws of self-interest was also to conform to the laws of God. Here as well there was no need to consult with any state bureaucracy or other outside church or other official body in order for a person to do the will of God. As the mention of God would gradually be dropped from free-market theories, the old individualism of the Protestant relationship to God would take a new secular form in the actions of individuals in the free market.

The Puritans had conceived of society as ruled by a set of "covenants" or contracts. A good Puritan not only entered into contracts with other members of society but also had a covenant with God. This Puritan contractual way of thinking would later be secularized in Locke's theory of an initial social contract that forms the basis for the establishment of government in society. The theories of the free market also seemed a logical and appropriate extension into the economic realm of the general Puritan view of the contractual and individualistic workings of society. The theologian Kenneth Latourette wrote of the great influence on the modern age of the characteristic Protestant "insistence of the individual that his conscience must not be surrendered to the authority of state or Church." In addition to asserting a freedom of the individual to pursue market opportunities without government restraint, the modern ideas of democratic government represented a further development and secularization of "the political principles of popular sovereignty which had arisen largely through the Puritans."[40]

As a result, the individual who pursued self-interest in the market—or those who in politics engaged in voting and other forms of individual action—now could be seen as carrying on in the theological traditions of Christian theology.* George Stigler would comment that "in Smith's time

* A leading contemporary student of the interrelationships of economics and religion, Anthony Waterman, offers an "Augustinian" interpretation of the theological content of The Wealth of Nations. (Augustine was held in particularly high regard by the Protestant Reformation—Luther had started off as an Augustinian monk. Luther, Calvin and other leaders of the Reformation believed that Augustine's theology had later often been abandoned by a Roman Catholic Church that had lost touch with God.)

> I have attempted to show that we may read The Wealth of Nations as containing, and possibly even as shaped by, an Augustinian account of the way in which God responds to human sin by using the consequences of sin both as a punishment and as a remedy.
>
> It is evident that the theology of The Wealth of Nations is entirely "natural theology," that is, putative knowledge of God arrived at by the study of nature alone, without any reliance upon the "revelation" supposed by the faithful to be recorded in sacred scripture. "Nature" is almost always viewed teleologically in The Wealth of Nations. It exists for and with a purpose, and part of that purpose is human welfare. And to say that must imply either a transcendent, Newtonian God *of* Nature, or an immanent, Leibnitzian God *in* Nature. Smith does not say which, and though his text is capacious of either interpretation, it is usually easier to read it in the second

and for a few decades thereafter the argument for efficiency [of the market] was embellished with a rhetoric of sacred and inviolable rights of natural liberty." [41] Or, as Thorstein Veblen had said, there was a clear line of continuity from theological concepts of "over-ruling providence" to the eighteenth-century ideas of "order of nature, natural rights and natural law." They all amounted to efforts "to formulate knowledge in terms of absolute truth; and this absolute truth is a spiritual fact." [42]

Substantively, medieval theology and the Enlightenment economic science of Adam Smith reached similar conclusions with respect to the proper workings of markets—the competitive price is the ethical ideal. The manner of operation of markets is less novel than twentieth-century economists—now seeking to develop a sophisticated mathematical "science" of the market—have often suggested. Indeed, as Schumpeter would note, "The skeleton of [Adam] Smith's analysis hails from the scholastics and natural law philosophers" of many centuries earlier. In medieval theology, "society was treated as a thoroughly human affair, and moreover, as a mere agglomeration of individuals brought together by their mundane needs." The social teachings of medieval theology were "remarkably individualist, utilitarian, and (in a sense) rationalist." This theology also shares these characteristics with the "body of ideas [associated] with the laical . . . political philosophies of the eighteenth century" as developed by Adam Smith and other free-market economists. [43]

To a much greater degree than most contemporary social scientists realize, their thinking follows in the lines of traditions of thought that are now centuries old, or in some cases even date back to ancient Roman and Greek times. The Judeo-Christian heritage has been a leading source of the individual political and economic freedoms that have characterized Western civilization. The belief in a monotheistic God has revolutionary implications; it means that there is one truth of the universe and that this truth transcends kings, priests, and all other earthly authorities. If every individual is in prin-

---

of these ways. Even on the first interpretation, however, Smith's God/Nature does not merely wind up the great machine, and leave it ticking, as the Deists were held to have believed. She continues to act in various ways, but always wisely and well, so as to make creative use of human folly and wickedness in ways which bring good out of evil. Such redemptive activity, we may assume, is only needed at all because humans have been endowed by God/Nature with freedom to choose; and though intended by God/Nature to choose well, suffer from some universal failing which may be primordial and which often impels them to choose ill.

See A. M. C. Waterman, " 'Pure and Rational Religion': A Theological Reading of Adam Smith's *Wealth of Nations*" (paper presented at the sixty-seventh annual meeting of the Southern Economic Association, Atlanta, Ga., November 21–23, 1997), 11.

ciple equal in the eyes of God, then kings and commoners alike, in fact any individuals, are in principle equal to every other in the ability to understand God's plan for the world. There can be no legitimate place for absolute authority and dictatorship such as that which characterized ancient Egypt and many other civilizations of old—as well as the many more recent manifestations of such thinking. The poor person is as likely—perhaps more likely—to be saved as the rich person and need feel no special respect for authority in the most important aspects of human existence. Michael Novak has commented, "The most distinctive contribution of Judaism and Christianity to social theory is the identification of the individual conscience as a major source of social energy. Not all energy comes from authority, as the ancients held; nor from social structures as the Marxists hold; nor from historical necessity; nor from 'class struggle,' etc. The individual is an originating source of insight, decision, and action [according to the fundamental tenets of Judeo-Christian religion]."[44]

ECONOMICS AS INSPIRATIONAL ART

As Adam Smith now interpreted the natural laws of economics, governments that sought to interfere with the individual pursuit of self-interest in the market were acting contrary to the divine plan. The results were only likely to cause wide social disruption and distress—just as would any government action that in the physical order might be foolishly taken in attempted defiance of the law of gravity. Indeed, Smith's efforts in *The Wealth of Nations* set an artistic standard of religious inspiration that few other modern economists could match—although Samuelson in *Economics* might be rated as a contender. Regarded as a work of art designed to portray a scientific enterprise, both Smith and Samuelson in their respective works used a number of similar methods. In neither case did the success of their efforts derive from any actual predictive power of their scientific demonstrations.

Rather, the key to success for Smith and Samuelson was in the overall quality of their artistic performance. Both presented masses of interesting and relevant information that met the needs of their audiences to better understand the economic world around them. If the claims to science of *The Wealth of Nations* and then two centuries later of *Economics* could not withstand subsequent sustained scrutiny, both books did contain a wealth of practical insight and useful discussion of particular economic topics. If both books failed in their goal to present a genuine new physics of society, both to some extent succeeded in another, if less prestigious, form of scientific endeavor.

One might say that *The Wealth of Nations* and *Economics* were valid classificatory exercises in the manner of the old study of the anatomy of the body, or the classification of various plant and animal species, the ways of doing biology before the discoveries of DNA and the biochemical revolution of the second half of the twentieth century. Smith and Samuelson gave their readers a set of terms and abstract categories—a beginning language for economic discourse—by which they could at least start to make some sense of the bewilderingly complex economic world that surrounded them.

Yet even as a classificatory exercise, *The Wealth of Nations* had some major failings. Rather than the claim that the free market is run by the harmonious operation of natural laws, it is more accurate to say that its success is derived from its transformative powers for rapid change, sweeping aside all the money-losing businesses, outmoded labor practices, and other failed economic institutions of the old order as no other instrument of social change can do. It is the impersonal absence of any regrets in the face of great transitional disruptions—as Charles Schultze once said, the "devil take the hindmost" attitude that the market exhibits toward anything standing in its way—that makes the market such an immensely powerful force for rapid economic growth and development.[45] In the great majority of societies in history, it has been just the opposite. Bureaucratic inertia and other barriers have tended to make large-scale changes difficult if not impossible. It is because there are so many losers who might object that the very existence of the market as an institution in society must be sustained by a powerful religious or other normative source of authority and legitimacy.

In its approach, the Austrian school of economics has been distinguished by its much greater interest in the dynamic factors of market change, as compared with the static equilibrium preoccupations of the economic mainstream. It should perhaps not be surprising, therefore, that it was Schumpeter, an émigré from Austria to the United States, who judged *The Wealth of Nations* especially harshly in terms of its overall scientific qualities. Schumpeter wrote that the book did not "contain a single analytical idea, principle, or method that was entirely new in 1776," and thus could offer little or no advancement in scientific economic theory.[46]★

★ Murray Rothbard, another member of the Austrian school of economics (if not himself from Austria), was even more critical (characteristically for his contentious temperament). Rothbard would write that in terms of a genuine scientific understanding of economic phenomena, Smith was in some areas "an unmitigated disaster." In Rothbard's view, Smith "tragically shunted economics on to a false path, a dead end from which the Austrians had to rescue economics a century later. Instead of subjective value, entrepreneurship and emphasis on real market pricing and market activity, Smith dropped all this and replaced it with a labour theory of value and a dominant focus on the unchanging long-run 'natural-price' equilibrium, a world where entrepreneurship was assumed out of existence. Under

If its scientific merits were few, Schumpeter was willing at least to grant that it offered a "great performance." Smith's imagery of the free market was so compelling because it provided the key "channel through which eighteenth-century ideas about human nature" were expressed in ways that would have great appeal to the late eighteenth and then much of the nineteenth century.[47] In short, although Schumpeter did not put it exactly this way, Smith took economic events from the humdrum study of ordinary commercial transactions and made them the centerpiece of God's plan for the natural order. If one should properly credit Smith as the first modern economist, it is equally true that one might call him the first modern economic theologian—the first modern thinker who clearly set out a route to a secular salvation in this world, achieved by following down a path laid out according to the prescriptions of a valid economic science.

From 1800 to 1900, the industrial revolution brought a vast economic transition to Europe. However, despite the Newtonian economic image of a world in happy equilibrium and harmony, it would be more accurate to say that in reality all hell broke loose in the industrial world of the West. In terms of human well-being, and despite Marxist, socialist, and many other objections (fundamentally "conservative" in character, in the sense of protesting against the great force and rapid pace of market change), Smith's new blessing for the market was in all likelihood a very positive development for most people. The economic progress of the modern age has radically transformed the material conditions of existence for the better for the great majority of people living in the developed parts of the world.★

This dynamic transition, however, has also involved large costs for many people. The greatest significance of Adam Smith to the economic history of the world was not in any power of economic explanation but in offering a "scientific" doctrine by which the many losers from all this radical change could be persuaded to accept their fate without active revolt—an act of rebellion against the market that in many cases might have been to their indi-

---

Ricardo, this unfortunate shift in focus was intensified and systematized." As a result, the correct marginalist understandings of earlier scholastics was lost to economics for one hundred years or more and had to be rediscovered in the late nineteenth century by the Austrian school. See Murray N. Rothbard, *Economic Thought Before Adam Smith: An Austrian Perspective on the History of Economic Thought*, vol. 1 (Brookfield, Vt.: Edward Elgar, 1995), 448, xi.

★ Speaking personally, my ancestors lived in poverty—the survivors, that is—as recently as 100–150 years ago as farmers and workers in the often dark and frozen recesses of Sweden and Finland. When one visits these areas, and considers the vast transformation in the quality of life brought about by things such as electric lighting and modern heating systems, it is not difficult to understand why Scandinavians, perhaps more than any people, have celebrated the successes of science in the modern era and transferred their deepest religious faith from the Lutheran Church of old to various forms of faith in scientific and economic progress.

vidual advantage. In the terms of the recent thinking of the new institutional economics, one might say that the *Wealth of Nations* provided an implicit contract for society by which opportunism in all the potential multiple forms in the market could be restrained. The scientific blessing for the market has opened the way for economic change at an unprecedented speed and scale in the Western world.*

In many other societies around the world, powerful religious and cultural forces typically did not support the market, but the very opposite. Reflecting the conservative role often played by religion, these traditional faiths have stood opposed to any such socially disruptive workings of market freedoms. Their populations remained mired in feudal and other premodern conditions well into the second half of the twentieth century—and some are still there as the twenty-first century begins.

As it happened, Smith's economic model of a harmony and equilibrium in society—partly because it was so far removed from the actual evolutionary processes of economic transformation—would eventually face a crisis of intellectual authority. By the late nineteenth century a brand-new way of thinking about the role of self-interested behavior in the market had supplanted Adam Smith in at least the popular mind (the university world, conservative as always, was somewhat more slow to change). It was not that a better scientific theory with a whole new range of predictive capabilities and corresponding powers to control the economic world had been discovered—as is typically the case when a revolution in a physical science occurs. Rather, the decisive event first took place in the world of natural science; economists would then recast the image of economics to conform more closely with the newest leading scientific theory of the age. Because modern economics has borrowed its social authority from the successes of physical sciences, its practitioners have always hastened to emulate the forms of physical or biological science that might be held in highest regard at any given moment.

In the nineteenth century the key scientific event was the publication, in 1859, of Charles Darwin's *On the Origin of Species*. The impact was so powerful in so many domains of society that the last part of the nineteenth century and the early twentieth century would later often be described as the Age of Darwin.

* A similar view on the role of the "theology" of the market, if with a more negative verdict on the social benefits of the overall market outcome, is found in Karl Polanyi. He writes that "economic liberalism" in the nineteenth century served the function of a "secular religion." This new religion had an "evangelical fervor" and "evolved into a veritable faith in man's secular salvation through a self-regulating market." In this way it justified and helped to sustain and advance the great social dislocations that the market was then creating. See Karl Polanyi, *The Great Transformation: The Political and Economic Origins of Our Times* (Boston: Beacon Press, 1957; 1st ed., 1944), 139, 134.

ECONOMIC SURVIVAL OF THE FITTEST

At the funeral of Karl Marx in 1883, Friedrich Engels would eulogize that "just as Darwin discovered the law of the evolution of organic nature, so Marx discovered the evolutionary law of human history."[48] Darwin had replaced Newton as the new messiah of scientific religion for modern men and women, now attracting a host of disciples to interpret the evolutionary meaning of survival of the fittest in the social domain. For Marx it was the fittest economic class that survived, an outcome predetermined by the particular stage of class struggle within the workings of economic history. For Herbert Spencer in England and for his follower in the United States, Yale economist William Graham Sumner, the most important form of evolutionary survival of the fittest took place in the competition of the marketplace. The true Darwinian survivor was the individual business firm that surpassed its competitors in the market.

Historian Sidney Fine reports that "it would be difficult to overestimate Spencer's popularity in the United States during the quarter century after the Civil War." At the end of the nineteenth century, "no authority was more often cited by the opponents of state action than Herbert Spencer."[49] When the Supreme Court took up the *Lochner* case in 1905, Spencer's version of social Darwinism was exerting such a powerful influence on American social thought that Justice Oliver Wendell Holmes felt compelled to remind his Court colleagues that it was not their place to implement the economic theories of Herbert Spencer.[50] As Fine explains, "Spencer's views appealed to Americans for a variety of reasons. His optimistic presentation of the beneficent operation of nature's laws was thoroughly consonant with the American faith in progress. His individualism, although it went too far for most Americans, was nevertheless in the best American tradition. Above all, his application to society of Darwin's theory suited the tastes of the American businessman."[51]

The new titans of American industry indeed looked to social Darwinism to bless their victories in the market and resulting accumulations of vast wealth—potentially a source of considerable anxiety in an America where Calvinist and Puritan impulses were still strong. Prior to the Civil War in the United States, there were few business corporations. By 1900, two-thirds of all U.S. manufacturing activity was being carried on in businesses operating under corporate ownership. Apparently, the survival of the fittest in the new industrial world would often mean the survival of the largest, a lesson that American businesses took newly to heart and for which the ideas of Spencer could offer a seemingly scientific justification. The workings of evolutionary biology that Darwin had discovered must surely also be the natural law of economic affairs.

Spencer is yet another of the economic determinists of the late nineteenth and early twentieth centuries. No less than for Marx, the underlying workings of economic forces in history determine everything important that happens in society. In the advance of the world, old ideals like social justice, fairness, equality, and so forth will do more harm than good; they impede—even though they can never permanently frustrate—the evolutionary workings of the iron laws of economic progress. Social planning is an impossibility because it is beyond human capacity to redirect the laws of nature, as they are embodied in the of survival of the economic fittest. Commenting on Spencer's views, Richard Hofstadter would write that for him "the conscious control of societal evolution" is "an absolute impossibility, and . . . the best that organized knowledge can do is teach men to submit more readily to the dynamic factors in progress"—as in an earlier day they had been required to submit to God.[52]

Like the false consciousness of the bourgeoisie in Marx, Spencer says that some people fool themselves into thinking that "by due skill an ill-working humanity may be framed into well working institutions" but any such conviction of the possibility of social planning should be understood to be "a delusion." Despite the hopes held out by socialists, Progressives, and many other modern economic thinkers, no "political alchemy" is possible for Spencer that would allow social control over economic forces (in the market and elsewhere) for human progress. In Christian theology, similarly, God has his own plan, known only to him, and human action can not affect or change the outcome. Indeed, Spencer argues that misguided efforts to achieve social advance and equality through better social planning and larger government are likely to backfire into lasting outcomes of "despotism" and "enslavement."[53]★

In short, for the new economics of the late nineteenth-century market, the prevailing image of the working of self-interest is now to be found in a new scientific model dominant for this time. Yet, although the Darwinian image is very far removed from the Newtonian market mechanism of Adam Smith, the actual competitive workings of markets at the end of the nineteenth century had not changed very much from the end of the eighteenth century. What had changed was the leading model of science and thus the

---

★ To be sure, Spencer seems here to be somewhat inconsistent—if positive efforts at social reform must always fail in the face of the iron laws of nature, it would then also seem impossible to do much harm as well.

"scientific" image of the market, and the manner in which a religious blessing could thereby be applied with the greatest authority. It was not a scientific requirement but an imperative of religious artistry—now in a secular mode—that demanded the shift from a Newtonian to a Darwinian portrayal of the marketplace. More traditional religions also have had different conceptions of religious art; the statuary and pictorial representations of biblical themes, for example, that were commonplace in Roman Catholic churches were forbidden in Jewish synagogues and were much less elaborate in Protestant churches.

With the shift in market metaphors went a further important change. In the Newtonian idea of market perfection, it would mean a true harmony with the natural laws of society. In the thinking of social Darwinism, hopes for the perfection of the world would shift to focus on ever greater material outputs. It was a time when leading social thinkers for the first time began to appreciate the enormous transformation in the material circumstances of human existence. As examined in Part I, the expectations of continuing rapid economic progress in the world led many people to expect the arrival in the near future at a state of perfect abundance—and thus as well the abolition of all the old fierce and debilitating conflicts over material possessions and resources. It would be nothing less than the end finally of original sin, now to be accomplished by economic methods.

Spencer offered a less apocalyptic image of the arrival at an ending stage of history, as compared with the Marxist triumph of the proletariat, but he envisioned as well that economic progress would eventually reach a steady state of perfection where the harsh evolutionary realities of survival of the fittest would no longer be necessary. For Spencer, it might be a different kind of "invisible hand," but some force beyond human control—some kind of secular divinity operating in history, one might say—was still acting to ensure that the common good would be served by the individual pursuit of self-interest in the market. It was necessary only that governments stay out of the way.

Calvinist theology had decreed in the sixteenth century that those predestined by God for salvation might be identified by their success in a business or other calling.[54] This notion would be carried over into social Darwinist thought where, as historian Robert McCloskey once commented, the economically successful—the survivers of the evolutionary struggle in the marketplace—constituted "the elite, the saints of the new religion." The market winners "had proved their native superiority by their survival value. This will be recognized as the Puritan [and Calvinist] idea of 'election' in modern dress."[55]

If the free market represented, in a new secular form, an expression of elements of Calvinist and Puritan thinking, it was bound—when combined with Adam Smith's invocation of the Newtonian image of market competition, and then with Spencer's appeal to Darwinist images of market survival of the fittest—to prove a potent brew indeed. In the United States at least, the influence of Calvinist thinking has been extraordinary since the founding days of the Puritans in the Massachusetts colony. Even today, as Paul Conkin comments, the strong "legacy of Puritanism" can still be found in the ever-continuing "search for redemptive experience" in American public life.[56]

If the most important function of economics seemingly is to provide an implicit contract, supported by—as Douglass North argues is often necessary—a strong religious bond, and by this means to inhibit rent seeking, opportunism and other "antisocial" actions that could undermine the workings of political and economic institutions, the Calvinist and Newtonian mechanics of Adam Smith, and then the Calvinist and social Darwinist evolutionary survival of the fittest of Herbert Spencer, proved to be modern gospels with an inspirational power to match traditional Jewish, Christian, and other religions of old.

AN INCENDIARY BREW

It would be the misfortune of the world, however, to discover in the first half of the twentieth century that the extension of Darwinist concepts into social and religious domains amounted to playing with fire on a global scale. Other interpretations of social Darwinism, much less favorable to human freedom and the protection of the market from predatory opportunism, were also possible. Indeed, by the middle of the twentieth century, the image of the market as an evolutionary and historical process would be abandoned by most American members of the economics profession. The association of Darwinist thought with German racial, Soviet world-class-struggle, and other much different interpretations of the evolutionary survival of the fittest had proven to have disastrous consequences for Western civilization.

In retrospect, the outcome should not be considered as surprising as many people today still seem to regard it. The injection of a social Darwinist framework of thought into Western social science, and combined with the religious crusading impulse in the West, in effect put a religious blessing on various forms of warfare within society, seemingly all part of God's design for the proper course of evolutionary progress in the world. The potential for disastrous conflict was all the greater because social Darwinism by its very framework of thought undermined many of the traditional restraints of Western religion and culture.

Both Judeo-Christian religion, and then physics and other sciences since their ascendance in the modern age, had grounded their authority in their claims to show the absolute truth of the world. The Darwinist forms of social thought, in essence, tended to say something radically new. It was no longer possible to argue for such a thing as truth in the old Christian and scientific sense; in a Darwinist framework the whole realm of ideas in the mind had to be regarded from the perspective of advancing or retarding the processes of evolutionary survival. From a valid Darwinist perspective, if an idea promoted survival of the human species (or the business entity, economic class, or racial group, as Darwinist thinking would successively be applied to competition among various elements within society), it would tend by this very fact to endure—whether true or not. If an idea stood in the way of competitive survival of a more powerful group, it would die out—even if it might be objectively true (assuming that any such thing remained).

Indeed, Marx would soon declare that all ideas in the mind were mere products of the material and biological workings of evolutionary conflicts among economic classes at different stages of economic history. The only "scientific" understanding of good and evil would be decreed by Marx's new god of economics; a "good" action would serve to advance and an "evil" action to retard the workings of the evolutionary laws of class struggle in economic history. If ordinary people might actually believe that traditioinal morality had an objective validity, it was merely because they were subject to "bourgeois" or other self-deceptions that themselves served in the grand scheme of things to advance the current stage of the class struggle. Spencer in essence said much the same thing, if seeing a different form of evolutionary advance and a difference source of modern illusions. For him the Marxist, socialist, progressive, and other government plans for eliminating inequality, educating the poor, achieving a just world and all manner of other "romantic" schemes for social engineering and improvement were signs of soft and weak minds unable to grasp the harsher decrees of nature, as manifested in the economic workings of the survival of the fittest businesses in the marketplace.

Sigmund Freud's theories of psychoanalysis, which Freud himself saw explicitly as a form of Darwinian evolutionary struggle in the mind, traced the progression of internal mental conflict (much like Marx's stages of class struggle) from oedipal and other mental stages in early childhood to adulthood.[57] Much like that of Marx and Spencer, the essence of the Freudian view of the world was to treat all ideas in the mind as outward manifestations of a more fundamental underlying reality—now the internal struggles of an evolutionary process driven by struggles within the psyche, involving the forces of the id, ego and superego. Much like Marx in his view of false consciousness, Freud saw religion, moral codes, and other ideas in the mind as mere "projections" or a "transference" of the more fundamental elements.

Taking the resulting undermining of the authority of traditional Western moral restraints, and combining it with the Darwinian view that the evolutionary laws of nature decree that human progress will be achieved by one or another form of internal competitive struggle in society, and then blessing this overall vision of pervasive conflict with the authority of religion, it is no wonder that the first half of the twentieth century was characterized by worldwide wars, genocides, and other forms of terrible conflict. By midcentury, the world had had enough. At least in models of society, if not with respect to evolutionary biology in the field of natural science, Darwin and all his works would have to go. One can say virtually anything in public today with respect to the contents of Christian religion, but any suggestion of truth in the old Darwinist categories of race (and to a lesser extent class) warfare will bring the full opprobrium of society on a true "heretic" of our time. If secular religion has largely displaced the old Jewish and Christian faiths in the public life of our day and age, real heresy can now take only secular forms.

BACK TO PHYSICS

The old Newtonian equilibrium in society, involving a harmonious—and peaceful!—working of the natural laws of the social order, seemed newly attractive to the second half of the twentieth century. Yet by then the old Newtonian scheme had been superceded in physics by the theories of Einstein, Niels Bohr, and other developers of relativity, quantum mechanics, and other modern twentieth-century physics. The scientific authority of economics might now depend on a new economic imagery modeled on this most recent picture of the workings of the physical universe. Indeed, when Keynes published *The General Theory* in 1936, he was implicitly making the claim that he was following in the footsteps of Einstein's general theory of relativity—or as one hostile reviewer noted, "Einstein has actually done for Physics what Mr. Keynes believes himself to have done for Economics."[58]

Samuelson's *Foundations of Economic Analysis* was published in 1947, and Samuelson here as well announced that economics must be done in the manner of physics. The key to the future success of economic analysis, Samuelson asserted, would be to employ the same mathematical and statistical methods that had recently proved once again to be so extraordinarily fruitful in investigating physical phenomena in nature. Samuelson thus declared that "the laborious literary working over of essentially simple mathematical concepts such as is characteristic of much of modern economic theory is not only unrewarding from the standpoint of advancing the science, but involves as well mental gymnastics of a peculiarly depraved type." [59] A prominent economist reviewing *Foundations* in 1948 optimistically declared that, much as in physics, Samuelson had been successful in unifying "all the various branches of economic analysis . . . by a small number of basic [mathematical] principles." [60]

Use of formal mathematical and statistical methods, to be sure, was about as close to the actual methods of twentieth-century physics as postwar economics would get. The ordinary person could be dazzled by a seeming endless series of technological miracles (television, radar, jet airplanes, computers, laser beams, and so forth) that would flow from the applications of theoretical discoveries of physics. Instead of offering a vague promise of miraculous events that few would ever witness directly, as found in the Bible, the applications of the understandings of modern physics delivered virtual miracles on a daily basis for all to see. But the actual scientific theories of relativity, quantum mechanics, and other twentieth-century physics offered no graphic mental images such as the mechanism of the solar system of Newton, or the evolutionary struggle of Darwin.

If twentieth-century physics had an image, it was that the world actually was incomprehensible and inscrutable to the ordinary person. How many people could actually understand what it might really mean for space and time to vary according to the speed of motion? The physics of the twentieth century itself had a mathematical meaning that did not correspond to any visual image accessible to ordinary understanding. Indeed, even among scientists, perhaps no more than ten thousand or so people in the world at any given time had the mental abilities and the scientific training to comprehend the full meaning of Einstein's special and general relativity. If they were the true elect, the only ones who could ever actually see the light directly (as the favored occupants of Plato's cave had once done), the god of twentieth-century physics was apparently designating a very small minority for his special favor.

As economics moved in the twentieth century to recapture the images of physics, the members of the economics profession thus would largely forgo the actual physics of the twentieth century. The next best thing apparently would be a return to earlier models of eighteenth-and nineteenth-century physics, including the old Newtonian imagery. Samuelson did introduce some new dynamic complications in his *Foundations* and did achieve some elegant theoretical results but the revolution in economic methods that his work promoted turned out to be pretty much the old economics in the mold of Newton.[61] Moving beyond Adam Smith and his followers, however, the vision of the market was now presented for the second half of the twentieth century in full mathematical dress—Adam Smith in a complete set of equations, one might say. As Milton Friedman commented in 1991, "The substance of professional economic discussion has remained remarkably unchanged over the past century while at the same time the language in which economic analysis is presented has changed so drastically that few economists who contributed to the early volumes would have been able to read most articles in recent volumes."[62]

In other words, the main developments in economics of the twentieth century, Friedman was acknowledging, had been more a matter of form than of substance. Friedman could have extended his observation even well beyond one hundred years. Little new of any great significance has been learned about the workings of markets since Adam Smith and, as noted above, Smith added much less to the discussion than most economists have commonly supposed. There have been great changes in the institutional framework in which the market functions—the rise of the modern corporation in the late nineteenth century, for example. These institutional developments might have provided grist for fundamental new insights into the workings of the American and world economy of potential social significance. However, institutional studies have never occupied more than a minority of American economists and were disavowed almost entirely by the leading economists of Samuelson's generation.

If required to make a choice between working in the accepted language of the scientific method and learning something important about the world, the majority of economists have almost opted for the former. Economics without the social authority and prestige of a science, most professional economists seem to believe, would not be worth having. And perhaps they are right. If the modern age required a priesthood, and science had displaced God as the source of authoritative truth of the time, economists perhaps had no choice. Even if God did not exist, many priests would still have done much good in the world. Even if it meant that they used the wrong methods and little substantive was learned, economists seemingly were nevertheless required to speak in the same language by which the new god of science had chosen to communicate with humankind. For them to have behaved otherwise would have been almost as though a priest of the Christian Church had begun speaking in the language of the Koran, asserting that Islam offered a more meaningful set of categories for understanding the workings of the economy than the traditional Christian vocabulary.

As examined in Part II, Samuelson did contribute new progressive ideas of scientific management of society based on "the market mechanism" subject to social control. Yet, even this side of Samuelson could also be traced to a Newtonian imagery, if by a different path. The American Progressives were followers in the tradition of nineteenth-century French socialism as found in the positivist writings of Saint-Simon, Auguste Comte, and their followers. Saint-Simon had imagined himself to be the Newton of society.[63] Comte believed that he had discovered a social physics in the mode of Newton that would make possible for the first time a true positive science of society, thus laying the basis for management of all aspects of society by a new scientific elite of engineers possessed of the requisite technical expertise. Other than the mathematics, the Newtonian familiarity of it all helps to explain why Samuelson and his followers have generated so little in the way of changed understandings of the basic workings of economic systems.

The economist Philip Mirowski has been one of the severest critics of what he characterizes as the "physics envy" of the economics profession throughout the modern era. He delivers an especially harsh verdict of Samuelson, describing him as virtually a scientific fraud. Mirowski writes that "the key to the comprehension of Samuelson's meteoric rise in the economics profession was his knack for evoking all the outward trappings and ornament of science without ever once coming to grips with the actual content or implications of physical theory for his neoclassical economics."[64] Samuelson, like Keynes, did make some efforts to relate his work to twentieth-century physics, but Mirowski finds them superficial. Niels Bohr formulated a "correspondence principle" in quantum mechanics and Samuelson published a paper about a "correspondence principle" in economics. Mirowski writes, however, that "there are no plausible analogies between Bohr's and Samuelson's Correspondence Principles" and that Samuelson was merely "straining to evoke parallels between neoclassical [economic] theory and twentieth-century physics."[65]

It was embarassing to Samuelson and his followers that the neoclassical models had their "origins" in "nineteenth-century physics" (or even seventeenth- and eighteenth-century physics). Hence, it was necessary to "disguise" this fact and adopt "superficial references to twentieth-century physics while simultaneously avoiding their characteristic formalisms and content." Mirowski finds that the making of claims to "scientific legitimacy by means of value innuendo abounds in Samuelson's oeuvre." Yet, in a profession anxiously seeking the social legitimacy of the physical sciences, fellow economists suspended their critical judgment, and even though the efforts to emulate physics represented "a tough act to get past the critics, . . . Samuelson pulled it off time after time," along with a large supporting cast made up of other economists of his generation.[66]

In his *Economics* textbook, to be sure, Samuelson necessarily had to abandon the formal mathematical language of physics to reach the several million students who would read it in order to learn about the economic world for the first time. Yet, as examined in Part II in the present book, while *Economics* is developed in the language of ordinary speech, the image Samuelson is presenting is still that of economics as the management of a physical system based on the precise scientific laws of the workings of that system. Following in a tradition that goes back to Saint-Simon, Auguste Comte, and other French socialists of the first half of the nineteenth century, economists are the latest engineers of society, now sitting at the steering wheel of the market mechanism.

However, as the new institutional economics of the 1980s and 1990s has been showing, the "Samuelson project" to do economics as physics spread fundamental errors of economic understanding. The Newtonian manner of understanding the economic system had already failed as an explanatory model in the nineteenth century, when the real-world processes of industrial change hardly fit an economic image of harmony and stability. Since the 1970s, American economists have increasingly recognized that any valid understanding of the workings of an economic system must be set in a fully dynamic context. In focusing on the role of transaction costs in the economy, there is little to be learned from the old forms of static analysis. Most of the interesting issues arise from the interactions of transaction costs with dynamic factors of adjustment in the economy. For the new institutional economics the setting is one of shifting solutions to information problems, signals of opportunistic motives, more efficient means of formal and implicit contracting, resolution of principal-agent problems, and other economic factors that influence the level of transaction costs. If the static analysis of the neoclassicals was all about comparing equilibrium positions, the new institutional analysis of transaction costs is—or should be—all about what happens between those positions.

CONCLUSION

To be sure, economics may perform a valuable social role without adding any significant understanding to knowledge of the economy—a "good myth," economically speaking, can work not only in primitive tribal cultures but also in modern societies. In this respect, Samuelson might be judged a large scientific failure and a great religious and economic success (at least until the basic value shifts in American society from the 1960s onward).

Economists can be valuable contributors to economic efficiency and progress—likely to be given positions of high respect in society—in the role merely of the latest class of priestly deliverers of authoritative blessings. As long as it is believed in (whether or not it is "true" is not essential), religion offers a common bond that can help to promote trust and to resolve the various large transaction-cost problems with which any real-world economy must contend.

Indeed, as in the analysis of this chapter suggests, the religious function may have been the most important role throughout the history of modern economics since the Enlightenment. For thousands of years all over the world, most societies have assigned a leading role to their priestly classes, and yet we would now judge that the great majority of these priesthoods have been mistaken in their preaching of objective religious truth (since the truths rarely coincide, almost by definition most of them must have been in error in some ways). Yet many of the multiple religious truths have been as important to the day-to-day functioning of their societies as current professional economists are today to contemporary American society.

If trust is a great economic asset, a critical form of "social capital," investments in religion may be a more effective means than achieving higher levels of physical and human capital in advancing economic growth and development. Reflecting a common American attitude, Dwight Eisenhower once remarked as president that "America makes no sense without a deeply held faith—and I don't care what it is."[67] Perhaps this can also be said as well for the workings of the American economy. A religious basis of civic-mindedness and social solidarity is necessary, whatever it is. The effective functioning of a market system requires a religious grounding to promote trust, inhibit opportunism, provide for implicit contracting, and serve in other ways to minimize transaction costs in society. The precise theological details of the religion (so long as the tenets of faith are not actively hostile to the market, or to other key economic institutions) may not be the most critical concern.

The Western tradition of religion, however, is that it should be "the truth." The truths of science displaced the truths of Judeo-Christian religion in many domains because science was able to make more authoritative claims to genuine knowledge. It will not be enough to say that a religion should be believed because as a practical matter it will "work"—whether the goal is promoting economic efficiency and rapid growth or any other social objective. Indeed, as argued earlier, the proselytizers of the various secular economic religions of the modern age have claimed a genuine scientific status. These economists were asserting that economic theories could deliver the same access to "truth" in the economic world that other scientific efforts were achieving in matters of the workings of physical nature.

In short, any old religion may do for economic purposes, as long as it is truly believed in and supports the market and other economic institutions, but a religion will not be believed in unless it can successfully assert a truth claim about the world. That extends the potential scope of research interest of members of the economics profession into a brand-new subject area—the very workings of theological argumentation and the manner by which truth claims are made and by which those claims can be sustained or discredited in active theological debate and controversy. A successful economic performance for the American nation (and the whole world eventually) may critically depend on the existence of a theological logic capable of being defended against vigorous attacks on its basic truthfulness.

To fully enter into this subject would take this book far beyond its intended scope. However, the final chapter will address one specific truth claim that has been of special importance to the secular economic religions of the modern age—the conviction that scientific and economic progress will transform the human condition for the better, and in the most optimistic expressions of this faith that the advance of progress will bring about the literal arrival of a new heaven on earth.

chapter **ELEVEN**

A CRISIS OF PROGRESS

Writing on the subject of utopias for *The New Palgrave* dictionary of economics, Gregory Claeys observed that "the period between 1700 and 1900 marks not only the great age of utopian speculation, but also the period in which economic practice and utopian precept become increasingly intertwined." It is in the eighteenth century that one first finds a strong connection between utopian thought and a devotion "to the notion of progress." Beginning in the nineteenth century, many utopian plans "concentrated upon the nation-state and the beneficial development of large-scale industry (Saint-Simon), a pattern which was to become increasingly dominant as the potential role of machinery in creating a new cornucopia became evident." By the end of the century one could find "a virtually continuous outpouring of planned-economy utopias" in at least Britain and America, expressing social ideals that would make their way into European socialist and American progressive thought of the first decades of the twentieth century.[1]

The term "utopian," to be sure, is being applied here after the fact. Most of the thinkers described by Claeys did not think they were being utopian at the time. Rather, they considered their ideas to be realistic prescriptions for the reworking of society in a brand-new mold. They were convinced that the following of their plans would lead over time to a perfection of the human condition—to the arrival of heaven on earth. Many millions of people made large personal sacrifices in the name of one or another of these promises of a future earthly paradise.

It is thus of particular significance for the future of the economics profession that, as Claeys finds, "in the 20th century utopianism has faltered in the face of some of the consequences of modernity, and speculation has often taken the form of the negative utopia or dystopia." * Long considered the path to a secular salvation, economic growth is no longer "an uncritically accepted ideal." Indeed, Claeys wonders whether there will be new visions of "progress" that "can be realized without 'growth.' " If so, it may be that such visions will also "first persuasively appear in utopian form." [2] And if the past is any guide, these new utopian elements will then find their way into wider patterns of thought that take less exaggerated forms.

In the United States, the performance of the economy during World War II, providing the material supplies to defeat German and Japan, and then the postwar economic boom, might have been taken to demonstrate that hopes for economic progress were being fulfilled. Whatever its other defects in matters of economic theory, Samuelson's *Economics* did in fact embody a continuing progressive—if now neoprogressive—outlook on the world that was close to the American consensus of the time. It proved, however, to be the calm before the storm. Looking back to the 1960s, this decade was the beginning of a crisis of legitimacy for the religions of economic progress that continues today.

A LOSS OF ECONOMIC FAITH

As a professor in the 1960s and 1970s at Yale Law School, Robert Bork was a prominent member of the law-and-economics movement and the author of a leading study of antitrust law. He seemed to view economic analysis as the key field of social inquiry. Today, however, Bork has a different assessment. He still considers "the vitality of our economy" to be an "important" subject for study. However, the United States has reached a "state of affluence" in which Bork finds that "social and cultural issues are more important to the good life." He now thinks that, rather than economic policies, the more central public issues are "battles over educational content, the content

---

* For example, the treatment of scientists in movies and television has betrayed new public anxieties concerning the benefits of science. As one TV producer commented at a conference, "Frankenstein gets a lot of business, Nova doesn't." For the American public, "science is out of reach as perceived by the vast, vast, vast majority of people. There are deep misgivings in the public consciousness about the devil's bargain science has made." Comments of David Milch, executive producer of the *NYPD Blue* television series, as reported in Andrew Pollack, "Scientists Seek a New Movie Role: Hero, Not Villain," *New York Times,* December 1, 1998, D1.

of popular culture, the feminization of the military, the understanding of the family, the proper spheres of reason and emotion, and much more" along these lines.[3]

Issues of this kind, Bork thinks, involve religion in critical ways. It is important, however, to understand religion in a broader sense than as encompassing only traditional Christian, Jewish, and other faiths. There was a "cultural and spiritual revolution" in the 1960s that has since triumphed in many areas of American life. At the heart of this transformation, Bork says, has been a "secular religion" that has promoted feminism, affirmative action, gay rights, equal treatment for the disabled, an end to age discrimination, and other "radical, emancipationist demands." This new secular faith rejects the traditional rational modes of analysis of public policy problems and instead "celebrates emotion, deplores reason."[4]

Bork's view that culture is more important than economics is now widely shared and is held by people who differ with him in value-outlook and policy conclusions. The very foundational premises of the old progressive gospel increasingly are being challenged across a wide front. John Lewis, a black Democratic congressperson from Georgia, declared in 1995 that "it is not only poverty that has caused crime. In a very real sense it is crime that has caused poverty, and is the most powerful cause of poverty today."[5] Writers in publications such as the *New Republic*—once a bastion of progressive faith— today assert that the time has come "not only to put economics in its place, but also to admit culture into the analysis," declaring that the real problem of the inner cities is a "crass, indulgent culture" that contains too many people "without the social wherewithal, or the personal confidence, to delay gratification."[6] A reporter for the *Washington Post* stated, as though it were now a truism, that "as common sense suggests and social science affirms, improving children's futures has more to do with time and values than with income."[7] Some social scientists now look to a revival of traditional religion, rather than to any conventional economic programs, as perhaps the most promising avenue to helping America's poor to solve their problems.★

Indeed, Bork's colleague at the American Enterprise Institute, Irving Kristol, declares that the continuing problems of the poor in America

---

★ The president of the Ford Foundation, Susan Berresford, announced a new focus on religion and the study of "moral resources and social change" in the foundation's grant-making patterns. She commented that "staff members at the Foundation recently began to explore the role that religion plays in the communities and the institutions we support. . . . We hope to learn more about how spiritual traditions can contribute to the reduction of poverty and injustice while increasing our capacity to foster tolerance, cooperation, and human achievement." See Susan V. Berresford, "Moral Resources and Social Change," *Ford Foundation Report* (Spring/Summer 1998): 2.

amount to a decisive refutation of the long-standing progressive "dogma of the Left," that "the persistence of economic inequality and the absence of economic opportunity are the root causes" of social maladies. Kristol declares that any full assessment of the future of the welfare and regulatory state must include an unavoidable "spiritual dimension," in addition to its "economic and social" aspects. It is not only the pocketbooks but also the "souls of the citizenry [that] are formed and shaped by the welfare state"—and it seems sometimes in less than desirable ways.[8]

Kristol also finds that there is today a powerful "alienation" from the progressive view of a large and powerful federal government acting "in the public interest," a new distrust of the old view of "society" making collective decisions to maximize social welfare, as so graphically portrayed in the inspirational imagery of Samuelson's *Economics*. The pervasiveness of interest-group politics, the Vietnam War, Watergate, frequent government scandals, and still other disappointments have been operating, Kristol observed, "to undermine the legitimacy of the state," rendering less effective the continuing efforts of older Progressives such as Samuelson to rally the American public to the greater cause of a secular economic salvation here on earth.[9]

Polls also tell the same story.* Asked to give the fundamental cause of the nation's most serious social and economic problems, a 1994 Peter D. Hart Research poll found 51 percent of Americans attributing these problems mainly to a basic "decline in moral values," while only 34 percent said they stemmed mainly "from economic and financial pressures on the family."[10] The National Commission on Civic Renewal in 1998 released a study containing a composite "index of national civic health," showing an overall 25 percent decline in the index from 1972 to 1996. For example, the willingness of Americans to turn out to vote in elections, one of the specific elements included in the index, had declined by about 20 percent over this period.[11]

From the late 1940s through the mid-1960s, *Economics* was a close mirror of the civic religion of America. Americans surely did not believe in the redeeming benefits of economic progress because they had read *Economics* in

---

* The new attitudes were also clearly making their presence felt in the summer of 1999 as various candidates were seeking to position themselves for the 2000 American presidential campaign. As the *Wall Street Journal* reported, "The values issue has gained gale force" in American public debate. Even at a time of great prosperity, there were grave national doubts concerning the state of "values" in American life. Contrary to the older thinking, prosperity was no assurance of a good life. Various candidates now each made their pronouncements to this effect—George W. Bush, Jr.: "Prosperity without purpose is simply materialism"; Al Gore: "As important as prosperity is, there is more to long for. There is a hunger and thirst for goodness among us"; Bill Bradley: "Even at a time of unparalleled prosperity, . . . people are worried about tomorrow. How will my child turn out?"; Dan Quayle: "Prosperity without values is no prosperity at all." See Jackie Calmes, "Prosperity Gives Politicians a Chance to Discuss Values," *Wall Street Journal,* June 24, 1999, A10.

college. However, they found in *Economics* a strong affirmation and further symbolic support for what they already knew. If this faith was waning at the end of the twentieth century, if the progressive imagery of *Economics* appeared increasingly dated, it was again not because of any subtle arguments by scholars and other intellectuals one way or the other. Rather, the matter was being decided on more empirical grounds that were easily accessible to common view. Until the 1930s, Germany had long been the leading scientific nation in the world, a leader also in music, philosophy, and the social sciences, among many other areas. It was possessed of an advanced economy. Yet, for all its scientific and material progress, Germany in the 1930s and 1940s had plunged the world into the horrors of World War II and the Holocaust.★

The development of the atomic and then the hydrogen bomb symbolized in an especially graphic way that science in the modern age could pose a great menace as well as provide a powerful force for the good. Rachel Carson in *Silent Spring* helped to spawn a whole generation of environmentalists, fearful that the modern products of scientific advance were destroying important parts of the biological heritage of the earth.[12] Other scientific developments in areas such as biotechnology with the recent cloning of animals (and potentially humans in the future), threaten to erode long-held moral beliefs. The implicit value system of *Economics,* with its unquestioning optimism about science and its elevation of economic efficiency to the highest value in society, could offer little effective response to these developments.

Many skeptics about science and progress would turn to environmentalism, where they found a new gospel often actively hostile to technology, economic growth, and the long-standing claims for the transforming benefits of material progress. Others who rejected the progressive gospel would turn in a libertarian direction, where they found a belief system dubious of any grand plans—progressive, environmental, Christian, or otherwise—for the salvation of society, and especially as proponents of these plans might seek to implement them through the exercise of governmental powers of coercion. Within economics, the values of the new libertarianism were symbolically affirmed in many of the writings of the members of the Chicago school, the successors to Samuelson and other leading economists in the progressive economic mainstream.

★ The new doubts about economic progress were succinctly captured in the following rebuttal made to an expression of hope for a strong middle class as the best solution to the social problems of a developing nation: "The only trouble with this postulate is the historical record. The centuries-long development of propertied middle classes in Europe did not lead to the emergence of liberal ideas in the 1920s and 1930s, but became the breeding ground for Nazi racism and fascism." See Adrian Karatnycky, "Still the Bedrock of a Better World," *Washington Post,* December 12, 1997, A17.

ENVIRONMENTAL CALVINISM

In an earlier time, the Puritan settlers of Massachusetts had seen human existence as precarious, constantly endangered by the workings of the devil. Now, as some much newer voices invoked these old Calvinist themes, it might be possible that the very gospel of economic growth and progress had been yet another of the devil's many snares and delusions. One environmental journal declared that, rather than growth being the path to heaven on earth, the most serious problems of the nation were attributable to the fact that "we in the United States are in a culture that worships growth." [13]

Indeed, many new voices would rise up to reassert the old Puritan skepticism of consumption and wealth.* Wendell Berry found that even many of the institutional churches of America had been corrupted by the same gospel of efficiency that Samuelson in *Economics* had preached to millions of students. Organized American religion was "increasingly industrialized: concerned with quantity, growth, fashionable thought and an inane sort of [progressive] expert piety." Berry complained that the official religious bodies of America had failed to understand that "the industrial economy is not just a part of a quasi-rational system of specializations, granting the needs of the body to the corporations and the needs of the spirit to the churches, but is in fact an opposing religion, assigning to technological progress and 'the market' the same omnipotence, omniscience, unquestionability, even the same beneficence, that the Christian teachings assign to God." [14]

America's churches had made a great mistake, Berry declared, in accepting the assurances of Progressives such as Samuelson who had so misleadingly asserted a "modern divorce between economy and religion—which is really just a version of the devastating old dualism of body and soul." [15] In other words, for Berry and others in his camp, the claim of *Economics* that it is practicing science, leaving the values of the nation to be decided in another domain, is a grand deception. Rather, economists and others of a progressive ilk have long sought to inculcate among Americans a harmful set of beliefs that are destructive of the most cherished values of the nation.

More recently, the old progressive conviction that science and religion must be kept in separate compartments has been breaking down on further

---

* A rejection of extensive material possessions can also be found in many other religions. In Judaism, for example, as one rabbi comments, there are important "moral and theological considerations" that lead to a significant "concern with limiting consumption." See Eliezer Diamond, " 'The Earth Is the Lord's and the Fullness Thereof': Jewish Perspectives on Consumption," in David A. Crocker and Toby Linden, eds., *Ethics of Consumption: The Good Life, Justice, and Global Stewardship* (Lanham, Md.: Rowman and Littlefield, 1998), 396.

fronts. Secretary of the Interior Bruce Babbitt in a 1995 speech to the League of Conservation Voters stated that his political enemies were out to get him because they were "so deeply disturbed by the prospect of religious values entering the national debate" over environmental and natural-resource policies.[16] In the management of the nation's physical environment, Babbitt thinks that human beings are acting today in an immoral fashion. They are putting their own material well-being above that of endangered species, wilderness areas, biological diversity, and other elements of the natural world. For example, Babbitt decried the proposed salvage logging of federally owned timber in the Pacific Northwest as an attempt to "sacrifice the integrity of God's creation at the altar of commercial timber production"— in other words, a false idolatry of economic outputs at the expense of a natural world that manifests God's original design for His Creation.[17] In this view he was far from alone; an enduring theme of American nature writing has long been "a belief that nature is an expression of God."[18]

As secretary of the interior, Babbitt has similarly defended the Endangered Species Act as a modern version of Noah's Ark. Some Republican critics of his policies have suggested—as many ordinary economists would—that not all species are as important as others, that perhaps some minor species can be allowed to go extinct, and that at a minimum, priorities should be set in the allocation of competing resources for the protection of endangered species (there are more than one thousand listed in the United States). In rejecting all this, Babbitt stated that "in Genesis, Noah was commanded to take into the ark two by two and seven by seven every living thing in creation, the clean and unclean. He did not specify that Noah should limit the ark to two charismatic species, two good for hunting, two species that might provide some cure down the road, and, say, two that draw crowds to the city zoo. No, He specified *the whole of Creation.*"[19] It may be one hundred years since an American cabinet secretary has actively defended an important government policy in terms of its conformance with the specific language of the Bible.[20]

There were many other signs that the progressive tide of modernism was ebbing in America at the end of the twentieth century.[21] Prominent environmentalists declared that their avowed purpose was to spread the truth of a new religion in opposition to the worship of science and progress.[22] Many environmental activists are proud to declare that their faith involves at its core "a peak, religious experience" that causes them to "approach earth's problems with religious fervor."[23] Among less sympathetic observers as well, it was readily apparent that environmentalism was "not ultimately about mere material things, but about the cleansing of sins and the saving of souls."[24]

If the progressive gospel also sought to save the world, environmentalism had a much different idea concerning the correct route. In what many consider a bible of environmental fundamentalism, Bill Devall and George Sessions in *Deep Ecology* condemn "the ultimate value judgment on which [current] technological society rests—*progress* conceived as the further development and expansion of the artificial environment at the expense of the natural world." This modern culture of environmental destruction is based on ideas of "modern scientific management" that seek to achieve "more efficient production of commodities." In the end, Devall and Sessions conclude that our present-day technological society has created a place where human beings are alienated not only "from the rest of Nature but also . . . from themselves and from each other." [25]

Devall and Sessions are of the view that, despite the claims of social scientists to leave out values in their professional capacities, the "scientists and technologists" actually do "not have objective, neutral answers." The values enter in ways that the technical experts may not themselves fully understand. Thus, when "resource economists look at wilderness," their professional orientation makes them simply incapable of really "seeing it." Economists automatically incorporate their core values based on "the premise of instrumental rationality—the narrowly utilitarian view"—into any thinking about the natural world. Devall and Sessions therefore call for a much diminished role in society for economists because they are unable "to distinguish vital human needs from mere desires, egotistical arrogance and adventurism in technology." [26]

Portrayals of utopia in the past commonly described urban settings of marvelous scientific invention and productivity where everyone could live in full material abundance with all the finer things of life. In a more recent popular utopia, however, this image has been turned on its head. Ernest Callenbach describes rural life in a Pacific Northwest "Ecotopia" that has seceded from the rest of the United States to provide a much simpler existence. A main reason for breaking away has been the deep offensiveness to the residents of Ecotopia of the "underlying national philosophy of America: ever-continuing progress, the fruits of industrialization for all, a rising Gross National Product." [27]

From this perspective, it is thus perhaps not surprising that many environmentalists have declared an antagonism toward the economics profession. A well-known journal of environmental opinion declared that "behind a facade of neutrality and analysis," economists traditionally have pushed for policies of "growth-at-all-costs." The members of the economics profession, fellow environmentalists were warned, should be recognized as the leading current "enemies of the environment."[28] Writing in another journal, *Environmental Ethics,* philosopher Bryan Norton posed the question for discussion of "why environmentalists hate mainstream economists." American environmentalism, Norton suggested, reflects a "fundamental rejection of the paradigm of neoclassical economics as a guide to environmental policy." Indeed, "environmental activists believe that an environmental policy based on purely economic reasoning results in the destruction, rather than the protection, of nature."[29]

Some environmentalists disagree and argue that the market can in fact be a powerful instrument for environmental improvement.* Most activists of the environmental movement are in fact typically ignorant of economic arguments; American environmentalism is a moral movement above all. Regarded as a practical matter, most air and water pollution and other environmental harms have resulted from past failures of economic policy. A market system without a suitable structure of property rights, for example, will inevitably yield "pollution" (nonmarket spillovers) in a host of forms. Environmental moralism may provide the political energy but the practical details for solving most environmental problems will have to come from improved economic policies.[30] Environmentalists who might wish to incorporate both moral and practical considerations in their thinking would do well to take a course in environmental economic policy.

Norton is more concerned, however, with the value implications of the economic way of thinking, not the technical efficiency of its proposed solutions or the use of economic instruments to find pragmatic solutions to real-world environmental problems. Part of the problem, Norton says, is that economists construct their social ideals exclusively in terms of human welfare; economics is strictly "anthropocentric."† A more basic problem, however, is the doctrine of consumer sovereignty by which human well-being is measured solely by the maximization of utility under given preferences. Environmentalists, Norton argues, instead want to "transform values." In contrast to the assumptions of neoclassical economic analysis, environmentalists

---

* The leading environmental organization that often takes this view is Environmental Defense (formerly the Environmental Defense Fund). Although not a part of the activist environmental movement, Resources for the Future in Washington, D.C., has also long argued in its research studies for the practical use of economic incentives and mechanisms to achieve environmental purposes.

† This common argument in environmental debates, it must be said, seems to reflect an element of confusion. Any policy action taken to protect the environment will be based on human thoughts and concerns, and in this respect will necessarily be "anthropocentric" as well. Until the day arrives that animals and trees are able to participate in public debates, and to propose government policy measures, any actions taken with respect to the environment would seem to be anthropocentric. The real issue is the proper form that the inevitable anthropocentrism should take.

have a "belief in the dynamic nature of human values" and—like adherents of other religions—seek above all to alter values in the right directions.[31] In reducing the impacts of modern civilization on the natural environment, Americans should accept a lower level of consumption as a central value and goal in and of itself.

Whatever one thinks of the practical feasibility of this idea, it is hardly without precedent.[32] Calvinist theology warned of the dangers to the soul of an excess of consumption.[33] The very purpose of most religions—Jewish and Christian in addition to environmental—is to change the way people think about the world. Religion is not as much about satisfying existing preferences it is as about changing preferences. Economics not only neglects this dimension of human existence but—intentionally or not—often seems actively hostile (it would undermine many economists' models, for one thing). It is yet another way in which a powerful implicit value judgment is often expressed in the methods of economic analysis.★

★ The winner of the 1993 Nobel Prize in economics, University of Chicago economist Robert Fogel, has recently departed from conventional methods of economic analysis to venture daringly into the realms of history and theology, as they interact with political and economic events. He offers a grand interpretation of the course of American history from its Massachusetts Puritan beginnings, focusing on four religious "great awakenings" as the defining moments in this history. The first Great Awakening took place in the 1740s and 1750s, and the forces it set loose in society eventually led to the American Revolution and the founding of the United States. The second Great Awakening reached a peak in the 1820s and 1830s, and its moral energies in opposition to slavery and other social evils led to the Civil War and the resulting triumph in the United States of a vision of a single national community of all Americans governed together by federal authority.

The third Great Awakening took place in the 1890s and early 1900s, associated with the social gospel movement and the reform movements of the Progressive Era. This third religious revival laid the foundations for the development in the twentieth century of the American welfare and regulatory state (as well as less lasting changes such as Prohibition). The most novel element of Fogel's new grand tour of American history is his belief that a fourth great religious awakening began in the United States in the 1960s. It offered once again powerful new challenges to the corruptions and follies of existing authority—eroding the influence not only of the secular religions of material progress but also the mainstream denominations of the old Protestant establishment. Christian energies shifted to more evangelical and fundamentalist faiths and sought to reform politics through efforts such as the Christian Coalition. Environmentalism offered a secular manifestation of related reform impulses. The ultimate political and social impact of this fourth American Great Awakening still remains to be seen.

Fogel comments that "this turn in perceptions [from the 1960s on] was not immediately obvious to those of us who inhabited the world of science"—a group that would include Samuelson and indeed most professional economists of the past half century who tended to be oblivious, as well as Fogel himself. They had failed to recognize that at the most fundamental level new and powerful moral and religious challenges were welling up from the depths of American society to the scientific and economic triumphalism of their own generational elite, associated with the progressive gospel of efficiency and other expressions of faith in progress. But Fogel has now come to a better understanding:

> The ethical crises, religious upsurge, and programmatic demands that heralded the opening decade of the Fourth Great Awakening were precipitated by a series of major technological breakthroughs that destabilized prevailing culture. Some of those unsettling advances were in

Economic religion is all the more irritating to many environmentalists today because it usually refuses to acknowledge its actual religious content. Attempts to promote dialogue have often failed in part because many of the differences between environmentalists and economists were religious in character and yet neither party wanted to—or perhaps knew how to—talk about these theological differences in any informed and sophisticated way.★ When economists claim that they are doing science, there is little room for a debate about values. As many economists regard the efforts of environmentalists, besides their ignorance of economic policy instruments being a negative element, it is also true that their plans to reduce the availability of goods and services would create new material shortages and would stir social tensions and antagonisms, in the worst case raising the grave possibility in a nuclear age of wars and other conflicts over control of resources. When they contemplate the prospect of a world of declining material outputs, progressive economists thus often reciprocate the hostile attitudes that members of the environmental movement frequently express toward the role in society of the members of the economics profession.

THE DAM VERSUS THE WILDERNESS

Samuelson's *Economics* depicts in symbols of technical economics the same kind of message as another favored setting of progressive artists, a dam construction site with heroic workers building a wonderful testimony to the

---

energy production (particularly nuclear energy), information retrieval, and communications. The unprecedented extension of control of human biology, particularly in the fields of reproductive technology and organ transplantation, also provoked widespread concern. The new technological breakthroughs raised profoundly difficult ethical and practical issues, including many that had never been considered previously, such as how to dispose of large quantities of radioactive waste. Among those who worried about these issues, some became alarmed that humanity was heading toward disaster, led by corrupt or mindless scientists and business leaders.

See Robert William Fogel, *The Fourth Great Awakening and the Future of Egalitarianism* (Chicago: University of Chicago Press, 2000), 44. See also Fogel, "Catching Up with the Economy," presidential address to the American Economic Association, January 4, 1999, *American Economic Review* 89 (March 1999).

★ There are, I believe, a number of problematic aspects to the environmental theology as explained by many leading environmentalists—especially in the more fundamentalist versions (see below). I disagree with most of my fellow economists, however, in that I think it is possible to have a theological conversation with respect to environmental policy matters. Theology was in the past and can again in the future be an area for useful discussion of leading economic, environmental, and other public issues. Indeed, theology is already heavily involved today but the theological elements tend to be submerged on both sides beneath a large body of "scientistic" camouflage that complicates the process of discussion.

powers of modern science and economics. The message in both *Economics* and in viewing a great dam is the wonderful new ability that scientific knowledge has given human beings to control nature and in general to direct outcomes in the world for human betterment. In contrast, David Brower, a former executive director of the Sierra Club and one of the inspirational leaders of the environmental movement for the past fifty years, said simply that "I hate all dams, large and small," and whatever their specific benefit-cost ratios might be.[34] One of his last crusades was to tear down the massive Glen Canyon Dam on the Colorado River, behind which Lake Powell has formed and on which two million Americans go boating and swimming each year.★

Instead of the old picture of a dam, the value system of American environmentalism today is expressed in the image of the wilderness. If a dam once symbolized human control over nature to provide water for growing crops to feed the people, and to generate electricity to light the cities, a wilderness area is defined by the Wilderness Act of 1964 as a place on earth where the impacts of human beings on nature have been minimized (where nature is "untrammeled by man" as the law reads). The remaining places in the natural world that are still free of human impacts should not be put to economic use but instead should be protected from any further human intrusion.[35] Symbolically, the creation of a wilderness area as the grandest "cathedral" of environmentalism is an affirmation of the basic value system of *Deep Ecology*—a statement that the most sacred sites on earth are precisely those places where evidence of the products of human technology and the pursuit of economic progress is the most limited.[36]

In Calvinist theology, those who aim the highest will often fall the farthest, owing to the grave weaknesses of reason and other incapacities of human beings in their deeply fallen condition. If in the eighteenth century the Enlightenment looked to human reason and to the redeeming powers of worldly progress, partly in reaction to the "doom and gloom" of sixteenth- and seventeenth-century Protestant religion, the environmental fundamentalists of today are asserting that those Calvinists of three hundred years ago had at least some important things right.[37]

Environmentalism can thus be seen in part as a traditional Christian critique of the moral failings of society, now repackaged for the many people (some of whom may consider themselves atheists) who in a secular age find traditional Christian language and settings less comfortable. The close affinity of environmentalism to long-standing Christian themes is suggested by the following critique, offered not long ago by a devout Christian funda-

★ The board of directors of the Sierra Club—with Brower as a member—endorsed the proposal to tear down Glen Canyon Dam.

mentalist of the old-fashioned kind. The concern here is more with the modern destruction of "natural" elements of family life than with the loss of natural elements of wilderness areas. In other respects, this Christian is barely distinguishable from the environmental critique of the moral failings of modern technological and industrial society. As Allan Carlson, president of the Rockford Institute, explains, there is today a "paradox of an age of abundance and wealth that is also an age of moral degeneration and family decline." Despite the existence of "a cornucopia of material goods, rising average incomes, and longer life spans," many things are getting worse rather than better, including "an unprecedented level of family breakup."[38] All this raises basic questions:

> Are these two developments related? Does the rise of industry cause family breakup? And if so, is it possible to find a way to have both material abundance and family virtue? Can we craft a virtuous economy?
>
> To the first question, the obvious . . . answer is "yes": Modern industrial production tends, by its very nature, to undermine the material and psychological foundations of the economy.
>
> Through the industrial production of physical goods, wealth does grow further by the extra gains that come from this exaggerated division of labor. But these material gains exact a price in loss of family solidarity and independence.
>
> [Society should instead pursue] models of an economic Third Way. . . . Family renewal would come *only* as certain tasks or functions were protected from immersion into industry, or deindustrialized and returned to the household. Under these models, the measure of economic success would not be monetary "growth" of the official, statistical economy, for, as we have seen, much of what is called growth is actually the obverse side of family decline.[39]

Carlson and David Brower, as surprised as each might have been to hear it, are bedfellows in their fears of the corrupting effects of modern economic influences. The devil still lurks around many corners. Sin still takes many forms, corrupting the innocence not only of the family but also of the world of wild nature as Adam and Eve first saw it.

AGAINST ENVIRONMENTAL FUNDAMENTALISM

Carried to its full logical conclusions, and whatever elements of truth it may contain, in the end a fundamentalist environmental theology grounded in an old-fashioned Calvinist way of thinking leads to an impossible outcome.[40] In the original Calvinism, the presence of God could always give meaning to the current depravity of human existence and hold out the prospect of a future salvation in the hereafter. When the Calvinist outlook takes a secular form, however, there is no god to rescue human beings, to offer them the hope at some point in the future of transcending their existing gravely sinful natures. As human populations grow rapidly and other species decline, the human presence might logically enough even come to be seen—as Brower, Dave Foreman, and some other leading environmental preachers have in fact already said—as the "cancer of the earth." In recently recanting the mistaken "misanthropic" attitudes of her youth, a current (and still radical, but now seeking radical human solutions as well) environmentalist, Anne Petermann, described that former outlook on the world: "When I was a teenager, I was deeply misanthropic. I loved nature and spent as much time as possible out of doors. But at night, I would look out the window at the Burger King across the street, at the gas stations on all sides, at the noisy stinking stream of traffic, and I would loathe humanity, dreaming of its demise. When I found Earth First!, the campfire chants of 'Billions are living that should be dead' or 'fuck the human race' appealed to me. Yes, I thought, humans are a cancer on the Earth."[41] As the distinguished environmental historian William Cronon explains, "If nature dies because we enter it, then the only way to save nature is to kill ourselves." In short, a narrowly Calvinist path—in the absence of any ultimate saving graces of the old Calvinist God—can today offer only "a self-defeating counsel of despair."[42]

The common environmental fundamentalist way of thinking about wilderness leads to a theological logic that is beset with a number of major problems. Wilderness is conceived by many environmentalists as true nature outside human impact. One problem is that—especially when native peoples are included in the picture, as they must be—there are almost no places on earth that are true wilderness; significant human impacts have already touched virtually every part of the globe. The most significant prehistoric impacts of native human populations on nature were often the result of the deliberate manipulation of fire. We now know that, for example, before European settlement, fire was a pervasive presence in the forests and rangelands of the Western United States. Native Americans actively used fire as a way of manipulating the landscape for hunting, transportation, farming, and other purposes. As the leading student of the history of fire, Stephen Pyne, has commented, "It is often assumed that the American Indian was incapable of greatly modifying his environment and that he would not have been much interested in doing so if he did have the capabilities." The truth is much dif-

ferent; "he possessed both the tool and the will to use it. That tool was fire."
Indeed, fire for American Indians was "a wonderful instrument, without
which most Indian economies would have collapsed."[43]

In suggesting that wilderness areas have been largely free of human impact, the manner of treatment of environmental fundamentalism is unfortunately reminiscent of earlier thinking about American Indians. To continue
to assert that pre-European conditions are "natural," and current conditions
are not, as Pyne has commented, amounts to "stripping American Indians of
the power to shape their environment;" it is an act that "is tantamount to dis-
missing their humanity."[44]

In other words, to suggest that Indian actions are "natural" is to put Indians in the same category as wolves, grizzly bears, and other nonhumans. In
effect, if unintentionally on the part of so many environmental thinkers, it
would revert to the most blatant of anti-Indian prejudices of the past—when
Indians could actually be treated as virtually nonhuman because they did not
worship the same God, because they were not rationally responsible for their
actions, or for other such theological reasons. Cotton Mather believed in his
deep Puritan convictions that the Massachusetts Indians were active disciples
of the devil. The Puritan settlers had been brought by God to the new world
to reclaim its territories for His greater glory. Such grounds were in fact then
and for many years to come offered for slaughtering Indian populations,
cheating on treaty obligations, moving Indians around from one place to another, and other actions now greatly regretted.

Surely, a return to such old ways of thinking about American Indians is
not what any environmental activist would wish to advocate. Yet in value
and philosophical terms—theological terms, broadly speaking—that is what
many of them are implicitly saying. In this newest incarnation of the old Indian prejudices, Indians once again do not count. Before European settlement, many environmentalists have in effect been telling us, there really was
only wild nature.

Another problem of theological reasoning in the environmental fundamentalist mode lies in the very concept of wilderness. Just as a church is
much more than the bundle of stone and bricks from which it is built,
wilderness does not exist in a physical sense alone. It is a creation of the
human mind. If a Roman Catholic cathedral has been transformed into a
place of spiritual inspiration by a set of church teachings and rituals and as an
exercise of human imagination, it requires an act of Congress to create a
wilderness. This legislative action transforms the very human perception of
the area (as is manifested concretely in the much larger number of visitors
who then are likely to come there to visit). Wilderness cannot be said to be

merely nature untouched by human action any more than the Bible is merely a large number of stories on paper all collected and bound together. Both the Bible and wilderness in fact are commonly seen by the faithful as ways of learning about God. Or as Cronon puts it, the idea of "Nature has become a secular deity in this post-romantic age." What is found in wilderness may not be nature at all but "virtual nature"—a vision of "nature as Eden" that amounts to "nature as artifice, nature as self-conscious cultural construction." [45]

Wilderness stands as a metaphor that makes a powerful symbolic statement of core tenets of environmental fundamentalist belief. Cronon explains that "wilderness serves as the unexamined foundation on which so many of the quasi-religious values of modern environmentalism rest." Yet, these values are problematic because "the romantic ideology of wilderness leaves precisely nowhere for human beings actually to make their living from the land." The Sierra Club has officially endorsed a goal of excluding timber harvesting altogether from the national forests of the United States—representing 10 percent of the land area of the lower forty-eight states, and as much as 40 percent of the land area of one state, Idaho. Even if the timber harvesting can be done in an environmentally sound fashion, that is not the point for the Sierra Club. Timber harvesting is an evil to be purged from the land. Similarly, rather than seeking ways to design a new ski area to accommodate outdoor recreation for large numbers of people in an attractive mountain setting, the environmental movement is increasingly opposed to any such intrusions on "nature." The environmental movement, as Cronon thinks, needs to spend more time working to improve the flower beds of the local public gardens and less time in campaigning to keep the land in Alaska as wilderness foreclosed to any further development. In the end, the unwillingness or inability of environmental fundamentalism to seek ways of reconciling human beings and nature, as reflected in the wilderness value system, exerts an influence on contemporary environmental policy making that Cronon believes is both "pervasive" and "insidious." [46]

SAMUELSON VERSUS THE POPE

When William F. Buckley attended Yale University in the late 1940s, Samuelson's *Economics* was just being introduced to introductory economics courses there. As he memorably detailed in his first book, *God and Man at Yale,* Buckley found the environment at Yale hostile to the Catholic faith in which he had been brought up. Reflecting the secular temper of the times, many of his professors, Buckley related, were actively hostile to Christianity and often ridiculed the faith in their lectures. The faculty of the Yale economics department did not say much about religion per se, but in other ways reflected the prevailing triumphal status of the progressive gospel.

Thus, in 1951 Buckley directed some specific barbs at *Economics,* that it preached a "brand of collectivism" and did not even bother to describe the long history of distinguished economic thought in Western civilization that had developed a set of "individualist" ideas.★ Any contemporaries who tried to criticize "the collectivists' program," if mentioned at all, were subject to a "savage" treatment in *Economics* and other economics textbooks used at Yale. Thus, as Buckley related with his customary sarcasm, "Samuelson states . . . one cannot believe in minimum government and be a 'modern man,' to which it is to be assumed, we all aspire." [47]

In the 1950s and 1960s, with the secularization of American society proceeding full bore, any Catholic or other religious prescriptions on economic matters tended to be met with indifference or dismissal. However, as the doubts about science and progress grew in the later part of the twentieth century, traditional religion began to make a comeback in the policy arena. According to a researcher at the Center for the Study of American Religion at Princeton University, there is a "religious revival" taking place today on college campuses. Students are exploring an "explosion of new religious forms" as they seek "new ways of believing and behaving in their search for a richer, more meaningful way of being in the world" and are seeking to apply these beliefs in concrete ways. [48]

Perhaps reflecting an emerging sense of a greater relevance of church teachings to public policy, the Catholic bishops of the United States by the mid-1980s issued a pastoral message titled "Catholic Social Teaching and the U.S. Economy." The American bishops stated that "to stand before God as the creator is to respect God's creation, both the world of nature and of human history. From the patristic period to the present, the Church has affirmed that misuse of the world's resources . . . betrays the gift of creation." [49] If economics is about the allocation of society's resources, including the management of natural resources, the American Catholic bishops were say-

---

★ Samuelson and Buckley represented different sides, one might say, of the Roman tradition of thought. Buckley put his faith in Rome, Samuelson in Washington, D.C. Buckley looked to the truths of God as revealed by the Catholic Church, Samuelson to the truths of nature and society as revealed by science. Yet both have had a faith in a rational world governed by the natural laws of their respective gods.

ing that God's plan for the world should be entering significantly into public decisions. *

Further church pronouncements have followed. In 1991 in *Centesimus Annis,* the leading encyclical of Pope John Paul II's papacy on economic matters, the pope warned against tendencies to find in "politics" an alternative belief system—a "secular religion," as he explicitly labeled such a creed—that offers the promise, rather than of a Christian heaven in the hereafter, of "creating paradise in this world."[50] The pope did not mention Samuelson, but *Economics* might have served to illustrate his point. In rich nations, the pope went on, there were tendencies toward "an excessive promotion of purely utilitarian values, with an appeal to the appetites and inclinations towards immediate gratification," all this in opposition to the "true values of human existence."[51] John Paul II endorsed "a society of free work, of enterprise and participation"—central to the workings of a market economy—but also declared that profit must not dominate "the life of a business." There were "other human and moral factors . . . which . . . are at least equally important" in the conduct of business affairs—such as "truth, beauty, goodness and communion with others." Indeed, "even the decision [by a business] to invest in one place rather than another, in one productive sector rather than another, is always *a moral and cultural choice"*—and the moral criteria, the pope did not have to say, were to be found in the teachings of the Roman Catholic Church.[52]

In a later encyclical, "Gospel of Life," the pope warned of the great dangers in a view of the human condition such as found in the writings of Gary Becker. As John Paul II declared, modern society affirmed false "cultural models" that depicted the historic teachings of the Roman Catholic Church on "fidelity, chastity, sacrifice, to which a host of Christian wives and mothers have borne . . . outstanding witness," as having become "obsolete." However, the pope regarded the modern values that had dominated intellectual views over much of the twentieth century as having promoted a series of

---

* The religious framework, if taken seriously, could have large effects on the character of resource-allocation decisions. The large distance between the mainstream of the American economics profession and the Roman Catholic vision is suggested by the following passage from the bishop's letter, typical of many Catholic pronouncements over the years. "The quality of the national discussion about our economic future will affect the poor most of all, in this country and throughout the world. The life and dignity of millions of men, women and children hang in the balance. [Economic] decisions must be judged in light of what they do for the poor, what they do to the poor, and what they enable the poor to do for themselves. The fundamental moral criterion for all economic decisions, policies, and institutions is this: They must be at the service of all people, especially the poor." See "Excerpts from Final Draft of Bishop's Letter on the Economy," *New York Times,* November 14, 1986, A14.

"massive attacks on life," including the pursuit of unjust "wars and a continual taking of innocent human life" in the Holocaust, other genocidal events, and (in the pope's view) the pervasive practice of abortion.[53]

At the heart of modern values such as both Samuelson and Becker preached, the pope found there existed a contemporary "culture [that] is actively fostered by powerful cultural, economic and political currents which encourage an idea of society excessively concerned with efficiency."[54] If modern economists had made "efficiency" and "inefficiency" the secular replacements for "good" and "evil," Pope John Paul II was announcing that such forms of economic thinking had promulgated a great anti-Christian heresy. The false preachings of the economists of the modern era bore a large responsibility for the breakdown of the family, the crime, the indifference to suffering, the assaults on the natural environment, and other grave failings of the world of the late twentieth century. The pope further explained his views in this regard:

> The eclipse of the sense of God and of man inevitably leads to a practical materialism, which breeds individualism, utilitarianism and hedonism. Here too we see the permanent validity of the words of the apostle: "And since they did not see fit to acknowledge God, God gave them up to a base mind and to improper conduct." The values of being are replaced by those of having. The only goal which counts is the pursuit of one's own material well-being. The so-called "quality of life" is interpreted primarily as economic efficiency, inordinate consumerism, physical beauty and pleasure, to the neglect of the more profound dimensions—interpersonal, spiritual and religious— of existence.[55]

The pope, and others in the Roman Catholic Church, have been articulate about the religious problems associated with modern values such as are preached in Samuelson's *Economics* or in Becker's writings on the family and many other subjects. However, they have been less successful in developing a viable alternative economic vision.[56] Much like contemporary environmental fundamentalists (with whom the pope shares an obvious large affinity), they offer a high moral sensitivity that has not been accompanied by a similar economic knowledge and sophistication. Like others in the Catholic tradition going all the way back to medieval theologians such as Aquinas, Pope John Paul II has no problem with the existence of competitive markets or the creation of material well-being per se.[57] His objection is to the elevation of material concerns to the sources of absolute religious truths, to the vision of the perfection of human existence here on earth by a route of economic salvation.★ In such beliefs one finds perhaps the most powerful religious competition to the historic teachings of the Roman Catholic Church.

How to maintain the practical benefits of free markets, while avoiding the elevation of a vision of the market into a religion unto itself, poses a dilemma that Catholic theologians and others in the Roman Catholic Church have found difficult to resolve.[58] The problem is made all the more complex because, as I have argued in this book, it takes a religious blessing for the market to overcome the large collective action obstacles that can greatly impede successful market performance. The poorer economic results in Catholic Latin America relative to Protestant North America, and most of the rest of the world as well, one is tempted to speculate, may be attributable at least in part to a failure of Catholic theologians there to satisfactorily resolve this theological conundrum that lies in the market paradox.†

MODERN CONSUMERISM

For most of human history, most people have been preoccupied with getting enough food to eat, seeking shelter from bad weather, obtaining relief from

---

★ Given the close identification of the civic religion of America with redemptive ideas of progress on earth, however, the pope and the Roman Catholic Church are left with a delicate problem of rejecting secular progressive religion without also rejecting the very idea of America itself. Indeed, some Roman Catholic writers have concluded that it is impossible to find a satisfactory compromise. And if a choice is necessary, they propose to opt for the Catholic Church with a full recognition of the corollary that much of what America stands for will have to be rejected as well.

Thus, a writer for a magazine dedicated to halting secularizing trends within the Roman Catholic Church finds that a chief obstacle is the very power of "American messianism." The historic role of the Roman Catholic Church (and other churches) has in America been "replaced with the secular principles of Americanism. As the social critic Will Herberg has said, 'the American Way of Life is the operative faith of the American people.'" Moreover, this "civil religion of Progress and the American Way of Life" is officially taught in school and otherwise has the powerful support of government and other institutions, leaving traditional Jewish and Christian religion "relegated to the private realm, at best a prop for personal morality or a solace." All in all, the very Church of America, grounded in its national religion of economic progress and opportunity for all, is a directly competing religion representing "a secular messianic dream which no orthodox Catholic can accept." See Thomas Storck, "The Americanization of the Globe," *New Oxford Review* 65 (February 1998): 27, 25–26, 26, 27.

This is in fact a long-standing issue in Roman Catholic theology, dating to a papal pronouncement of the late nineteenth century rejecting the Americanization of the church in the United States. Many Catholic theologians have since struggled with the question of the degree to which the idea of America is itself a competing religious vision that represents a heretical threat to the true faith. See John Courtney Murray, *We Hold These Truths: Catholic Reflections on the American Proposition* (New York: Sheed and Ward, 1960).

† On a long-term basis, Latin America has had a poorer record of economic growth than any other part of the world except sub-Saharan Africa, falling behind China, India, the rest of Asia, and Northern Africa. See Richard A. Easterlin, "The Worldwide Standard of Living Since 1800," *Journal of Economic Perspectives* 14 (Winter 2000): 11.

disease, finding clothing to wear, and meeting of other basic needs. By now, however, these basic requirements have been largely met for most people living in the developed parts of the world. Why, then, do so many people still seem to pursue consumption as aggressively as ever? The operating assumption of economic religion had long been that as material needs were more and more satisfied, people would increasingly turn their attention to other, higher parts of life.

One possible answer might be that there are much different motives at work in "modern" consumer behavior. Such consumptive efforts may involve the active pursuit of consumption well beyond the point of satisfaction of material needs. It is a subject of obvious great importance to the religions that seek salvation along a path of economic progress. If consumer appetites are insatiable, there will be no prospect of attaining a heaven on earth by the expected material route. There may instead be a never ending cycle of higher consumer demands, higher production to meet these demands, higher incomes and then still higher demands, and so forth and so on. Thorstein Veblen many years ago had suggested that this might be the case in his discussion of "conspicuous consumption" in the *Theory of the Leisure Class*.[59] Fred Hirsch, in 1976, developed a similar argument.[60] People often did not acquire more and more goods and services to meet physical material needs. Rather, they were seeking to obtain "positional" goods—such as an expensive diamond, or a "trophy house" at a ski resort—as a means of demonstrating to others their higher status in the social hierarchy.

To the extent that this is true, if present-day consumption has become mainly a race for status, achieving ever higher levels of production of goods and services will have limited effects on human welfare. It will be like an arms race where each side acquires more and more weapons but with no resulting increase in their overall military security. In this light economist Robert Frank suggests, for example, that higher levels of income taxation would be desirable.[61] Even if the higher taxation created a major disincentive for increased material production, there would be little or no loss of welfare in society—the tax would be the functional equivalent of a disarmament treaty negotiated to end an arms race. Taxing the income of the wealthy at a significantly higher rate, Frank believes, would work even better because it would generate the money for the government to take care of those few remaining people in American society who still face any real consumptive deprivation in ordinary material terms.

Robert Lane, professor emeritus of political science at Yale, also thinks that the basic character of modern consumption has changed. As he states, historically there has been a "preoccupation with scarcity that is our inheritance from millenia of hunter-gatherer and peasant life." This has fooled many people into thinking that "more material resources are a prime source of happiness." Yet, as Lane observes, the twentieth century has put this proposition to various forms of empirical test. Most people in the United States, western Europe, and other economically advanced countries experienced rapid growth over the course of the twentieth century to the extent that their basic material needs were met. It is surprising that on the basis of psychological studies of the incidence of clinical depression, Lane finds that "precisely those countries that have experienced or are currently experiencing rapid economic growth have the highest incidence of depression." It was during the 1960s, when there was a "marked increase in disposable income," that there was a rapid rise in cases of depression in the United States, along with other signs of general "decreased happiness."[62] The dynamic processes of rapid economic change—upsetting old habits and causing people constantly to be on guard against losses of income or status—may in themselves be a source of great disutility.*

Having surveyed various studies on this matter, Lane finds that "there is ample evidence that within advanced economies, the rich are no happier than the less rich. In general, above the poverty line, happiness (or its pale, vulgar companion, average utility) does not change much or at all as level of income increases." Rather than with money, happiness in Lane's view is more closely correlated with "self-esteem" that is "unrelated to levels of income" but is instead closely associated with circles of "friendship" and a sense of being a member of one or another "intimate groups"—yet another person who is in basic agreement with the arguments of Frank Knight in this regard.[63] To the extent that the processes of economic progress may at the same time undermine networks of friendship and other stable personal associations, many people may find themselves affected in negative ways by economic growth and development.

At least for those who can maintain their good physical health (perhaps the one area where more money and the products of a modern economic system can still bring clear additional benefits in well-being), nonmodern cultures that offer strong social cohesiveness are often happier than economically richer societies where people live more atomistic, lonelier lives.[64] Lane argues elsewhere that the workings of markets are a main contributing factor

---

* Admittedly, this does not necessarily undermine the hopes of the progressive gospel. One could argue that current generations have to suffer (perhaps including greater incidences of depression) in order that their sacrifice can make it possible for future generations to reach heaven on earth. However, the idea that people might feel worse in a time of rising material possessions does call into question the basic relationship between the satisfaction of material requirements of life and the achievement of human happiness and contentment.

in this outcome.[65] As discussed previously in Part II of the present book, if the value considerations Lane is raising were taken seriously, it would be virtually impossible to derive any policy conclusions from the methods of most economic theory at present. Economists and economics derive their strong policy views from a longstanding implicit agreement simply to set aside such matters of transitional impacts of economic growth on communities and other groups.

Colin Campbell is yet another social scientist who has taken up the subject of why we consume and what impact it actually has on our sense of well-being. Campbell argues that modern consumption is not really about finding pleasure at all but about acts of self-improvement. In a wide-ranging intellectual history addressing the formation of attitudes toward consumption over several centuries, Campbell shows how "much of the Puritan tradition was carried forward into [nineteenth-century] Romanticism," which in turn fostered the habits of thought characteristic of the modern consumer.[66] On the whole, surprising as it may seem at first, the modern impulse to seek happiness and pleasure in the act of consumption is in Campbell's view a displaced and secularized set of Calvinist habits of thought.

> It is now possible to state the general nature of the conclusion reached concerning the relationship between the romantic ethic and the spirit of modern consumerism. The latter, labeled self-illusory hedonism, is characterized by a longing to experience in reality those pleasures created and enjoyed in imagination, a longing which results in the ceaseless consumption of novelty. Such an outlook, with its characteristic dissatisfaction with real life and an eagerness for new experiences, lies at the heart of much conduct that is most typical of modern life, and underpins such central institutions as fashion and romantic love. . . . In particular, romantic teachings concerning the good, the true and the beautiful, provide both the legitimation and motivation necessary for modern consumer behavior to become prevalent throughout the contemporary industrial world.[67]

Campbell observes that "traditional consumption" at an earlier stage of history was directed to meeting essential requirements of survival but that "as the advance of civilization causes fewer people to experience the frequent deprivation of their basic needs, . . . the pleasure associated with need fulfillment tends to become more and more elusive." In the transition to modern consumption, "the basic motivation underlying consumerism is the desire to experience in reality that pleasurable experience the consumer has always enjoyed imaginatively." That is to say, the stepping into "daydreams" motivates the modern consumer, who looks to the realization of such fantasies virtually as his or her own artistic project.[68] If one daydream is realized, however, it is promptly succeeded by another. Thus, modern consumer wants are never met: "No sooner is one want satisfied than another appears, and subsequently another, in an apparently endless series." If the progressive hopes for heaven on earth rested on an assumption that a state of total abundance would end all consumptive concerns in life, Campbell's thinking suggests that any such view is based on a grand misconception. The reality of modern consumption is that it is grounded in a constant search for novelty and therefore yields "inexhaustible wants."[69]

CONCLUSION

In their daily interactions in the political arena, environmentalists and libertarians often do not get along. This has tended to obscure a fundamental area of agreement.[70] Both the environmental and libertarian movements emerged in significant part to protest the false claims of the progressive value system. Both have been hostile to the claims of national governments that they should be given the power and autonomy to realize a regime of scientific management of society. The antagonism of libertarians in this regard requires no elaboration but many environmental activists also began their careers protesting new highways, power plants, dams, and other federal government projects designed to provide energy, water, and other outputs, all part of the scientific management of society for economic progress.

Until the "revolution of 1989," the old Soviet Union and the countries of Eastern Europe were the last bastions of true faith in the redeeming benefits of technology and industrial advance. Their lack of democracy limited other views in society from being heard or having much say in the workings of government. Libertarians condemned these governments for their abuses of human freedom but it was also no coincidence that the same governments were among the worst abusers of the environment in the world, all in the name of particular versions of "scientific management" of society.

Over the years, the Chicago school of economics has opposed the progressive vision of scientific management, but has typically defended the basic values of material progress and economic efficiency. The one large exception was Frank Knight, who also doubted the possibilities for any improvement in the human condition based on material progress. He rejected the prevailing euphoria with respect to science, including the efforts of the economics profession to develop in a scientific mode. Knight instead saw the attempts to extend scientific methods into human domains as a basic threat to human liberty. If Knight was in essence a "secular Calvinist," he regarded scientific management by the government in Washington with about the same degree of mistrust that the original Calvin had felt for the efforts of the church in Rome. Knight in effect called for a new Protestant revolution against the illegitimate central usurpers of authority, now including the modern welfare and regulatory state in this category.

Almost uniquely among leading American economists of the twentieth century, Knight thus achieves a form of synthesis of libertarian and environmental strains of thought. It seems likely that the American progressive gospel is on its last legs; it survives today by inertia and habit more than by any remaining depth of conviction.* It follows that the legitimacy of American government in the twenty-first century is likely to require some new governing vision. As the most articulate critics of the progressive gospel, the libertarian and environmental movements are likely to be important con-

---

* Harry Boyte, best known as the author of *The Backyard Revolution* in favor of a new localism, has recently commented that "today, we are like the citizens of the Soviet bloc in 1989, governed by a dead ideology few believe in, but one that shapes our lives." The economics profession has been the leading priesthood of this secular religion:

> American graduate students in economics learned an ethos of scientific "objectivity" and a model of policy making in private consultation with political leadership, far removed from public involvement. It was fed by the philosophers of positivism, who argued that science rested on the discovery of permanent, atemporal standards of rationality that could be found and applied. Scientific method was purported to be pure. Its aim was to find abstract, universal truths "out there" that could be brought back to enlighten the masses, like the philosopher king returns to Plato's cave.
>
> Despite its all-pervasiveness in practice, few theorists of knowledge or science any longer defend this notion of the "objective search for truth." Science, as many have demonstrated, is itself a process full of trial-and-error, messiness, ambiguity, and social interaction and cooperation, far different than positivists imagined. More broadly, thinkers from an enormous range of fields—from pragmatic philosophy and interpretive social theory to women's studies and action research—have shaped an alternative pragmatic ground for knowledge theory. . . . It is provisional, contextually relevant, open-ended, evolving, best emerged from real world problems, and needs constant testing through practical action.

See Harry C. Boyte, "The Public Sides of Work: Building Mediating Institutions for the Information Age," *The Good Society* 9, no. 3 (2000): 28–29. See also Boyte, *The Backyard Revolution: Understanding the New Citizen Movement* (Philadelphia: Temple University Press, 1980).

The task for political philosophy of the next generation will in one perspective be to adapt American political and economic institutions to this new conception of social knowledge, so different from that of the progressive gospel of efficiency and its hopes for the scientific management of society—the underlying knowledge vision of social science and the basis for the welfare and regulatory state of the twentieth century. While there are obviously great uncertainties, as Boyte suggests, it also seems clear that the new philosophies of knowledge will imply a significant decentralization of political authority, as compared with the centralizing impetus associated with past hopes for one "scientific" truth of society.

tributors. The moral and political philosophy of Frank Knight is only one of many possible ways of seeking a synthesis. His Calvinistic vision of fallen humanity in the iron grip of sin may be too pessimistic for the basic American temperament. Yet the very fact of Knight's having made the effort—to find a new governing model that rejects the redemptive hopes for science and progress as a starting point, but yet is also sophisticated in its economic understanding—is a significant development in itself. In the future other economists may have to look more to Knight's work for inspiration as they seek to reconcile science, economics, and religion.

CONCLUSION

The most vital religion of the modern age has been economic progress. If economists have had a modest impact in actually generating this progress, or even understanding the actual mechanisms by which it has occurred, they have had a large role in giving it social legitimacy. They have been the modern priesthood of the religion of progress, interpreting its forms, refining its messages, and assuring the faithful that progress would continue. Without the blessings of an authoritative priesthood, all kinds of opportunistic and predatory forces are always lurking in wait in society, holding the potential to undermine the workings of the market as well as other core institutions. By promoting a culture of civic commitment to the market system, economists have put the power of religion to work in fending off these newer temptations of a modern kind of "devil." ★

In their routine professional activities, economists spend much of their time giving the belief in progress a set of compelling religious symbols. If economists are closer to Thomas Aquinas than to Isaac Newton, it is also true that they are related to Michelangelo. In writing the *Summa Theologica,* Aquinas produced a great work of religious inspiration; in painting the Sistine Chapel, Michelangelo was also engaged in a mission of inspiring faith. Samuelson had a related purpose—if not likely such lasting success—in *Economics.*

In the modern age, the symbols that have been capable of arousing the most powerful religious devotion have not been scenes from the Bible, or other renditions of traditional Jewish and Christian themes. Rather, like the heroic portrayals of workers occupied in the construction of a large dam, or the images of the U.S. space program of men landing on the moon and other

★ As sociologist Peter Berger, writing on the failure of current sociology to address the central questions of society, has said (and with equal applicability to economics):

> This is a basic theoretical point that much of sociologizing has routinely overlooked. The "problem" is not social disorganization, but social organization—marriage rather than divorce, law-abidingness rather than crime, racial harmony rather than strife, and so on. We may safely assume that . . . the "common human pattern" is faithlessness, violence and hate. These manifestations of human nature hardly need explanation, except perhaps by zoologists. What needs explaining is those instances in which, amazingly, societies manage to curb and civilize these propensities.

See Peter Berger, "Sociology: A Disinvitation?" *Society* (December 1992): 16.

explorations, they have been pictures of science and technology at work, achieving wonderful results, controlling natural processes for human benefit, contributing to the economic progress of humankind here on earth. When the object of human mastery is the economic workings of society, the scientific imagery is perhaps less graphic and less obviously compelling. It required an artist of Samuelson's skill to produce a work capable in its time of genuine inspirational qualities.

This should not be taken to suggest that professional economists have not had a great deal of useful and practical advice to give. This book is not an argument against the application of economic ideas to policy problems or against economists in government having a significant influence. I spent many years in such efforts myself. Instead, I am saying that economists have been defending their professional status in society under false pretenses. The emperor of high economic theory has no clothes. Economists have been saying one thing as a matter of theory and doing another as a matter of the daily practice of economic policy—and the doing part has often yielded significant social benefits. If the objection might be raised that this assertion presupposes a subjective definition of "benefit," the objection would be valid. However, the conclusion that economics can be useful in the policy arena requires only a minimal agreement on a desirable outcome—that health is better than illness, for example, or that being warm in winter is better than being cold.

A few rather simple economic ideas can have a great power to illuminate a wide variety of actions and events in society. Much of what economists know reduces to the observation that "incentives matter." The most important incentives are the price incentives of the marketplace. It has been important to spell these out explicitly and to consider their potential consequences. A very important message of economics is that "the market works." Economists have also played a critical role in designing and collecting the statistics by which macroeconomic trends in society are measured and monitored. They have usefully evaluated government programs for their benefits and costs and have tried to stand as an obstacle (if often with limited success) to the opportunistic forces that seek to convert many government actions to private gain.

However, these practical contributions of economists for the most part did not require any great scientific apparatus.* The argument that "the market

---

* And the parts of applied economics that have involved new scientific thinking such as econometric techniques are the areas that have particularly lost credibility. For example, *Forbes* magazine of January 21, 1991, ran a cover story titled "Goodby Economists: Why Companies Are Sacking Their Soothsayers." *Forbes* commented that "like kings of old dispensing with their astrologers, big business is sacking its economic soothsayers. Their stargazing proved entertaining and interesting—but not very useful." See Dana Wechsler Linden, "Dreary Days in the Dismal Science," *Forbes*, January 21, 1991, 68.

works" has been known for many centuries, even well before Adam Smith. It often amounts to little more than saying that a money system with prices for goods and services will outperform a barter system as an arrangement for their exchange—something recognized by all kinds of societies and stated in many times and places before modern "technical" economics. Historically, the greatest obstacle to the market is not a failure to understand its workings. Rather, the larger obstacles lie in two forms. First, many people have objected to the market for moral and ethical reasons—that is to say, they had strong religious (or quasi-religious) objections of one form or another to the wide scope for the expression of self-interest as found in the market. Second, the individual pursuit of opportunistic actions such as corruption and dishonest behavior—creating a climate in which "trust" does not exist in society—have the potential to undermine the efficient workings of markets.

The answer to both, one might say, is a religious defense of the market. If a suitable religion can be found, like other religions in other societies, it will have the potential to significantly reduce (if never eliminate altogether) the opportunistic forms of behavior that can be such a threat to market workings. And this religion should also bless the normal workings of exchange of goods and services in pursuit of individual gain within the specific context of the market system.

Beyond these practical religious functions central to the role of economic professionals in modern society, their other practical functions might be described as engaging in the "science of common sense." As a matter of intellectual content, the basic economic principles of price theory could be learned in a few days if not hours. The resistance of many students is more moral than intellectual.★ If they must be exposed to many concrete examples that show how "the market works," it is because there is a strong initial ethical predisposition to reject the message (one that many noneconomists never overcome). If the private pursuit of self-interest was long seen in Christianity as a sign of the continuing presence of sin in the world—a reminder of the fallen condition of humanity since the transgression of Adam and Eve in the Garden—a blessing for a market economy has appeared to many people as the religious equivalent of approving of the existence of sin.

Although the scientific content of economics is limited in its practical application, the economics profession still requires years of study of economic

★ The editor of a publication as much in the mainstream of American society as the *Christian Century* not long ago professed the view that: "the market is a monster because it has no conscience; it produces and sells what some segment of society will buy. And if children are harmed along the way, that is no concern to the monster; its does what its internal drive system tells it to do: defend itself against anything that interferes with its profits." See James M. Wall, "The Market Monster," *Christian Century*, August 16–23, 1995, 763.

theory to win full acceptance among its members. Part of this can be seen as developing a mastery of the religious artistry of economic progress—the capability of producing inspirational economic poetry in scientific language. Part of this long training period also serves to instill the ethics of economic professionalism involving a sense of commitment among economists to advance the common good. A further purpose of professional training is to require the budding economist to make a large investment of time and money—to offer a "hostage" that serves to "signal" his or her continuing commitment over the long run to the norms of the profession.

Yet another function served by a long professional apprenticeship is to select out those individual economists of the highest qualities. If the policy advice of economists is mainly a matter of applying their native wits, it is still important that economists should have high intellectual abilities. The process of becoming a leading economist within the profession does in fact pose a formidable obstacle course. Anyone who succeeds in this intense competition is likely to possess a high intellectual ability and other valuable skills for society. Advancing in the economics profession, in short, provides a good indication of a much broader set of competencies beyond economic theory.

Economists, like other priestly classes of history, live a secure and protected existence, often in the groves of the academy. Even if they were of ordinary intellectual capability, they would be freer to offer views independent of private interests in society. In this sense the university members of the economics profession are somewhat like the members of the Supreme Court (or the federal judicial system in general), given a lifetime tenure in hopes that they will be better able to exercise good judgment for the broader benefit of society. The Federal Reserve Bank—which conducts itself in secrecy and otherwise follows many of the rituals found at the Supreme Court—provides a similarly protected status for economists (if not for a lifetime) in a particular area of great economic importance, the conduct of national monetary policy.

It is customary in a book by an economist to address the question, What are the policy recommendations? or, What are the implications for the future?[1] However, with respect to the subjects of this book, the members of the economics profession are not likely to decide the issue in the end. Economists did not create their current role in society. They have been following a script prescribed by the broader rituals of the religion of economic progress. If in the future most Americans continue to believe in the transformative powers of economic progress, there will be a continuing demand for a priestly class to produce appropriate religious interpretation and symbolism.

Many members of the economics profession will probably be available to serve in this capacity.

However, if newer religions take hold in American society, if the religion of economic progress loses favor, society may seek altogether different groups to perform in its priestly roles, and the economics profession as we know it could well disappear altogether (although some organized group would still have to assemble economic facts and figures and provide other nuts-and-bolts advice relating to the production-and-consumption side of life). Hence, to speculate about the future of professional economics does not require economic insight as much as theological wisdom.★

As someone trained as an economist and essentially an informed amateur in theological matters, I have no special claims to predictive powers in religious areas.[2] However, it might also be said that the predictive record of those formally trained in theology is not much (or any) better—even in theological domains—than those formally trained in economics. Indeed, in some sense in this book I have been arguing that the modern members of the economics profession have proved themselves better "theologians" than those formally and officially designated by society as its experts in religion. When it comes to predicting the future of religion, there may not be any "experts."

Chapter 11, on the crisis of progress, represented the main form of specifically theological commentary included in this book. It is thus mainly a negative conclusion—that the faith in the redeeming power of material progress is fading, and in that sense perhaps the days of the various religions of progress are numbered. Some of them, including Marxism and the more doctrinaire versions of orthodox socialism, have already largely disappeared. Many people today are actively searching for religious alternatives, some of them turning to environmental fundamentalism, others to Eastern religions, or in the Middle East to Islamic fundamentalism, and still others to a rediscovery of the strengths of traditional Jewish and Christian faiths (often these days in their more evangelical and fundamentalist forms).[3] The modern propensity to find God in the laws of the material realms of society is apparently in decline.† It would be folly to try to predict exactly where this will

★ The longtime editor of the editorial page of the *Wall Street Journal*, Robert Bartley, predicts that in the twenty-first century "the big issues of society will be moral issues, that the dawn of the new millennium will witness fervent moral searching and even, at least for some, religious rebirth." See Robert L. Bartley, "A Time for Moralism," *Wall Street Journal*, May 26, 1995, A10.

† A sign of the changing thinking in the past two decades of the twentieth century was a 1980s cover story in the *Washingtonian* magazine with the headline "God Is Back: To Restore Something Lost, to Find a Date, to Add Meaning to Their Lives, to Help Their Kids, to Find Some Peace, to Save Their Marriages, Washingtonians Are Returning to Religion." Two main explanations offered for this new phenomenon were that "churches are an answer to a secular world that is losing faith in the fu-

all end up, religiously speaking. I will thus confine my final thoughts to a few conjectures that reflect my best "judgment," and that cannot be "scientifically" defended. I take it as a starting point that the institutions in society that today derive their legitimacy from the various religions of economic progress are facing a crisis of authority.

1. The modern university may be facing fundamental change, including the abolition of many of its current organizational forms. The university historically is a religious institution. Harvard, Princeton, and other American universities initially had the responsibility of educating the ministry of the nation. In the Progressive Era, as belief in economic progress for many people eroded traditional Jewish and Christian faith, the university was reorganized to fit a new religious mission—serving the requirements of the progressive gospel of efficiency for expertise in many fields, and the hopes for the scientific management of society. If progressive religion fades from the American scene, one can confidently expect (although the process of transition may be slow) to see the university remolded to fit the tenets of whatever new religious beliefs may take the place of the progressive aspirations for a salvation in this world by material progress.

2. As part of this likely reorganization of the university world, the existing social sciences—the particular instruments of the progressive hopes for the scientific management of society—are the most vulnerable. They will probably disappear in their current forms. If economic progress is no longer the religion of society, the economics profession will no longer have its special status as the leading priestly class of our time. There will still be many people who study economic subjects, however, because the economic sphere of society will still demand careful attention, whatever the ultimate religious significance may be. But the students of material progress will no longer be the holders of the keys to a secular salvation, the members of society capable of giving the most authoritative priestly blessings. Rather, economists may well be more like accountants, lawyers or, doctors, administering a necessary practical service.

3. The field of study most likely to be revived will be history. Marx knew what he was doing when he put his economic religion in the form of a the-

---

ture," and that "the substitutes for religion have proved thin gruel." For Washingtonians it had long been a tradition that "religion is not the opiate of the masses here; politics is." It was through politics that in practice the instruments of government could be put to use to save the world. Moreover, this secular salvation would take an economic form: "God manifests His favor in material ways." However, Washingtonians by the 1980s were confronting a loss of faith because politics and economics—despite the enormous resources available to the government—had "not provided the answers: to hunger, to poverty, to the dissolution of the family, to the empty spot in the center of our being that religion insists is an immortal soul." See Howard Means, "God Is Back," *Washingtonian,* December 1986, 157, 156, 158.

ory of history. The Bible is in essence a story of history from the very beginnings of a human presence in the world. From its earliest days, Judeo-
Christian religion has been in essence the discovery of the true meaning of
history. This central impulse to find meaning in history has survived even
when the formal trappings of Judeo-Christian religion have disappeared.
Darwinism posed such a severe challenge to Christianity—more than Newtonian physics—because it offered an alternative interpretation of the history
of the world directly at odds with that of the Bible. The progressive belief in
the redeeming powers of economic progress is yet another historical guide to
and prediction of a path to heaven on earth.

However, current professional historians are not likely to provide the history that will matter the most. They too are a specialized product of the progressive impulse to expertise over "vision" and in some cases have even been
caught up themselves in making claims to "scientific" history. The people
who develop the most influential forms of history in the twenty-first century
will have to integrate contributions from multiple perspectives. Their
method of analysis will be closer to the long-run traditions of theology than
to those of modern social science.

4. It is not only the institution of the existing university that is endangered by the current crisis of progressive religion. Many other institutions
derive their legitimacy from this source. Ultimately, the modern nation-state
has been a church of progressive faith. The end of Marxism in the old Soviet
Union did not just mean a new economic system but soon led to the
breakup of the Soviet Union itself. There was no unifying religion left to
hold the center. If the eroding faith of the religions of economic progress
makes way for some new world religion, there may be a common world culture, and more-centralized institutions may prosper to some extent based on
this unifying vision. Otherwise, if a new wider pluralism of religions
emerges, there may be powerful centripetal forces leading to the breakup of
existing nation-states and the reordering of national and regional authority.

5. A very important practical question, if the preceding is true, will be the
issue of the legitimacy of secession. Secession would be a key practical means
by which a fundamental reordering of national boundaries—possibly including a widespread decentralization to arrange the boundaries of smaller
nations to correspond more closely to older ethnic and religious group-
ings—might take place. The bonds of the old universal economic religions
such as socialism are no longer holding. The proper place of a "right of free
secession" along with other such rights as free speech and assembly is a critical issue of political philosophy facing the twenty-first century.

In a modern context, the right of secession amounts to the right to leave
the church of the welfare and regulatory state; in this respect it also in a mod-

ern context raises fundamental questions about the meaning of religious free-dom. To deny the right to leave the nation-state and to employ coercive measures for this purpose is the modern equivalent of the old waging of war upon and the burning of heretics who sought to leave the established church (as the medieval Roman Catholic Church in fact coercively denied a right of exit for centuries). The very idea of the separation of church and state re-quires brand-new thinking, once it is recognized that modern secular reli-gions should be regarded in much the same religious light as more traditional Jewish and Christian faiths. The nation-state today is in essence the church of a secular religion. As presently applied, the arguments for separation of church and state have been used hypocritically by advocates of the secular re-ligions of the modern state, who seek in fact to maintain a privileged position relative to other older institutional-faith traditions.

6. The cutting edge of social thought today, probably the best indicator of future trends, can be found in the libertarian and environmental move-ments. Both have the advantage that they define themselves in significant part by a rejection of the scientific management aspirations that have been at the heart of the progressive gospel. They thus have greater freedom to aban-don current social and economic orthodoxies. The one economist of the twentieth century who comes closest to an integration of libertarian and en-vironmental sensibilities is Frank Knight. Among the many professional economists of the twentieth century, Knight may thus be rated the highest in the histories of the future.

But that is enough of these sheer speculations. They can be left as possible subjects for another book. In the end, only history will tell.

A CLOSING NOTE

As this book was approaching its final stages of the production process for publication, the Re-publican and Democratic Parties were holding their national conventions in 2000. Such occasions are moments for invoking the fundamental values that each party represents—which are in many, perhaps most, respects the same. The most eloquent speech was no doubt that of John McCain. With few orig-inal expectations and little money at first for campaigning, McCain had touched a nerve in American life and almost defeated the ordained candidate of the Republican Party establishment, Texas gover-nor George W. Bush. McCain was unique among the candidates in that he was a genuine war hero who had honorably endured torture and other sufferings for many years as a prisoner of war in North Vietnam. As a result, McCain could say things that others in politics could not. In the current cynical age, the words would have sounded phony and calculating from almost any other political candidate. What McCain said to the assembled regulars of the Republic Party amounted to an inspirational state-ment of the American civic religion of the twentieth century—the beliefs that had sustained McCain during his own prison years.

What the fate of this immensely powerful secular religion of America will be in the twenty-first century remains to be seen. It is much the same religion as that of Samuelson and many other leading twentieth-century economists, if expressed in a more evangelical and overtly proselytizing rhetoric by McCain. It will be well worth keeping McCain's words in mind as we ponder the next steps, politically and economically, of the twenty-first century.

> When we nominate Governor Bush for president, here in the city where our great nation was born, we invest him with the faith of our founding fathers, and charge him with the care of the cause they called glorious.
> We are blessed to be Americans, not just in times of prosperity, but at all times. We are part of something providential; a great experiment to prove to the world that democracy is not only the most effective form of government, but the only moral government. And through the years, generation after generation of Americans has held fast to the belief that we were meant to transform history.
> On an early December morning, many years ago, I watched my father leave for war. He joined millions of Americans to leave for war. He joined millions of Americans to fight a world war that would decide the fate of humanity. They fought against a cruel and formidable enemy bent on world domination. They fought not just for themselves and their families, not just to preserve the quality of their own lives. They fought for love, for love of an idea: that American stood for something greater than the sum of our individual interests.
> From where did the courage come to make the maximum effort in that decisive moment in history? It marched with the sons of a nation that believed deeply in itself, in its history, in the justice of its cause, in its magnificent destiny. Americans went into battle armed against despair with the common conviction that the country that sent them there was worth their sacrifice. Their families, their schools, their faith, their history, their heroes taught them that the freedom with which they were blessed deserved patriots to defend it.
> Many would never come home—many would never come home. But those who did returned with an even deeper civic love. They believed that if America were worth dying for, then surely she was worth living for. They were, as Tocqueville said of Americans, "haunted by visions of what will be."
> They built an even greater nation than the one they had left their homes to defend; an America that offered more opportunities to more of its people than ever before; an America that began to redress the injustices that had been visited on too many of her citizens for too long.
> They bound up the wounds of war for ally and enemy alike. And when faced with a new, terrible threat to the security and freedom of the world, they fought that, too. As did their sons and daughters. And they prevailed [in this Cold War against the Soviet Union and the forces of international communism].
> Now we stand unsurpassed in our wealth and power. What shall we make of it? Let us take courage from their example and, from the new world they built, build a better one.
> This new century will be an age of untold possibilities for us and for all mankind. Many nations now share our love of liberty and aspire to the ordered progress of democracy. But the world is still home to tyrants, haters and aggressors hostile to America and our ideals. We are obliged to seize this moment to help build a safer, freer and more prosperous world, completely free of the tyranny that made the last century such a violent age.
> We are strong, confident people. We know that our ideals, our courage, our ingenuity ensure our success. Isolationism and protectionism are fool's errands. We shouldn't build walls to the global success of our interests and values. Walls are for cowards, my friends, not for Americans.
> I am so grateful to have seen America rise to such prominence. But America's greatness is a quest without end, the object beyond the horizon. And it is an inescapable and bittersweet irony of life, that the older we are the more distant the horizon becomes. I will not see what's over

America's horizon. The years that remain are not too few, I trust, but the immortality that was the aspiration of my youth, like all the treasures of youth, quietly slipped away.

But I have faith. I have faith in you. I have faith in your patriotism, in your passion to build upon the accomplishments of our storied past. I have faith the people who are free to act in their own interests will perceive their interests in an enlightened way and live as one nation, in a kinship of ideals, served by a government that kindles the pride of every one of you.

I have faith that just beyond the distant horizon live a people who gratefully accept the obligation of their freedom to make of their power and wealth a civilization for the ages—a civilization in which all people share the promise of freedom.

I have such faith in you, my fellow Americans. And I am haunted by the vision of what will be.

See "McCain Says His Support for Bush Serves the Nation," excerpts from remarks delivered by Senator John McCain [of Arizona] at the Republican National Convention, *New York Times,* August 2, 2000, A20.

NOTES

PREFACE

1. I describe the federal policy-making process, as seen from the viewpoint of one government economist, in Robert H. Nelson, "The Office of Policy Analysis in the Department of the Interior," *Journal of Policy Analysis and Management* 8 (Summer 1989); reprinted in Carol H. Weiss, *Organizations for Policy Analysis: Helping Government Think* (Newbury Park, Calif.: Sage, 1992). See also Nelson, "The Economics Profession and the Making of Public Policy," *Journal of Economic Literature* 25 (March 1987); "Introduction and Summary," in Joseph A. Pechman, ed., *The Role of the Economist in Government: An International Perspective* (New York: New York University Press, 1989); and "Economists as Policy Analysts: Historical Overview," in David L. Weimer, ed., *Policy Analysis and Economics: Developments, Tensions, Prospects* (Boston: Kluwer, 1991).

2. William C. Dennis, "Wilderness Cathedrals and the Public Good," *Freeman* (May 1987).

3. Charles C. Mann and Mark L. Plummer, *Noah's Choice: The Future of Endangered Species* (New York: Alfred A. Knopf, 1995).

4. Robert H. Nelson, "Bruce Babbitt, Pipeline to the Almighty," *Weekly Standard*, June 24, 1996.

5. See, for example, Arthur O. Lovejoy, *The Great Chain of Being: A Study of the History of an Idea* (Cambridge, Mass.: Harvard University Press, 1966); John Passmore, *Man's Responsibility for Nature: Ecological Problems and Western Traditions* (New York: Charles Scribner's, 1974); and Roderick Frazier Nash, *The Rights of Nature: A History of Environmental Ethics* (Madison: University of Wisconsin Press, 1989).

6. See, for example, W. C. Heath, M. S. Waters, and J. K. Watson, "Religion and Economic Welfare: An Empirical Analysis of State Per Capita Income," *Journal of Economic Behavior and Organization* 27 (June 1995).

7. A few economists, to be sure, have joined with leading theologians to discuss economic subjects in terms both could understand. See Walter Block, Geoffrey Brennan, and Kenneth Elzinga, eds., *The Morality of the Market: Religious and Economic Perspectives* (proceedings of an international symposium, Vancouver, B.C.: Fraser Institute, 1985); and Walter Block and Irving Hexham, eds., *Religion, Economics, and Social Thought* (proceedings of an international symposium, Vancouver: Fraser Institute, 1986).

8. Robert H. Nelson, "Does 'Existence Value' Exist: Economics Encroaches on Religion," *Independent Review* 1 (March 1997).

9. The majority of the literature on economics and religion in recent years has been produced by theologians; economists have mostly declined to enter the discussion. A comprehensive collection is included in Max L. Stackhouse, Dennis P. McCann, and Shirley J. Roels, eds., *On Moral Business: Classical and Contemporary Resources for Ethics in Economic Life* (Grand Rapids, Mich.: William B. Eerdmans, 1995). See also Robert Benne, *The Ethic of Democratic Capitalism: A Moral Reassessment* (Philadelphia: Fortress Press, 1981); M. Douglas Meeks, *God the Economist: The Doctrine of God and Political Economy* (Minneapolis: Fortress Press, 1989); Michael Novak, *The Spirit of Democratic Capitalism* (New York: Simon and Schuster, 1982); Max L. Stackhouse, *Public Theology and Political Economy: Christian Stewardship in Modern Society* (Grand Rapids, Mich.: W. B. Eerdmans, 1987); Max L. Stackhouse, Peter L. Berger, Dennis P. McCann, and M. Douglas Meeks, *Christian Social Ethics in a Global Era* (Nashville, Tenn.: Abingdon Press, 1995); Meir Tamari, *With All Your Possessions: Jewish Ethics and Economic Life*

(New York: Free Press, 1987); and Philip Wogaman, *The Great Economic Debate: An Ethical Analysis* (Philadelphia: Westminster Press, 1977).

10. The focus of much of this literature is on the meaning of rationality in economics. Three of the most important contributors here are Jon Elster, Thomas Schelling, and Amartya Sen. See Jon Elster, *Solomonic Judgements: Studies in the Limitations of Rationality* (New York: Cambridge University Press, 1989); Amartya Sen, *On Ethics and Economics* (New York: Basil Blackwell, 1987); Thomas C. Schelling, *Choice and Consequence: Perspectives of an Errant Economist* (Cambridge: Harvard University Press, 1984); and Thomas C. Schelling, "Coping Rationally with Lapses from Rationality," *Eastern Economic Journal* 22 (Summer 1996). For recent surveys reflecting a new questioning of traditional rationality assumptions among economists, see Matthew Rabin, "Psychology and Economics," *Journal of Economic Literature* 36 (March 1998); and Jon Elster, "Emotions and Economic Theory," *Journal of Economic Literature* 36 (March 1998).

11. See Jaroslav Pelikan, *The Christian Tradition: A History of the Development of Doctrine*, vol. 1, *The Emergence of the Catholic Tradition (100–600)* (Chicago: University of Chicago Press, 1971); vol. 2, *The Spirit of Eastern Christendom (600–1700)* (1974); vol. 3, *The Growth of Medieval Theology (600–1300)* (1978); vol. 4, *Reformation of Church and Dogma (1300–1700)* (1984); and vol. 5, *Christian Doctrine and Modern Culture (Since 1700)* (1989). See also Kenneth Scott Latourette, *A History of Christianity*, vol. 1, *Beginnings to 1500* (New York: Harper and Row, 1975); vol. 2, *Reformation to the Present* (1975); and William C. Placher, *A History of Christian Theology: An Introduction* (Philadelphia: Westminster Press, 1983).

12. Robert H. Nelson, *Reaching for Heaven on Earth: The Theological Meaning of Economics* (Lanham, Md.: Rowman and Littlefield, 1991).

13. A short summary of the argument is contained in Robert H. Nelson, "The Theological Meaning of Economics," *Christian Century*, August 11–18, 1993.

14. Among many theologians who have commented on a basic divide running through two traditions in Western theology, see the comments of a leading Roman Catholic theologian, John Courtney Murray, on the "two tendencies" in Christian religion. John Courtney Murray, *We Hold These Truths: Catholic Reflections on the American Proposition* (New York: Sheed and Ward, 1960), 184–93. Paul Tillich similarly comments on two "great lines of thought" that run through the history of Christianity in the West. See Paul Tillich, *A History of Christian Thought: From Its Judaic and Hellenistic Origins to Existentialism* (New York: Simon and Schuster, 1967), 488–91.

15. For readable introductory surveys of the history of Jewish and Christian religion, see Paul Johnson, *A History of the Jews* (New York: Harper and Row, 1987); and Paul Johnson, *A History of Christianity* (New York: Atheneum, 1987; 1st ed., 1976).

16. See Robert H. Nelson, "Unoriginal Sin: The Judeo-Christian Roots of Ecotheology," *Policy Review*, no. 53 (Summer 1990); "Environmental Calvinism: The Judeo-Christian Roots of Environmental Theology," in Roger E. Meiner and Bruce Yandle, eds., *Taking the Environment Seriously* (Lanham, Md.: Rowman and Littlefield, 1993); "Sustainability, Efficiency, and God: Economic Values and the Sustainability Debate," *Annual Review of Ecology and Systematics* 26 (1995); Robert H. Nelson, "Does 'Existence Value' Exist; and "Calvinism Minus God: Environmental Restoration as a Theological Concept," in L. Anathea Brooks and Stacy D. Van Deever, eds., *Saving the Seas: Values, Scientists and International Governance* (College Park, Md.: Maryland Sea Grant, 1997).

17. Joseph L. Sax, *Mountains Without Handrails: Reflections on the National Parks* (Ann Arbor: University of Michigan Press, 1980), 104.

18. For commentary from an economic point of view on the tensions between the economic and the environmental worldviews, see Irwin M. Stelzer, "Irrational Element of Environmental Policy Making," in Stelzer and Paul R. Portney, *Making Environmental Policy: Two Views* (Washington, D.C.: American Enterprise Institute, 1998).

19. See Willis B. Glover, *Biblical Origins of Modern Secular Culture: An Essay in the Interpretation of Western History* (Macon, Ga.: Mercer University Press, 1984); also Arend T. Van Leeuwen, *Christianity in World History: The Meeting of the Faiths of East and West* (New York: Charles Scribner's, 1964).

20. Larry Owens, "Free-Marketing Science," *Science* 277 (July 11, 1997): 189.

21. Robert Bellah, "The Power of Religion in the Contemporary Society" (1981), quoted in Arthur J. Vidich and Stanford M. Lyman, *American Sociology: Worldly Rejections of Religion and Their Directions* (New Haven: Yale University Press, 1985), 305.

22. Donald N. McCloskey, *The Rhetoric of Economics* (University of Wisconsin Press, 1985); and "The Rhetoric of Economics," *Journal of Economic Literature* 21 (June 1983). See also John S. Nelson, Allan Megill, and Donald N. McCloskey, eds., *The Rhetoric of the Human Sciences: Language and Argument in Scholarship and Public Affairs* (Madison: University of Wisconsin Press, 1987).

23. For the value assumptions of economics, see also Sen, *On Ethics and Economics*. Although not written by economists, further studies of interest included Amitai Etzioni, *The Moral Dimension: Toward a New Economics* (New York: Free Press, 1988); and Allen Buchanen, *Ethics, Efficiency, and the Market* (Totowa, N.J.: Rowman and Littlefield, 1988).

24. McCloskey, *The Rhetoric of Economics*, 4–9.

25. Mark Sagoff, "Muddle or Muddle Through? Takings Jurisprudence Meets the Endangered Species Act," *William and Mary Law Review* 38 (March 1997): 968, 972, 980. See also Christopher Lasch, *The True and Only Heaven: Progress and Its Critics* (New York: W. W. Norton, 1991)

26. Richard Rorty, *Philosophy and the Mirror of Nature* (Princeton: Princeton University Press, 1979). See also Ian Mitroff, *The Subjective Side of Science: A Philosophical Inquiry into the Psychology of the Apollo Moon Scientists* (New York: Elsevier, 1974).

27. See Morris Kline, *Mathematics: The Loss of Certainty* (New York: Oxford University Press, 1980); David Oldroyd, *The Arch of Knowledge: An Introductory Study of the History of the Philosophy and Methodology of Science* (New York: Metheun, 1986).

28. See Laurence H. Tribe, "Policy Science: Analysis or Ideology?" *Philosophy and Public Affairs* 2 (Fall 1972).

29. David Colander and Arjo Klamer, "The Making of an Economist," *Journal of Economic Perspectives* 1 (Fall 1987): 102. See also Arjo Klamer and David Colander, *The Making of an Economist* (Boulder, Colo.: Westview Press, 1990).

30. Quoted on cover of Paul Tillich, *Theology of Culture* (New York: Oxford University Press, 1959).

31. Tillich, *Theology of Culture,* 130.

32. Ibid., 61.

33. Paul Tillich, *A History of Christian Thought: From Its Judaic and Hellenistic Origins to Existentialism* (New York: Simon and Schuster, 1967), 476.

34. Anand Agneshwar, "Rediscovering God in the Constitution," *New York University Law Review* 67 (May 1992): 296, 300.

35. Daniel G. Reid, Robert D. Linder, Bruce L. Shelley, and Harry S. Stout, eds., *Dictionary of Christianity in America* (Downers Grove, Ill.: InterVarsity Press, 1990), 1069.

INTRODUCTION

1. James S. Coleman, "Norms as Social Capital," in Gerard Radnitzky and Peter Bernholz, eds., *Economic Imperialism: The Economic Method Applied Outside the Field of Economics* (New York: Paragon House Publishers, 1987), 153.

2. See Rafael La Porta, Florencio Lopez-De-Silanes, Andrei Shleifer, and Robert W. Vishny, "Trust in Large Organizations," *American Economic Review* 87 (May 1997); Rafael La Porta, Florencio Lopez-de-Silanes, Andrei Shleifer, and Robert Vishny, "The Quality of Government," NBER working paper 6727, National Bureau of Economic Research, Cambridge, Mass. (September 1998); and William Easterly and Ross Levine, "Africa's Growth Tragedy: Policies and Ethnic Divisions," *Quarterly Journal of Economics* 112 (November 1997).

3. Robert D. Putnam, *Making Democracy Work: Civic Traditions in Modern Italy* (Princeton: Princeton University Press, 1993), 155–57.

4. See, for example, Francis Fukuyama, *Trust: The Social Virtues and the Creation of Prosperity* (New

York: Free Press, 1995) and Lawrence E. Harrison, *Who Prospers: How Cultural Values Shape Economic and Political Success* (New York: Basic Books, 1992).

5. Kenneth J. Arrow, "Methodological Individualism and Social Knowledge," *American Economic Review* 84 (May 1994).

6. Elinor Ostrom, *Governing the Commons: The Evolution of Institutions for Collective Action* (New York: Cambridge University Press, 1990).

7. See William A. Galston, "Liberal Virtues," *American Political Science Review* 82 (December 1988), 1278–79.

8. World Bank, *1998/99 World Development Report: Knowledge for Development* (New York: Oxford University Press, 1999), 72.

9. The World Bank, *Assessing Aid: What Works, What Doesn't, and Why* (New York: Oxford University Press, 1998), 10.

10. Goran Hyden, *No Shortcuts to Progress: African Development Management in Perspective* (London: Heineman, 1983), 111. See also Jean-Francois Bayart, Stephen Ellis, and Beatrice Hibou, *The Criminalization of the State in Africa* (Bloomington: Indiana University Press, 1999).

11. Mancur Olson, Jr., "Big Bills Left on the Sidewalk: Why Some Nations Are Rich, and Others Poor," *Journal of Economic Perspectives* 10 (Spring 1996): 22.

12. See Paul Collier and Jan Willem Gunning, "Why Has Africa Grown Slowly?" *Journal of Economic Perspectives* 13 (Summer 1999); and Benno J. Ndulu and Stephen A. O'Connell, "Governance and Growth in Sub-Saharan Africa," *Journal of Economic Perspectives* 13 (Summer 1999).

13. Daniel M. Hausman and Michael S. McPherson, "Taking Ethics Seriously: Economics and Contemporary Moral Philosophy," *Journal of Economic Literature* 31 (June 1993): 686.

14. George Eliot, *Middlemarch* (New York: Modern Library, 1994; 1st ed., 1872), 799.

15. James Q. Wilson, "Two Cheers for Capitalism," *Public Interest* (Spring 2000): 75.

16. Francis Fukuyama, "Lecture I: The Great Disruption"; "Lecture II: Technology, Hierarchy, and Networks"; and "Lecture III: The Origins of Order," all in Grethe Peterson, ed., *The Tanner Lectures on Human Values, 1998* (Salt Lake City: University of Utah Press, 1998).

17. One version of such an argument was offered by Max Weber in his classic study of the Protestant ethic as found in Calvinist theology. See Max Weber, *The Protestant Ethic and the Spirit of Capitalism* (New York: Charles Scribner, 1958; 1st ed., 1905). For commentary on Weber, including criticisms of his analysis, see S. N. Eisenstadt, ed., *The Protestant Ethic and Modernization: A Comparative View* (New York: Basic Books, 1968).

18. Although the reasons given are different from those in the present book, a view of an economics profession in crisis is offered in Robert Heilbroner and William Milberg, *The Crisis of Vision in Modern Economic Thought* (New York: Cambridge University Press, 1996). See also Robert Heibroner, "Analysis and Vision in the History of Modern Economic Thought," *Journal of Economic Literature* 28 (September 1990).

19. See Richard A. Easterlin, "The Worldwide Standard of Living Since 1800," *Journal of Economic Perspectives* 14 (Winter 2000).

20. Outside the economics profession, the growing criticism of claims to a "scientific" status of economics is illustrated by John Cassidy, "The Decline of Economics," *New Yorker*, December 2, 1996.

21. Some economists now go further to argue that growth can be a positive harm, by endangering the natural resource base and the environmental quality of the future. See Herman E. Daly and John B. Cobb, Jr., *For the Common Good*, 2d ed. (Boston: Beacon Press, 1994); and Herman E. Daly, *Beyond Growth: The Economics of Sustainable Development* (Boston: Beacon Press, 1996). For discussion of underlying theological dimensions to this debate, see also Robert H. Nelson, "Sustainability, Efficiency, and God: Economic Values and the Sustainability Debate," *Annual Review of Ecology and Systematics* 26 (1995).

22. George M. Marsden, *The Soul of the American University: From Protestant Establishment to Established Nonbelief* (New York: Oxford University Press, 1994), 396, 394.

23. Eliza Wing-yee Lee, "Political Science, Public Administration and the Rise of the American Administrative State," *Public Administration Review* 55 (November/December 1995); Dwight Waldo,

The Administrative State: A Study of the Political Theory of American Public Administration (New York: Holmes and Meier, 1984; 1st ed., 1948); and Robert H. Wiebe, *The Search for Order, 1877–1920* (New York: Hill and Wang, 1967).

24. Among what is now a large and growing literature, a limited selection includes Peter G. Brown, *Restoring the Public Trust: A Fresh Vision for Progressive Government in America* (Boston: Beacon Press, 1994); Herman E. Daly and John B. Cobb., Jr., *For the Common Good* (Boston: Beacon Press, 1989); E. J. Dione, ed., *Community Works: The Revival of Civil Society in America* (Washington, D.C.: Brookings Institution Press, 1998); Bruce Frohnen, *The New Communitarians: The Crisis of Modern Liberalism* (Lawrence: University Press of Kansas, 1996); William A. Galston, *Liberal Purposes: Goods, Virtues, and Diversity in the Liberal State* (New York: Cambridge University Press, 1989); Mary Ann Glendon, *Rights Talk: The Impoverishment of Political Discourse* (New York: Free Press, 1991); Michael Novak, ed., *To Empower People: From State to Civil Society*, 2d ed. (Washington, D.C.: AEI Press, 1996); Robert Putnam, "The Prosperous Community: Social Capital and Public Life," *American Prospect* 4 (Spring 1993); Theda Skocpol, *Social Policy in the United States: Future Possibilities in Historical Perspective* (Princeton: Princeton University Press, 1995); and Robert Wuthnow, *Sharing the Journey: Support Groups and America's New Quest for Community* (New York: Free Press, 1994). See also the recent report of the National Commission on Civic Renewal, *A Nation of Spectators: How Civic Disengagement Weakens America and What We Can Do About It* (1998), obtainable from the Institute for Philosophy and Public Policy, University of Maryland, College, Park, Md.

25. See Dorothy Ross, *The Origins of American Social Science* (New York: Cambridge University Press, 1991); Benjamin G. Rader, *The Academic Mind and Reform: The Influence of Richard T. Ely in American Life* (Lexington: University of Kentucky Press, 1966); and Mary O. Furner, *Advocacy and Objectivity: A Crisis in the Professionalization of American Social Science, 1865–1905* (Lexington: University of Kentucky Press, 1975).

26. A. W. Coats has been one of the few economists to explore the historic origins of the idea of the economic professional. See A. W. Coats, "The First Two Decades of the American Economic Association," *American Economic Review* 50 (September 1960); and "The American Economic Association and the Economics Profession," *Journal of Economic Literature* 23 (December 1985).

27. Alison Schneider, "A Harvard Economist Hits the Jackpot with a $1.4-Million Advance for a Textbook," *Chronicle of Higher Education,* October 10, 1997, A12.

28. Mark Skousen, "The Perseverance of Paul Samuelson's *Economics,*" *Journal of Economic Perspectives* 11 (Spring 1997); and Paul A. Samuelson, "Credo of a Lucky Textbook Author," *Journal of Economic Perspectives* 11 (Spring 1997).

29. Kenneth G. Elzinga, "The Eleven Principles of Economics," *Southern Economic Journal* 58 (April 1992).

30. Paul A. Samuelson, *Economics* (New York: McGraw Hill, 1948). In celebration of the fiftieth anniversary of the original publication of *Economics,* McGraw Hill in 1998 issued a new commemorative edition with a new foreword by Samuelson.

31. Paul A. Samuelson, "My Life Philosophy: Policy Credos and Working Ways," in Michael Szenberg, ed., *Eminent Economists: Their Life Philosophies* (New York: Cambridge University Press, 1992), 238.

32. For an interesting discussion of these broader developments, see James C. Scott, *Seeing Like a State: How Certain Schemes to Improve the Human Condition Have Failed* (New Haven: Yale University Press, 1998).

33. Samuel P. Hays, *Conservationism and the Gospel of Efficiency: The Progressive Conservation Movement, 1890–1920* (Cambridge: Harvard University Press, 1959).

34. See Eirik G. Furubotn and Rudolf Richter, *Institutions and Economic Theory: The Contribution of the New Institutional Economics* (Ann Arbor: University of Michigan Press, 1997).

35. See, for example, Douglas C. North, *Institutions, Institutional Change, and Economic Performance* (New York: Cambridge University Press, 1990).

CHAPTER ONE

1. See Frank E. Manuel and Fritzie P. Manuel, *Utopian Thought in the Western World* (Cambridge: Harvard University Press, 1979); J. L. Talmon, *Politican Messianism:The Romantic Phase* (Boulder, Colo.: Westview Press, 1985; 1st ed., 1960).

2. Isaiah Berlin, *Karl Marx: His Life and Environment* (New York: Time Books, 1963; 1st ed., 1939).

3. Paul Tillich, *A History of Christian Thought: From Its Judaic and Hellenistic Origins to Existentialism* (New York: Simon and Schuster, 1967), 476.

4. See G. N. Kitching, *Marxism and Science: Analysis of an Obsession* (University Park: Penn State Press, 1994).

5. Murray N. Rothbard, *Classical Economics: An Austrian Perspective on the History of Economic Thought* (Brookfield, Vt.: Edward Elgar, 1995), 433, 299, 301.

6. Ibid., 317.

7. Mitchell Cohen, "Theories of Stalinism," *Dissent* 39 (Spring 1992): 180–82, 184.

8. *Quotations from Mao Tse-tung* (Peking: Foreign Language Press, 1966), 222. This publication was widely known as the red book.

9. J. W. Harris, *Property and Justice* (Oxford: Clarendon Press, 1996), 292.

10. Charles W. Hendel, Jr., ed., *Hume Selections* (New York: Charles Scribner's Sons, 1927), 203–4.

11. Charles A. Beard, *An Economic Interpretation of the Constitution* (New York: Macmillan, 1913).

12. Thorstein Veblen, "The Preconceptions of Economic Science, I," *Quarterly Journal of Economics* (January 1899): 143. See also Thorstein Veblen, *The Engineers and the Price System* (New York: Augustus Kelley, 1965; 1st ed., 1921).

13. John Kenneth Galbraith, *The New Industrial State* (Boston: Houghton Mifflin, 1979; 1st ed., 1967).

14. Max Weber, *The Protestant Ethic and the Spirit of Capitalism* (New York: Charles Scribner, 1958; 1st ed., 1905).

15. Kate Soper, "Socialism and Personal Morality," in David McLellan and Sean Sayers, eds., *Socialism and Morality* (New York: St. Martin's Press, 1990), 111.

16. See Steven Lukes, *Marxism and Morality* (New York: Oxford University Press, 1985); and Eugene Kamenka, *Marxism and Ethics* (London: Macmillan, 1969).

17. Will Kymlicka, *Liberalism, Community, and Culture* (New York: Oxford University Press, 1989), 114, 119, 114–15, 119.

18. Karl Marx, *Critique of the Gotha Programme* (1875), quoted in Kymlicka, *Liberalism, Community, and Culture,* 119.

19. Quoted in Rothbard, *Classical Economics,* 327.

20. Ibid., 374.

21. For the life history of Keynes, see Robert Skidelsky, *John Maynard Keynes: Hopes Betrayed, 1883–1920* (New York: Viking, 1986); and, *John Maynard Keynes:The Economist as Savior, 1920–1937* (New York: Viking, 1994).

22. John Maynard Keynes, "Economic Possibilities for Our Grandchildren," (1930) in Keynes, *Essays in Persuasion* (New York: W. W. Norton, 1963), 369, 371–72.

23. Ibid., 369–372.

24. Ibid., 372.

25. See Robert G. Clouse, ed., *The Meaning of the Millennium: Four Views* (Downers Grove, Ill.: InterVarsity Press, 1977), 7–9.

26. Keynes, "Economic Possibilities for Our Grandchildren," 369–73.

27. John Maynard Keynes, *The General Theory of Employment, Interest, and Money* (New York: Harcourt, Brace, and World, 1965; 1st ed., 1936), 374.

28. Ibid., 376.

29. David C. Colander and Harry Landreth, introduction to Colander and Landreth, eds., *The Coming of Keynesianism to America: Conversations with the Founders of Keynesian Economics* (Brookfield, Vt.: Edward Elgar, 1996), 9.

30. Milton Friedman, "John Maynard Keynes,", *Economic Quarterly* (Federal Reserve Bank of Richmond) 83 (Spring 1997): 22.

31. Letter from Keynes to Friedrich Hayek praising his *The Road to Serfdom,* quoted in Friedman, "John Maynard Keynes," 22.

32. Joseph A. Schumeter, *Ten Great Economists from Marx to Keynes* (1951), quoted in Colander and Landreth's introduction to *The Coming of Keynesianism,* 9–10.

33. Paul A. Samuelson, *Economics* (New York: McGraw Hill, 1948), 253.

CHAPTER TWO

1. Sean Wilentz, "Speedy Fred's Revolution," *New York Review of Books,* November 20, 1997, 32.

2. Gifford Pinchot, *The Fight for Conservation* (Seattle: University of Washington Press, 1967), 95.

3. Quoted in Ashley L. Schiff, *Fire and Water: Scientific Heresy in the Forest Service* (Cambridge: Harvard University Press, 1962), 5.

4. Samuel P. Hays, *Conservation and the Gospel of Efficiency: The Progressive Conservation Movement, 1890–1920* (Cambridge: Harvard University Press, 1959).

5. Samuel Haber, *Efficiency and Uplift: Scientific Management in the Progressive Era, 1890–1920* (Chicago: University of Chicago Press, 1964), ix.

6. Raymond E. Callahan, *Education and the Cult of Efficiency: A Study of the Social Forces That Have Shaped the Administration of the Public Schools* (Chicago: University of Chicago Press, 1962), 24–25.

7. Dwight Waldo, *The Administrative State: A Study of the Political Theory of American Public Administration* (New York: Holme and Meier, 1984; 1st ed., 1948), 19–20.

8. Observation of G. K. Chesterton, cited in Michael Novak, "The Nation with the Soul of a Church," in Richard J. Bishirjian, ed., *A Public Philosophy Reader* (New York: Arlington House, 1978), 92.

9. See Robert H. Nelson, "Calvinism Minus God: Environmental Restoration as a Theological Subject," in Anathea Brookes and Stacy Van Deever, eds., *Saving the Seas: Values, Scientists, and International Governance* (College Park, Md.: University of Maryland Sea Grant, 1997).

10. Charles Howard Hopkins, *The Rise of the Social Gospel in American Protestantism, 1865–1915* (New Haven: Yale University Press, 1940), 320–21.

11. See George M. Marsden, *The Soul of the American University: From Protestant Establishment to Established Nonbelief* (New York: Oxford University Press, 1994).

12. Quoted in Eldon Eisenach, "Bookends: Seven Stories Excised from the Lost Promise of Progressivism," *Studies in American Political Development* 10 (Spring 1996): 174.

13. Ibid., 175.

14. Eliza Wing-yee Lee, "Political Science, Public Administration, and the Rise of the American Administrative State," *Public Administration Review* 55 (November/December 1995): 543, 539, 541.

15. Ibid., 539, 540, 543.

16. Ibid., 544.

17. Robert M. Crunden, *Ministers of Reform: The Progressive's Achievement in American Civilization, 1889–1920* (Chicago: University of Illinois Press, 1984), 77.

18. William A. Schambra, "Is There Civic Life Beyond the Great National Community?" working paper no. 5, National Commission on Civic Renewal (1998), 24, 25–26. Available from the Institute for Philosophy and Public Policy, University of Maryland, College Park, Md.

19. Ibid., 22.

20. Ibid., 23–24.

21. C. Bernard Ruffin, *Profiles of Faith: The Religious Beliefs of Eminent Americans* (Liguiri, Mo.: Liguiri, 1997), 245.

22. Quoted in Ruffin, *Profiles of Faith,* 243.

23. Ruffin, *Profiles of Faith,* 243.

24. See A. W. Coats, "The American Economic Association and the Economics Profession," *Journal of Economic Literature* 23 (December 1985).

25. See John Rutherford Everett, *Religion in Economics: A Study of John Bates Clark, Richard T. Ely, Simon N. Patten* (Philadelphia: Porcupine Press, 1982; 1st ed. 1946).

26. Richard T. Ely, *Social Aspects of Christianity and Other Essays* (New York: Thomas Y. Crowell, 1889), 15, 53.

27. Ibid., 73.

28. Crunden, *Ministers of Reform,* 71.

29. Edwin R. A. Seligman, *The Economic Interpretation of History* (New York: Columbia University Press, 1903), 120.

30. Ibid., 126.

31. Ibid., 131, 130.

32. Ibid., 131, 132.

33. Ibid., 132–33.

34. Ibid., 132.

35. Quoted in Joseph Dorfman, *Thorstein Veblen and His America* (New York: Viking, 1934), 505.

36. Thorstein Veblen, "Why Is Economics Not an Evolutionary Science?" *Quarterly Journal of Economics* 12 (July 1898): 379, 382.

37. Thorstein Veblen, "The Preconceptions of Economic Science, II," *Quarterly Journal of Economics* 13 (July 1899): 412.

38. Thorstein Veblen, *The Engineers and the Price System* (New York: Augustus M. Kelly, 1965; 1st ed., 1921), 64, 115, 144, 152.

39. Ibid., 79–80.

40. Ibid., 69–70.

41. Robert H. Wiebe, *The Search for Order, 1877–1920* (New York: Hill and Wang, 1967), 113, 161.

42. Quoted in Joseph Dorfman, *The Economic Mind in American Civilization,* vols. 4 and 5, 1918–1933 (New York: Viking, 1959), 62.

43. Quoted in Dorfman, *The Economic Mind in American Civilization,* 62–63.

44. See Gary North, "Millennialism and the Progressive Movement," *Journal of Libertarian Studies* 12 (Spring 1996).

45. Richard Hofstadter, *The Age of Reform: From Bryan to F.D.R.* (New York: Vintage, 1955), 152.

46. Sidney Fine, *Laissez Faire and the General-Welfare State: A Study of Conflict in American Thought, 1865–1901* (Ann Arbor: University of Michigan Press, 1964; 1st ed., 1956), 381.

47. Arthur J. Vidich and Sanford M. Lyman, *American Sociology: Worldly Rejections of Religion and their Directions* (New Haven: Yale University Press, 1985), 134.

48. Ibid., 82, 132, 35.

49. Ibid., 111.

50. Ibid., 304.

INTRODUCTION TO PART TWO

1. See James C. Scott, *Seeing Like a State: How Certain Schemes to Improve the Human Condition Have Failed* (New Haven: Yale University Press, 1998).

2. David B. Truman, *The Governmental Process: Political Interests and Public Opinion* (New York: Knopf, 1951); and Norton E. Long, "Public Policy and Administration: The Goals of Rationality and Responsibility," *Public Administration Review* 14 (Winter 1954).

3. Charles E. Lindblom, "The Science of 'Muddling Through,' " *Public Administration Review* 19 (Spring 1959).

4. For testimonies to Samuelson's importance for the economics profession, see Kenneth J. Arrow, "Samuelson Collected," *Journal of Political Economy* 75 (October 1967); Assar Lindbeck, "Paul Samuelson's Contributions to Economics," *Swedish Journal of Economics* 72 (1970): 341–54; E. C. Brown and Robert Solow, eds., *Paul Samuelson and Modern Economic Theory* (New York: McGraw-Hill,

1983); George Feiwel, ed., *Samuelson and Neoclassical Economics* (Boston: Kluwer Nijhoff, 1982); and Stanley Fischer, "Paul Samuelson," in John Eatwell, Murray Milgate, and Peter Newman, *The New Palgrave: A Dictionary of Economics* (New York: Stockton Press, 1987).

CHAPTER THREE

1. Dorothy Ross, "American Social Science and the Idea of Progress," in Thomas L. Haskell, ed., *The Authority of Experts: Studies in History and Theory* (Bloomington: Indiana University Press, 1984), 164.

2. Following the radicalism of the 1960s, Samuelson would come under attack from those who thought he had made too many compromises, that Samuelson was an apologist for the American capitalist system. See Marc Linder, *The Anti-Samuelson*, vol. 1, *Macroeconomics: Basic Problems of a Capitalist Economy* (New York: Urizen Books, 1977); and Marc Linder, *The Anti-Samuelson*, vol. 2, *Microeconomics: Basic Problems of a Capitalist Economy* (New York: Urizen Books, 1977).

3. George R. Feiwel, "Samuelson and Contemporary Economics: An Introduction," in Feiwel, ed., *Samuelson and Neoclassical Economics* (Boston: Kluwer Nijhoff, 1982), 22.

4. Paul A. Samuelson, "My Life Philosophy: Policy Credos and Working Ways," in Michael Szenberg, ed., *Eminent Economists: Their Life Philosophies* (New York: Cambridge University Press, 1992), 237, 236.

5. Ibid., 238, 243.

6. Lawrence Klein, *The Keynesian Revolution* (New York: Macmillan, 1961; 1st ed., 1947), 153.

7. Kenneth J. Arrow, "Rationality of Self and Others in an Economic System," in Robin M. Hogarth and Melvin W. Reder, eds., *Rational Choice: The Contrast Between Economics and Psychology* (Chicago: University of Chicago Press, 1987), 208.

8. George J. Stigler, "The Economics of Information," *Journal of Political Economy* 69 (June 1961).

9. Ronald H. Coase, "The Problem of Social Cost," *Journal of Law and Economics* 3 (October 1960).

10. Rachel McCulloch, "The Optimality of Free Trade: Science or Religion?" *American Economic Review* 83 (May 1993), 370, 369.

11. Eirik G. Furubotn and Rudolf Richer, *Institutions and Economic Theory: The Contribution of the New Institutional Economics* (Ann Arbor: University of Michigan Press, 1997), 436.

12. Avinash K. Dixit, *The Making of Economic Policy: A Transaction-Cost Politics Perspective* (Cambridge: MIT Press, 1998), 51.

13. Joseph E. Stiglitz, *Wither Socialism?* (Cambridge: MIT Press, 1994), 5, 13.

14. George Akerlof, 1988 interview published in Richard Swedberg, *Economics and Sociology, Refining Their Boundaries: Conversations with Economists and Sociologists* (Princeton: Princeton University Press, 1990), 65.

15. Peter J. Boettke, "Where Did Economics Go Wrong? Modern Economics as a Flight from Reality," *Critical Review* 11 (Winter 1997): 20.

16. Ibid., 28. See also Karen I. Vaughn, "Economic Policy for an Imperfect World," *Southern Economic Review* 62 (April 1996).

17. Douglass C. North, *Institutions, Institutional Change, and Economic Performance* (New York: Cambridge University Press, 1990), 80, 108, 81.

18. Ibid., 111.

19. Oliver E. Williamson, *Markets and Hierarchies: Analysis and Antitrust Implications* (New York: Free Press, 1975).

20. Oliver E. Williamson, *Economic Organization: Firms, Markets and Policy Control* (New York: New York University Press, 1986), 131.

21. Ibid., 177.

22. Herbert A. Simon, "Rationality in Psychology and Economics," in Hogarth and Reder, *Rational Choice*, 38–39.

23. Donald N. McCloskey, *The Rhetoric of Economics* (Madison: University of Wisconsin Press, 1985), 16. See also McCloskey, *If You're So Smart: The Narrative of Economic Expertise* (Chicago: University of Chicago Press, 1990).

24. See also John S. Nelson, Allan Megill, and Donald N. McCloskey, eds., *The Rhetoric of the Human Sciences: Language and Argument in Scholarship and Public Affairs* (Madison: University of Wisconsin Press, 1987).

25. See Robert H. Nelson, "Does 'Existence Value' Exist: Economics Encroaches on Religion," *Independent Review* 1 (March 1997); also Donald H. Rosenthal and Robert H. Nelson, "Why Existence Values Should Not Be Used in Cost-Benefit Analysis," *Journal of Policy Analysis and Management* 11 (Winter 1992).

26. See A. Dan Tarlock, "Can Cowboys Become Indians? Protecting Western Communities as Endangered Cultural Remnants," *Arizona State Law Journal* (Summer 1999).

27. Ibid., 549, 546, 550, 546–47.

28. Ibid., 550–51, 554.

29. Ibid., 582, 552, 550.

30. See Robert H. Nelson, "In Memoriam: On the Death of the 'Market Mechanism,' " *Ecological Economics* 20 (March 1997).

31. Matthew Rabin, "Pyschology and Economics," *Journal of Economic Literature* 36 (March 1998): 13–14.

32. Martha S. Feldman and James G. March, "Information in Organizations as Signal and Symbol," *Administrative Science Quarterly* 26 (June 1981): 182.

33. A. Michael Spence, *Market Signalling: Information Transfer in Hiring and Related Screening Processes* (Cambridge: Harvard University Press, 1974).

34. George J. Stigler, "Economics or Ethics?" *The Tanner Lectures on Human Values* (Salt Lake City: University of Utah Press, 1981), reprinted in Kurt R. Leube and Thomas Gale Moore, eds., *The Essence of Stigler* (Stanford, Calif.: Hoover Institution Press, 1986), 307.

35. R. A. Mundell, "A Reconsideration of the Twentieth Century," *American Economic Review* 90 (June 2000), 327, 331.

36. Charles L. Schultze, *The Politics and Economics of Public Spending* (Washington, D.C.: Brookings Institution, 1968), 2–3.

37. Charles L. Schultze, "The Role and Responsibilities of the Economist in Government," *American Economic Review* 72 (May 1982): 62.

38. William J. Baumol, "On My Attitudes: Sociopolitical and Methodological," in Michael Szenberg, ed., *Eminent Economists: Their Life Philosophies* (New York: Cambridge University Press, 1992), 51.

39. See Richard A. Posner, "The Ethical and Political Basis of the Efficiency Norm in Common Law Adjudication," *Hofstra Law Review* 8 (Spring 1980); Ronald Dworkin, "Why Efficiency?" *Hofstra Law Review* (Summer 1980); and other articles from the "Symposium on Efficiency as a Legal Concern" included in the summer 1980 issue of the *Hofstra Law Review.*

40. Wade Roush, "Conflict Marks Crime Conference," *Science,* September 29, 1995, 1808.

41. Quoted in Patricia Cohen, "One Angry Man," *Washington Post,* May 30, 1997, B2.

42. David Ostendorf, "Rural Frustrations," *Christian Century,* September 27–October 4, 1995, 877.

43. Jerome H. Skolnick, "Passions of Crime," *American Prospect,* 25 (March–April 1996): 92. For an example of the conservative view, see Marvin Olasky, "Welfare States," *National Review,* October 23, 1995.

44. Gordon F. Sander, "Sweden: After the Fall," *Wilson Quarterly* 20 (Spring 1996): 60.

45. Nurith C. Aizenman, "What's Cooking in the Ivory Tower," *Washington Monthly,* September 1997, 13.

46. Robert J. Samuelson, "It's Not the Economy, Stupid," *Washington Post,* January 7, 1994, A19.

47. Robert J. Samuelson, "How Our American Dream Unraveled," *Newsweek,* March 2, 1992, 32. See also Samuelson, *The Good Life and its Discontents: The American Dream in the Age of Entitlement, 1945–1995* (New York: Times Books, 1995).

48. See John V. Krutilla, "Conservation Reconsidered," *American Economic Review* 57 (September 1967); W. Michael Hanemann, "Valuing the Environment Through Contingent Valuation," *Journal of Economic Perspectives* 8 (Fall 1994); Robert Mitchell and Richard Carson, *Using Surveys to Value Public Goods: The Contingent Valuation Method* (Washington, D.C.: Resources for the Future, 1989); and Paul R. Portney, "The Contingent Valuation Debate: Why Economists Should Care," *Journal of Economic Perspectives* 8 (Fall 1994).

49. For criticisms of the use of existence value in economic studies, see Jerry A. Hausman, ed., *Contingent Valuation: A Critical Assessment* (New York: North Holland, 1993); William H. Desvousges et al., "Measuring Natural Resource Damages with Contingent Valuation: Tests of Validity and Reliability," in Hausman, ed., *Contingent Valuation;* and Peter A. Diamond and Jerry A. Hausman, "Contingent Valuation: Is Some Number Better Than No Number?," *Journal of Economic Perspectives* 8 (Fall 1994).

50. For further discussion of this issue, see Robert H. Nelson, "Does 'Existence Value' Exist: Economics Encroaches on Religion," *Independent Review* 1 (March 1997); also Donald H. Rosenthal and Robert H. Nelson, "Why Existence Values Should Not Be Used in Cost-Benefit Analysis," *Journal of Policy Analysis and Management* 11 (Winter 1992).

51. Kenneth J. Arrow, *Social Choice and Individual Values* (New Haven: Yale University Press, 1972; 1st ed., 1951), 1.

52. See Timur Kuran, "Islam and Underdevelopment: An Old Puzzle Revisited," *Journal of Institutional and Theoretical Economics* 153 (March 1997); "Fundamentalisms and the Economy," in Martin Marty and Scott Appleby, eds, *Fundamentalisms and the State: Remaking Politics, Economics, and Militance* (Chicago: University of Chicago Press, 1993); and "The Economic System in Contemporary Islamic Thought: Interpretation and Assessment," *International Journal of Middle East Studies* 18, no. 2 (1986).

CHAPTER FOUR

1. For studies in the failures of progressive theories of scientific management as applied to specific policy issues facing American government, see Robert H. Nelson, *Zoning and Property Rights: An Analysis of the American System of Land Use Regulation* (Cambridge: MIT Press, 1977); *The Making of Federal Coal Policy* (Durham: Duke University Press, 1983); *Public Lands and Private Rights: The Failure of Scientific Management* (Lanham, Md.: Rowman & Littlefield, 1995); and *A Burning Issue: A Case for Abolishing the U.S. Forest Service* (Lanham, Md.: Rowman & Littlefield, 2000).

2. For a short survey, see N. Gregory Mankiw, "A Quick Refresher Course in Macroeconomics," *Journal of Economic Literature* 28 (December 1990).

3. Kenneth J. Arrow, "Rationality of Self and Others in an Economic System," in Robin W. Hogarth and Melvin W. Reder, eds., *Rational Choice: The Contrast Between Economics and Psychology* (Chicago: University of Chicago Press, 1987), 202.

4. Paul Samuelson, *Economics from the Heart: A Samuelson Sampler* (Sun Lakes, Ariz.: Thomas Horton and Daughters, 1983), 99–100.

5. Ibid., 100

6. Milton Friedman, "John Maynard Keynes," *Economic Quarterly* (Federal Reserve Bank of Richmond) 83 (Spring 1997): 20, 21.

7. James M. Buchanan, Robert D. Tollison, and Gordon Tullock, eds., *Toward a Theory of a Rent-Seeking Society* (College Station: Texas A&M University Press, 1980); Robert D. Tollison, "Rent-Seeking: A Survey," *Kyklos* 35 (1982); and Gordon Tullock, *The Economics of Special Privilege and Rent Seeking* (Dordrecht: Kluwer, 1989).

8. Theodore J. Lowi, *The End of Liberalism: Ideology, Policy, and the Crisis of Public Authority* (New York: W. W. Norton, 1969).

9. See James M. Buchanan, *What Should Economists Do?* (Indianapolis, Ind.: Liberty Press, 1979).

10. Mancur Olson, *The Logic of Collective Action: Public Goods and the Theory of Groups* (Cambridge: Harvard University Press, 1965).

11. See Gary J. Miller, "The Impact of Economics on Contemporary Political Science," *Journal of Economic Literature* 35 (September 1997).

12. An authoritative source on the natural-law foundations of medieval philosophy and theology is Etienne Gilson, *The Spirit of Medieval Philosophy* (New York: Charles Scribner's, 1936).

13. Lynn White, Jr., "The Historic Roots of Our Ecologic Crisis," *Science*, March 10, 1967, 1204–5.

14. John Nef, *The Conquest of the Material World* (Chicago: University of Chicago Press, 1964), 62–63, 116.

15. Carl L. Becker, *The Heavenly City of the Eighteenth-Century Philosophers* (New Haven: Yale University Press, 1968; 1st ed., 1932), 60.

16. Isaiah Berlin, *The Age of Enlightenment: The Eighteenth Century Philosophers*, in *Great Ages of Western Philosophy* (Boston: Houghton Mifflin, 1962), 16.

17. John F. Henry, "John Bates Clark: The Religious Imperative," in H. Geoffrey Brennan and A. M. C. Waterman, *Economics and Religion: Are They Distinct?* (Boston: Kluwer, 1994), 76.

18. For discussion of the key role of medieval scholastic thought in setting the "foundations for modern rationalism and individualism" in the economic domain, see Franz-Xavier Kaufman, "Religion and Modernization in Europe," *Journal of Institutional and Theoretical Economics* 153 (March 1997): 80.

19. Herbert A. Simon, "The Failure of Armchair Economics," *Challenge* 29 (November–December 1986): 23.

20. This is a main theme of Nelson, *Reaching for Heaven on Earth*.

21. For an excellent survey of the follies of the past three hundred years, see Frank E. Manuel and Fritzie P. Manuel, *Utopian Thought in the Western World* (Cambridge: Harvard University Press, 1979).

22. Elinor Ostrom, *Governing the Commons: The Evolution of Institutions for Collective Action* (New York: Cambridge University Press, 1990).

23. Ibid., 184.

24. Daniel J. Mahoney, review of *Community of Citizens: On the Modern Idea of Nationality*, by Dominique Schnapper, *Society* 37 (March/April 2000): 91–93.

25. Jon Elster, *Solomonic Judgements: Studies in the Limitations of Rationality* (New York: Cambridge University Press, 1989), 179. See also Elster, *The Cement of Society: A Study of Social Order* (New York: Cambridge University Press, 1989), 186–215; and "Emotions and Economic Theory," *Journal of Economic Literature* 36 (March 1998).

26. Albert O. Hirschman, *A Propensity to Self-Subversion* (Cambridge: Harvard University Press, 1995), 151.

27. Samuelson interview in Carla Ravaioli, *Economists and the Environment* (London: Zed Books, 1995), 122.

28. John Maynard Keynes, "Economic Possibilities for Our Grandchildren," quoted in Paul A. Samuelson and William D. Nordhaus, *Economics*, 16th ed. (New York: McGraw-Hill, 1998), 735.

29. Samuelson and Nordhaus, *Economics*, 735.

INTRODUCTION TO PART THREE

1. The impact of libertarian ideas is described in Gerald F. Seib, "Libertarian Impulses Show Growing Appeal Among the Disaffected," *The Wall Street Journal*, January 20, 1995, 1.

2. Paul Samuelson, *Economics from the Heart: A Samuelson Sampler* (Sun Lakes, Ariz.: Thomas Horton and Daughters, 1983), 60.

3. See T. Patrick Raines and Clarence R. Jung, "Knight on Religion and Ethics as Agents of Social Change," *American Journal of Economics and Sociology* 45 (October 1986): 430–31.

4. George J. Stigler, autobiographical statement in William Breit and Roger W. Spencer, eds., *Lives of the Laureates: Thirteen Nobel Economists*, 3d ed. (Cambridge: MIT Press, 1995), 98.

5. Milton Friedman, *Capitalism and Freedom* (Chicago: University of Chicago Press, 1962).

6. George J. Stigler and Claire Friedland, "What Can Regulators Regulate? The Case of Electricity," *Journal of Law and Economics* 5 (October 1962).

7. George J. Stigler, "The Theory of Economic Regulation," *Bell Journal of Economics and Management Science* 2 (Spring 1971).

8. The worldwide impact of Chicago thinking in the last three decades of the twentieth century is usefully reviewed in Daniel Yergin and Joseph Stanislaw, *The Commanding Heights: The Battle Between Government and the Marketplace That Is Remaking the Modern World* (New York: Simon and Schuster, 1998). Privatization in the United States is discussed in *Privatization: Toward More Effective Government*, report of the President's Commission on Privatization (Washington, D.C., March 1988).

9. Gary S. Becker, *The Economic Approach to Human Behavior* (Chicago: University of Chicago Press, 1976); and Gary S. Becker, *A Treatise on the Family* (Cambridge: Harvard University Press, 1991; 1st ed., 1981).

10. A Chicago professor of law (and now federal judge), Richard Posner, would apply an economic method not only to the workings of the legal system but also to many other corners of American society—exceeding even Becker as a prolific and visible spokesperson for the application of the Chicago school's economic way of thinking.

11. See Robert E. Hall, "Robert Lucas, Recipient of the 1995 Memorial Prize in Economics," *Scandinavian Journal of Economics* 98 (March 1996); and Stanley Fischer, "Robert Lucas's Nobel Prize," *Scandinavian Journal of Economics* 98 (March 1996).

12. The citations data were provided by Zvi Griliches and Liran Einav, in the Correspondence Section, *Journal of Economic Perspectives* 12 (Fall 1998): 234.

13. See Sylvia Nasar, "New Breed of College All Star," *New York Times,* April 8, 1998.

14. Paul Heyne, "Theological Visions in Economics and Religion," paper presented to the Atlantic Economic Society, Allied Social Science Association, San Francisco, Calif., January 5, 1996, 1.

15. A. W. Coats, "The Origins of the 'Chicago School(s)'?" *Journal of Political Economy* 71 (October 1963). See also Warren J. Samuels, ed., *The Chicago School of Political Economy* (New Brunswick: Transaction, 1993; 1st ed., 1976).

16. A collection of leading Chicago writings is contained in George J. Stigler, ed., *Chicago Studies in Political Economy* (Chicago: University of Chicago Press, 1988).

CHAPTER FIVE

1. Milton Friedman and Rose Friedman, *Free to Choose: A Personal Statement* (New York: Avon Books, 1981), 117.

2. James M. Buchanan, foreword to Liberty Press edition of Frank Knight, *Freedom and Reform: Essays in Economics and Social Philosophy* (Indianapolis, Ind.: Liberty Press, 1982; 1st ed., 1947), xi. See also James M. Buchanan, "Frank H. Knight," in Edward Shils, *Remembering the University of Chicago: Teachers, Scientists, and Scholars* (Chicago: University of Chicago Press, 1991).

3. Quoted in Buchanan, foreword to Knight, *Freedom and Reform,* xiv.

4. Don Patinkin, *Essays On and In the Chicago Tradition* (Durham, N.C.: Duke University Press, 1981), 26, 25.

5. Buchanan, foreword to Knight, *Freedom and Reform,* x.

6. See William S. Kern, "Frank Knight on Preachers and Economic Policy: A Nineteenth Century Anti-Religionist, He Thought Religion Should Support the Status Quo," *American Journal of Economics and Sociology* 47 (January 1988).

7. Frank H. Knight and Thornton W. Merriam, *The Economic Order and Religion* (Westport, Conn.: Greenwood Press, 1979; 1st ed., 1945).

8. Frank H. Knight, "The Role of Principles in Economics and Politics," presidential address to American Economic Association, December 28, 1950, *American Economic Review* 41 (March 1951), reprinted in Frank H. Knight, *On the History and Method of Economics* (Chicago: University of Chicago Press, 1956), 252.

9. Patinkin, *Essays on and in the Chicago Tradition*, 46.

10. Frank H. Knight, "Pragmatism and Social Action," *International Journal of Ethics* 46 (1936), reprinted in Knight, *Freedom and Reform*, 52.

11. Frank H. Knight, *Risk, Uncertainty, and Profit* (New York: Harper and Row, 1965; 1st ed., 1921). This was Knight's first book, based on his doctoral dissertation.

12. For Knight's early years, see Donald Dewey, "Frank Knight Before Cornell: Some Light on the Dark Years," in Warren Samuels, ed., *Research in the History of Economic Thought and Methodology*, vol. 8 (Greenwich, Conn.: JAI Press, 1990).

13. Razeen Sally, "The Political Economy of Frank Knight: Classical Liberalism from Chicago," *Constitutional Political Economy* 8, no. 2 (1997).

14. Richard Schlatter, *Private Property: The History of an Idea* (New York: Russell and Russell, 1973; 1st ed., 1951), 35.

15. Richard T. Ely, *Social Aspects of Christianity and Other Essays* (New York: Thomas Y. Crowell, 1889), 1, 6–7.

16. Charles Howard Hopkins, *The Rise of the Social Gospel in American Protestantism, 1865–1915* (New Haven: Yale University Press, 1940).

17. Frank H. Knight, "Ethics and Economic Reform," *Economica* 6 (1939), reprinted in Knight, *Freedom and Reform*, 129, 127.

18. Ibid., 63.

19. Ibid., 63–64.

20. Ibid, 131.

21. Ibid., 67.

22. Frank H. Knight, "Liberalism and Christianity," in Frank H. Knight and Thornton W. Merriam, *Economic Order and Religion* (New York: Harper and Brothers, 1945), 100.

23. Kern, "Frank Knight on Preachers and Economic Policy."

24. Frank H. Knight "The Rights of Man and Natural Law," *Ethics* 44 (1944), reprinted in Knight, *Freedom and Reform*, 332.

25. Knight, "Ethics and Economic Reform," 125.

26. Knight, "The Rights of Man and Natural Law," 320.

27. Knight, "Pragmatism and Social Action," 53.

28. Frank H. Knight, "Salvation by Science: The Gospel According to Professor Lundberg," *Journal of Political Economy* (December 1947), reprinted in Knight, *On the History and Method of Economics*.

29. Daniel J. Hammond, "Frank Knight's Antipositivism," *History of Political Economy* 23 (Fall 1991).

30. Knight, "The Role of Principles in Economics and Politics," 277.

31. Ibid., 275.

32. Frank H. Knight, "The Limitations of Scientific Method in Economics," in Rexford G. Tugwell, ed., *The Trend of Economics*, reprinted in Frank Hyneman Knight, *The Ethics of Competition* (New Brunswick, N.J.: Transactions, 1997; 1st ed., 1935).

33. Frank H. Knight, "Free Society: Its Basic Nature and Problem," *Philosophical Review* (January 1948), reprinted in Knight, *Essays on the History and Method of Economics*, 299.

34. Richard A. Gonce, "Frank H. Knight on Social Control and the Scope and Method of Economics," *Southern Economic Journal* 38 (April 1972).

35. Frank H. Knight, "Abstract Economics as Absolute Ethics," *Ethics* 76 (April 1966): 166.

36. Knight, "Salvation by Science," 229, 235.

37. Ibid., 230.

38. Knight, "The Role of Principles in Economics and Politics," 261, 258, 260.

39. Frank H. Knight, "Economic Psychology and the Value Problem," *Quarterly Journal of Economics* 39 (1925), reprinted in Knight, *The Ethics of Competition*.

40. Knight, "The Role of Principles in Economics and Politics," 279.

41. Knight, "Free Society," 299.

42. See John Kohl, "Christianity: Protestantism," in R. C. Zaehner, *Encyclopedia of the World's Religions* (New York: Barnes and Noble, 1997), 101.

43. Ross B. Emmett, "Frank Knight: Economics versus Religion," in H. Geoffrey Brennan and A. M. C. Waterman, eds., *Economics and Religion: Are They Distinct?* (Boston: Kluwer, 1994), 118–19.

44. Buchanan, "Frank H. Knight," 247, 246. See also James M. Buchanan, "The Economizing Element in Knight's Ethical Critique of Capitalist Order," *Ethics* 98 (October 1987).

45. For a full exploration of the Puritan mentality, see Michael Walzer, *The Revolution of the Saints: A Study in the Origins of Radical Politics* (New York: Atheneum, 1974). See also Duncan B. Forrester, "Martin Luther and John Calvin," in Leo Strauss and Joseph Cropsey, eds., *History of Political Philosophy* (Chicago: University of Chicago Press, 1981).

46. Knight, "Liberalism and Christianity," 38–39.

47. Knight, "The Role of Principles in Economics and Politics," 273, 269, 262.

48. A classic study of the powerful role of Calvinist (and Quaker) religion in American life is found in E. Digby Baltzell, *Puritan Boston and Quaker Philadelphia: Two Protestant Ethics and the Spirit of Class Authority and Leadership* (New York: Free Press, 1979).

49. Paula Baker, *The Moral Frameworks of Public Life: Gender, Politics, and the State in Rural New York, 1870–1930* (New York: Oxford University Press, 1991), 14.

50. Frank H. Knight, "The Ethics of Competition," *Quarterly Journal of Economics* 37 (August 1923), reprinted in Knight, *The Ethics of Competition*, 33.

51. Paul K. Conkin, *Puritans and Pragmatists: Eight Eminent American Thinkers* (Bloomington: Indiana University Press, 1976), 3–4.

52. Patinkin, *Essays on and in the Chicago Tradition*, 34.

53. Richard Boyd, "Frank Knight's Pluralism," *Critical Review* 11 (Fall 1997): 537.

54. For further discussion of these theological traditions, see Robert H. Nelson, *Reaching for Heaven on Earth: The Theological Meaning of Economics* (Lanham, Md.: Rowman and Littlefield, 1991).

55. Boyd, "Frank Knight's Pluralism," 537.

56. See Knight, "The Ethics of Competition"; also Frank H. Knight, "Ethics and the Economic Interpretation," *Quarterly Journal of Economics* 36 (May 1922), reprinted in Knight, *The Ethics of Competition*.

57. Knight, "Liberalism and Christianity," 71.

58. Knight, "Ethics and Economic Reform," 84.

59. Frank H. Knight, "Social Science," *Ethics* 51 (January 1941), reprinted in Knight, *On the History and Method of Economics*, 134.

60. Knight, "Ethics and Economic Reform," 55.

61. J. Patrick Raines and Clarence R. Jung, "Knight on Religion and Ethics as Agents of Social Change: An Essay to Commemorate the Centennial of Frank H. Knight's Birth," *American Journal of Economics and Sociology* 45 (October 1986).

62. Knight, "The Role of Principles in Economics and Politics," 266.

63. Knight, "Free Society," 295.

64. Frank H. Knight, "Social Science and the Political Trend," *University of Toronto Quarterly* 3 (1934), reprinted in Knight, *Freedom and Reform*, 32.

65. Knight, "Ethics and Economic Reform," 73.

66. Knight, "Social Science and the Political Trend," 39–40.

67. Knight, "The Role of Principles in Economics and Politics," 265.

68. Ernest Troeltsch, *Protestantism and Progress: A Historical Study of the Relation of Protestantism to the Modern World* (Boston: Beacon Press, 1958; 1st ed., 1912), 125–26.

69. Conkin, *Puritans and Pragmatists*, 18.

CHAPTER SIX

1. See H. Laurence Miller, Jr. "On the 'Chicago School of Economics,' " *Journal of Political Economy* 70 (February 1962): 64.

2. Don Patinkin, *Essays on and in the Chicago Tradition* (Durham: Duke University Press, 1981), 45.

3. William Niskanen, *Policy Analyis and Public Choice: Selected Papers by William Niskanen* (Northhampton, Mass.: Edward Elgar, 1998), 307.

4. Cited in Daniel Yergin and Joseph Stanislaw, *The Commanding Heights: The Battle Between Government and the Marketplace That Is Remaking the Modern World* (New York: Simon and Schuster, 1998), 151.

5. Milton Friedman and Rose Friedman, *Free to Choose* (New York: Avon Books, 1979), xv, 28, 129.

6. Ibid., 54.

7. Ibid., 47, 137, 138, 129.

8. Luke 18:24–25.

9. George Stigler, *The Intellectual and the Marketplace* (Cambridge: Harvard University Press, 1984), 157–58.

10. Raymond Seidelman, *Disenchanted Realists: Political Science and the American Crisis, 1884–1984* (Albany: State University of New York Press, 1985).

11. David B. Truman, *The Governmental Process: Political Interests and Public Opinion* (New York: Alfred A. Knopf, 1951).

12. John Kenneth Galbraith, *American Capitalism: The Concept of Countervailing Power* (Boston: Houghton Mifflin, 1956).

13. Gunnar Myrdal, *Beyond the Welfare State: Economic Planning and Its International Implications* (New Haven: Yale University Press, 1960), 96.

14. Truman, *The Governmental Process,* 50–51.

15. Herbert Simon, "The Proverbs of Administration," *Public Administration Review* 6 (Winter 1946); see also Herbert A. Simon, *Administrative Behavior: A Study of Decision-Making Processes in Administrative Organization* (New York: Free Press, 1965; 1st ed., 1945).

16. Charles E. Lindblom, "The Science of 'Muddling Through,' " *Public Administration Review* 19 (Spring 1959).

17. Pendleton Herring, "Research on Government, Politics, and Administration," in *Research for Public Policy,* Brookings Dedication Lectures (Washington, D.C.: Brookings Institution, 1961), 13.

18. Theodore J. Lowi, *The End of Liberalism: Ideology, Policy, and the Crisis of Public Authority* (New York: W. W. Norton, 1969), 86–89. See also Mancur Olson, *The Rise and Decline of Nations: Economic Growth, Stagflation, and Social Rigidities* (New Haven: Yale University Press, 1982).

19. Paul Anthony Samuelson, *Foundations of Economic Analysis* (New York: Atheneum 1965; 1st ed., 1947).

20. Deirdre N. McCloskey, *The Vices of Economists: The Virtues of the Bourgeoisie* (Amsterdam: Amsterdam University Press, distributed by the University of Michigan Press, 1996), 75.

21. Milton Friedman, *Capitalism and Freedom* (Chicago: University of Chicago Press, 1962), 13, 2, 3, 13.

22. Laurence A. Boland, "A Critique of Friedman's Critics," *Journal of Economic Literature* 17 (June 1979).

23. Robert Heilbroner, "Analysis and Vision in the History of Modern Economic Thought," *Journal of Economic Literature* 28 (September 1990): 1106.

24. Friedman, *Capitalism and Freedom,* 25.

25. These proposals are summarized in Friedman, *Capitalism and Freedom,* 35–36.

26. *Privatization: Toward More Effective Government,* report of the President's Commission on Privatization (Washington, D.C., March 1988), 243.

27. Yergin and Stanislaw, *The Commanding Heights.*

28. Lewis Evans, Arthur Grimes, Bryce Wilkinson, and David Teece, "Economic Reform in New Zealand, 1984–95: The Pursuit of Efficiency," *Journal of Economic Literature* 34 (December 1996).

29. Friedman autobiographical statement in William Breit and Roger W. Spencer, eds., *Lives of the Laureates: Thirteen Nobel Economists* (Cambridge: MIT Press, 1995), 92.

30. Norman Pearlstine, "Big Wheels Turning," *Time,* December 7, 1998, 73.

31. George J. Stigler, *Memoirs of an Unregulated Economist* (New York: Basic Books, 1988), 146–47.

32. George J. Stigler, *Citizen and the State: Essays on Regulation* (Chicago: University of Chicago Press, 1975), 18–19.

33. See Milton Friedman and Rose D. Friedman, *Two Lucky People: Memoirs* (Chicago: University of Chicago Press, 1998), 333–65.

34. George J. Stigler, "Bernard Shaw, Sidney Webb and the Theory of Fabian Socialism," *Proceedings of the American Philosophical Society* 103 (June 1959), reprinted in Kurt R. Leube and Thomas Gale Moore, eds., *The Essence of Stigler* (Stanford, Calif.: Hoover Institution Press, 1986), 299.

35. James Buchanan and Gordon Tullock, *The Calculus of Consent: Logical Foundations of Constitutional Democracy* (Ann Arbor: University of Michigan Press, 1962). For a review of Buchanan's thinking, see Agnar Sandmo, "Buchanan on Political Economy," *Journal of Economic Literature* 28 (March 1990). See also Mancur Olson, *The Logic of Collective Action: Public Goods and the Theory of Groups* (Cambridge: Harvard University Press, 1965).

36. George J. Stigler, "Why Have the Socialists Been Winning?" *Ordo* 30 (1979), reprinted in Leube and Moore, eds., *The Essence of Stigler,* 340, 338.

37. George J. Stigler, "The Process and Progress of Economics," Nobel Memorial Lecture, December 8, 1982, reprinted in Leube and Moore, eds., *The Essence of Stigler,* 145.

38. Government powers can be particularly effective in reducing transaction costs in the land market. See Robert H. Nelson, *Zoning and Property Rights: An Analysis of the American System of Land Use Regulation* (Cambridge: MIT Press, 1977).

39. George J. Stigler, "The Theory of Economic Regulation," *Bell Journal of Economics and Management Science* 2 (Spring 1971), reprinted in Stigler, *The Citizen and the State,* 115.

40. Ibid., 114, 116, 126.

41. See Robert H. Nelson, "Private Rights to Government Actions: How Modern Property Rights Evolve," *University of Illinois Law Review* 1986, no. 2 (1986).

42. Stigler, "The Theory of Economic Regulation," 123.

43. Stigler, "Process and Progress of Economics," 155.

44. Ibid.

45. Melvin W. Reder, "Chicago Economics: Permanence and Change," *Journal of Economic Literature* 20 (March 1982): 26.

46. Ibid.

47. Ronald Coase, "George J. Stigler," in Edward Shils, ed., *Remembering the University of Chicago* (Chicago: University of Chicago Press, 1991), 477.

48. Quoted in Friedman and Friedman, *Two Lucky People,* 231.

49. Timur Kuran, *Private Truths, Public Lies: The Social Consequences of Preference Falsification* (Cambridge: Harvard University Press, 1995).

50. Ibid., 205–21.

51. Ibid., 300–302.

52. Niels Thygesen, "The Scientific Contributions of Milton Friedman," *Scandinavian Journal of Economics,* 79, no. 1 (1977): 83, 56.

53. Quoted in Friedman and Friedman, *Two Lucky People,* 230.

54. Ibid., 446–49.

55. Ibid., 220.

56. Martha Derthick and Paul J. Quirk, *The Politics of Deregulation* (Washington, D.C.: Brookings Institution, 1985).

57. Gary Becker, "Milton Friedman," in Shils, *Remembering the University of Chicago,* 145, 146.

58. See Edward Shils, "Harry Johnson," in Shils, *Remembering the University of Chicago,* 209, 201.

59. George J. Stigler, "Economics or Ethics?" *The Tanner Lectures on Human Values* (Salt Lake City: University of Utah Press, 1981), 146.

60. Caption for 1965 picture of Frank Knight, Ronald Coase, George Stigler, and Harold Demsetz, in Stigler, *Memoirs of an Unregulated Economist.*

61. Ibid., 103, 95, 180.

62. George J. Stigler, "The Economist and the State," presidential address to the American Economic Association, December 29, 1964, *American Economic Review* 55 (March 1965), reprinted in Stigler, *The Citizen and the State,* 55–56.

CHAPTER SEVEN

1. Cindy Kelly, "The Most Cited Economists," *Margin* (Fall 1992), 75.

2. Sherwin Rosen, "Risks and Rewards: Gary Becker's Contributions to Economics," *Scandinavian Journal of Economics* 95 (March 1993): 34, 25. See also Agnar Sandmo, "Gary Becker's Contributions to Economics," *Scandinavian Journal of Economics* 95 (March 1993).

3. Victor R. Fuchs, "Gary S. Becker: Ideas About Facts," *Journal of Economic Perspectives* 8 (Spring 1994): 183, 190.

4. See Richard Swedberg, *Economics and Sociology* (Princeton: Princeton University Press, 1990).

5. A selection of Becker's *Business Week* columns is contained in Gary S. Becker and Guity Nashat Becker, *The Economics of Life* (New York: McGraw-Hill, 1997).

6. Religion has never fared well in libertarian circles. Many libertarians have been atheists. Friedrich Hayek considered that "religious beliefs seem to be almost the only ground on which general rules seriously restrictive of liberty have ever been universally enforced." See Friedrich A. Hayek, *The Constitution of Liberty* (Chicago: Henry Regnery, 1972; 1st ed., 1960), 155.

7. Gary S. Becker, "The Economic Way of Looking at Behavior," 1992 Nobel Lecture, reprinted in Ramon Febrero and Pedro S. Schwartz, eds., *The Essence of Becker* (Stanford, Calif.: Hoover Institution Press, 1995), 633–34.

8. Robert B. Ekelund, Robert F. Hebert, Robert D. Tollison, Gary M. Anderson, and Audrey B. Davidson, *Sacred Trust: The Medieval Church as an Economic Firm* (New York: Oxford University Press, 1996).

9. George J. Stigler and Gary S. Becker, "De Gustibus Non Est Disputandum," *American Economic Review* 67 (March 1977): 76, 89.

10. Gary S. Becker, *The Economics of Discrimination* (Chicago: University of Chicago Press, 1971; 1st ed., 1957), 14.

11. Ibid., 21.

12. Jon Elster, "Emotions and Economic Theory," *Journal of Economic Literature* 36 (March 1998): 59.

13. Gary S. Becker, "Crime and Punishment: An Economic Approach," *Journal of Political Economy* 76 (March/April 1968); reprinted in Becker, *The Economic Approach to Human Behavior* (Chicago: University of Chicago Press, 1976), 41.

14. Stigler was also a contributor to this literature. See George J. Stigler, "The Optimum Enforcement of Laws," *Journal of Political Economy* 78 (May/June 1970).

15. Becker, "Crime and Punishment," 46.

16. Ibid., 41.

17. Ibid., 43.

18. Ibid., 71.

19. Becker, *The Economics of Discrimination,* 161.

20. Richard A. Posner, "Euthanasia and Health Care: Two Essays on the Policy Dilemmas of Aging and Old Age," Tanner Lectures in Human Values, Yale University, October 10 and 11, 1994, in Grethe B. Peterson, ed., *The Tanner Lectures in Human Values, 1996* (Salt Lake City: University of Utah Press, 1996).

21. Posner, "Euthanasia and Health Care," 16.

22. Ibid.

23. For a similar approach reflecting a more general effort to model the "optimal length of life," see Isaac Ehrlich and Hiroyuki Chuma, "A Model of the Demand for Longevity and the Value of Life Extension," *Journal of Political Economy* 98 (August 1990). For a broad criticism of the utilitarian ap-

proach to resolving questions of law, see Laurence H. Tribe, "Constitutional Calculus: Equal Justice or Economic Efficiency?" *Harvard Law Review* 98 (January 1985).

24. Gary S. Becker, "An Economic Analysis of Fertility," in *Demographic and Economic Change in Developed Countries,* a report of the National Bureau of Economic Research (Princeton: Princeton University Press, 1960).

25. Gary S. Becker, "A Theory of Marriage: Part I," *Journal of Political Economy* 81 (July/August 1973); and "A Theory of Marriage: Part II," *Journal of Political Economy* 82 (March/April 1974).

26. Gary S. Becker, *A Treatise on the Family* (Cambridge: Harvard University Press, 1991). The 1991 edition is a rewritten and enlarged version of the first 1981 edition (also Harvard University Press).

27. Becker, "The Economic Way of Looking at Behavior," 649.

28. Gary S. Becker, *The Economic Approach to Human Behavior* (Chicago: University of Chicago Press, 1976), 82.

29. Ibid., 83.

30. Ibid., 346.

31. Ibid., 124.

32. Ibid., 96.

33. Ibid., 288.

34. Richard A. Posner, *Sex and Reason* (Cambridge: Harvard University Press, 1992), 131.

35. Posner's most important scholarly contributions have come in the area of law and economics. See Richard A. Posner, *Economic Analysis of Law* (Boston: Little Brown, 1972); *The Problems of Jurisprudence* (Cambridge: Harvard University Press, 1990); and *Overcoming Law* (Cambridge: Harvard University Press, 1995).

36. Becker, *A Treatise on the Family,* 346 n. 3.

37. Elizabeth Cady Stanton, Susan B. Anthony, and Matilda Joslyn Gage, *The History of Woman Suffrage,* vol. 1 (New York: Arno Press, 1969), 70.

38. The Seneca Falls Declaration of Sentiments and Resolutions, prepared by Elizabeth Cady Stanton and committee, signed at Seneca, Falls, New York, July 19, 1848.

39. See Elizabeth S. Scott and Robert E. Scott, "A Contract Theory of Marriage," in F. H. Buckley, ed., *The Fall and Rise of Freedom of Contract* (Durham: Duke University Press, 1999).

40. Ramon Febrero and Pedro S. Schwartz, introduction to Febrero and Schwartz, *The Essence of Becker,* xliv.

41. Becker, "The Economic Way of Looking at Behavior," 648.

42. I base this statement about Hay's unique religious status among his Oxford economist colleagues on a personal conversation with Hay in January 1998.

43. Donald A. Hay, *Economics Today: A Christian Critique* (Leicester, U.K.: Inter-Varsity Press, 1989).

44. Ibid., 166, 163.

45. Ibid., 124, 71.

46. J. Budziszewski, "The Problem with Conservatism," *First Things,* April 1996, 42.

47. See also Roland Hoksbergen, "Is There a Christian Economics? Some Thoughts in the Light of the Rise of Postmodernism," *Christian Scholar's Review* 14 (December 1994).

48. Hay, *Economics Today,* 143, 142, 140.

49. See Christoph Schonborn, "The Hope of Heaven, the Hope of Earth," *First Things,* April 1995, 32.

50. Jennifer Roback Morse, *The Family in a Free Society,* draft book manuscript, July 1998. See also Morse, "Who Puts the Self in Self-Interest?" *Religion and Liberty* 8 (November/December 1998).

51. Jennifer Roback Morse, "Natural Law and Modern Economics," *Religion and Liberty* 8 (March/April 1998): 7.

52. Paul Tillich, *A History of Christian Thought: From Its Judaic and Hellenistic Origins to Existentialism* (New York: Simon and Schuster, 1967), 338, 334.

53. See James Davison Hunter, "When Psychotherapy Replaces Religion," *Public Interest,* no. 139 (Spring 2000): 19, 21, 11, 12.

54. Ibid., 12, 14.

55. Ibid., 5–6.

56. Ronald Inglehart, "Postmaterialist Values and the Erosion of Institutional Authority," in Joseph S. Nye, Jr., Philip D. Zelikow, and David C. King, eds., *Why People Don't Trust Government* (Cambridge: Harvard University Press, 1997), 217, 220, 221. See also Ronald Inglehart, *Silent Revolution: Changing Values and Political Styles Among Western Publics* (Princeton: Princeton University Press, 1977).

57. Inglehart, "Postmaterialist Values and the Erosion of Institutional Authority," 220.

58. Ibid., 219–20.

59. See also Jeffrey M. Berry, *The New Liberalism: The Rising Power of Citizen Groups* (Washington, D.C.: Brookings Institution Press, 1999).

60. David S. Broder and Richard Morin, "Struggle over New Standards," *Washington Post,* December 27, 1998, A1. The poll results for 1998 reported in this and other *Post* articles were the product of a collaboration between the *Post,* the Kaiser Family Foundation, and researchers at Harvard University.

61. See Robert H. Nelson, "Economic Religion versus Christian Values," *Journal of Markets and Morality* 1 (October 1998).

INTRODUCTION TO PART FOUR

1. See Karl Brunner, "Ronald Coase—Old-Fashioned Scholar," *Scandinavian Journal of Economics* 94 (March 1992).

2. Ronald H. Coase, "The Nature of the Firm," *Economica* 4 (November 1937); and "The Problem of Social Cost," *Journal of Law and Economics* 3 (October 1960). Both essays are reprinted in R. H. Coase, *The Firm, The Market, and the Law* (Chicago: University of Chicago Press, 1988). See also Yoram Barzel and Levis A. Kochin, "Ronald Coase on the Nature of Social Cost as a Key to the Problem of the Firm," *Scandinavian Journal of Economics* 94 (March 1992).

3. Douglass C. North, autobiographical statement, in William Breit and Roger W. Spencer, eds., *Lives of the Laureates: Thirteen Nobel Economists* (Cambridge: MIT Press, 1995), 259. North's most important contribution to institutional economics has been *Institutions, Institutional Change, and Economic Performance* (New York: Cambridge University Press, 1990).

4. Oliver E. Williamson, *Economic Organization: Firms, Markets, and Policy Control* (New York: New York University Press, 1986), xvi.

5. Oliver E. Williamson, *Markets and Hierarchies: Analysis and Antitrust Implications* (New York: Free Press, 1975); and *The Economic Institutions of Capitalism: Firms, Markets, Relational Contracting* (New York: Free Press, 1985).

6. A. Michael Spence, "The Economics of Internal Organization: An Introduction," *Bell Journal of Economics* 6 (Spring 1975): 164.

7. Eirik G. Furubotn and Rudolf Richter, *Institutions and Economic Theory: The Contribution of the New Institutional Economics* (Ann Arbor: University of Michigan Press, 1997), 436, 437.

8. Viktor J. Vanberg, "Institutional Evolution Through Purposeful Selection: The Constitutional Economics of John R. Commons," *Constitutional Political Economy* 8, no. 2 (1997): 105; see also Terence W. Hutchison, "Institutionalist Economics Old and New," *Journal of Institutional and Theoretical Economics* 140 (March 1984); and R. A. Gonce, "The Social Gospel, Ely, and Common's Initial Stage of Thought," *Journal of Economic Issues* 30 (September 1996).

9. In a literature that is now very large, and in addition to the comprehensive survey found in the Furubotn and Richter volume, useful overviews can also be found in Paul Milgrom and John Roberts, "Economic Theories of the Firm: Past, Present, and Future," *Canadian Journal of Economics* 21 (August 1988); *Economics, Organizations, and Management* (Englewood Cliffs, N.J.: Prentice-Hall, 1992); and Thrainn Eggertsson, *Economic Behavior and Institutions* (Cambridge: Cambridge University Press,

1990); and Oliver E. Williamson and Sidney G. Winter, eds., *The Nature of the Firm: Origins, Evolution, and Development* (New York: Oxford University Press, 1993).

CHAPTER EIGHT

1. Richard Miller, *Fact and Method: Explanation, Confirmation, and Reality in the Natural and Social Sciences* (Princeton: Princeton University Press, 1987).
2. George A. Akerlof, "The Market for 'Lemons': Quality Uncertainty and the Market Mechanism," *Quarterly Journal of Economics* 84 (August 1970).
3. See Daniel B. Botkin, *Discordant Harmonies: A New Ecology for the Twenty-First Century* (New York: Oxford University Press, 1990).
4. Donald Worster, "The Ecology of Order and Chaos," in Donald Worster, ed., *The Wealth of Nature* (New York: Oxford University Press, 1993); also Robert H. Nelson, "The Religions of Forestry," *Journal of Forestry* 96 (April 1998).
5. See Mark Sagoff, "Muddle or Muddle Through? Takings Jurisprudence Meets the Endangered Species Act," *William and Mary Law Review* 38 (March 1997).
6. Ronald H. Coase, autobiographical statement, in William Breit and Roger W. Spencer, eds., *Lives of the Laureates: Thirteen Nobel Economists* (Cambridge: MIT Press, 1995), 233.
7. Ibid.
8. Alfred P. Sloan, *My Years with General Motors* (Garden City, N.Y.: Doubleday, 1972).
9. See Steven G. Medema, *Ronald H. Coase* (New York: St. Martin's Press, 1994); also Medema, ed., *The Legacy of Ronald Coase in Economic Analysis*, 2 vols. (Aldershot: Edward Elgar, 1995); and Medema, ed., *Coasean Economics: Law and Economics and the New Institutional Economics* (Boston: Kluwer, 1998).
10. J. Wallis and D. North, "Measuring the Transaction Sector in the United States Economy, 1870–1970," in S. Engerman and R. Gallman, eds., *Long-Term Factors in American Economic Growth* (Chicago: University of Chicago Press, 1986), 121.
11. See Robert H. Nelson, "The Economics of Honest Trade Practices," *Journal of Industrial Economics* 24 (June 1976).
12. Akerlof, "The Market for 'Lemons.'"
13. See Phillip Nelson, "Information and Consumer Behavior," *Journal of Political Economy* 78 (March/April 1970); and Phillip Nelson, "Advertising as Information," *Journal of Political Economy* 82 (July/August 1974).
14. See also Carl Shapiro, "Premiums for High Quality Products as Returns to Reputations," *Quarterly Journal of Economics* 97 (November 1983); and Paul Milgrom and John Roberts, "Price and Advertising Signals of Product Quality," *Journal of Political Economy* 94 (August 1986).
15. Joanne Salop and Steven Salop, "Self-Selection and Turnover in the Labor Market," *Quarterly Journal of Economics* 90 (November 1976).
16. A. Michael Spence, "Job Market Signaling," *Quarterly Journal of Economics* 87 (August 1973).
17. Ronald H. Coase, "Industrial Organization: A Proposal for Research" (1972), reprinted in Coase, *The Firm, The Market, and the Law* (Chicago: University of Chicago Press, 1988), 63.
18. Oliver E. Williamson, *Markets and Hierarchies: Analysis and Antitrust Implications* (New York: Free Press, 1975); *The Economic Institutions of Capitalism: Firms, Markets, Relational Contracting* (New York: Free Press, 1985); and *Economic Organization: Firms, Markets, and Policy Control* (New York: New York University Press, 1986). For a good overview summary, see Armen A. Alchian and Susan Woodward, "The Firm is Dead, Long Live the Firm: A Review of Oliver E. Williamson's *The Economic Institutions of Capitalism*," *Journal of Economic Literature* 26 (March 1988).
19. Oliver E. Williamson, "Reflections on the New Institutional Economics," *Journal of Institutional and Theoretical Economics* 141 (March 1985); and "The Evolving Science of Organization," *Journal of Institutional and Theoretical Economics* 149 (March 1993).

20. Armen A. Alchian and Harold Demsetz, "Production, Information Costs, and Economic Organization," *American Economic Review* 62 (December 1972). See also Armen A. Alchian and Susan Woodward, "Reflections on the Theory of the Firm," *Journal of Institutional and Theoretical Economics* 143 (March 1987).

21. For a good review see also Louis De Alessi, "The Economics of Property Rights: A Review of the Evidence," *Research in Law and Economics* 2 (1980).

22. Paul Milgrom and John Roberts, "Economic Theories of the Firm: Past, Present and Future," *Canadian Journal of Economics* 21 (August 1988): 447.

23. Benjamin Klein, Robert G. Crawford, and Armen A. Alchian, "Vertical Integration, Appropriable Rents, and the Competitive Contracting Process," *Journal of Law and Economics* 21 (October 1978).

24. Williamson, *Economic Organization*, 142.

25. See Robert Wilson, "Informational Economies of Scale," *Bell Journal of Economics* 6 (Spring 1975).

26. Bruce C. Greenwald and Joseph E. Stiglitz, "Externalities in Economies with Imperfect Information and Incomplete Markets," *Quarterly Journal of Economics* 101 (May 1986).

27. One of the early articles to highlight this problem is Michael C. Jensen and William H. Meckling, "Theory of the Firm: Managerial Behavior, Agency Costs, and Ownership Structure," *Journal of Financial Economics* 3 (October 1976). Another early article is Stephen A. Ross, "The Economic Theory of Agency: The Principal's Problem," *American Economic Review* 63 (May 1973). See more recently David E. M. Sappington, "Incentives in Principal-Agent Relationships," *Journal of Economic Perspectives* 5 (Spring 1991).

28. Jean Tirole, "The Multicontract Organization," *Canadian Journal of Economics* 21 (August 1988): 459.

29. See, for example, Oliver D. Hart, "Optimal Labour Contracts Under Asymmetric Information: An Introduction," *Review of Economic Studies* 50 (January 1983).

30. Guillermo A. Calvo and Stanislaw Wellisz, "Supervision, Loss of Control and the Optimum Size of the Firm," *Journal of Political Economy* 86 (October 1978). Sanford J. Grossman and Oliver D. Hart, "Takeover Bids, the Free Rider Problem, and the Theory of the Corporation," *The Bell Journal of Economics* 11 (Spring 1980).

31. Oliver E. Williamson, *Markets and Hierarchies: Analysis and Antitrust Implications* (New York: Free Press, 1975), 7.

32. Herbert A. Simon, "Theories of Decision Making in Economics and Behavioral Science," *American Economic Review* 49 (June 1959); and "Rationality as Process and as Product of Thought," *American Economic Review* 68 (May 1978).

33. Eirik G. Furubotn and Rudolf Richter, *Institutions and Economic Theory: The Contribution of the New Institutional Economics* (Ann Arbor: University of Michigan Press, 1997), 408.

34. Williamson, *Markets and Hierarchies*, 9.

35. Joseph E. Stiglitz, "Another Century of Economic Science," *Economic Journal* 101 (January 1991): 136.

36. Joseph E. Stiglitz, *Wither Socialism?* (Cambridge: MIT Press, 1994), 11, 201. See also Stiglitz, *Information and Economic Analysis* (New York: Oxford University Press, 1993).

37. Stiglitz, *Wither Socialism?* 211, 6.

38. Stiglitz is the author of an introductory economics textbook that seeks to give the new "information paradigm" wider exposure in a more accessible language. See Joseph E. Stiglitz, *Economics* (New York: W. W. Norton, 1993).

39. An expression of a related concept is that economics should begin from a state of "unknowledge." See Jack Wiseman, "The Black Box," 101 *Economic Journal* (January 1991): 151.

40. Stiglitz, *Wither Socialism?* 149.

41. Ibid., 154, 155.

42. Ibid., 5.

43. Mark Pingle, "Costly Optimization: An Experiment," *Journal of Economic Behavior and Organization* 17 (January 1992): 11.

44. Peter J. Boettke and David L. Prychitko, "The Future of Austrian Economics," in Boettke and Prychitko, eds., *The Market Process: Essays in Contemporary Austrian Economics* (Brookfield, Vt.: Edward Elgar, 1994), 288. See also Karen Iverson Vaughn, *Austrian Economics in America: The Migration of a Tradition* (New York: Cambridge University Press, 1994).

45. Furubotn and Richter, *Institutions and Economic Theory*, 442–43.

46. Ibid., 442, 445.

47. Ibid., 446.

48. See, for example, James G. March and Herbert A. Simon, *Organizations* (New York: Willey, 1958); and Herbert A. Simon, *Models of Bounded Rationality: Behaviorial Economics and Business Organization*, vols. 1 and 2 (Cambridge: MIT Press, 1982).

49. Kenneth J. Arrow, "Methodological Individualism and Social Knowledge," *American Economic Review* 84 (May 1994): 4, 8.

50. Furubotn and Richter, *Institutions and Economic Theory*, 480.

51. Ibid, 481.

52. Avinash K. Dixit, *The Making of Economic Policy: A Transaction-Cost Politics Perspective* (Cambridge: MIT Press, 1996), 28–29, 19.

53. A. Michael Spence, "The Economics of Internal Organization: An Introduction" *Bell Journal of Economics* 6 (Spring 1975): 169.

54. Milgrom and Roberts, "Economic Theories of the Firm," 449–50.

55. Oliver Hart, "An Economist's Perspective on the Theory of the Firm," *Columbia Law Review* 89 (November 1989): 1757.

56. Robert Gibbons, "Incentives in Organizations," *Journal of Economic Perspectives* 12 (Fall 1998): 130.

57. Bengt Holmstrom and John Roberts, "The Boundaries of the Firm Revisited," *Journal of Economic Perspectives* 12 (Fall 1998): 75, 77, 75.

58. Stiglitz, *Wither Socialism?* 269.

59. See also Herbert A. Simon, "The Failure of Armchair Economics," *Challenge* 29 (November/December 1986).

CHAPTER NINE

1. Frank H. Knight, "Ethics and Economic Reform, *Economica* 6 (1939), reprinted in *Freedom and Reform: Essays in Economics and Social Philosophy* (Indianapolis: Liberty Press, 1982; 1st ed., 1947), 70.

2. These changing citizen attitudes as found in Gallup polls over many years were summarized in David S. Broder and Richard Morin, "Struggle over New Standards," *Washington Post,* December 27, 1998, A1.

3. Douglass C. North, autobiographical statement, in William Breit and Roger W. Spencer, eds., *Lives of the Laureates: Thirteen Nobel Economists* (Cambridge: MIT Press, 1995), 259.

4. See Douglass C. North, *Institutions, Institutional Change, and Economic Performance* (New York: Cambridge Univerity Press, 1990); for a more recent overview, see North, "Economic Performance Through Time," *American Economic Review* 84 (June 1994).

5. Kenneth J. Arrow, *The Limits of Organization* (New York: W. W. Norton, 1974), 26.

6. Ibid., 26–27.

7. Oliver E. Williamson, *Markets and Hierarchies: Analysis and Antitrust Implications* (New York: Free Press, 1975), 38–39.

8. For treatments emphasizing the economic importance of trust, see also Francis Fukuyama, *Trust: The Social Virtues and the Creation of Prosperity* (New York: Free Press, 1995); Adam Seligman, *The*

Problem of Trust (Princeton: Princeton University Press, 1997); and Lawrence E. Harrison, *Who Prospers: How Cultural Values Shape Economic and Political Success* (New York: Basic Books, 1992).

9. Chester I. Barnard, *The Functions of the Executive,* 2d edition (Cambridge: Harvard University Press, 1962).

10. See Michael Novak and John W. Cooper, eds., *The Corporation: A Theological Inquiry* (Washington, D.C.: American Enterprise Institute, 1981); and Oliver Williams and John Houck, eds., *The Judeo-Christian Vision and the Modern Corporation* (Notre Dame: University of Notre Dame Press, 1982). See also Michael Novak, *The Spirit of Democratic Capitalism* (New York: Simon and Schuster, 1982); and *Free Persons and the Common Good* (Lanham, Md.: Madison Books, 1989).

11. Williamson, *Markets and Hierarchies,* 39.

12. Michael C. Jensen and William H. Meckling, "Theory of the Firm: Managerial Behavior, Agency Costs, and Ownership Structure," *Journal of Financial Economics* 3 (October 1976): 310.

13. Paul Milgrom and John Roberts, "Economic Theories of the Firm: Past, Present, and Future," *Canadian Journal of Economics* 21 (August 1988): 456.

14. David Kreps, "Corporate Culture and Economic Theory," in James E. Alt and Kenneth A. Shepsle, eds., *Perspectives on Positive Political Economy* (New York: Cambridge University Press, 1990).

15. Eirik G. Furubotn and Rudolf Richter, *Institutions and Economic Theory: The Contribution of the New Institutional Economics* (Ann Arbor: University of Michigan Press, 1997), 407.

16. See, among many possible examples, John P. Kotter and James L. Heskett, *Corporate Culture and Performance* (New York: Free Press, 1992).

17. Martha S. Feldman and James G. March, "Information in Organizations as Signal and Symbol," *Administrative Science Quarterly* 26 (June 1981): 176.

18. Furubotn and Richter, *Institutions and Economic Theory,* 334.

19. Ibid., 335.

20. Robert Gibbons, "Incentives in Organizations," *Journal of Economic Perspectives* 12 (Fall 1998): 130.

21. For discussion of this issue, see Robert Frank, *Passions Within Reason: The Strategic Role of the Emotions* (New York: W. W. Norton, 1988).

22. Howard Margolis, "Religion as Paradigm," *Journal of Institutional and Theoretical Economics* 153, (March 1997): 248–49.

23. Fernando L. Flores and Robert C. Solomon, "Rethinking Trust," *Business and Professional Ethics Journal* 16, nos. 1–3 (1997): 48–49.

24. Russell Hardin is one of those who make an attempt to analyze the development of religious belief as a matter of economic choice. See Russell Hardin, "The Economics of Religious Belief," *Journal of Institutional and Theoretical Economics* 153 (March 1997).

25. Margolis, "Religion as Paradigm, 248, 250.

26. Jon Elster, *The Cement of Society: A Study of Social Order* (New York: Cambridge University Press, 1989), 195.

27. Gary J. Miller, "The Impact of Economics on Contemporary Political Science," *Journal of Economic Literature* 35 (September 1997): 1181. See also Herbert A. Simon, "Altruism and Economics," *American Economic Review* 83 (May 1993).

28. See Benedict Anderson, *Imagined Communities: Reflections on the Origin and Spread of Nationalism* (New York: Verso, 1991).

29. See Daniel Kahneman and Amos Tversky, "Prospect Thoery: An Analysis of Decision Under Risk," *Econometrica* 47 (March 1979); and Daniel Kahneman, "New Challenges to the Rationality Assumption," *Journal of Institutional and Theoretical Economics* 150 (March 1994).

30. See Vernon L. Smith, *Bargaining and Market Behavior: Essays in Experimental Economics* (New York: Cambridge University Press, 2000).

31. Kahneman, "New Challenges to the Rationality Assumption"; Daniel Kahneman, Jack L. Knetsch, and Richard H. Thaler, "Anomalies: The Endowment Effect, Loss Aversion, and Status Quo Bias," *Journal of Economic Perspectives* 5 (Winter 1991); and Robert H. Frank, "Frames of Reference and the Quality of Life," *American Economic Review* 79 (May 1989).

32. Matthew Rabin, "Psychology and Economics," *Journal of Economic Literature* 36 (March 1998): 37, 34, 35. See also Jon Elster, "Emotions and Economic Theory," *Journal of Economic Literature* 36 (March 1998).

33. Terence W. Hutchison, "Institutionalist Economics Old and New," *Journal of Institutional and Theoretical Economics* 150 (March 1994).

34. See Robert H. Nelson, *Reaching for Heaven on Earth: The Theological Meaning of Economics* (Lanham, Md.: Rowman and Littlefield, 1991).

35. J. L. Talmon, *Political Messianism: The Romantic Phase* (Boulder, Colo.: Westview Press, 1985; 1st ed., 1960), 25, 24.

36. Frank Hahn, "The Next Hundred Years," *Economic Journal* 101 (January 1991): 47, 49.

37. Richard A. Easterlin, "The Worldwide Standard of Living Since 1800," *Journal of Economic Perspectives* 14 (Winter 2000): 24.

38. North, *Institutions, Institutional Change and Economic Performance*, 57. See also Douglass C. North, *Structure and Change in Economic History* (New York: W. W. Norton, 1981).

39. Mancur Olson, 1988 interview published in Richard Swedberg, *Economics and Sociology* (Princeton: Princeton University Press, 1990), 184. See Olson, *The Rise and Decline of Nations: Economic Growth, Stagflation, and Social Rigidities* (New Haven: Yale University Press, 1982).

40. Robert E. Hall and Charles I. Jones, "Levels of Economic Activity Across Countries," *American Economic Review* 87 (May 1997): 173.

41. Paul Collier and Jan Willem Gunning, "Why Has Africa Grown Slowly?" *Journal of Economic Perspectives* 13 (Summer 1999): 18–19. See also Benno J. Ndulu and Stephen A. O'Connell, "Governance and Growth in Sub-Saharan Africa," *Journal of Economic Perspectives* 13 (Summer 1999); and World Bank, *Assessing Aid: What Works, What Doesn't, and Why* (New York: Oxford University Press, 1998).

42. North, *Institutions, Institutional Change, and Economic Performance*, 54, 52.

43. Ibid., 55, 138.

44. Ibid., 138, 44.

45. In an effort reminiscent of Weber's explorations of the relationship between religious belief and economic development in various cultures, Timur Kuran has examined the links between Islam and the low level of development often associated with nations where Muslims are heavily represented in the population. See Timur Kuran, "Islam and Underdevelopment: An Old Puzzle Revisited," *Journal of Institutional and Theoretical Economics* 153, no. 1 (1997).

46. Max Weber, *The Religion of China: Confucianism and Taoism* (New York: Macmillan, 1964; 1st ed., 1916); *The Religion of India: The Sociology of Hinduism and Buddhism* (Glencoe, Ill.: Free Press, 1958; 1st ed., 1916). See also Weber, *Economy and Society*, vols. 1 and 2, edited by Guenther Roth and Claus Wittich (Berkeley and Los Angeles: University of California Press, 1978).

47. H. Stuart Hughes, "Weber's Search for Rationality in Western Society," in Robert W. Green, ed., *Protestantism, Capitalism, and Social Science: The Weber Thesis Controversy* (Lexington, Mass.: D.C. Heath, 1973), 165.

48. Max Weber, *The Protestant Ethic and the Spirit of Capitalism* (New York: Charles Scribner, 1958; 1st ed., 1905).

49. Nathan Rosenberg and L. E. Birdzell, Jr., *How the West Grew Rich: The Economic Transformation of the Industrial World* (New York: Basic Books, 1986), 124, 125, 130.

50. North, *Institutions, Institutional Change, and Economic Performance*, 76, 111. See also William Kingston, "Property Rights and the Making of Christendom," *Journal of Law and Religion* 9, no. 2 (1992); and "Monks, Liturgy, and Labor," *Studies* (1995): 181–89.

51. North, *Institutions, Institutional Change and Economic Performance*, 111.

52. See W. B. Arthur, "Competing Technologies, Increasing Returns, and Lock-In by Historical Events," *Economic Journal* 9 (March 1989); Paul A. David, "Clio and the Economics of QWERTY," *American Economic Review* 75 (May 1985). For a history, see M. Mitchell Waldrop, *Complexity: The Emerging Science at the Edge of Order and Chaos* (New York: Simon and Schuster, 1992).

53. W. Brian Arthur, *Increasing Returns and Path Dependence in the Economy* (Ann Arbor: University of Michigan Press, 1994), 100, 109.

54. See Steven N. Durlauf, "What Policy Makers Should Know About Economic Complexity," *Washington Quarterly* 20 (Winter 1998).

55. See James Gleick, *Chaos: Making a New Science* (New York: Penguin, 1987).

56. A leading recent example is David S. Landes, *The Wealth and Poverty of Nations: Why Some Are So Rich and Some Are So Poor* (New York: W. W. Norton, 1998).

57. Putnam has been a leading contributor to a rapidly expanding literature on the state of "civil society" in the United States. His most recent study is Robert D. Putnam, *Bowling Alone: The Collapse and Revival of American Community* (New York: Simon and Schuster, 2000). See also E. J. Dionne, Jr., ed., *Community Works: The Revival of Civil Society in America* (Washington, D.C.: Brookings Institution Press, 1998); National Commission on Civil Renewal, *A Nation of Spectators: How Civic Disengagement Weakens America and What We Can Do About It* (1998), available from the Institute for Philosophy and Public Policy, University of Maryland, College Park, Md.; Theda Skocpol, *Social Policy in the United States: Future Possibilities in Historical Perspective* (Princeton: Princeton University Press, 1995); and Robert Wuthnow, *Sharing the Journey: Support Groups and America's New Quest for Community* (New York: Free Press, 1994).

58. For an earlier study of Italy, see Edward C. Banfield, *The Moral Basis of a Backward Society* (New York: Free Press, 1958).

59. Robert D. Putnam, *Making Democracy Work: Civic Traditions in Modern Italy* (Princeton: Princeton University Press, 1993).

60. Ibid., 114.

61. Ibid., 155–57.

62. Ibid., 154, 167.

63. Ibid., 177, 178.

64. Sisela Bok, *Lying* (New York: Pantheon Books, 1978), 28.

65. Putnam, *Making Democracy Work*, 183.

66. Ibid., 179.

67. Ibid., 183.

68. Quoted in James Q. Wilson, "The History and Future of Democracy," address at the Reagan Presidential Library, November 15, 1999 (Malibu, Calif.: Pepperdine University School of Public Policy, 1999), 12.

69. Alex Inkeles and Larry Diamond, "Personal Development and National Development: A Cross-Cultural Perspective," in Alexander Szalai and Frank M. Andrews, eds., *The Quality of Life: Comparative Studies* (London: Sage, 1980), 97.

70. Fukuyama, *Trust,* 18.

71. Rafael La Porta, Florencio Lopez-De-Silanes, Andrei Shleifer, and Robert W. Vishny, "Trust in Large Organizations," *American Economic Review* 87 (May 1997): 335. See also William Easterly and Ross Levine, "Africa's Growth Tragedy: Policies and Ethnic Divisions," *Quarterly Journal of Economics* 112 (November 1997).

72. Rafael La Porta, Florencio Lopez-de-Silanes, Andrei Shleifer, and Robert Vishny, "The Quality of Government," NBER working paper 6727, National Bureau of Economic Research, Cambridge, Mass., September 1998, 2.

73. Elinor Ostrom, *Governing the Commons: The Evolution of Institutions for Collective Action* (New York: Cambridge University Press, 1990).

74. Ibid., 184, 202.

75. Ibid., 36.

76. Ibid., 63.

INTRODUCTION TO PART FIVE

1. The mainstream economic understanding of rationality is, to be sure, a rather constricted understanding. See Amartya Sen, "Rational Fools," *Philosophy and Public Affairs* 6 (Summer 1977) and "Rationality and Uncertainty," *Theory and Decision* 18 (March 1985).

2. See Andrei Shleifer and Robert W. Vishny, "Corruption," *Quarterly Journal of Economics* 108 (August 1993); and Paulo Mauro, "Corruption and Growth," *Quarterly Journal of Economics* 110 (August 1995).

3. The role of culture and values in economic development is gaining wider recognition. See, for example, Lawrence E. Harrison and Samuel P. Huntington, eds., *Culture Matters: How Values Shape Human Progress* (New York: Basic Books, 2000).

4. Michael Novak, "The Nation with the Soul of a Church," in Richard J. Bishirjian, ed., *A Public Philosophy Reader* (New Rochelle, N.Y.: Arlington House, 1978), 92–93, 94. See also Sanford Levinson, *Constitutional Faith* (Princeton: Princeton University Press, 1988).

CHAPTER TEN

1. Francis Fukuyama, *Trust: The Social Virtues and the Creation of Prosperity* (New York: Free Press, 1995), 356.

2. Eirik G. Furubotn and Rudolf Richter, *Institutions and Economic Theory: The Contribution of the New Institutional Economics* (Ann Arbor: University of Michigan Press, 1997), 11–12.

3. For attempts to develop explanations for why rapid economic growth and development has occurred in the past thousand years in a few places such as western Europe but in few others (until at least the second half of the twentieth century), see David S. Landes, *The Wealth and Poverty of Nations: Why Some Are So Rich and Some So Poor* (New York: W. W. Norton, 1998); Joel Mokyr, *The Lever of Riches: Technological Creativity and Economic Progress* (New York: Oxford University Press, 1990); Eric L. Jones, *The European Miracle: Environments, Economies, and Geopolitics in the History of Europe and Asia* (New York: Cambridge University Press, 1981); *Growth Recurring: Economic Change in World History* (New York: Oxford University Press, 1988); and Douglass C. North and Robert P. Thomas, *The Rise of the Western World* (New York: Cambridge University Press, 1973).

4. Karl R. Popper, *The Open Society and Its Enemies*, vol. 1, *The Spell of Plato* (Princeton, N.J.: Princeton University Press, 1971; 1st ed., 1962), 38, 164.

5. Aristotle, *The Politics*, trans. B. Jowett (London: Oxford University Press, 1885), 33–34.

6. See Richard Schlatter, *Private Property: The History of an Idea* (New York: Russell and Russell, 1973; 1st ed., 1951), 35.

7. Randall Collins, *Weberian Sociological Theory* (New York: Cambridge University Press, 1986); Odd Langholm, *Economics in the Medieval Schools* (Leiden: E. J. Brill, 1992); and Franz-Xaver Kaufman, "Religion and Modernization in Europe," *Journal of Institutional and Theoretical Economics* 153 (March 1997).

8. See, for example, Raymond de Roover, "Scholastic Economics: Survival and Lasting Influence from the Sixteenth Century to Adam Smith," *Quarterly Journal of Economics* 69 (May 1955). For recent reviews of this body of scholarship, see Alejandro A. Chaufen, *Christians for Freedom: Late-Scholastic Economics* (San Francisco: Ignatius Press, 1986); Robert A. Sirico, "The Economics of the Late Scholastics," *Journal of Markets and Morality* 1 (October 1998).

9. Joseph A. Schumpeter, *History of Economic Analysis* (New York: Oxford University Press, 1954), 93.

10. Ibid.

11. Jacob Viner, *Religious Thought and Economic Society: Four Chapters of an Unfinished Work*, edited by Jacques Melitz and Donald Winch (Durham: Duke University Press, 1978), 84–85. See also Viner, *The Role of Providence in the Social Order* (Princeton: Princeton University Press, 1976).

12. Ephraim Kleiman, "'Just Price' in Talmudic Literature," *History of Political Economy* 19 (Spring 1987): 26, 35.

13. Stephen Theodore Worland, *Scholasticism and Welfare Economics* (Notre Dame: University of Notre Dame Press, 1967).

14. George O'Brien, *An Essay on Medieval Economic Teaching* (New York: Augustus M. Kelley, 1967; 1st ed., 1920).

15. For further development of this argument, see chap. 5 of Robert H. Nelson, *Reaching for*

Heaven on Earth: The Theological Meaning of Economics (Lanham, Md.: Rowman and Littlefield, 1991).

16. Jean Starobinski, *Jean-Jacques Rousseau: Transparency and Obstruction* (Chicago: University of Chicago Press, 1988; 1st ed., 1971), 112.

17. Arend T. van Leeuwen, *Christianity in World History: The Meeting of the Faiths of East and West* (New York: Charles Scribner's, 1964), 333, 107, 268.

18. Murray Rothbard, *Economic Thought Before Adam Smith: An Austrian Perspective on the History of Economic Thought,* vol. 1 (Brookfield, Vt.: Edward Elgar, 1995), 53, 54, 316.

19. Patrick D. Miller, "Theology and Science in Conversation," *Theology Today* 55 (October 1998): 301, 303.

20. Unpublished paper by John Polkinghorne and Michael Welker, quoted approving in Miller, "Theology and Science in Conversation," 303.

21. Joyce Oldham Appleby, *Economic Thought and Ideology in Seventeenth-Century England* (Princeton, N.J.: Princeton University Press, 1978), 115.

22. Ibid., 93–94.

23. Ibid., 128, 94.

24. For a recent analysis of Smith's thinking, see Susan E. Gallagher, *The Rule of the Rich: Adam Smith's Argument Against Political Power* (University Park: Penn State Press, 1998).

25. The connections from Roman Catholic scholastic writers to Protestant natural-law theorists to Adam Smith are traced in Jeffrey T. Young, *Economics as a Moral Science: The Political Economy of Adam Smith* (Cheltenham, U.K.: Edward Elgar, 1997).

26. This created significant tensions between existing religions and the new field of economics. See A. M. C. Waterman, *Revolution, Economics, and Religion: Christian Political Economy* (New York: Cambridge University Press, 1991).

27. J. L. Talmon, *The Origins of Totalitarian Democracy* (New York: W. W. Norton, 1970), 31.

28. Louis I. Bredvold, *The Brave New World of the Enlightenment* (Ann Arbor: University of Michigan Press, 1961), 50.

29. Quoted in Milton L. Myers, *The Soul of Modern Economic Man: Ideas of Self-Interest, Thomas Hobbes to Adam Smith* (Chicago: University of Chicago Press, 1983), 69.

30. James Halteman, review of *Economics as a Moral Science,* by Jeffrey T. Young, *Bulletin of the Association of Christian Economists,* no. 32 (Fall 1998): 27.

31. Fukuyama, *Trust,* 360.

32. James Moore and Michael Silverthorne, "Gershom Carmichael and the Natural Jurisprudence Tradition in Eighteenth-Century Scotland," in Istvan Hont and Michael Ignatieff, eds., *Wealth and Virtue: The Shaping of Political Economy in the Scottish Enlightenment* (New York: Cambridge University Press, 1983), 73.

33. Myers, *The Soul of Modern Economic Man,* 102.

34. Andrew S. Skinner, "Adam Smith," in John Eatwell, Murray Milgate, and Peter Newman, eds., *The New Palgrave: The Invisible Hand* (New York: W. W. Norton, 1989), 37.

35. Quoted from the *Wealth of Nations* in Skinner, "Adam Smith," 34.

36. Skinner, "Adam Smith," 39.

37. Marci A. Hamilton, "The People: The Least Accountable Branch," *The University of Chicago Law School Roundtable* 4, no. 1 (1997): 3–4.

38. Istvan Hont and Michael Ignatieff, "Needs and Justice in the *Wealth of Nations:* An Introductory Essay," in Hont and Ignatieff, *Wealth and Virtue,* 26, 43.

39. See R. H. Tawney, *Religion and the Rise of Capitalism: A Historical Study* (New York: Harcourt Brace, 1926); and Ernt Troeltsch, *The Social Teaching of the Christian Churches,* 2 vols. (Chicago: University of Chicago Press, 1981; 1st ed., 1931). For more recent studies, see S. N. Eisenstadt, ed., *The Protestant Ethic and Modernization: A Comparative View* (New York: Basic Books, 1968); and David Little, *Religion, Order, and Law: A Study of Prerevolutionary England* (New York: Harper and Row, 1969).

40. See Kenneth Scott Latourette, *A History of Christianity,* vol. 2, *Reformation to the Present* (New York: Harper and Row, 1975), 838, 826.

41. George J. Stigler, "Economics or Ethics?" *The Tanner Lectures on Human Values* (Salt Lake City:

University of Utah Press, 1981), reprinted in Kurt R. Leube and Thomas Gale Moore, eds., *The Essence of Stigler* (Stanford, Calif.: Hoover Institution Press, 1986), 307–8.

42. Thorstein Veblen, "Why Is Economics Not an Evolutionary Science," *Quarterly Journal of Economics* 12 (July 1898): 378.

43. Schumpeter, *History of Economic Analysis,* 182, 91–92.

44. Michael Novak, "God and Man in the Corporation," *Policy Review,* no. 13 (Summer 1980), 22.

45. Charles L. Schultze, *The Public Use of Private Interest* (Washington, D.C.: Brookings Institution, 1977), 21.

46. Schumpeter, *History of Economic Analysis,* 184.

47. Ibid., 185, 186.

48. Friedrich Engels, "Eulogy for Marx," quoted in Harry W. Laidler, *A History of Socialist Thought* (New York: Thomas Crowell, 1927), 196.

49. Sidney Fine, *Laissez Faire and the General-Welfare State: A Study of Conflict in American Thought, 1865–1901* (Ann Arbor: University of Michigan Press, 1964), 41, 43.

50. *Lochner v. New York,* 198 U.S. 45 (1905).

51. Fine, *Laissez-Faire and the General-Welfare State,* 43.

52. Richard Hofstadter, *Social Darwinism in American Thought* (Boston: Beacon Press, 1955; 1st ed., 1944), 49.

53. Herbert Spencer, "The Coming Slavery" (1884), in Spencer, *The Man Versus the State: With Six Essays on Government, Society, and Freedom* (Indianapolis, Ind.: Liberty Classics, 1981), 69, 67, 57.

54. Max Weber, *The Protestant Ethic and the Spirit of Capitalism* (New York: Charles Scribner's, 1958; 1st ed., 1905).

55. Robert Green McCloskey, *American Conservatism in the Age of Enterprise* (Cambridge: Harvard University Press, 1951), 27–28.

56. Paul Conkin, *Puritans and Pragmatists: Eight Eminent American Thinkers* (Bloomington: University of Indiana Press, 1976).

57. See Robert H. Nelson, *Reaching for Heaven on Earth: The Theological Meaning of Economics* (Lanham, MD: Rowman and Littlefield, 1991), 150–61.

58. Quoted in Robert L. Heilbroner, *The Worldly Philosophers: The Lives, Times, and Ideas of the Great Economic Thinkers* (New York: Simon and Schuster, 1972; 1st ed., 1953), 272.

59. Paul Anthony Samuelson, *Foundations of Economic Analysis* (New York: Atheneum, 1965; 1st ed., 1947), 6.

60. Lloyd A. Metzler, "Review of Foundations of Economic Analysis," *American Economic Review* 38 (December 1948): 905.

61. Philip Mirowski, *More Heat Than Light: Economics as Social Physics, Physics as Nature's Economics* (New York: Cambridge University Press, 1989), 378–86.

62. Milton Friedman, "Old Wine in New Bottles," *Economic Journal* 101 (January 1991): 33.

63. F. A. Hayek, *The Counter-Revolution of Science: Studies on the Abuse of Reason* (Indianapolis, Ind.: Liberty Press, 1979; 1st ed., 1951), 221. See also Frank Edward Manuel, *The New World of Henri Saint-Simon* (Cambridge: Harvard University Press, 1956).

64. Mirowski, *More Heat Than Light,* 383.

65. Ibid., 379–80.

66. Ibid., 380, 385, 384, 380.

67. Quoted in Duane M. Oldfield, *The Right and the Righteous: The Christian Right Confronts the Republican Party* (Lanham, Md.: Rowman and Littlefield, 1996), 224.

CHAPTER ELEVEN

1. Gregory Claeys, "Utopias," in John Eatwell, Murray Milgate, and Peter Newman, eds., *The New Palgrave: The Invisible Hand* (New York: W. W. Norton, 1989), 273, 274.

2. Ibid., 275.

3. Robert H. Bork, "Good Reasons for Despair on the Right," *Wall Street Journal* (October 9, 1997), op-ed, A18.

4. Ibid.

5. John Lewis, "Crime as a Cause of Poverty," *Atlantic Monthly,* July 1995, 49.

6. Joe Klein, "The True Disadvantage," *New Republic,* October 28, 1996, 32. Klein's article is a book review of *When Work Disappears: The World of the New Urban Poor,* by William Julius Wilson.

7. Katherine Boo, "Painful Choices," *Washington Post,* October 19, 1997, A1.

8. Irving Kristol, "The Welfare State's Spiritual Crisis," *Wall Street Journal,* February 3, 1997, A14.

9. Ibid.

10. Thomas B. Edsall, "Christian Coalition on Comeback Trail?" *Washington Post,* September 16, 1994.

11. National Commission on Civic Renewal, *A Nation of Spectators: How Civic Disengagement Weakens America and What We Can Do About It* (College Park, Md.: Institute for Philosophy and Public Policy, University of Maryland, 1998), 27–28.

12. Rachel Carson, *Silent Spring* (Boston: Houghton Mifflin, 1962).

13. Albert A. Bartlett, "Is There a Population Problem?" *Wild Earth,* Fall 1997, 89.

14. "Toward a Healthy Community: An Interview with Wendell Berry," *Christian Century,* October 15, 1997, 915–16.

15. Ibid., 913.

16. Bruce Babbitt, "Our Covenant: To Protect the *Whole* of Creation," circulated to top staff of the Interior Department by E-mail, December 14, 1995. This speech was delivered on several occasions, including to the League of Conservation Voters in New York City in December 1995.

17. Quoted in Stephen Stuebner, "Government Plans More Fires to Prevent Fires," *New York Times,* February 9, 1997, 30.

18. Edward Hoagland (editor of the Penguin Nature Library), preface to Frank Bergon, ed., *The Journals of Lewis and Clark* (New York: Penguin Books, 1989).

19. Babbitt, "Our Covenant."

20. See Robert Booth Fowler, *The Greening of Protestant Thought* (Chapel Hill: University of North Carolina Press, 1995); Sean McDonagh, *The Greening of the Church* (Maryknoll, N.Y.: Orbis Books, 1990).

21. See Stephen Fox, *The American Conservation Movement: John Muir and His Legacy* (Madison: University of Wisconsin Press, 1985; 1st ed., 1981).

22. See the portrayal of David Brower in John McPhee, *Encounters with the Archruid* (New York: Farrar, Straus and Giroux, 1971); also David Brower, *For Earth's Sake: The Life and Times of David Brower* (Salt Lake City, Ut.: Peregrine Books, 1990).

23. Brooke Williams, "Love or Power?" *Northern Lights,* Fall 1991, 19.

24. "O Holy Day," editorial, *Wall Street Journal,* April 19, 1990, A14.

25. Bill Devall and George Sessions, *Deep Ecology: Living As If Nature Mattered* (Salt Lake City, Ut.: Peregrine Books, 1985), 48, 56, 48.

26. Ibid., 107, 115, 125.

27. Ernest Callenbach, *Ecotopia* (New York: Bantam Books, 1977), 5.

28. *High Country News,* October 10, 1988, 10.

29. Bryan G. Norton, "Thoreau's Insect Analogies: Or, Why Environmentalists Hate Mainstream Economists," *Environmental Ethics* 13 (Fall 1991): 236, 248.

30. See, for example, Paul R. Portney and Robert N. Stavins, eds., *Public Policies for Environmental Protection,* 2d ed. (Washington, D.C.: Resources for the Future, 2000).

31. Norton, "Thoreau's Insect Analogies," 248, 249, 248.

32. See Robert H. Nelson, "Environmental Calvinism: The Judeo-Christian Roots of Environmental Theology," in Roger E. Meiners and Bruce Yandle, eds., *Taking the Environment Seriously* (Lanham, Md.: Rowman and Littlefield, 1993).

33. See Hugh T. Kerr, *Calvin's Institutes: A New Compend* (Louisville, Ky.: Westminster/John Knox Press, 1989). This is an abridgement of John Calvin's *Institutes of the Christian Religion.*

34. Quoted in McPhee, *Encounters with the Archdruid,* 159.

35. On the clash between economic and environmental values with respect to wilderness, see Christopher Manes, "Economic Man in the Wilderness," *Northern Lights,* Fall 1992.

36. William C. Dennis, "Wilderness Cathedrals and the Public Good," *Freeman* (May 1987).

37. See Perry Miller, *The New England Mind: The Seventeenth Century* (Cambridge, Mass.: Harvard University Press, 1954); also Perry Miller, *Errand into the Wilderness* (New York: Harper and Row, 1964).

38. Allan C. Carlson, "Toward a Family-Centered Economy," *New Oxford Review* 64 (December 1997): 28.

39. Ibid., 29, 32.

40. For criticisms of the assumptions and logic of many leading environmental thinkers, see Robert H. Nelson, "Unoriginal Sin: The Judeo-Christian Roots of Ecotheology," *Policy Review* no. 53 (Summer 1990); "Environmental Calvinism: The Judeo-Christian Roots of Environmental Theology," in Roger E. Meiners and Bruce Yandle, eds., *Taking the Environment Seriously* (Lanham, Md.: Rowman and Littlefield, 1993); "Calvinism Minus God: Environmental Restoration as a Theological Concept," in Anathea Brooks and Stacey Vandever, eds., *Saving the Seas* (College Park, Md.: University of Maryland Sea Grant, 1997); and "Does 'Existence Value' Exist? An Essay on Religions, Old and New," *Independent Review* 1 (March 1997).

41. Anne Petermann, "Tales of a Recovering Misanthrope," *Earth First! The Radical Environmental Journal* 19 (June–July 1999): 3.

42. William Cronon, "The Trouble with Wilderness; or, Getting Back to the Wrong Nature," in Cronon, ed., *Uncommon Ground: Toward Reinventing Nature* (New York: W. W. Norton, 1995), 83. Cronon is also the author of the environmental history *Changes in the Land: Indians, Colonists, and the Ecology of New England* (New York: Hill and Wang, 1983).

43. Stephen J. Pyne, *Fire in America: A Cultural History of Wildland and Rural Fire* (Princeton: Princeton University Press, 1982), 71.

44. Stephen J. Pyne, *World Fire: The Culture of Fire on Earth* (New York: Holt, 1995), 244.

45. William Cronon, "In Search of Nature," introduction to Cronon, ed., *Uncommon Ground,* 41, 32, 35.

46. Cronon, "The Trouble with Wilderness," 80, 73.

47. William F. Buckley, *God and Man at Yale: The Superstitions of "Academic Freedom"* (Chicago: Henry Regnery Company, 1951), 81.

48. Diane Winston, "Campuses Are a Bellwether for Society's Religious Revival," *Chronicle of Higher Education,* January 16, 1998, A60.

49. National Conference of Catholic Bishops, *Economic Justice for All: Catholic Social Teaching and the U.S. Economy* (Washington, D.C.: United States Catholic Conference, November 18, 1986), 18–19. For discussion of an earlier draft of the Catholic bishops' statement, see the various articles in the Symposium on the Economy, *Notre Dame Journal of Law, Ethics, and Public Policy* 2, no. 1 (1985).

50. Pope John Paul II, *Centesimus Annus* (Vatican City: Libreria Editrice Vaticana, May 1, 1991), 49. See also George Weigel, *A New Worldly Order: John Paul II and Human Freedom, A 'Centesimus Annus' Reader* (Washington, D.C.: Ethics and Public Policy Center, 1992).

51. Pope John Paul II, *Centesimus Annus,* 57.

52. Ibid., 68, 69, 72.

53. John Paul II, *Evangelium Vitae* (Gospel of Life), reprinted in *Origins,* April 6, 1995, 719, 696.

54. Ibid, 694.

55. Ibid., 698.

56. See Dennis P. McCann, "Capitalism in the Light of Catholic Moral Claims," *Christian Century,* October 6, 1993. This is a book review of Richard John Neuhaus, *Doing Well and Doing Good: The Challenge to the Christian Capitalist* (New York: Doubleday, 1993).

57. See Alejandro A. Chafuen, *Christians for Freedom: Late-Scholastic Economics* (San Francisco: Ignatius Press, 1986); Joseph A. Schumpeter, *History of Economic Analysis* (New York: Oxford University Press, 1954), chap. 2; Raymond de Roover, "Scholastic Economics: Survival and Lasting Influence from the Sixteenth Century to Adam Smith," *Quarterly Journal of Economics* 69 (May 1955).

58. Over the past twenty years, Michael Novak has been a leading Catholic interpreter of the moral dimensions of the market. His many works include *The Spirit of Democratic Capitalism* (New York: Simon and Schuster, 1982); *Free Persons and the Common Good* (Lanham, Md.: Madison Books, 1989); and Novak, ed., *Liberation South, Liberation North* (Washington, D.C.: American Enterprise Institute, 1981).

59. Thorstein Veblen, *The Theory of the Leisure Class* (New York: Penguin Books, 1994; 1st ed., 1899).

60. Fred Hirsch, *The Social Limits to Growth* (Cambridge: Harvard University Press, 1976). See also Robert H. Frank, *Passions Within Reason: The Strategic Role of the Emotions* (New York: W. W. Norton, 1988).

61. Robert H. Frank, *Choosing the Right Pond: Human Behavior and the Quest for Status* (New York: Oxford University Press, 1985).

62. Robert E. Lane, "The Road Not Taken: Friendship, Consumerism, and Happiness," in David A. Crocker and Toby Linden, *Ethics of Consumption: The Good Life, Justice, and Global Stewardship* (Lanham, Md.: Rowman and Littlefield, 1998), 226, 238, 235.

63. Ibid., 223, 225.

64. See also Tibor Scitovsky, *The Joyless Economy: The Psychology of Human Satisfaction* (New York: Oxford University Press, 1992; 1st ed., 1976).

65. Robert E. Lane, *The Market Experience* (New York: Cambridge University Press, 1991).

66. Colin Campbell, *The Romantic Ethic and the Spirit of Modern Consumerism* (New York: Basil Blackwell, 1987), 217.

67. Ibid., 205–6.

68. Colin Campbell, "Consuming Goods and the Good of Consuming," in Crocker and Linden, eds., *Ethics of Consumption,* 144, 147, 145.

69. Ibid., 142, 143.

70. See Robert H. Nelson, "Is 'Libertarian Environmentalist' an Oxymoron?" in Donald Snow, ed. *The Next West: Public Lands, Community, and Economy in the American West* (Washington, D.C.: Island Press, 1997).

CONCLUSION

1. Economists were attracted as well by the urge to speculate on the long term future of the profession at the end of both a century and a millennium. See the symposium issue of the *Journal of Economic Perspectives* 14 (Winter 2000) for various articles addressing the past and future of the American economics professor.

2. For recent writings addressing the future role of religion in American public life, see Paul J. Weithman, ed., *Religion and Contemporary Liberalism* (Notre Dame: University of Notre Dame Press, !997); and Barry A. Kosmin and Seymour P. Lachman, *One Nation Under God: Religion in Contemporary American Society* (New York: Crown, 1993).

3. See Diane Winston, "Campuses Are a Bellwether for Society's Religious Revival," *Chronicle of Higher Education,* January 16, 1998, A60.

INDEX